A FLEET STREET IN EVERY TOWN

A Fleet Street in Every Town

The Provincial Press in England, 1855–1900

Andrew Hobbs

OpenBook Publishers

http://www.openbookpublishers.com

Updated digital material and resources associated with this volume are available at, https://www.openbookpublishers.com/product/835#resources

Every effort has been made to identify and contact copyright holders and any omission or error will be corrected if notification is made to the publisher.

ISBN Paperback: 978-1-78374-559-3
ISBN Hardback: 978-1-78374-560-9
ISBN Digital (PDF): 978-1-78374-561-6
ISBN Digital ebook (epub): 978-1-78374-562-3
ISBN Digital ebook (mobi): 978-1-78374-563-0
ISBN XML: 978-1-78374-654-5
DOI: 10.11647/OBP.0152

Cover image: Offices of rival newspapers the *Manchester Guardian/Manchester Evening News* and the *Manchester Courier*, Cross Street, Manchester, 1902 (image M56243). Courtesy of Manchester Libraries, Information and Archives, Manchester City Council. All rights reserved. Cover design: Anna Gatti.

All paper used by Open Book Publishers is SFI (Sustainable Forestry Initiative), PEFC (Programme for the Endorsement of Forest Certification Schemes) and Forest Stewardship Council® (FSC® certified).

Printed in the United Kingdom, United States, and Australia by Lightning Source for Open Book Publishers (Cambridge, UK)

Contents

To Rosa and Lynne

Acknowledgements

I love being part of a scholarly community, and I owe so much to the generosity, time, encouragement and practical help of other members of this community.

Thanks to Dave Russell and Steve Caunce for taking this project seriously in the first place, and for their excellent supervision, with the help of Dawn Archer; to other historians at the University of Central Lancashire, past and present, who have offered encouragement and inspiration to so many mature students like myself, including Annemarie McAllister, Andy Gritt, Robert Poole, David Stewart, Billy Frank, Máirtín Ó Catháin, Keith Vernon, Geoff Timmins, John Walton and Jack Southern; the UCLan MRes History students; to members of the wonderfully supportive and friendly Research Society for Victorian Periodicals, especially Laurel Brake, Margaret Beetham, Andrew King, Bob Nicholson, Brian Maidment, Jim Mussell, Patrick Leary, John North, David Finkelstein, Catherine Waters and Leslie Howsam; to members of the North-West Print Culture Research Network, the VICTORIA and SHARP-L email discussion lists, and to others who have helped along the way, given encouragement and/or read drafts: Martin Hewitt, Brian Hollingworth, Jonathan Rose, Victoria Gardner, Helen Rogers, Fred Milton, Kirstie Blair, Alison Chapman, Rachel Matthews, Carole O'Reilly, Andrew J. H. Jackson, Will Slauter, Felix Larkin, Melodee Beals, Nick Foggo and Margaret Dickinson; to the Black Horse History Society (Steve Tate, Alex Jackson and Peter Park); to the patient librarians and archivists, particularly Jacquie Crosby of Lancashire Archives and David Shuttleworth, Ann Dennison and Victoria Roberts, all formerly of the Harris Library, Preston, Jane Hodkinson of Manchester Archives and Roger Hull of Liverpool Archives; to Rachel Riggs and Adam Bennett, whose freelance commission first made me realise how much I loved history; to the members of the National Union of Journalists West Lancashire branch, who care about journalism, and to all involved in the *Preston Other Paper*, who believed local journalism could be part of a progressive politics of place. The Arts & Humanities Research Council funded the original PhD research on which this book is based, and the University of Central Lancashire and the Marc Fitch Fund have generously supported publication costs.

Introduction

Karl Marx was not always right (he thought world revolution would begin in Preston, for example), but his throw-away assessment of the impact of ending Stamp Duty taxation on newspapers in 1855 was correct, forecasting a

> revolution in the provincial press caused by the abolition of stamp duty. In Glasgow alone four new daily penny papers are to appear. In Liverpool and Manchester the papers that have hitherto only appeared weekly or twice weekly are to turn into dailies at 3d., 2d., and 1d. The emancipation from London of the provincial press, the decentralisation of journalism was, in fact, the main aim of the Manchester School in their fierce and protracted campaign against stamp duty.[1]

'Decentralisation', a desire attributed to Richard Cobden, John Bright and other northern Liberal MPs of the 'Manchester School', may be too strong a word, but for the next eighty years, at the heart of almost every town and city, on the high street or town square, there was a miniature version of Fleet Street, the London newspaper publishing centre. The cover of this book shows two rival Manchester dailies, the *Guardian* and the *Courier*, on Cross Street in 1902; similarly, in Liverpool in the 1860s, five of the city's twelve newspapers jostled with each other on Castle Street, the *Mail* at 11, South Castle Street, then *Gore's General Advertiser* at 4 Castle Street, the *Chronicle* at 32, the *Albion* at 36 and the *Courier* at 60 Castle Street.

Fifteen years after Marx's prediction, a trade magazine, the *Printers' Register*, declared that:

---

1   Karl Marx, 'Prince Albert's Toast.— The Stamp Duty on Newspapers', *Neue Oder Zeitung*, 21 June 1855, http://marxengels.public-archive.net/en/ME0913en.html

    https://doi.org/10.11647/OBP.0152.12

> Nothing, in the history of the Newspaper Press of the nineteenth century, is more remarkable than the rapid development of provincial journalism since the abolition of the Paper, the Stamp, and the Advertisement Duties. Every city, town, village, and we may almost say hamlet, has now its local organ.[2]

In every place, anywhere between one and a dozen local newspapers thrived as catalysts and chronicles of small (and not so small) centres of distinctive local cultures. These regions, cities, towns and villages were connected to each other and to England's biggest newspaper centre, London, as nodes in a national network (a 'national' made from many 'local' elements). Books, magazines and London newspapers were important, but the national reach of the local press gave it a greater influence on Victorian culture than any other type of print. The local newspaper shaped popular understandings of politics, poetry, government (local and central), citizenship, fiction, and history, for example. Such claims, which promise to rewrite a great deal of nineteenth-century cultural history, can only be made by starting with Victorian readers. The vast majority of them preferred the local newspaper, which, in aggregate, outsold London papers until the 1930s at least.

There had been more provincial newspapers than London newspapers since the late eighteenth century. By 1856 there were more than twice as many provincial papers (370, compared to 152 London papers). As Marx predicted, the number of provincial titles nearly doubled after the abolition of compulsory stamp duty (see Table 0.1 below), while the increase in London publications, by about 50 per cent, was smaller (with half of that increase due to local newspapers such as the *Hackney Gazette*, in London's districts, as opposed to larger papers such as *The Times* that circulated more widely). By the end of the century, provincial titles (exluding London local papers) had increased six-fold, rising from 224 to 1340, while those published from London had roughly doubled, going from 131 to 298 (if we exclude London local papers). Table 0.1 also shows that the weekly or bi-weekly provincial paper, the focus of this book, was by far the most common type, accounting for all but seven provincial papers in 1856, and even at the end of the century, there were about ten times as many provincial weeklies and bi-weeklies as provincial daily papers. These figures underestimate the number of

---

2   Anon., 'Provincial Journalistic Enterprise', *Printers' Register*, 7 March 1870, p. 49.

papers, as not all of them appeared in the newspaper directories used to compile this table.[3] The greater numbers of provincial titles, and their networked, co-operative working methods, gave them greater economic and political power as a body. As Victoria Gardner has pointed out, the government consulted provincial rather than metropolitan newspaper publishers when they were considering changes in newspaper taxation, as early as 1797.[4] They continued to have more influence on government as a trade body, in discussions of Stamp Duty reduction in 1836, and in the unprecedented nationalisation of a private business, the telegraphs, on their terms, in 1870. In consequence, Julius Reuter, the owner of the world's largest news agency, made an exclusive deal with the provincial press rather than the more prestigious but smaller London press.[5]

Of course, numbers of titles are not the same as copies sold or read, but provincial papers outsold London ones from the 1860s until around the 1950s. Before the abolition of compulsory stamp duty in 1855, London papers outsold provincial ones, with 65 million London papers sold in 1854, compared to 25 million for provincial titles.[6] But ten years later the situation was reversed, with 340 million copies of provincial papers sold per year, compared to 206 million London papers.[7] In 1920, the circulation of the provincial morning and evening papers alone, ignoring weekly papers, was still one-third greater than the London dailies.[8] Records from newsagents, reading rooms, libraries and early oral history interviews all confirm that the vast majority of the population preferred the local paper. A Bradford teacher, the father of the novelist J. B. Priestley, for example, 'never dreamt of taking anything but our morning penny

---

3   In Preston alone, five of the fifty-one nineteenth-century titles traced so far do not appear in the British Library catalogue nor in the *Waterloo Directory of Nineteenth Century Newspapers and Periodicals* online edition.

4   Victoria E. M. Gardner, *The Business of News in England, 1760–1820* (Basingstoke: Palgrave, 2016), pp. 46–47, https://doi.org/10.1057/9781137336392

5   Jonathan Silberstein-Loeb, 'The Structure of the News Market in Britain, 1870–1914', *Business History Review*, 83 (2009), 759–88 (pp. 771–72), https://doi.org/10.1017/s0007680500000908

6   House of Commons, 'Return of Number of Stamps issued at One Penny to Newspapers in United Kingdom', 1854–55 (83), 1854.

7   Edward Baines, *Extension of the Franchise: Speech of Edward Baines on Moving the Second Reading of the Borough Franchise Bill, in the House of Commons, on the 11th May, 1864* (London, 1864).

8   Colin Seymour-Ure, *The British Press and Broadcasting since 1945* (Oxford: Blackwell, 1996), p. 16.

paper, which was then a very dignified organ of [local] opinion'.[9] For most of the population, provincial newspapers were not on the fringes of nineteenth-century print culture, but at the very heart of it.

Table 0.1. Numbers of English newspapers by place of publication, 1846–96.[10]

Newspapers	1846	1856	1866	1875	1886	1896
London						
Mornings	8	8	11	13	13	18
Evenings	4	7	10	5	8	12
Weekly / bi-weekly	119	137	172	244	273	268
London local			33	52	140	201
London total	131	152	226	314	434	499
Provincial						
Mornings		7	23	55	53	42
Evenings			2	25	70	82
Weekly / bi-weekly	224	363	698	807	1139	1216
Provincial total	224	370	723	887	1262	1340
All newspapers	**355**	**522**	**949**	**1201**	**1696**	**1839**

This book begins with these readers, devoting four chapters to who they were (Chapter 1), where they read (Chapter 2), when they read (Chapter 3) and what they read (Chapter 6). This focus on the circumstances of reading the local paper helps us to understand what the Victorian local paper was. It acknowledges the power of the reader, individually and

---

9   J. B. Priestley, 'An Outpost', in *The Book of Fleet Street*, ed. by T. Michael Pope (London: Cassell, 1930), pp. 174–82 (p. 174).

10   Source: *Mitchell's Newspaper Press Directories*, British Library. The volume for 1876 is missing, so 1875 was used instead. Excludes Monmouthshire. These figures supersede those in Andrew Hobbs, 'The Deleterious Dominance of *The Times* in Nineteenth-Century Scholarship', *Journal of Victorian Culture*, 18 (2013), p. 482, https://doi.org/10.1080/13555502.2013.854519 and Andrew Hobbs, 'Reading the Local Paper: Social and Cultural Functions of the Local Press in Preston, Lancashire, 1855–1900' (unpublished PhD dissertation, University of Central Lancashire, 2010), p. 41 (Table 4), which mistakenly mixed British and English figures. Thanks to Beth Gaskell for assistance in finding this information.

as a community, to shape the text and to use it in their own way, whilst also identifying some of the inequalities in power between reader and publisher.[11]

A Counter-Factual

It was not inevitable that there would be English local newspapers, or that they would prove so popular. Many countries have no history of an independent, networked provincial press, and from the 1850s to the 1870s, some publishers and commentators wished for a more centralised press, whilst others believed that the local newspaper was threatened by the advance of the railway and the telegraph. In 1851, Frederick Knight Hunt, then sub-editor of the London *Daily News*, told a select committee that the abolition of the compulsory newspaper stamp would free London and big-city newspapers to become 'national', with only a minor role for smaller local newspapers:

> a paper emanating from the metropolis, having a manifest national character, is much more likely to be useful over the country [...] instead of entering into little local bickerings [...] there would be little papers like the "Cheltenham Looker-On," to give local news, but papers emanating from large towns, such as London, Manchester, and Liverpool, would circulate over the country, and give more than ever a tone to national opinion.[12]

In 1863, Mortimer Collins, former editor of the *Lancaster Gazette*, now a poet and novelist, wrote: 'The country newspaper is essentially a thing of the past [...] We suspect that the days will soon arrive when there will, with an exception or two, be no country newspapers in England; when London will supply all the journalism of the kingdom.'[13] In the same year, an anonymous writer described 'the dream [...] of enthusiastic persons, that some three or four leviathan London, Manchester,

---

11   These ideas are taken from Gardner, especially Chapter 4; Stuart Hall, 'Encoding/ Decoding', in *Media and Cultural Studies: Keyworks*, ed. by Meenakshi Gigi Durham and Douglas Kellner (Malden: Blackwell, 2006); James Carey, 'A Cultural Approach to Communication', in *Communication as Culture: Essays on Media and Society* (London: Routledge, 1989), pp. 13–36, https://doi.org/10.4324/9780203928912

12   House of Commons, 'Report from the Select Committee on Newspaper Stamps; Together with the Proceedings of the Committee, Minutes of Evidence, Appendix, and Index' 1851 (558) XVII.1 (minutes 2358–60).

13   Mortimer Collins, 'Country Newspapers', *Temple Bar*, 10 (1863), pp. 128–41 (p. 141).

or Dublin prints, sold at a penny, will be carried everywhere by rail and steamboat, to the final extinguishment of local journalism'.[14] The Provincial Newspaper Society used these fears in the late 1860s, in their lobbying for the nationalisation of the private telegraph companies.[15]

The growing number of successful local newspaper proprietors knew that these fears were unfounded, as they watched their circulations increase. The spread of the railways from the 1840s onwards probably helped to distribute London papers more than provincial ones, but they also speeded up the arrival of London news (as distinct from newspapers) in provincial towns. The news service provided by the 'intelligence departments' of the private telegraph companies from the 1850s was slow and sometimes inaccurate and irrelevant, but was a boon to those provincial papers that could afford it; they received the news in their own town at the same time as it arrived in the London newspaper offices, but it was only a matter of minutes to typeset, print and publish that news, whereas the London papers, containing the same news, took hours to arrive by train. The penny newspaper stamp doubled as a tax and a postage charge, so had provided cheap postal distribution for London papers, but it was simply a tax for those provincial papers which had no need of the post because they sold within a restricted geographical area; its change to a postal charge only, in 1855, made local newspapers cheaper whilst significantly cutting the provincial circulation of London papers. The nationalisation of the telegraphs in 1870, and the creation of the Press Association, a co-operative news agency controlled by the provincial press, provided news from London, the rest of the UK and from around the world at preferential rates for local papers.[16] Finally, the advent of slightly earlier 'newspaper trains' from London in the 1870s was a favourite topic for journalists at the time, but had little impact on London newspaper sales in the regions.[17] These conditions helped the local press to flourish, but they do not explain its popularity.

---

14   Anon., 'The British Newspaper: The Penny Theory and Its Solution', *Dublin University Magazine*, 61 (1863), 359–76 (p. 371).

15   Jonathan Silberstein-Loeb, *The International Distribution of News: The Associated Press, Press Association, and Reuters, 1848–1947* (New York, NY: Cambridge University Press, 2014), p. 93, https://doi.org/10.1017/cbo9781139522489

16   Silberstein-Loeb, *The International Distribution of News*, p. 5.

17   Alexander Paterson, 'Provincial Newspapers', in *Progress of British Newspapers in the Nineteenth Century* (London: Simpkin, Marshall, Hamilton, Kent & Co., 1901), p. 79.

Why Were Local Newspapers so Popular?

So why were post-1855 provincial newspapers far more successful than London papers? Few people have asked this question, about one of the most significant developments in nineteenth-century print culture, and even fewer have suggested answers. As the provincial newspaper industry shrinks in the early twenty-first century, its phenomenal popularity in the past can now be seen as contingent and puzzling, rather than taken for granted. Was its popularity due to the growth of Victorian localism, expressed in newly incorporated boroughs, neo-classical town halls and associational culture? Perhaps, but those trends began decades before 1855, and a strong interest in local news was constant throughout the century. Was it because of a differential growth in literacy, with the provinces catching up with London?[18] Perhaps, but why did these new readers choose the local paper? Or was it the faster news service that local daily papers could provide, thanks to the shorter distances between publishing office and reader, in each local market, compared to the distance between London publishing offices and provincial readers? Perhaps, but the local press (most of it weekly rather than daily) was in the ascendant before many papers began to use telegraphic news, and certainly before the launch of the Press Association in 1870.

This book argues that, for morning and evening newspapers in particular, the national structure of the local press meant that local Fleet Streets could deliver news to local readers faster than papers produced on London's Fleet Street. But more importantly, the provincial press was so popular in the second half of the nineteenth century because it built upon, and built, local and regional identities.

George Gissing's 1891 novel *New Grub Street* gives the impression of a London-centred press in the Victorian era, but, as Margaret Stetz notes, newspapers and books were published from many centres.[19] While Stetz's focus is on a global network, this book explores a national network of local publishing (Chapters 4 and 5). This paradox, the

---

18 David Vincent, *Literacy and Popular Culture: England 1750–1914* (Cambridge: Cambridge University Press, 1989), p. 41, https://doi.org/10.1017/cbo9780511560880

19 Margaret D. Stetz, 'Internationalizing Authorship: Beyond New Grub Street to the Bookman in 1891', *Victorian Periodicals Review*, 48 (2015), 1–14 (p. 3), https://doi.org/10.1353/vpr.2015.0011

national aspect of the local press, was a commonplace in the second half of the nineteenth century. As an anonymous contributor to the *Dublin University Magazine* explained in 1863:

> We are not to regard the newspapers of this highly developed country as so many distinct productions, each independent of the other; they all hang together, and in union form a system of intelligence which ministers to good government, social peace, and the interests of trade.[20]

In the twenty-first century we are comfortable with the idea of a national thing made up of local things, such as a national House of Commons full of MPs from constituencies around the country, a national Church of England comprising local parishes, or a national rail network made up of pieces of local track connecting local stations. Graham Law's work on national publication of serial fiction through ad hoc syndicates of local newspapers reminds us of this local/national structure, and I have found Simon Potter's work on international press systems and networks useful for understanding the structure of the English local press.[21] However, many historians struggle with this idea when applied to nineteenth-century newspapers, falling back instead on anachronistic twenty-first-century concepts.

We need to be clear about the meanings of 'local' and 'national' in the nineteenth century. Victorian 'local' newspapers were distributed within one district or group of districts, as distinct from county or regional papers and their wider circulation areas. However, there is no simple division between local, sub-regional, county and regional papers, partly because such areas are difficult to define exactly, and partly because of changes over time in the nature and extent of the circulation areas of newspapers. Nineteenth-century local papers were less local in their content and control than has been assumed, while the other side of the twenty-first-century binary, the 'national' press, is an anachronism when applied to the nineteenth century. The London papers were more regional than national; they combined coverage of national institutions

---

20   Anon., 'British Newspaper: Penny Theory', p. 371.
21   Graham Law, *Serializing Fiction in the Victorian Press* (Basingstoke: Palgrave, 2000); Simon Potter, 'Webs, Networks, and Systems: Globalization and the Mass Media in the Nineteenth- and Twentieth-Century British Empire', *Journal of British Studies*, 46 (2007), 621–46, https://doi.org/10.1086/515446; Andrew Hobbs, 'When the Provincial Press Was the National Press (c.1836–c.1900)', *International Journal of Regional and Local Studies*, 5 (2009), 16–43, https://doi.org/10.1179/jrl.2009.5.1.16

based in London with coverage of London and the south-east.[22] In 1870 Walter Bagehot despaired of the provincialism of London papers: 'Of municipal news there is next to nothing, — of county news nothing at all unconnected with imperial politics […] Manchester might be almost on the verge of civil war without London knowing that anything had occurred in Manchester.'[23] Consequently, the terms 'local', 'regional', 'metropolitan' and 'national' must be used carefully, specifying whether these terms apply to the place of production, to the circulation area, the content or merely editorial aspirations; in the twenty-first century, media regulators have similar problems when trying to define 'local'.[24] Readers wanted national information as well as local news, and much of the content of the 'local' press was about non-local topics. This included significant amounts of material such as Parliamentary reports, foreign news and snippets from around the UK, leader columns on national politics, serialised fiction and so on.

Conversely, the term 'national' as we understand it today (implying a large, nationwide circulation, containing news from across the nation plus Parliamentary and foreign news) was barely used. A search of forty-eight digitised London and provincial newspapers found only ten instances of the phrase 'national newspaper' used in the modern sense, across the whole century.[25] The twenty-first-century meaning of 'national' newspaper was very occasionally applied in the nineteenth century, to the Chartist *Northern Star* and to the *Times*. It was not used to describe other titles, even the handful that were truly national in content

---

22 Maurice Milne, *The Newspapers of Northumberland and Durham: A Study of Their Progress during the 'Golden Age' of the Provincial Press* (Newcastle upon Tyne: Graham, 1971), p. 14; Alan J. Lee, 'The Structure, Ownership and Control of the Press, 1855–1914', in *Newspaper History from the Seventeenth Century to the Present Day*, ed. by David George Boyce, James Curran, and Pauline Wingate (London: Constable, 1978), p. 120. For an opposing view, see Stephen Koss, *The Rise and Fall of the Political Press in Britain, Vol. 1, The Nineteenth Century* (London: Hamish Hamilton, 1981), p. 21 and passim.

23 [Walter Bagehot], 'The Position of the Metropolitan Press', *The Economist*, 14 May 1870, pp. 595–96.

24 Christopher Ali, *Media Localism: The Policies of Place* (Urbana: University of Illinois Press, 2017), p. 18, https://doi.org/10.5406/illinois/9780252040726.001.0001

25 Even this figure exaggerates how often 'national' was used — the four instances from the 1830s were self-descriptions in advertisements for two failed journals, the *United Kingdom* and the *Britannia*, both using nationalistic rhetoric: advertisement for *United Kingdom* in *Hull Packet*, 19 October 1830; advertisement for *The Britannia* in *Morning Chronicle*, 22 April 1839.

and distribution, such as *Cobbett's Political Register*, Sunday papers such as *Reynolds' News*, *Lloyd's Weekly Newspaper* and the *News of the World*, the *Illustrated London News* or trade and professional titles, such as *Alliance News* (an anti-alcohol temperance periodical) or the *Lancet* (a professional newspaper for doctors). Newspaper publishers did not use the term 'national', with the *Newspaper Press Directory* continuing to use the classification of 'London' rather than 'national' newspapers well into the twentieth century.[26] 'National' publications could be published from the provinces, of course, such as the *Northern Star* from Leeds, the Band of Hope journal *Onward* and the football weekly *Athletic News*, both from Manchester. And there were hybrid national-local publications such as Anglican parish magazines, their 'middles' produced centrally, to be supplemented by local editorial and advertising, on the model of partly printed newspapers.[27]

The continuing use of the term 'local newspaper', and the survival of many nineteenth-century local titles, mislead us into thinking that their twenty-first-century content, their system of production and their current place in society is similar to the situation 150 years ago. It is not. They contained more national news, more scholarly and literary content (George Eliot and the Brontës were first published in local newspapers), and more general information, and were more 'magaziney' than today's local papers. They were more likely to be owned by a local proprietor rather than being part of a national chain, they were more politically partisan, were more open to 'amateur' local contributors, their buildings were visible in town and city centres, not hidden on commercial estates on the edge of town, and they had more competition from other local papers, but less competition from London papers or other types of media. Thus there have been big changes in the logistical, structural side of the local newspaper; but in other ways, there is continuity.

> One thing stays relatively constant. We base ourselves somewhere in the world, for family, work or social reasons. We develop affinities with some places where we come to consider ourselves 'local', part of a 'community' or feel a 'sense of place' [...] information about our 'place'

---

26   Hobbs, 'When the Provincial Press'.
27   Jane Platt, *Subscribing to Faith? The Anglican Parish Magazine 1859–1929* (Basingstoke: Palgrave Macmillan, 2015), pp. 3–5, https://doi.org/10.1057/9781137362445

in the world is important for us to navigate our day-to-day lives or to fulfil a basic desire to belong somewhere and be connected to others.[28]

In their 2017 book, Kristy Hess and Lisa Waller argue that 'place still matters in a digital world', and this connection between people and a particular place radiates from every page of a Victorian local newspaper. They expressed it and exploited it. For good or ill, they used their power to define each place.[29] Belatedly, media history is beginning to adopt the 'spatial turn' and acknowledge that the category of place is crucial — history always happens *somewhere*, after all. Victorians were not disembodied repositories of ideas: they created, and were created by, particular localities, counties, regions and nations.[30] The study of journalism lags behind literary studies in acknowledging the importance of sense of place: T. S. Eliot wrote that he doubted 'whether a poet or novelist can be universal without being local too.'[31] Fiona Stafford believes that Wordsworth's *Lyrical Ballads* helped Charles Lamb 'to recognise what he already felt — that local attachment depended, not on conventional ideas of picturesque beauty, but on the psychological bonds fostered there', in the same way that love for one's mother does not depend on the beauty of the mother.[32] The growing interest, among historians and literary scholars (but not geographers, surprisingly) in the relationship between place and less literary print can lead to new understandings:[33]

> place is not just a thing in the world but a way of understanding the world [...] When we look at the world as a world of places, we see

---

28   Kristy Hess and Lisa Waller, *Local Journalism in a Digital World: Theory and Practice in the Digital Age* (London: Palgrave, 2017), pp. vi, 6. See also Meryl Aldridge, *Understanding the Local Media* (Maidenhead: Open University Press, 2007), ch. 1.

29   Tim Cresswell, *Place: An Introduction*, 2nd edition (Chichester: Wiley-Blackwell, 2014), p. 45.

30   Denis G. Paz, *Popular Anti-Catholicism in Mid-Victorian England* (Stanford: Stanford University Press, 1992), pp. 299–300.

31   T. S. Eliot, 'American Literature and the American Language', in *To Criticize the Critic and Other Writings* (University of Nebraska Press, 1965), pp. 43–60 (p. 56).

32   Fiona J. Stafford, *Local Attachments: The Province of Poetry* (Oxford: Oxford University Press, 2010), p. 274.

33   For a good survey, see Sydney Shep, 'Books in Global Perspectives', in *The Cambridge Companion to the History of the Book*, ed. by Leslie Howsam (Cambridge: Cambridge University Press, 2014), https://doi.org/10.1017/CCO9781139152242.005. But no mention of local media in the otherwise excellent Cresswell.

different things. We see attachments and connections between people
and place. We see worlds of meaning and experience.[34]

Some writers have explored how newspapers 'wrote' urban places.
Peter Fritzsche's insightful exploration of how daily papers represented
and influenced Berlin from 1900 to 1914, and David Henkin's study
of newspapers and other ephemeral texts in pre-Civil War New York
City, both reveal the complexity of newspapers and their connection to
place. However, they focus on the writing only, and conjure up implied
readers and their responses purely from the texts.[35] Sense of place is
much more localised in Mary Shannon's study of one Victorian London
street, Wellington Street, where Dickens, Reynolds and other writers,
journalists and publishers congregated.[36] For once, London is specific
and local, rather than vaguely national, somehow above geography. But
again, Shannon concentrates on the production and circulation of texts,
rather than their reading.

Newspapers and other ephemeral texts could create communities,
these writers all agree. They take Benedict Anderson's idea of an 'imagined
community' of other readers and apply it to the physical community of
a city or even a street.[37] In English towns, readers spoke and wrote of
feeling connected to other readers of the same newspaper, even though
they had never met most of them. Mid-twentieth-century Chicago School
sociologists found similar connections between newspaper reading and
sense of community in the United States.[38] However, we should be wary
of over-claiming for the power of print — as we will see in Chapter 7, there
were many other factors in the creation and sustenance of local identities.

---

34   Cresswell, p. 18.

35   Peter Fritzsche, *Reading Berlin 1900* (London: Harvard University Press, 1996);
     David M. Henkin, *City Reading: Written Words and Public Spaces in Antebellum New
     York* (New York: Columbia University Press, 1998).

36   Mary L. Shannon, *Dickens, Reynolds, and Mayhew on Wellington Street: The Print Culture
     of a Victorian Street* (London: Routledge, 2015), https://doi.org/10.4324/9781315577067

37   Benedict Anderson, *Imagined Communities: Reflections on the Origin and Spread of
     Nationalism* (London: Verso, 2006).

38   Morris Janowitz, 'The Imagery of the Urban Press', *Public Opinion Quarterly*, 15
     (1951), 519–31; Eric W. Rothenbuhler and others, 'Communication, Community
     Attachment, and Involvement', *Journalism and Mass Communication Quarterly*,
     73 (1996), 445–66, https://doi.org/10.1177/107769909607300214; see also Keith R.
     Stamm, Arthur G. Emig, and Michael B. Hesse, 'The Contribution of Local Media
     to Community Involvement', *Journalism & Mass Communication Quarterly*, 74 (1997),
     97–107, https://doi.org/10.1177/107769909707400108

While the writing of place is a well-established idea, the *reading* of place has received less attention. Christine Pawley's analysis of print culture in the town of Osage, Iowa in the late nineteenth century explores how 'Osage inhabitants created and re-created their own print culture, both literally — by producing printed artifacts — and metaphorically — by producing distinct meanings and interpretations of print.' She describes how local reading and publishing patched together a sense of the national from the local.[39] Pawley includes some discussion of reading, but there is little about the reading of newspapers, beyond general description and implied readership deduced from the text. Another study of one town, Lancaster in northern England, by David Barton and Mary Hamilton, is an ethnographic project from the late twentieth century, which focuses on real readers, and comes to the same conclusions as Janowitz, that the local newspaper is important in people's lives, creating a sense of community.[40]

It is peculiarly difficult to empathise with someone else's sense of place, even if we have an attachment to a different place; it is only tangible from 'inside' a place, and meaningless or invisible to outsiders.[41] If we have no commitment to any place, local papers seem trivial; but the historical evidence presented in this book says that others felt differently. On historical grounds alone, the trivial and the mundane offer us the flavour of everyday life from a time now gone. Dickens's mockery of the *Eatanswill Gazette* and the *Eatanswill Independent* in the *Pickwick Papers* is well known; but his journal *All The Year Round* defended the local press and its place in local democracy. Referring to a comically detailed local newspaper account of the ancient custom of beating the bounds, the anonymous writer (possibly Dickens) adds: 'these things may appear very small, but life is made up of small things.'[42] James Carey encourages us to pay attention to the small things which together constitute everyday communication.[43] Local newspapers used this type of communication

39 Christine Pawley, *Reading on the Middle Border: The Culture of Print in Late-Nineteenth-Century Osage, Iowa* (Amherst: University of Massachusetts Press, 2001), pp. 4–5.

40 David Barton and Mary Hamilton, *Local Literacies: Reading and Writing in One Community* (London: Routledge, 1998).

41 Lucy R. Lippard, *The Lure of the Local: Senses of Place in a Multicentered Society* (New York: The New Press, 1998), p. 7.

42 Anon., 'On the Parish', *All The Year Round*, December 29 (1860), 273–76.

43 James Carey, *Communication as Culture: Essays on Media and Society* (London: Routledge, 1989), p. 24, https://doi.org/10.4324/9780203928912

in an explicit project of promoting local identity, or appealing to local patriotism, as Aled Jones and Patrick Joyce have noted, often using simple, even banal techniques.[44] Chapters 7, 8 and 9 of this book analyse some of the techniques for evoking sense of place. Indeed, one of these — the inclusion of hundreds of names of local people — is the chief attraction of digitised Victorian local newspapers for today's family historians.

This book charts new territory in recovering the readers' uses of the local newspaper's local content, to build and sustain local identities (Chapter 10). Readers used the local paper individually, such as the workhouse inmate who guarded his weekly copy as his only remaining comfort, or the exile who read a posted paper avidly to take his mind back to the places and people from whom he was separated. They used it for affirmation and validation, as James Carey notes, to confirm what they already knew, whether it was a football score or the report of a meeting at which they spoke. They used it as part of comforting daily routines, with favourite armchairs and a good fire often appearing in accounts of how the local paper was read. They used it publicly and communally as a forum for debate, a historical embodiment of Jurgen Habermas's public sphere, in which private citizens held rational debates in the public pages of newspapers.[45] And when local identity was threatened, as when traditionally distinct towns were combined in local government reorganisation, sales rose as the local paper spoke on the public's behalf.

The Local Newspaper is History

There is renewed interest in the local newspaper, from politicians and commentators concerned about its future, and from historians and literary scholars studying its past. In 2018 the British government announced a review of the news media market, expressing concerns about the impact of its decline on democracy.[46] History may soon be all that remains of provincial papers that have survived into the twenty-first century with remarkably few changes from their Victorian beginnings.

---

44   Patrick Joyce, *The Rule of Freedom: Liberalism and the Modern City* (London: Verso, 2003), p. 125; Aled Gruffydd Jones, *Press, Politics and Society: A History of Journalism in Wales* (Cardiff: University of Wales Press, 1993), p. 199.

45   Jurgen Habermas, *The Structural Transformation of the Public Sphere: An Inquiry into a Category of Bourgeois Society* (Oxford: Polity, 1992).

46   'Tackling the Threat to High-Quality Journalism in the UK', GOV.UK, https://www.gov.uk/government/news/tackling-the-threat-to-high-quality-journalism-in-the-uk

Yet nineteenth-century local papers are being read by more people than ever before thanks to digitisation, aimed primarily at family historians. Hundreds of titles are available in the commercial British Newspaper Archive, and some of the same titles are also available free of charge via British local libraries.[47] Digitisation has encouraged historians and literary scholars to once again use, and study, the nineteenth-century press.

While decline has sparked interest today, it was the phenomenal rise of provincial newspapers, alongside metropolitan newspapers, that encouraged five significant historical studies of the press between 1850 and 1887.[48] It took twice as long for the next five to be published, but by the 1950s historians were generally showing a new interest in the nineteenth century. The academic journal *Victorian Studies* was founded in 1956, and the centrality of the press to Victorian culture was recognised in the establishment of the Research Society for Victorian Periodicals (RSVP) in 1968. Many of the methods and sources pioneered by RSVP members have shaped this book, although most of their scholarship has concerned elite metropolitan literary periodicals rather than newspapers until recent years.

There was a burst of scholarship on the nineteenth-century newspaper in the 1980s and 1990s, producing four major works, all acknowledging the importance of the provincial press, by Alan Lee, Lucy Brown and Aled Jones, although only Jones tackles the whole century, and treats newspapers as cultural and not just political phenomena.[49] More recently,

---

47 British Newspaper Archive, https://www.britishnewspaperarchive.co.uk/; 19th Century British Library Newspapers database http://www.bl.uk/reshelp/findhelprestype/news/newspdigproj/database/. For a practical research guide, see Denise Bates, *Historical Research Using British Newspapers* (Barnsley: Pen & Sword, 2016).

48 Frederick Knight Hunt, *The Fourth Estate: Contributions Towards a History of Newspapers, and of the Liberty of the Press* (London: Bogue, 1850); Alexander Andrews, *The History of British Journalism: From the Foundation of the Newspaper Press in England to the Repeal of the Stamp Act in 1855, with Sketches of Press Celebrities* (London: Richard Bentley, 1859); James Grant, *The Newspaper Press: Its Origin, Progress and Present Position* (London: Routledge, 1872), especially vol. 3 for the provincial press; Charles Pebody, *English Journalism, and the Men Who Have Made It* (London: Cassell, Petter, Galpin & Co., 1882); H. R. Fox Bourne, *English Newspapers: Chapters in the History of Journalism* (London: Routledge, 1887).

49 Alan J. Lee, *The Origins of the Popular Press in England: 1855–1914* (London: Croom Helm, 1976); Lucy Brown, *Victorian News and Newspapers* (Oxford: Clarendon Press, 1985); Aled Gruffydd Jones, *Powers of the Press: Newspapers, Power and the Public in Nineteenth-Century England* (Aldershot: Scolar Press, 1996); Jones, *Press, Politics and Society*.

RSVP members have provided essential scholarly infrastructure for a field embarrassed by the riches of thousands of nineteenth-century newspapers and periodicals. The monumental *Dictionary of Nineteenth Century Journalism* has some entries on the provincial press, with more in cumulative digital updates. The equally ambitious *Waterloo Directory* is a superb source, although its information should always be cross-checked; its potential for quantitative research has yet to be realised. Palmegiano's well indexed bibliography of magazine commentary on the nineteenth-century press has plenty of material on provincial serials, and Dixon's various bibliographies on the provincial press are useful, alongside the *Cambridge Bibliography of English Literature*, particularly for non-academic sources such as company histories and anniversary supplements.[50] Two new edited collections with a focus on magazines and periodicals nevertheless offer much for the newspaper historian, from the vibrant field of Victorian periodical studies.[51]

The field is broadening out from an early focus on newspapers as purely political phenomena, in otherwise excellent work on early nineteenth-century provincial newspapers by Aspinall (good on readership), Read (on northern middle-class reforming papers), and Lopatin (on the 1830s radical reform movement).[52] Valuable work has been done on the political and economic roles of newspaper owners

---

50 *Dictionary of Nineteenth Century Journalism*, ed. by Laurel Brake and Marysa Demoor, online edition, in C19: The Nineteenth Century Index (ProQuest); *The Waterloo Directory of English Newspapers and Periodicals, 1800–1900*, ed. by John S. North, online edition (North Waterloo Academic Press), www.victorianperiodicals. com/series3/; Eugenia M. Palmegiano, *Perceptions of the Press in Nineteenth-Century British Periodicals: A Bibliography* (London: Anthem, 2012), https://doi. org/10.7135/upo9781843317562; Diana Dixon, 'Navigating the Maze: Sources for Press Historians', *Media History*, 9 (2003), 79–90, https://doi.org/10.1080/13688800 32000060005; *The Cambridge Bibliography of English Literature. Vol.4*, ed. by Joanne Shattock (Cambridge: Cambridge University Press, 1999), https://doi.org/10.1017/ cbo9780511518683

51 *The Routledge Handbook to Nineteenth-Century British Periodicals and Newspapers*, ed. by Andrew King, Alexis Easley, and John Morton (London: Routledge, 2016), https://doi.org/10.4324/9781315613345; *Researching the Nineteenth-Century Periodical Press: Case Studies*, ed. by Alexis Easley, Andrew King, and John Morton (London New York: Routledge, 2017), https://doi.org/10.4324/9781315605616

52 Arthur Aspinall, *Politics and the Press, c.1780–1850* (Brighton: Harvester Press, 1973); Donald Read, *Press and People, 1790–1850: Opinion in Three English Cities* (London: Edward Arnold, 1961); Nancy P. Lopatin, 'Refining the Limits of Political Reporting: The Provincial Press, Political Unions, and The Great Reform Act', *Victorian Periodicals Newsletter*, 31 (1998), 337–55.

and editors in the early years of the century.[53] The *Northern Star* and other Chartist or sympathetic local papers have stimulated some excellent scholarship examining newspaper language, the relationship of local and national, the nature of newspaper-reading and the role of the newspaper as poetry publisher.[54] Victoria Gardner approaches the provincial press of the late eighteenth and early nineteenth centuries primarily as businesses, whilst acknowledging their other functions, and bringing many new insights, about the collective power of the provincial press, its co-operative ethos, the ways in which entire communities could influence a newspaper, and the distinctive local economies and cultures from which each paper sprang.[55] Rachel Matthews, in her sweeping history of the provincial press from its beginnings to today, also sees it primarily as a business, and challenges its rhetoric of community. Matthews argues that 'the provincial newspaper is, and always has been, a commercial venture to its core' and that 'profit is the principle around which all other elements of the newspaper [...] are organised'.[56] But this is undermined by her own evidence of political subsidy, and acknowledgement of political purpose as a 'pillar' of the newspaper's business model.[57] Her critique of publishers' rhetoric is based on ahistorical twenty-first-century criteria, and does not acknowledge how much of this rhetoric was sincere.

Nineteenth-century newspapers developed rapidly. But few have attempted to explain how politics, business and government policy combined between the 1830s and 1850s to transform the newspaper world, from the equivalent of a rowdy radical meeting to a vibrant but unthreatening street market in the space of a generation. Martin Hewitt

---

53 Victoria E. M. Gardner, 'The Communications Broker and the Public Sphere: John Ware and the Cumberland Pacquet', *Cultural and Social History*, 10 (2013), 533–57 https://doi.org/10.2752/147800413X13727009732164; F. David Roberts, 'Still More Early Victorian Newspaper Editors', *Victorian Periodicals Newsletter*, 18 (1972), 12–26; Derek Fraser, 'The Editor as Activist: Editors and Urban Politics in Early Victorian England', in *Innovators and Preachers: The Role of the Editor in Victorian England*, ed. by Joel Wiener (Westport, Conn: Greenwood Press, 1985).

54 See bibliography in Joan Allen and Owen R. Ashton, *Papers for the People: A Study of the Chartist Press* (London: Merlin Press, 2005).

55 Gardner, *Business of News*.

56 Rachel Matthews, *The History of the Provincial Press in England* (New York: Bloomsbury Academic, 2017), p. 4, https://doi.org/10.5040/9781501324680

57 Matthews, pp. 59, 89.

recounts the political lobbying for the abolition of newspaper taxes at mid-century, but the best account is Brian Maidment's modest yet profound essay on Manchester newsagent and publisher Abel Heywood, who went from imprisoned agent for the radical *Poor Man's Guardian* to mayor of Manchester without changing his views. Instead, society changed around him.[58] Maidment has written perceptively on other aspects of Manchester print culture, including the role of the local press in fostering 'bardic communities' of working-class poets, and edited a significant collection of essays on the Manchester press.[59] Some of the writers of those essays — Beetham, Michael Powell, Terry Wyke and Eddie Cass — and others have created an impressive body of scholarship on Manchester, Britain's second publishing centre (Powell and Wyke's edition of Leary's unpublished history of the city's press is eagerly awaited).[60] The press of northern England has received more attention than other English regions, perhaps because it was more dynamic.

Scholarship increases in proportion to the growing scale of the provincial press, with most work devoted to post-1855 developments. Shattock and Wolff's excellent 1982 collection takes a holistic approach, including newspaper-reading, but their agenda is only now being picked up.[61] More recent work on the provincial press appears in three

---

58 Martin Hewitt, *The Dawn of the Cheap Press in Victorian Britain: The End of the 'Taxes on Knowledge', 1849–1869* (London: Bloomsbury Academic, 2014); Brian E. Maidment, 'The Manchester Common Reader — Abel Heywood's "Evidence" and the Early Victorian Reading Public', in 'Printing and the Book in Manchester, 1700–1850', special issue of *Transactions of the Lancashire and Cheshire Antiquarian Society*, 97, ed. by Eddie Cass and Morris Garratt (2001), pp. 99–120.

59 Brian E. Maidment, 'Class and Cultural Production in the Industrial City: Poetry in Victorian Manchester', in *City, Class and Culture: Studies of Cultural Production and Social Policy in Victorian Manchester*, ed. by Alan J. Kidd and Kenneth Roberts (Manchester: Manchester University Press, 1985), pp. 148–66; 'The Literary Culture of Nineteenth-Century Manchester', special issue of *Manchester Region History Review*, 17, ed. by Brian E. Maidment, 2006.

60 Margaret Beetham, 'Healthy Reading', in Kidd and Roberts; Michael Winstanley, 'News from Oldham: Edwin Butterworth and the Manchester Press, 1829–1848', *Manchester Region History Review*, 4 (1990), 3–10; John Nicholson, 'Popular Imperialism and the Provincial Press: Manchester Evening and Weekly Papers, 1895–1902', *Victorian Periodicals Review*, 13 (1980), 85–96; Colin Buckley, 'The Search for "a Really Smart Sheet": The Conservative Evening Newspaper Project in Edwardian Manchester', *Manchester Region History Review*, 8 (1994), 21–28.

61 *The Victorian Periodical Press: Samplings and Soundings*, ed. by Joanne Shattock and Michael Wolff (Leicester: Leicester University Press, 1982). For readers, see chapters by Harrison, James and Wolff.

special issues of journals, and in the annual Print Networks volumes.[62] Beyond this body of work, research on provincial newspapers and magazines can be found scattered among works of political, social, economic, cultural and literary history.

Reasons to Ignore the Provincial Press

The renewed interest in the provincial press is heartening, but it is still misunderstood by many scholars. It is seen as an inferior, scaled-down version of the London press; it is dismissed because it was not produced, or read, by powerful people, and because local topics are to be avoided if one wants to say something significant (or be someone significant, in career terms). Some still see newspapers, particularly local papers, as simple, banal texts, in contrast to sophisticated literary texts. This is all wrong, of course.

Victorian local newspapers were not poor-quality imitations of London papers; they were a different beast. Content, both advertising and editorial, was different — it was either local or locally relevant. They used form and content to evoke a sense of place and capitalise on local patriotism, which made them more varied across the nation, more open to local influences on their form and content.[63] This local loyalty could clash with the journalistic ideal of objectivity more than on London papers, where journalists could more easily see themselves as aloof from the society on which they reported and commented.[64] Miscellaneity, seen as fundamental to the form of the newspaper, was less pronounced in local papers because news items had the unifying theme of place. They were more 'magaziney', a hybrid of newspaper and magazine. This point is worth developing: the idea that all newspapers contained mainly news comes from the misleading example of London dailies such as the *Times*.[65] But the *Times* was an

---

62 Maidment, 'Literary culture'; *Journalism Studies* 7 (2006); *International Journal of Regional and Local Studies* 5.1 (2009); for example, *Periodicals and Publishers: The Newspaper and Journal Trade, 1750–1914*, ed. by John Hinks, Catherine Armstrong, and Matthew Day (New Castle, DE: Oak Knoll Press, 2009).

63 Margaret Beetham, 'Ben Brierley's Journal', *Manchester Region History Review*, 17 (2006), 73–83 (p. 75).

64 Hess and Waller, pp. 86–88.

65 For a contemporary view of the restricted content of the newspaper, see Anon., 'Journalism', *Cornhill Magazine*, 6.31 (1862), 52–63 (p. 52).

anomaly in its concentration on political, foreign and commercial news, and its lack of non-news, 'feature' content.[66] Non-political news from around Britain accounted for less than ten per cent of content, although this did increase at the end of the century. Sports coverage was minimal, there were occasional book reviews, travelogues and reports of cultural events, but this was a very small proportion of the paper's content. The *Times* lacked the variety of content found in most provincial papers and in popular Sunday newspapers, making it a very atypical nineteenth-century newspaper.[67]

Provincial newspapers worked to a different business model, with more of their income coming from advertising, and less opportunity for economies of scale, particularly before the abolition of the newspaper taxes. They tended to control their own distribution, rather than using wholesale newsagents, the post, or trains. The structure of their industry was more national, more networked and more collaborative. This national structure made them, in aggregate, a significant publishing platform for many genres of content, in the pages of their newspapers, and in books, often compiled from previously published newspaper content; this publishing function was a smaller part of London newspapers' business. Provincial newspaper personnel were more likely to be personally known to their readers, making them more accountable, and therefore more trustworthy. Related to this, they were more open to 'amateur' contributors, making them a more culturally democratic form of print. A decentred view of the Victorian press enables us to move away from Matthew Arnold's dream of London as the headquarters of culture, from which new elements could be distributed to the provinces. Instead, innovations moved between many centres, provincial and metropolitan, sometimes arising far from London and eventually reaching the capital, sometimes reaching the provinces direct from other countries, carried in American newspapers by boat to Liverpool, for example.

A second reason to ignore the provincial press is that important people did not read it or write for it, unlike the London dailies. The standard work on the politics of the nineteenth-century press, by Stephen Koss, defines politics as the activities of government ministers

---

66   Brown, p. 108.
67   Hobbs, 'Deleterious'.

and senior party figures, and categorises as political only those London newspapers which contemporary politicians tried to influence.[68] But, as James Vernon has demonstrated, political participation of a kind was even available to those outside the franchise, and local government had a great deal of autonomy, which it used to the full.[69] Rich and poor, literate and illiterate took part in public meetings and the carnival and drama of elections and other political rituals, as demonstrated in the name of the Bury Non-Electors' Reform Association, for example.[70] Local issues and local rituals ensured that politics was an arena in which local identities were contested and confirmed, but national politics was also constructed at local level.[71] These vibrant, argumentative local political cultures continued into the Victorian era, even after 1872, when the secret ballot made elections less rumbustious. Nineteenth-century local newspapers were intensely political phenomena, in their circumstances of production, their content and in many of the uses to which readers put them. Publishers, journalists and readers were involved in a power struggle to define reality, locally and nationally, and newspapers were far from politically neutral in this argument, even if they claimed to be (the pretence of neutrality became more common after the 1886 Liberal party split).[72]

More broadly, this book is about the marginalised majority: those citizens who lived outside London, and the majority press that they read, most of it published weekly rather than daily. A focus on the higher-status but lower-circulation London press has produced many theories that do not adequately describe or explain local and regional newspapers, the mainstream of the Victorian press. Habermas's 'decline of the public sphere' retains its value as a theoretical framework despite its lack of historical evidence, but the restatements of this theory by Chalaby and Hampton, and Curran's view that the press became an

---

68   Koss, pp. 21, 23–24.
69   James Vernon, *Politics and the People: A Study in English Political Culture, c. 1815–1867* (Cambridge: Cambridge University Press, 1993).
70   V. C. Barbary, 'Reinterpreting "Factory Politics" in Bury, Lancashire, 1868–1880', *Historical Journal*, 51 (2008), 115–44 (p. 134).
71   Vincent, p. 238.
72   Carey, *Communication as Culture*, p. 86, Jones, *Press, Politics and Society*, p. 141; Jean Chalaby, *The Invention of Journalism* (Basingstoke: Macmillan, 1998), p. 77 ('it is false to assume that a depoliticised newspaper conveys less ideology than a political organ').

agent of control or the Whiggish account of the growing freedom of the 'Fourth Estate' all focus on metropolitan publications.[73] It is difficult to find evidence of such a decline in the reading rooms and newspapers of the provinces. Joel Wiener's focus on London dailies in his account of the 'Americanisation' of the British press from the 1880s onwards ignores the more complex, dispersed influences on what was in fact the 'magazinization' of the newspapers, partly influenced by the provincial press.[74] These matters are explored in more detail in Chapter 5. Neither does Chalaby's decline of the political publicist and the rise of 'objective' journalistic discourse in Britain fit the majority of newspapers, those of the provinces, where smaller local markets dictated a localist, rather than objective, style of journalism.[75] A final example is Rowbotham et al's narrative of crime reporting, which erases an army of local court reporters from history by concentrating on the London press.[76]

Few scholars even acknowledge their choice to study the minority of the press, let alone explain that choice. Before digitisation some scholars may have decided that the seemingly unmanageable quantity of local newspapers required too much effort. That practical reason is being overcome as hundreds of titles can be searched and analysed quickly in digital databases. All that remains is the notion of 'influence', which has led some researchers towards publications produced at the centre of cultural power, London. The assumption has been that texts worth studying are 'influential' texts, those that changed the attitudes or behaviour of influential people, such as cabinet ministers or a small elite

---

73 Chalaby, *Invention*; Mark Hampton, *Visions of the Press in Britain, 1850–1950* (Urbana: University of Illinois Press, 2004); James Curran, 'Media and the Making of British Society, c.1700–2000', *Media History*, 8 (2002), 135–54, https://doi.org/10.1080/1368880022000047137

74 Joel H. Wiener, *The Americanization of the British Press, 1830s–1914: Speed in the Age of Transatlantic Journalism* (Basingstoke: Palgrave Macmillan, 2011), https://doi.org/10.1057/9780230347953; his analysis is much subtler in an earlier, briefer account: Joel H. Wiener, 'How New Was the New Journalism?', in *Papers for the Millions: The New Journalism in Britain, 1850s to 1914*, ed. by Joel H. Wiener (London: Greenwood, 1988). The word 'magazinization' was coined by John Tulloch, in 'The Eternal Recurrence of New Journalism', in *Tabloid Tales: Global Debates Over Media Standards*, ed. by Colin Sparks and John Tulloch (Oxford: Rowman & Littlefield, 2000), pp. 131–146 (p. 139).

75 Hess and Waller, p. 9.

76 Judith Rowbotham, Kim Stevenson, and Samantha Pegg, *Crime News in Modern Britain: Press Reporting and Responsibility, 1820–2010* (Basingstoke: Palgrave Macmillan, 2013), https://doi.org/10.1057/9781137317971

of metropolitan literary writers and editors. 'All too often [...] English history, and even British history, turn out to be the history of what was happening in the West End, ignoring what was happening North of the Thames, or North of the Trent.'[77] But political and cultural power was widely distributed in the long nineteenth century, across classes and across the country.

The third reason to ignore local papers is because of their very localness. In any notional hierarchy of nineteenth-century print, books and periodicals would have higher status than newspapers, and metropolitan papers would rank more highly than provincial ones.[78] The derogatory sense of the words 'provincial' and 'provinces' was invented by London newspapers in the late eighteenth century, no doubt partly to position themselves in a competitive market.[79] In the 1860s Matthew Arnold added a new inflection when he identified the provinces with the 'philistinism' of dissenting chapel-goers; to Victorian readers this also reflected on provincial newspapers, which can be seen as an outgrowth of provincial Nonconformity.[80] The metropolitan is the default; Raymond Williams's description of the literary category of the 'regional novel' as an 'expression of centralized cultural dominance' applies also to the regional and local newspaper: 'The life and people of certain favoured regions are seen as essentially general, even perhaps normal, while the life and people of certain other regions [...] are, well, regional.'[81] The low status of 'local' history within academia may be a further reason for the relative neglect of the local press. To be considered a merely local historian is anathema, yet some of the best history has been based on small numbers of very local case studies, while some of the worst has generalised from local examples and ignored huge regional variations.

---

77 Paz, p. 19.

78 Lee Erickson, *The Economy of Literary Form: English Literature and the Industrialization of Publishing, 1800–1850* (London: Johns Hopkins University Press, 1996), p. 13; John S. North, 'The Importance of Newspapers', *Waterloo Directory of English Newspapers and Periodicals*, series 2, 'Tour site: Overview: Section 2', www.victorianperiodicals.com/series2/TourOverview.asp

79 Donald Read, *The English Provinces, 1760–1960: A Study in Influence* (London: Edward Arnold, 1964), p. 2.

80 Simon Goldsworthy, 'English Nonconconformity and the Pioneering of the Modern Newspaper Campaign', *Journalism Studies*, 7 (2006), 387–402 (p. 395), https://doi.org/10.1080/14616700600680690

81 Raymond Williams, 'Region and Class in the Novel', in *Writing in Society* (London: Verso, 1983), pp. 229–38 (p. 230).

The fourth reason is that newspapers, particularly provincial newspapers, are considered to be simplistic, transparent, ephemeral, banal texts, not worthy of one's analytical powers. This is to take them at their word.[82] But newspapers are not what they seem, and their stories about themselves are not always trustworthy. Margaret Beetham, the great theorist of the periodical, takes on this myth with a deft comparison of a local magazine, *Ben Brierley's Journal* (containing much material also found in local newspapers) and Isabella Banks's novel *The Manchester Man*:

> Because the magazine is essentially fragmented and fractured in terms of authorial voice and genre, it can encompass complexity and even contradiction which other genres cannot. Because it comes out over time and must engage its readers over time, encouraging them to continue to buy but also inviting them to write in as contributors, it involves negotiations between producers and readers not available even to the author of a serialised novel.[83]

The History of Reading the Local Paper

The overlapping histories of the book (taken to include newspapers and periodicals) and of reading are very good at following texts as they move from place to place. But this book is less about the mobility of texts, and more about their 'whereness', how place gives them meaning and flavour, like the 'terroir' of a French wine. It takes many of its techniques from the study of newspapers in the United States, where a decentralised newspaper geography is better understood. The ingenious methods of David Paul Nord, the Zborays and Uriel Heyd have proved particularly useful; they have shown that the fleeting act of newspaper reading *has* left traces in the record, if you look in the right places.[84] I have gathered these traces, in the records of reading places such as news rooms and

---

82 Dallas Liddle, *The Dynamics of Genre: Journalism and the Practice of Literature in Mid-Victorian Britain* (Charlottesville: University of Virginia Press, 2009), p. 4.

83 Beetham, 'Ben Brierley's Journal', p. 76.

84 David Paul Nord, *Communities of Journalism: A History of American Newspapers and Their Readers* (Urbana: University of Illinois Press, 2001); Ronald J. Zboray and Mary Saracino Zboray, 'Political News and Female Readership in Antebellum Boston and Its Region', *Journalism History*, 22 (1996), 2–14; Uriel Heyd, *Reading Newspapers: Press and Public in Eighteenth-Century Britain and America* (Oxford: Voltaire Foundation, 2012).

libraries, in letters to the editor, diaries, autobiographies and oral history interviews. This evidence has been used to reconstruct the 'reading world' of one Lancashire town, Preston, and to explore the many uses to which readers put the local press, not least the confirmation of local identities. Other evidence suggests that the local press was equally important and used in similar ways in other towns and cities. Taken together, these fragmentary and imperfect sources are greater than the sum of their parts, and tell a consistent story, of the significance of the local press, in both its production and use.

Reading the local paper was a social and ritual activity, to borrow the ideas of Stanley Fish and James Carey. There is concrete evidence that some readers' behaviour was directly affected by the content of the local press, for example the Blackburn shoemakers who picketed a local cobbler in reaction to a letter he wrote to the local paper (Chapter 10), but such clear influence is probably not representative of the way in which most readers used the local press. The connection between what journalists wrote and how readers responded was usually much looser. Victorian journalists' memoirs and diaries, and my experience of modern-day journalism, suggest that the primary audience for journalists was other journalists and close non-journalistic friends, and the ordinary reader was almost an after-thought. Conversely, most readers' primary relationships — as readers — were with *other* readers, as seen in readers' letters, where dialogue was usually between readers rather than with what journalists had written.

Despite this gulf between journalists and readers, there was a shared understanding. In Fish's terms they were all members of the same 'interpretive community', meaning a group of readers who interpret texts in similar ways, constrained by the 'codes and conventions that regulate the practices of a membership community'.[85] Although Fish did not use it in this way, this term is particularly helpful in enabling reading to be put into geographical *place*, to characterise particular groups of readers in a particular town; it can also be usefully combined with ideas from research on media effects, such as journalistic 'framing' of stories, i.e. the selection and emphasis of certain aspects of a story over others.

---

85   Stanley Eugene Fish, 'Interpreting the Variorum', *Critical Inquiry*, 2 (1976), 465–85, https://doi.org/10.1086/447852; see also Stephen Colclough, *Consuming Texts: Readers and Reading Communities, 1695–1870* (Basingstoke: Palgrave Macmillan, 2007), p. 9, https://doi.org/10.1057/9780230590540

Interpretive communities are taken to be groups of readers *and writers*, who can be members of multiple, overlapping interpretive communities but who share 'interpretive strategies' with other members of each community. Fish's 'interpretive strategies' are similar to the 'primary frameworks' or frames of reference, 'relatively stable and socially shared category systems that human beings use to classify information' discussed by Erving Goffman. Journalists have a choice of frames when telling a story, but only among a limited set with 'commonly shared cultural roots' — a frame needs to be part of the surrounding culture. A person can share an interpretation of a text, and be part of a culture shaped by that interpretation, without having read or heard the text.[86] However, one crucial notion absent from Fish's interpretive communities is power: cultural, economic and political power were all displayed and negotiated in the Victorian local press, and there was unequal access to publishing and reading.

The concept of interpretive communities helps us to see reading as a communal activity, embedded in social relationships (not always friendly ones), in which discussion is central. It also helps us to understand the nature of nineteenth-century local newspapers: how the interactive nature of newspapers made interpretive communities dynamic and historically and geographically specific, how tropes such as oppositional journalism could bind communities of readers together, how they were expressions of cultures such as Nonconformism, how the serial nature of newspapers enabled the repetition of frames, and the building of trust or 'source credibility', and how techniques such as 'kite-flying' (trying out ideas in print, to gauge public reaction) can be seen as a gentle repositioning of frames or interpretive strategies.[87] Later chapters will demonstrate how printers, booksellers, newspaper

---

86   Fish, pp. 483, 484; Erving Goffman, *Frame Analysis: An Essay on the Organization of Experience* (Cambridge, Mass: Harvard University Press, 1974), p. 24; elaborated in David Tewksbury and Dietram A. Scheufele, 'News Framing Theory and Research', in *Media Effects: Advances in Theory and Research*, ed. by Jennings Bryant and Mary Beth Oliver (New York: Routledge, 2009), pp. 18, 24, https://doi.org/10.4324/9780203877111. For more on the many possibilities that lie between reading and non-reading, see Pierre Bayard, *How to Talk About Books You Haven't Read* (Granta Books, 2008); Hall, 'Encoding/Decoding'.

87   Jones, *Press, Politics and Society*, pp. 154–55; Goldsworthy; Koss, p. 25; Tewksbury and Scheufele, p. 20; Harold Richard Grant Whates, *The Birmingham Post, 1857–1957. A Centenary Retrospect* (Birmingham: Birmingham Post & Mail, 1957), p. 215.

publishers, journalists, part-time newspaper correspondents, letter-writers and members of news rooms created interpretive communities in one town. Participation in the 'public sphere' identified by Habermas can be seen as one of the activities of an interpretive community, in which private individuals can come together as a public, and discuss public issues and hold authority to account. Habermas saw the press as central to this activity, and it is not necessary to accept his narrative of decline to find his approach useful.[88]

While Habermas compares reading the news to arguing in a coffee-house, Carey likens it to 'attending a mass, a situation in which nothing new is learned but in which a particular view of the world is portrayed and confirmed.'[89] Thus, the various interpretive communities within and beyond a small town such as Preston integrated the local press into reassuring rituals of everyday life, at the personal and communal level. Such a view makes only qualified claims about the influence of the local press. There is, however, a popular and persuasive theory that argues boldly for the pre-eminent influence of texts — novels and newspapers — to change people's minds about who they were and where they lived, rather than merely confirm their established beliefs; Benedict Anderson's idea of the imagined community. Using the example of the nineteenth-century Philippines, Anderson argues that, to read a novel in one's mother tongue, or a newspaper that is known to circulate over a particular area, makes one aware of other readers of the same texts, and thus creates an 'imagined community'.[90] This book makes smaller claims about the impact of being part of an imagined community created by the local paper — but the awareness of other readers, known or unknown, was important.

A Place: Preston

This book gathers historical evidence from across England, but it is grounded in a study of the reading, production and circulation of local

---

88 Habermas, pp. 27, 51.

89 Carey, *Communication as Culture*, p. 21; see also Georg Wilhelm Friedrich Hegel, *Hegel's Political Writings*, ed. by Z. A. Pelczynski and T. M. Knox (Oxford: Clarendon Press, 1964), p. 6.

90 Benedict Anderson, *Imagined Communities: Reflections on the Origin and Spread of Nationalism* (London: Verso, 2006).

newspapers in one place, the town of Preston in Lancashire.[91] The case study approach is a concrete and manageable way to bring this book's themes together and to test the theories of other scholars. It embraces the specificity of a place, recovering the concrete details of the readers, the where and when of what they read. Preston was small enough for its reading places and practices, and its newspapers, to be studied as a whole. The reader is invited to imagine an emotional connection to this town in the second half of the nineteenth century. From the inside, every place is unique (despite their sameness from the outside, when we hurtle past them on a train) and, to many of those who live in any particular place, it is numinous in its specialness. Some background information about Preston is therefore needed.

Fig. 0.1. Location map of Preston. Outline map by D-maps.com, CC BY 4.0, https://d-maps.com/carte.php?num_car=2555&lang=en

Halfway between London and Edinburgh, Preston was Lancashire's second oldest borough, and was a market centre for the agricultural areas of north Lancashire. This geography, and the rhythms of its

---

91   Other studies of local press ecologies (but lacking a focus on readers) include Maurice Milne, *The Newspapers of Northumberland and Durham: a Study of Their Progress During the 'Golden Age' of the Provincial Press* (Newcastle upon Tyne: Graham, 1971), and Peter J. Lucas, 'The First Furness Newspapers: the History of the Furness Press From 1846 to c.1880' (unpublished M.Litt. dissertation, University of Lancaster, 1971).

weekly markets, became visible in the circulation areas and publishing schedules — the where and the when — of its many newspapers. Preston was the administrative centre for all parts of Lancashire outside the cities and large towns, giving it a greater number of lawyers and other professionals. Geographically isolated from the main industrial areas of Lancashire, it drew many immigrants from the rural areas north, east and west of the town, and this reservoir of labour enabled its mills to pay lower wages than in other parts of Lancashire. Many of these immigrants were 'old' (as opposed to Irish) Roman Catholics, making Preston the most Catholic town in England.[92] Industrial relations in Preston were more acrimonious than in most other Lancashire textile towns, and were at their worst during the 1853–54 lock-out, which inspired writers such as Charles Dickens, Elizabeth Gaskell and Karl Marx, the first two using the dispute as inspiration for their novels *Hard Times* and *North and South* respectively, while Marx predicted that world revolution would begin there, as the working class began to cry, 'our St Petersburg is at Preston!'[93] The town's population grew from some 69,000 in 1851 to 125,000 in 1901. The railway arrived in 1838, the telegraph in 1854, but neither technology harmed Preston's newspapers, in fact quite the opposite. As geographers of place have argued, distinctiveness and sense of place are not necessarily threatened by connections to other places, or by the globalisation of the international telegraph system; the local and the global are not opposites, they are 'entangled' with each other.[94]

Preston's sense of its own significance was not based solely on its size and industry, but also on its social, administrative and commercial functions, and its long history, so that it saw itself as Lancashire's third centre, after Manchester and Liverpool. Spinning and weaving mills dominated the economy at mid-century, although its status as a market centre and county town gave it a more mixed economy than some other textile towns. It became the headquarters of the new county council in 1889, and its economy continued to diversify, particularly

---

92 Thirty-six per cent of Preston church attenders on March 30, 1851 were Roman Catholics: *Census of Great Britain, 1851: Religious Worship in England and Wales Abridged from the Official Report* (London: Routledge, 1854), p. 128.

93 Karl Marx, 'The English Middle Classes' [1 August 1854], in *Dispatches for the New York Tribune: Selected Journalism of Karl Marx*, ed. by James Ledbetter (London: Penguin Classics, 2007), pp. 142–45.

94 Shep, pp. 62–63.

into engineering (including print machinery), enabling it to survive the late nineteenth-century depression better than most Lancashire towns.[95] Its established river port was greatly expanded in 1892, by the controversial creation of a new deep water dock, at enormous cost. Its ship-building and maritime trade linked it to the empire and the wider world, as did its barracks, where regiments were stationed between deployments, including Waterloo, the Crimea, Afghanistan and South Africa.

Politically, Preston was a two-member Parliamentary constituency, with a tradition of electing one Whig and one Tory. This custom ended in 1865, when the Conservatives began an unbroken forty-one years of control of both seats. Michael Savage argues that working-class Conservatism in Preston was created by the party's cultural populism, and its support for redevelopment of the port. The town's Liberals, in contrast, were seen as the party of the mill and factory owners, and their Nonconformist, teetotal tendencies threatened a working-class Anglican culture which included drinking, gambling and blood sports.[96] The large Catholic electorate voted en bloc for Whig-Liberal candidates until 1858, after which Liberal foreign policy divided them.[97] These divisions were reflected in rival Liberal and Tory newspapers, and, from the 1880s, Roman Catholic publications.

An unusually high proportion of Preston residents had the vote until the 1880s. There had been a tradition of universal male suffrage in Preston that had officially ended in 1832; however, those with a vote under the old franchise retained it for the rest of their lives. These 'old franchise men' still accounted for more than 25 per cent of the electorate in 1865, giving Preston a more working-class franchise than most other towns.[98] In consequence, one might expect a wider political culture,

---

95 Michael Savage, *The Dynamics of Working-Class Politics: The Labour Movement in Preston 1880–1940* (Cambridge: Cambridge University Press, 1987), pp. 66, 95, https://doi.org/10.1017/cbo9780511898280; David Hunt, *A History of Preston* (Preston: Carnegie/Preston Borough Council, 1992), pp. 230, 234.

96 Jon Lawrence, 'Class and Gender in the Making of Urban Toryism, 1880–1914', *English Historical Review*, 108 (1993), 629–52 (p. 635).

97 Savage, *Dynamics*; Tom Smith, 'Religion or Party? Attitudes of Catholic Electors in Mid-Victorian Preston', *North West Catholic History*, 33 (2006), 19–35 (pp. 22, 24).

98 Smith, 'Religion or Party?'; Tom Smith, '"Let Justice Be Done and We Will Be Silent": A Study of Preston's Catholic Voters and Their Parliamentary Elections Campaigns, 1832 to 1867', *North West Catholic History*, 28 (2001), 5–54 (p. 8).

resulting in higher newspaper readership, but there is no evidence that levels of newspaper reading in Preston were unusually high in this period. After the 1867 Reform Act the middle classes dominated the town's Parliamentary electorate, which expanded enormously from 2,649 men in 1865 to 11,312 in 1868.[99] The municipal electorate was broader than that for Parliament, and included some working-class men throughout the period. From 1869, single women could also vote in corporation elections, with married women eligible after 1894.[100]

How to Use this Book

Parts of this book focus on readers and reading (Chapters 1, 2, 3, 6 and 10), others on the production of local newspapers (Chapters 4 and 5) and their content (Chapters 7, 8 and 9). The Preston case study, alongside evidence from other parts of England, reveals historical readers (Chapter 1), how they grew in number, particularly among the working classes, and moved from reading and listening to the local newspaper in public to buying their own copies for consumption at home. The particular places (Chapter 2) and times (Chapter 3) of reading the local newspaper help us to understand what readers looked for in a paper, and how they integrated it into their weekly and daily rituals and routines. The atmosphere of the reading rooms and pubs where newspapers were read and argued over had many similarities to the eighteenth-century coffee houses conjured up by Habermas, where discussion in person mingled with discussion in print to create a public sphere.

In a small town like Preston, hundreds of these readers were known to reporters like Anthony Hewitson, whose diaries are used to explain how the local newspaper was produced, and how it fitted into a national newspaper ecology, which was also connected to magazine and book publishing (Chapters 4 and 5). Hewitson went on to become an editor and newspaper owner, but he still understood the texts he wrote and published in similar ways to his readers, as part of the same interpretive community, one of a number in Preston, differentiated by politics, religion,

---

99 J. C. Lowe, 'The Tory Triumph of 1868 in Blackburn and in Lancashire', *The Historical Journal*, 16 (1973), 733–48 (p. 747), https://doi.org/10.1017/s0018246x00003927

100 Brian Keith-Lucas, *The English Local Government Franchise: A Short History* (Oxford: Blackwell, 1952), pp. 55, 59, 69, 74; Smith, 'Justice', p. 16.

class and gender (Chapter 6). Hewitson was not a native of Preston, but he became committed to the place, and used the same established journalistic techniques as his rival newspaper publishers, to promote and profit from local patriotism (Chapters 7, 8 and 9). These chapters reveal a dialogue between the interests and desires of local newspaper readers on the one hand, and newspaper publishers and journalists on the other. The final chapter (Chapter 10) comes back to the readers, and how individuals used the local paper for many different purposes, including the sustenance and defence of deeply felt local identities.

If you read all of this book, I hope to persuade you that beginning with the reader enables us to move from our twenty-first-century perceptions of the local press to the very different world in which the nineteenth-century English local press was produced and read. This approach, encompassing what Robert Darnton calls the 'communication circuit' of production, distribution and reading, enables a more holistic view of the local press, treating it as multi-dimensional: a material, cultural, economic and social phenomenon; it places newspapers in their most significant context, and it brings out the centrality of newspapers to the nineteenth-century reading experience. Evidence of readers' use of the local press ('use' is a broader, less misleading term than 'response', as Leah Price notes) can illuminate many issues that have previously been addressed speculatively, or with evidence only from newspaper content and production.[101] These issues include the function of newspapers in culture and society, their readership and their influence, on local identities in particular. More broadly, if texts have historically and geographically specific meanings, as argued here, then evidence of local newspaper readers, reading in particular places, at particular times, is more than an add-on; it is central to any history of texts such as newspapers.[102]

---

101 Mark Hampton, 'Newspapers in Victorian Britain', *History Compass*, 2 (2004), 1–8 (p. 4), https://doi.org/10.1111/j.1478-0542.2004.00101.x; Leah Price, *How to Do Things with Books in Victorian Britain* (Princeton, N.J: Princeton University Press, 2012), ch. 1, 'Reader's block', https://doi.org/10.23943/princeton/9780691114170.001.0001

102 Guglielmo Cavallo and Roger Chartier, 'Introduction', in *A History of Reading in the West*, ed. by Guglielmo Cavallo and Roger Chartier (University of Massachusetts Press, 1999), p. 2; Jones, *Powers of the Press*, p. 3.

1. The Readers of the Local Press

If we want to read periodicals because they were what the Victorians read, the work that must be done to bring them to life suggests they are not quite what they were.[1]

– James Mussell

As Mussell's epigram suggests, we see Victorian local newspapers very differently to how their original readers saw them, and we must work hard to recreate that original reading experience. Reading the local paper in the second half of the nineteenth century was different in almost every way from our experience today. These early chapters aim to 'defamiliarize what is an all too familiar practice', and show how the circumstances of reading shaped the content of the local press, which in turn shaped the way that people read it.[2]

Literacy

Who read the local paper in the second half of the nineteenth century? The short answer is, all kinds of people — young and old, from labourers to lords, literate and illiterate. But literacy is a spectrum of abilities, rather than a binary division between the literate and the illiterate, and the local paper was particularly attractive to those who

---

1 James Mussell, 'Repetition: Or, "In Our Last"', *Victorian Periodicals Review*, 48 (2015), 343–58 (p. 344).

2 Miles Ogborn and Charles W. J. Withers, 'Introduction: Book Geography, Book History', in *Geographies of the Book* (Farnham: Ashgate, 2010), p. 20, https://doi.org/10.4324/9781315584454

     https://doi.org/10.11647/OBP.0152.01

could barely read and perhaps could not write. Two readers in Charles Dickens's novel *Our Mutual Friend* — the impoverished childminder Betty Higden and the simple, honest Sloppy — show that literacy is not a simple idea. Mrs Higden reveals some of the complexities to a visitor:

> 'Mrs. Milvey had the kindness to write to me, ma'am, and I got Sloppy to read it [...] For I aint, you must know,' said Betty, 'much of a hand at reading writing-hand, though I can read my Bible and most print. And I do love a newspaper. You mightn't think it, but Sloppy is a beautiful reader of a newspaper. He do the Police in different voices.'[3]

Mrs Higden suggests that Raymond Williams's distinction between the reading public and the read-to public is too simplistic — she could read the Bible 'and most print', struggled to read handwriting and preferred to have newspapers read to her.[4] She makes no reference to writing, which was taught separately from reading, or sometimes not at all, particularly for girls. Meanwhile Sloppy's dramatic reading skills can bring to life the characters of a newspaper court report.

Beyond the pages of a Dickens novel, flesh-and-blood Victorians also complicate our ideas of literacy. In the 1850s the Clitheroe weaver John O'Neil could read and write, but would sometimes receive news in the same way as his less literate workmates, by word of mouth.[5] At the turn of the century (before radio), a working-class Middlesbrough household was described as 'not a reading family, but like to hear the news.'[6] Literacy was a shared communal asset, enabling individuals who could not read or write to enjoy the newspaper. This sociable, communal aspect of local newspaper reading was still present in the early twentieth century, as in Preston, where an oral history interviewee identified as Mr T2P, born in 1903, remembered the eagerness of his grandmother's neighbours to hear the news:

---

3   Charles Dickens, *Our Mutual Friend* (London: Chapman and Hall, 1865), p. 162.

4   Raymond Williams, *The Long Revolution* (Harmondsworth: Penguin, 1965), p. 184.

5   John O'Neil, *The Journals of a Lancashire Weaver: 1856–60, 1860–64, 1872–75*, ed. by Mary Brigg (Chester: Record Society of Lancashire and Cheshire, 1982), 5 February 1856.

6   Florence Eveleen Eleanore Olliffe Bell, *At the Works: A Study of a Manufacturing Town* (London: E. Arnold, 1907; repr. Middlesbrough: University of Teesside, 1997), p. 107. Her reading survey was originally published in the *Independent Review* 7 (1905), 426–40.

> I used to go down the road for the newspaper and when I came up with
> it all the old people in Rigby Street used to follow me up because my
> grandmother was the only one that could read.[7]

Readers like Betty Higden, who could be described crudely as semi-
literate, were particularly attracted to the local newspaper, because
it was about familiar people and places, and was woven into their
relationships. *Westminster Review* editor and social reformer William
Edward Hickson, giving evidence to the 1851 Select Committee on
Newspaper Stamps, argued that poorly educated agricultural labourers
in his native Kent would prefer a newspaper

> that related to local events which they really understood [...] a paper
> that gave a good account of some trial at Maidstone assizes [...] a paper
> that gave a good account of some farmer's stackyard having been burnt
> down, and what steps were taken in consequence [...] a paper that gave
> an account of what became of a ship that sailed with some families from
> their neighbourhood with which they might be connected.[8]

Some semi-literate readers could struggle through the local paper
themselves. Tom Stephenson, born in Chorley, Lancashire, in 1893,
remembered as a child reading the local paper with his grandmother:

> She had had no schooling but had somehow learned to read in middle
> age. We would tackle the *Chorley Guardian* together, stumbling over the
> long words and improvising the pronunciation.[9]

The appeal to the semi-literate continued. In early-twentieth-century
Preston, the *Lancashire Daily Post*, an evening paper, was the sole
reading matter of the semi-literate parents of two women interviewed
by oral historian Elizabeth Roberts. 'Mrs W4P', born in 1900, described
her mother in terms Betty Higden would have recognised:

---

7   'Social and family life in Preston, 1890–1940', transcripts of recorded interviews,
    Elizabeth Roberts archive, Lancaster University Library (hereafter *ER*; the letters
    P, B or L at the end of the interviewee's identifier denotes whether the interviewee
    was from Preston, Barrow or Lancaster): Mr T2P (b. 1903). The transcripts are being
    digitised, with some available at www.regional-heritage-centre.org

8   House of Commons, 'Report from the Select Committee on Newspaper Stamps;
    Together with the Proceedings of the Committee, Minutes of Evidence, Appendix,
    and Index'1851 (558) XVII. 1 (questions 3175, 3198).

9   Tom Stephenson, *Forbidden Land: The Struggle for Access to Mountain and Moorland*
    (Manchester: Manchester University Press, 1989), p. 15.

> [My mother] would read the *Post*. She could read and she could write but
> she wouldn't sit and read a long book because she was never used to it.[10]

'Mrs B2P', born in 1916, gave a similar answer in response to the
interviewer's question, 'When your mother and father were at home,
did any of you ever do any reading?' 'No,' she replied, 'they just used
to like the *Lancashire Daily Post*. They didn't read books or anything.'[11]

This attitude, that newspaper-reading is not real reading, was shared
by the social investigator Lady Florence Bell, the wife of Sir Hugh Bell,
owner of a Middlesbrough ironworks. In 1905 Lady Bell interviewed 200
households to discover the reading habits of her husband's employees,
reporting that 'about a quarter of the men do not read at all: that is to
say, if there is anything coming off in the way of sport that they are
interested in, they buy a paper to see the result. That hardly comes under
the head of reading.'[12] She found that three-quarters of the iron workers
only read newspapers, 'the favourite being a local halfpenny evening
paper, which seems to be in the hands of every man and woman, and
almost every child.'[13]

The idea of 'functional literacy' helps to explain this preference for
the local paper among semi-literate men and women. This approach
recognises that literacy is not an abstract set of skills; it comprises
a range of activities that are specific and meaningful in particular
times and places, for particular purposes.[14] Dramatic reading ability
like Sloppy's was more important in a time when communal reading
aloud was necessary; local references in news articles, advertising,
historical features or dialect writing are meaningful in the paper's
circulation area, less so in the next town ten miles away. Readers used
local newspapers for many purposes that could not be supplied by
other reading matter, harnessing them to create local public spheres,
to share gossip, or to feel connected to their home area when far
away. Many of these purposes are about feeling connected, to family,

---

10   Mrs W4P (b. 1900), *ER*.

11   Mrs B2P (b. 1916), *ER*.

12   Bell, p. 145.

13   Ibid., p. 144.

14   David Vincent, *Literacy and Popular Culture: England 1750–1914* (Cambridge: Cambridge University Press, 1989), pp. 15–16, https://doi.org/10.1017/cbo9780511560880; David Barton and Mary Hamilton, *Local Literacies: Reading and Writing in One Community* (London: Routledge, 1998), p. 7.

friends and neighbours, making the local newspaper a resource for relationships.[15]

The ability to read, in all its complexity, became more widespread in the second half of the nineteenth century, in the case study town of Preston as elsewhere. The change from hearing to reading the news influenced the newspapers, in their form and content, and affected the reading environment. These changes can be tracked in a crude way by measuring the ability to sign the marriage register. There has been much debate about how this ability relates to other aspects of literacy, but the current consensus is that women and men who could sign their own names rather than marking an 'X' could also read at a basic level (but could not necessarily write anything more than their name). While marriage register evidence ignores the subtle gradations described by Betty Higden, they are unique as a standardised form of evidence across time and place, and for every level of society, thereby allowing objective comparisons.[16]

The marriage registers suggest that basic reading ability had spread to more than ninety-five per cent of the population by the end of the century, but at mid-century literacy in Lancashire was significantly below the English average, with figures for Preston even lower. Across England, two thirds (sixty-seven per cent) of men of marriageable age could sign their names in 1840 but the average for Lancashire was sixty-two per cent, and in Preston barely more than half of bridegrooms (fifty-five per cent) could write their names. By 1880 (local figures are not available beyond 1884), Lancashire men had caught up with the rest of the country, while in Preston they had overtaken the national average, with ninety-two per cent able to sign their name, compared with eighty-six per cent nationally. The trends were broadly similar for women, but from a much lower starting point, with only a quarter of Preston women able to write their name in 1840, compared to a national average of fifty-one per cent. By 1880, Preston women's literacy was the same as

---

15   Barton and Hamilton, p. 7.

16   Vincent, pp. 17–18, 23; Carl F. Kaestle, 'Studying the History of Literacy', in *Literacy in the United States: Readers and Reading since 1880*, ed. by Carl F. Kaestle and others (New Haven: Yale University Press, 1991), pp. 1–32 (pp. 4, 11–12). For a critique of marriage registers as a source, see Richard Altick, *The English Common Reader: A Social History of the Mass Reading Public, 1800–1900* (Chicago: University of Chicago Press, 1963), p. 170.

the national average, at eighty-one per cent — still significantly below that of men. Note that literacy was already relatively high, before the introduction of universal elementary education in 1870.

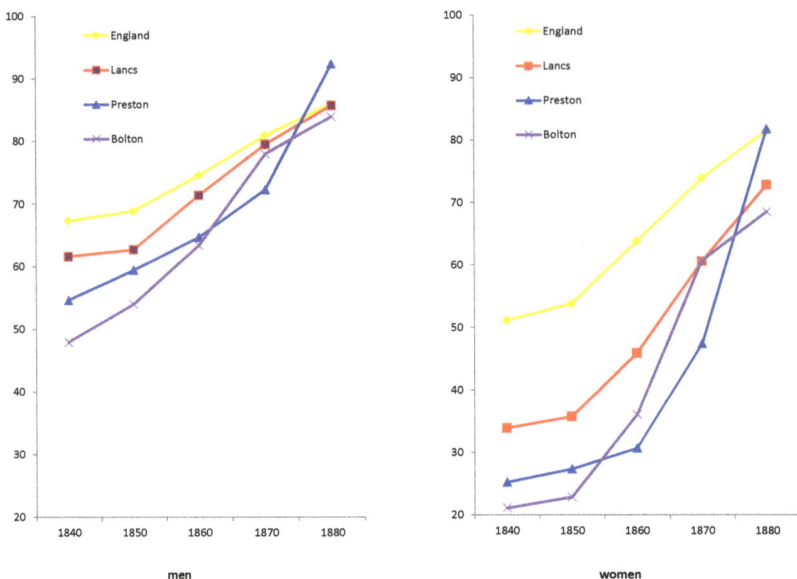

men   women

Fig. 1.1. Men (left) and women (right) signing marriage register (%) 1840–1880, selected areas. Source: Registrar General annual reports.
Diagram by the author, CC-BY 4.0.

The low figures at the start of the period can be explained by the lack of demand for literacy in the cotton industry, and the inability of voluntary and informal working-class schools to cope with the influx of population into towns in the early decades of the century (assuming that literacy rates at marrying age reflect schooling from ten to fifteen years previously). Indeed, literacy actually declined in most industrialising Lancashire towns between the 1750s and the 1830s.[17] Beyond that, we come up against the limits of these numbers. There are too many contradictory strands to unpick here — on the one hand, Preston's legal and administrative status required more literacy, it attracted immigrants from more literate rural areas, and was part of Lancashire's dynamic

---

17   For detailed discussion of literacy rates, see Vincent, pp. 24, 97; William B. Stephens, *Education, Literacy and Society, 1830–1870: The Geography of Diversity in Provincial England* (Manchester: Manchester University Press, 1987), pp. 5–7, 10–11, 19, 96, 327.

print culture; on the other, Preston had a poor educational reputation and was the largest town in the country without a school board, from their creation in 1870 to their abolition in 1902, leaving educational administration to the churches. By 1862, Preston had enough school places for every child between three and thirteen years of age, but one commentator claimed that it had 'a larger proportion of totally ignorant children than any other town of equal size [...] the majority of children of the infant stage in Preston are constantly found in the streets.'[18] Elementary schooling became compulsory in 1876, but local byelaws in Preston and other textile towns allowed older children to attend school half-time, spending the other half of the week working in the mills, so that, on any one day, roughly a quarter of Preston school-age children were not in school. Related factors may have been the influence of the Catholic church (generally less interested in education than the other denominations), lower Sunday School attendance and lower incomes (in comparison to most Lancashire cotton towns) leaving less to spend on reading matter.[19] Crucially, there may have been many people who could read a newspaper but could not write their own name, since writing was often taught after reading, or not at all for some children, particularly girls. However, we can be confident that literacy increased in Preston, as elsewhere, becoming less a collective, more an individual resource, thus requiring less reading aloud for the benefit of those who could not read themselves.

Reading Has a History

The marriage register figures show that literacy varied according to when and where it was measured. This means that reading has a history (and a geography, addressed in the next chapter). The history of reading is a relatively new field of scholarship, overlapping with the history of the book and of print culture, and combines historical and

---

18 Letter from Mr T. Paynter Allen, *National Education League Monthly Paper*, May 1872, reprinted in 'Education in Preston and Blackburn', *Preston Chronicle* (hereafter *PC*) May 16, 1872; for Preston's lack of school board, see House of Commons Debate on Voluntary Schools Bill, 16 February 1897 vol 46 col. 544, in *Historic Hansard*, https://api.parliament.uk/historic-hansard/commons/1897/feb/16/voluntary-schools-bill

19 Michael Savage, *The Dynamics of Working-Class Politics: The Labour Movement in Preston 1880–1940* (Cambridge: Cambridge University Press, 1987), pp. 69–70, https://doi.org/10.1017/cbo9780511898280

literary strands.[20] This dynamic and fruitful new discipline has much to offer a study of reading the local newspaper. The founding text for the history of reading is Richard Altick's 1957 *The English Common Reader*, which used a huge array of sources to reconstruct the reading world of ordinary people across the centuries. Although Altick dealt with the reading of newspapers (mainly metropolitan rather than provincial publications), his focus was on books. This bias can be justified when studying periods before the nineteenth century, but from then on, books became a minority of the reading material available, although the scholarship does not reflect this.[21] The bias to books in the history of reading is partly explained by the discipline's literary roots and by its implicit hierarchy of print, in which newspapers rank far below books, as seen in the comments of Lady Bell and the oral history interviewees. Altick's approach has most recently been developed by Jonathan Rose, focusing on the reading habits revealed by working-class autobiographies. Rose also prioritises book-reading, perhaps because of his explicit aim of showing that the proletariat read Proust.[22]

Books also dominate the most exciting development in the recent historiography of reading, the Reading Experience Database, which collects and classifies historical evidence of reading from 1450 to 1945. With more than 30,000 records as of February 2018, it now enables scholars to make less tentative generalisations about reading behaviour. However, the literary origins of the project have led to a focus on book-reading, creating a misleading picture of nineteenth-century reading habits. In February 2018 the database held 524 records of newspaper reading between 1850 and 1899, mostly of London papers, compared with 4,224 records of book reading.[23] Simon Eliot, a founder of the database, acknowledges that

---

20   Christine Pawley, 'Retrieving Readers: Library Experiences', *Library Quarterly*, 76 (2006), 379–87 (p. 380), https://doi.org/10.1086/511761; Stephen Colclough, *Consuming Texts: Readers and Reading Communities, 1695–1870* (Basingstoke: Palgrave Macmillan, 2007), Chapter 1, 'Reading has a history', https://doi.org/10.1057/9780230590540

21   The director of the *Waterloo Directory of Victorian Periodicals* project, John North, estimates there were more than one hundred times as many individual editions of periodicals and newspapers published in the nineteenth century as books: 'Compared to books,' *Waterloo Directory of English Newspapers and Periodicals: 1800–1900*, online edition, www.victorianperiodicals.com/series2/TourOverview.asp

22   Jonathan Rose, *The Intellectual Life of the British Working Classes* (London: Yale University Press, 2001), pp. 4–5.

23   *Reading Experience Database*, www.open.ac.uk/Arts/RED

the book was not the predominant form of text and, more than likely, was not therefore the thing most commonly or widely read [...] The most common reading experience, by the mid-nineteenth century at latest, would most likely be the advertising poster, all the tickets, handbills and forms generated by an industrial society, and the daily or weekly paper. Most of this reading was, of course, never recorded or commented upon for it was too much a part of the fabric of everyday life to be noticed.[24]

Eliot's point is that starting from the reader rather than the text allows a new picture of nineteenth-century reading to emerge, in which books are less important than newspapers and magazines.

Implying a Reader

The reading habits of real-life historical readers are only surprising because literary scholars have traditionally worked backwards, deducing an imaginary 'implied reader' from the text.[25] But such readers, conjured solely from a single book or newspaper, are strange creatures, as in this 1853 reconstruction of a reader from the advertisements of the mythical *Brocksop, Garringham and Washby Standard*, in Dickens's magazine *Household Words*:

a native of those parts in luxuriant whiskers, riding forth after a light breakfast of Wind Pills, on a steed watered with British Remedy, or well rubbed down with Synovitic Lotion. He would be going out to buy a windmill, or to engage a governess who did not want remuneration, and he would meet by the road, perhaps, a neighbour with magnificent legs who would talk over with him the news supplied by their gratuitous paper, and speculate upon the chance of the odd hundred pounds that might be paid them for the job of reading it.[26]

---

24 Simon Eliot, *The Reading Experience Database; or, What Are We to Do About the History of Reading?*, http://www.open.ac.uk/Arts/RED/redback.htm. On the reading of non-literary texts, see Mike Esbester, 'Nineteenth-Century Timetables and the History of Reading,' *Book History* 12 (2009), 156–85, https://doi.org/10.1353/bh.0.0018; Sadiah Qureshi, *Peoples on Parade: Exhibitions, Empire, and Anthropology in Nineteenth-Century Britain* (University of Chicago Press, 2011), ch. 2, 'Artful promotion', https://doi.org/10.7208/chicago/9780226700984.001.0001

25 For a defence of this technique, see Susan J. Douglas, 'Does Textual Analysis Tell Us Anything about Past Audiences?,' in *Explorations in Communication and History*, ed. Barbie Zelizer (London: Routledge, 2008), https://doi.org/10.4324/9780203888605

26 Anon., 'Country News', *Household Words*, 2 July 1853, pp. 426–30 (p. 427), found in *Dickens Journals Online*, http://www.djo.org.uk/household-words/volume-vii/page-426.html

Less absurdly, when we eavesdrop on a telephone conversation, the unseen, unheard person on the other end of the call is like an implied reader. We can make some reliable guesses about them, from the half of the conversation audible to us, but such evidence has its limits. As a case study in reconstructing the reader from the text, take Preston's most popular paper at the start of the period, the bi-weekly *Preston Guardian* of 1 September 1860. We can draw some conclusions about the readers from the newspaper's name, its price and its content: they lived in and around Preston, and were apparently teetotal Nonconformists, with politics allied to the Free-Trader Radical middle-class 'Manchester School' of Cobden and Bright, and they were not Irish. Beyond those generalisations, it gets complicated — there were readers from all social classes, mainly men but some women, some Roman Catholics, interested in world affairs, and at least some were highly cultured. We can make these assumptions from the inclusion of Preston in the title of the paper and the amount of local editorial and advertising content; the paper advertised and reported temperance events, and its church coverage mainly concerned Baptist, Congregational and Methodist chapels, with occasional digs at disreputable vicars and the greed of the Church of England. Its editorial line supported advanced Liberalism and condemned the Tories, and it reprinted anti-Irish jokes from *Punch*. While most of its job adverts were for servants and apprentices, of interest only to working-class readers, it made fun of working-class defendants and witnesses in its court reporting, and it advertised fresh oysters, fee-paying schools and auctions of farms and estates, presumably to wealthy middle-class readers, some of them living in country areas. Some adverts and reports were about Roman Catholic activities, while a fashion article and adverts for dancing and deportment classes and for the supposedly abortion-inducing Widow Welch's Female Pills (for 'removing obstructions, and relieving all other inconveniences to which the female frame is liable') seem to be aimed at women readers.[27] Large amounts of foreign news and details of last posting times for overseas mails suggest a cosmopolitan readership, or at least readers with friends and family overseas, while the literary extracts and a feature on the Manchester Academy of Fine Arts suggest an interest in what Matthew Arnold would call culture.

---

27   P. S. Brown, 'Female Pills and the Reputation of Iron as an Abortifacient', *Medical History*, 21 (1977), 291–304, https://doi.org/10.1017/S0025727300038278

The implied readers of the rival *Preston Herald*, on the other hand, were Anglican Tory beer-drinkers, of a more female persuasion. In other respects, they were similar to *Guardian* readers, local people from all classes (although with less advertising aimed at middle-class readers), and some of them Catholic (although the *Herald* carried more anti-Catholic material than the *Guardian*).

The implied reader is not as ridiculous as the *Household Words* article suggests. Changes in the text do reveal changes in readership. Forty years later, at the end of the century, the two papers had dropped their price to a penny, to cater for poorer readers. In 1884 the *Preston Guardian* had cut the price of its Saturday edition from 2d to 1½d, to bring 'an accession of readers of the industrial class [...] to whom the former price of our Saturday's publication might operate in some measure as a deterrent [...]'[28] In 1893 the price fell again, to a penny. A year later, the book review column, entitled 'Books I Have Read, By a Provincial', made assumptions about the limited spending power of the typical *Preston Guardian* reader: 'Now if one wrote of 31s. 6d. books, how many in Preston would have a chance of seeing them? Very few.'[29] The two papers still catered for readers of opposing political and religious views, and the *Guardian* now had more trade-unionists and children among their readers, apparently. Otherwise, both papers' clientele had changed in similar ways — they had more time for hobbies such as cycling, gardening, angling and keeping chickens, and more money to spend on these interests; there were also more women readers — and rural readers, judging from the pages of detailed advice and news about agriculture. Despite their price cut, both papers appealed across the classes, from country gentry and urban factory owners to servants in need of a situation. Surprisingly, the readers appeared to have little interest in sport.

However, the evidence of the newspapers themselves may be telling us more about the fiscal and economic environment and the people who produced them, than about those who read them. George and James Toulmin, owners of the *Preston Guardian* in 1860, were teetotal Methodists, part of a national network of advanced Liberals, while the *Herald* had just been bought by the local Conservative association. Were there no adverts for pubs in the *Guardian* because advertisers knew that all the readers were

---

28   *Preston Guardian* (hereafter *PG*), 4 October 1884, p. 5.
29   *PG*, 26 May 1894, p. 9.

teetotal, or because the publishers refused such ads on principle? In later chapters we will see that publishers sometimes refused to give readers what they wanted (football news, for instance) and that many people read papers without endorsing their editorial line. The texts themselves are not consistent, with the generally anti-Catholic *Herald* occasionally reporting and even praising the activities of Roman Catholics.

The texts tell us nothing about the aspiring reader, the curious, interested general reader nor the person reading on another's behalf. The Cycling Notes, the Angling Notes, the Gardening Notes, the Poultry Notes and the Allotment Notes probably were read by cyclists, anglers, gardeners, poultry-keepers and allotment-holders. But they were also probably read by armchair cyclists, anglers and so on, in the same way that we watch a cookery programme whilst eating a takeaway today. As for the general reader, Clitheroe weaver John O'Neil notes in his diary in 1856 that 'a person was telling me that he has seen the paper last night and wheat had fallen 6/- per quarter at Mark Lane on Monday.'[30] His informant is more likely to have been a weaver like himself than a corn merchant — both of them probably general readers, interested in the state of the economy and its impact on Clitheroe. The *Preston Guardian* in 1860 reprinted its 'Fashions for September' article from the leading French fashion magazine *Le Follet*, and between them these Preston papers carried adverts for women's fashions, abortion pills, prams, dancing and deportment lessons and job adverts for female occupations. However, men may have bought clothes for women, and men may have helped women obtain abortions.

The lack of sport is explained only if we move beyond the study of one or two publications to the whole of the print ecology available to readers in Preston. From the 1860s onwards, halfpenny evening papers began to be published, aimed chiefly (but not exclusively) at working-class readers. In 1886 two halfpenny evening newspapers were launched within weeks of each other, the *Lancashire Evening Post* (later renamed the *Lancashire Daily Post*) in Preston and the *Northern Daily Telegraph* in Blackburn (with a publishing and editorial office in Preston), designed to be read by the 'mill hands' as well as the 'middle classes'.[31] The *Post*, a sister title to the *Preston Guardian*, soon cornered the Preston

---

30   O'Neil diaries, 6 March 1856.
31   *The Journalist*, 3 December 1886, pp. 114–15.

newspaper market in sports journalism. By 1900, on the first Saturday of September, as the end of the cricket season overlapped with the start of the football season, four out of six pages of the *Post* were devoted to sport, mainly football. Its low price and its content — more 'working-class' ads, for a Co-op concert, a gipsy fortune-teller, and situations vacant for apprentices, gardeners and insurance agents — confirm that it was aimed mainly at working-class readers, but readers' letters and memoirs tell us that doctors and landed gentry also read this paper.

Inferences about readers are safer when based on the most successful publications, those that survived for decades without subsidy, such as the *Preston Guardian* and the *Lancashire Daily Post*, their large circulations requiring some editorial understanding of the readers, creating an alignment between what readers wanted and what publishers offered. The repetition over a long period of certain types of content suggests the presence of readers interested in that content — but the opposite does not follow. The absence of other types of content, for example news of Preston's Catholic churches and societies, does not signify the absence of readers interested in such content. De Certeau captures this distance between the producers and readers of texts, describing readers as 'travellers; they move across lands belonging to someone else, like nomads poaching their way across fields they did not write [...]'[32]

Readers as poachers, and 'oppositional' and unrepresented readers are hard to discern from one newspaper alone. We need to ask, 'what else were they reading?'[33] An 'oppositional' reader, to use Stuart Hall's terminology, actively resisted the intended meaning of the newspaper text. In Preston, a Tory oppositional reader might write a letter to the Tory *Preston Herald*, expressing his anger and rejection of what he read in the Liberal *Preston Chronicle*.[34] Alton Locke, Charles Kingsley's fictional Chartist poet, highlights how differently the same text can be

---

32 Michel de Certeau, *The Practice of Everyday Life* (Berkeley: University of California Press, 1988), p. 174. Here is a perfect example of poaching readers from 1928: 'In Norwich any three or four householders may ask the free library committee to buy for the library a book they need. Mr Charles Row, in his *Practical Guide to the Game Laws* (Longmans) [...] says some poachers requisitioned the first edition of this book in this way and when he conducted prosecutions used to pull him up with such remarks as, 'No, no, Charlie, you're wrong there; your book in the free library doesn't say that': Anon., 'Country Books of the Quarter', *Countryman*, April 1928, p. 90.

33 Rose, p. 93.

34 For example, 'Borough registration', letter contradicting the *Preston Chronicle's* account of voter registration, *Preston Herald* (hereafter *PH*), 13 October 1860, p. 6.

read as he describes his oppositional reading of an attack on working-class radicals like himself in a 'respectable' newspaper: '*We* see those insults, and feel them bitterly enough; and do not forget them, alas! soon enough, while they pass unheeded by your delicate eyes as trivial truisms.'[35] As one of de Certeau's 'poaching' readers, Alton Locke was an eavesdropper who hears nothing good about himself. Eavesdropping readers cannot be implied from the text, yet at a time of communal newspaper reading, they made up a large proportion of readers. As late as 1893, one commentator described how:

> In all directions one sees   Unionists [Conservatives] reading papers the politics of which are diametrically opposed to their own, because in those papers they get what they want, and even enjoy the clever, if sometimes coarse, attacks on their own Party.[36]

Unrepresented readers are also not apparent from the text, such as Preston's Roman Catholic population, who until 1889, 'had not Catholic journals to fairly represent their cause', in the words of Fr Bond of St Ignatius's church, welcoming the newly launched *Catholic News* from the pulpit.[37]

Finding Historical Readers

Historical readers are much more interesting, and complex, than implied readers, but they can be hard to find. Reading the local paper was 'so commonplace and unremarkable and therefore so commonly unremarked upon in the historical record', yet there is a surprising amount and variety of evidence.[38] In the United States, David Paul Nord has skilfully interpreted unpublished letters to the editor, letters published at times of civic crisis, and nineteenth-century government household expenditure surveys, among other sources; the Zborays have

---

35 Charles Kingsley, *Alton Locke: Tailor and Poet* (Cassell, 1969), p. 48; Stuart Hall, 'Encoding/Decoding', in *Media and Cultural Studies: Keyworks*, ed. by Meenakshi Gigi Durham and Douglas Kellner (Malden: Blackwell, 2006).

36 FitzRoy Gardner, 'The Tory Press and the Tory Party, I. — a Complaint', *National Review*, 21 (1893), p. 358.

37 *Catholic News*, 16 February 1889, p. 3.

38 David Paul Nord, 'Reading the Newspaper: Strategies and Politics of Reader Response, Chicago, 1912–1917', in *Communities of Journalism: A History of American Newspapers and Their Readers* (Urbana: University of Illinois Press, 2001), pp. 246–77 (p. 269).

used family papers, diaries and correspondence, while Garvey has used scrapbooks to reveal those who did their reading — and writing — with scissors in hand.[39] For England and Wales, Jones has revealed readers' responses to the press through records of debating societies, libraries, correspondence, articles in trade journals and literary reviews.[40] I have used two types of evidence, individual and collective. At the individual level there were people who bothered to mention reading the local paper, in their diaries, correspondence and autobiographies; oral history material and published readers' letters are also valuable. The diaries of Clitheroe weaver John O'Neil allow a detailed study of an individual reader, akin to those of Colclough on the Sheffield apprentice Joseph Hunter and Secord on the Halifax apprentice surveyor Thomas Hirst.[41] At the collective level, annual reports of libraries and other reading places list periodicals and newspapers taken, including numbers of multiple copies, and social investigators such as Lady Bell conducted contemporary surveys of reading habits.

Oral history material comes from the Elizabeth Roberts archive at Lancaster University. Roberts interviewed approximately sixty men and women from Preston, fifty-four from Barrow and forty-six from Lancaster, and was 'confident that they are a representative sample of the working class in all three areas.'[42] However, John Walton believes that the number

---

39   Nord, *Communities of Journalism*; Ronald J. Zboray and Mary Saracino Zboray, 'Political News and Female Readership in Antebellum Boston and Its Region', *Journalism History*, 22 (1996), 2–14; Ronald J. Zboray and Mary Saracino Zboray, '"Have You Read…?": Real Readers and Their Responses in Antebellum Boston and Its Region', *Nineteenth-Century Literature*, 52 (1997), 139–70, https://doi. org/10.2307/2933905; Ellen Gruber Garvey, *Writing with Scissors: American Scrapbooks from the Civil War to the Harlem Renaissance* (Oxford: Oxford University Press, 2012), https://doi.org/10.1093/acprof:oso/9780195390346.001.0001

40   Aled Gruffydd Jones, *Powers of the Press: Newspapers, Power and the Public in Nineteenth-Century England* (Aldershot: Scolar Press, 1996), p. 181; for other types of newspaper reading evidence, see Peter J. Lucas, 'The First Furness Newspapers: The History of the Furness Press from 1846 to c.1880' (unpublished M.Litt, University of Lancaster, 1971) and Marie-Louise Legg, *Newspapers and Nationalism: The Irish Provincial Press, 1850–1892* (Dublin: Four Courts Press, 1999).

41   Stephen Colclough, 'Procuring Books and Consuming Texts: The Reading Experience of a Sheffield Apprentice, 1798', *Book History* 3 (2000), https://doi. org/10.1353/bh.2000.0004; James A. Secord, *Victorian Sensation: The Extraordinary Publication, Reception, and Secret Authorship of Vestiges of the Natural History of Creation* (Chicago: University of Chicago Press, 2003), chap. 10.

42   Elizabeth Roberts, *A Woman's Place: An Oral History of Working-Class Women 1890– 1940* (Oxford: Blackwell, 1985), p. 6; John K. Walton, *Lancashire: A Social History, 1558–1939* (Manchester: Manchester University Press, 1987), pp. 293–94.

of interviews is too small for quantitative conclusions, while the lack of information about recruitment and selection of interviewees means that we do not know how socially representative they are. Nonetheless, the indexed transcripts have been used here because their testimony is consistent with other evidence. Fortunately, Roberts included a question about newspaper-reading, although the transcripts reveal her assumption that newspaper-reading was a domestic rather than public activity, an assumption that probably coloured the responses. Interviewees were born between 1884 and 1927, so that memories of their childhood homes date from the 1880s to the 1930s.[43] These oral history interviews, and other evidence, enable us to move beyond the default, male, middle-class implied reader, and to recognise other readers, differentiated by age, gender and social class, and by their enthusiasm for newspaper-reading.

Age

Children were a small part of the readership of the local paper. However, the rapid expansion of literacy meant that, for a generation or two, it was not unusual for children to be more literate than their parents, and therefore it was quite likely that they would be asked to read the newspaper to their elders. The slightly stagey photograph (Fig. 1.1) below is confirmed by oral history interviewees such as Mrs S4L (b. 1896), who remembered only one paper, the *Lancaster Observer*, and 'my mother always used to have that. Do you know I used to have to read that to her, word for word.' Between 1862 and 1882, older children who stayed on at school would have encountered a newspaper (not necessarily local) as the pinnacle of reading material, as the Revised Code stipulated that pupils must be able to read 'a short ordinary paragraph in a newspaper, or other modern narrative', to reach Standard VI, the highest (one headmaster, not from Preston, described using the London evening paper, the *Echo*, for this purpose).[44] However, only two per cent of pupils reached this Standard VI, even fewer in

---

43   For a summary of references to reading and writing in the Roberts material, see Barton and Hamilton, *Local Literacies*, pp. 28–31 and David Barton, 'Exploring the Historical Basis of Contemporary Literacy', *The Quarterly Newsletter of the Laboratory of Comparative Human Cognition*, 10 (1988), 70–76.

44   Royal Commission Appointed to Inquire into the Working of the Elementary Education Acts in England and Wales (P.P. 1887, C. 5158, Third Report, Evidence), p. 356.

Preston, according to a commentator in 1874 who claimed that 'Preston, with her possible school population of nearly 20,000 can never in any year present so many as one hundred in Standard VI.'[45] Unfortunately, a 'payment by results' inspection regime encouraged reading without understanding. The educationalist William Ballantyne Hodgson wrote in 1867 of a boy taught to read from the Bible 'who, having been asked by his mother to read a passage in a newspaper, was suddenly roused from his monotonous chaunt by a box on the ear, accompanied by these words — "How dare ye, ye scoundrel, read the newspaper with the Bible twang?"'[46]

Fig. 1.2. Photographic study of child reading to old man, 1907, 'A Good Friend' by CF Inston FRPS, Northern Photographic Exhibition, Walker Art Gallery, Liverpool 1907, programme, opp. p. 16, used by permission of Liverpool Archives.

---

45   Altick, p. 158; Vincent, p. 43. The Preston figures may have been exaggerated, as the writer was using them to argue for the establishment of a School Board in the town: Letter from Mr T. Paynter Allen.

46   Harvey J. Graff and W. B. Hodgson, 'Exaggerated Estimates of Reading and Writing as Means of Education (1867), by W. B. Hodgson', *History of Education Quarterly*, 26 (1986), 377–93 (p. 389), https://doi.org/10.2307/368244

Those who learnt to read as children did not necessarily have an unbroken reading career, as literacy skills often declined when education ended. The attractions of 'trashy' reading or the familiarity of the local paper may have kept those skills alive for many of Wilkie Collins's 'unknown public'.[47] *Westminster Review* editor and social reformer William Edward Hickson told the 1851 Newspaper Stamp Committee that 'the only effectual thing to induce them to keep up or create the habit of reading was some local newspaper. If you began in that way, by asking them to read an account of somebody's rick that was burnt down, you would find that you would succeed.'[48] In later years some children were forbidden to read the local paper, such as the oral history interviewees Mr R1P (b. 1897) and Mrs B5P (b. 1898). 'We weren't allowed to look at the [*Lancashire Daily*] *Post*, you know!'[49] Yet children read or heard the news, and sometimes incorporated it into their games, as with the 500 Preston boys, aged 8 and upwards, who had followed the battles of the Franco-Prussian War (1870–71). They were 'assembled under commanders who impersonated the Crown Prince of Prussia, Prince Frederick Charles, Steinmetz, Marshals Bassine, M'Mahon and other leaders' in the Lark Hill district of the town. They were 'drawn up in line of battle on the opposite sides of the street [...] with drums beating and colours (in the shape of dirty handkerchiefs) waving', receiving final orders, when a policeman chanced upon the battlefield.[50] This information must have reached these boys via a newspaper, directly or indirectly.

The *Preston Guardian* was probably the most popular paper among children in Preston and North Lancashire, because of its column, 'Our Children's Corner', launched in 1884. It was similar in content to the children's magazines that had flourished from the early nineteenth century onwards, part of the 'magazinization' of newspapers that became known as New Journalism in the 1880s and 1890s. The most influential children's column was the *Newcastle Weekly Chronicle*'s 'Corner for Children', launched in 1876 and hosted by 'Uncle Toby', the pseudonym of the editor, W. E. Adams. Imitations of this successful format sprang up across the country, exclusively in the provincial press

---

47 [Wilkie Collins], 'The Unknown Public', *Household Words*, 18 (1858), 217–22.

48 Evidence of William Hickson, 1851 Newspaper Stamps Committee, Q3240.

49 Quote from Mrs B5P, *ER*.

50 'French and Prussians on a small scale', *PH* supplement w/e 3 September 1870, p. 4.

and particularly in Liberal weeklies like the *Preston Guardian*.[51] This was something new, as the *Aberdeen Weekly Journal* explained in 1881:

> Hitherto Newspapers [...] have contained little of real interest and pleasure for Girls and Boys, who, although called upon to read the paper for the benefit of others, seldom find anything in it to suit their own tastes and feelings.[52]

A distinctive aspect of many such children's columns was their associated nature conservation clubs, whose members had to promise not to harm any creature. These clubs were hugely popular — the *Newcastle Weekly Chronicle*'s 'Dicky Bird Society' had 50,000 members within five years of its founding in 1876. The columns printed contributions from young readers, such as the staggering 20,183 letters, essays and drawings sent to the *West Cumberland Times* in just 12 months during 1904–05. The *Preston Guardian* too had its own 'Animal's Friend Society', which boasted 10,000 members within four years of its launch. Any boy or girl could join by taking this pledge:

> I hereby promise never to tease or torture any living thing, or to destroy a bird's nest, but to promote as much as possible the comfort and happiness of all the creatures over which God has given man dominion.[53]

Fig. 1.3. Membership badge for provincial newspaper animal welfare club: *Preston Guardian* Animals' Friend Society membership badge, twentieth century. Photograph by the author, CC BY 4.0.

---

51 *PG*, 17 February 1894, p. 16.

52 *Aberdeen Weekly Journal*, 2 August 1881, cited in Frederick Milton, 'Uncle Toby's Legacy: Children's Columns in the Provincial Newspaper Press, 1873–1914', *International Journal of Regional and Local Studies*, 5 (2009), 104–20 (p. 104).

53 *PG*, 22 December 1888, p. 4; *PG*, 17 February 1894, p. 16. For more on animal welfare organisations associated with the provincial press, see Milton.

An oral history interviewee born in 1895 recalled his class entering their drawings in a *Preston Guardian* competition.[54]

Gender

Men were more likely to read newspapers and magazines than women, at least in the memories of oral history interviewees, and this is consistent with women's lower literacy in the marriage registers seen above. The oral history material suggests that men were twice as likely to read newspapers and periodicals as women: twenty-nine men to thirteen women in Preston, twenty-seven to fourteen in Barrow, but — intriguingly — a more even fifteen to twelve in Lancaster. Eight boys read comics, but only one girl, across all three towns. Girls and women had less time than men for reading, because of their domestic workload, on top of paid work for many women in areas like the textile districts of Lancashire. Bell's door-to-door survey of reading habits in Middlesbrough in the early years of the twentieth century includes many instances where 'wife no time for reading'.[55]

Fig. 1.4. A woman reading a newspaper was an unusual sight. 'At the Bar' by Marcus Stone, wood engraving by Dalziel, illustration of pub landlady Abbey Potterson, for original monthly serial of Charles Dickens, *Our Mutual Friend*, 1864, Chapter 6, 'Cut Adrift', facing p. 54. Scanned by Philip V. Allingham, Victorian Web, CC BY 4.0, http://www.victorianweb.org/art/illustration/mstone/14.html

54   Mr G4P (b. 1895), *ER*.

55   Bell, *passim*.

A woman reading a newspaper by herself in a public place was probably unusual at any time in the nineteenth century, so Dickens's description of such behaviour by pub landlady Miss Abbey Potterson suggests a rather 'masculine' character by the standards of the 1860s. Even by 1889, men outnumbered women in the segregated news rooms of Barrow's public library by a factor of fifteen to one, 'a fair average of the number of persons who enter the rooms daily, for the purpose of reading the Newspapers and Periodicals'.[56] Women were more likely to read a newspaper at home, even at the end of the century: 'A lady who has much time on her hands' would read and re-read the morning paper throughout the day, according to an article in *The Journalist and Newspaper Proprietor* of 1900. Alternatively, according to the same article, 'husbands [...] in some cases [...] mark the daily paper as they read it, to indicate to their wives on their return home in the evening with what portion of the day's news they should make themselves acquainted.'[57] Men could also control women's newspaper consumption by reading aloud, such as the Preston husband who read extracts from *John Bull* (a London weekly news miscellany) to his illiterate wife.[58] It was more noteworthy for women to read to their husbands.[59]

The newspaper was by default male reading matter, although most local newspapers described themselves as suitable for family reading, meaning women as well as men. In the text of the newspaper itself, women are misleadingly invisible, with the exception of fashion columns, advertisements for items usually bought by women, price lists for bread, eggs and other household staples at local markets, poetry, and women's columns and serial fiction in later decades. They are glaringly absent from the correspondence columns of the local press, if we take the male names and pseudonyms at face value. This did not change even when women began to take a more active part in the public

---

56 Barrow Library annual reports, 1887–89, Cumbria Archive and Local Studies Centre, Barrow, p. 220.

57 'Getting Through the Morning Newspaper', *The Journalist and Newspaper Proprietor*, 20 October 1900, p. 329.

58 See also Mrs M6L (b.1885), *ER*. For the expectation that fathers should read aloud to the family, see Thomas Wright [The 'Journeyman Engineer'], 'Readers and Reading', *Good Words*, 17 (1876), 315–20 (p. 316).

59 See for example 'Daring Attempt To Rob A House — Beware Of General Dealers', London *Standard*, 22 April 1858, p. 7; 'Quips and Cranks', *North-Eastern Daily Gazette*, 27 November 1890, British Newspaper Archive.

life of Preston, with single women gaining the municipal franchise in 1869, the right to stand for the Board of Guardians from 1875, and the right to vote for and serve on parish, urban and rural district councils in 1894.[60] Only 12 out of some 900 letters sampled from the Preston papers between 1855 and 1900 purported to be from women, and only 9 in the newspapers of the Furness area of North Lancashire between 1846 and 1880.[61] This may have been censorship by editors — the *Ulverston Advertiser* reported 'a deluge of letters from Miss A or Miss B requesting a few words' in support of women's suffrage in 1872, but refused to publish any of them — and self-censorship by female correspondents, who knew they would be mocked for daring to take part in public debate (something familiar to female Twitter users today). When housemaids dared to respond to a critical article about them in the London *Daily Telegraph*, a leader in the *Huddersfield Daily Chronicle* dismissed the 'interesting house girls' whose letters were published by the *Telegraph*, attributing their 'intense masculine style' to the help they must have received from the butler or the groom.[62] The working-class Carlisle school teacher Mary Smith often used initials or male pseudonyms to write to her local papers, and this was probably a common tactic: 'In writing on politics, which I often did, I used some other initial, "Z" very often, or other signature. I considered that if men knew who the writer was, they would say, "What does a woman know about politics?"'[63]

Smith is just one example of the many women who, we know, did read newspapers, both local and metropolitan. She recalled how, in the year of revolutions, 1848, 'we shared all the excitement of the great world in that small northern village [Scotby, near Carlisle], rejoicing with the best when unkingly kings were uncrowned [...] We kept our best sympathies, as well as our intelligence, up to the stroke of the great

60   Brian Keith-Lucas, *The English Local Government Franchise: A Short History* (Oxford: Blackwell, 1952), pp. 55, 59, 69; Patricia Hollis, *Ladies Elect: Women in English Local Government 1865–1914* (Oxford: Clarendon Press, 1987), pp. 207, 357, 392. Women gained the right to serve on borough councils such as Preston's in 1907.

61   Peter J. Lucas, 'The Regional Roots of Feminism: A Victorian Woman Newspaper Owner', *Transactions of the Cumberland & Westmorland Antiquarian & Archaeological Society*, Series 3, 2 (2002), 277–300 (p. 293); Lucas, 'First Furness Newspapers', p. 73.

62   *Huddersfield Daily Chronicle*, 13 March 1876, p. 2, British Newspaper Archive.

63   Mary Smith, *The Autobiography of Mary Smith, Schoolmistress and Nonconformist, a Fragment of a Life (Volume 1); With Letters from Jane Welsh Carlyle and Thomas Carlyle* (Carlisle: Wordsworth Press, 1892), p. 259. I am grateful to Dr Helen Rogers for this reference.

world, and shared the cares of its life struggles.'[64] Besides the fictional examples of Betty Higden and Abbey Potterson, there were the three women newspaper readers described in memoir and oral history interviews at the beginning of this chapter.

Class

Traditional local weekly newspapers tried to be all things to all men (with women as an afterthought). By the second half of the century, they aimed to appeal to working-class as much as middle-class readers, and their popularity in working-class reading rooms attests to their success. Radical newspapers had targeted this audience in the 1830s, when illegal, untaxed papers flourished, and in the 1840s, when the Chartist movement produced a vibrant provincial press, led by the Leeds-based *Northern Star* — but this competition to the politically mainstream local press had waned by the 1850s. From this decade on, as the newspaper taxes were abolished, penny and halfpenny weekly and evening papers began to appear, aimed squarely at working-class readers. The weekly news-miscellanies such as the *Bolton Journal*, the *Manchester Weekly Times* or the *Liverpool Weekly Post*, now extinct, were hugely popular, and had an overwhelmingly working-class readership.[65] One of the first, Birmingham's *Saturday Evening Post*, was

> specially intended to meet the wants of the great body of the working classes, whose necessities, it is evident, are not to any great extent supplied by the existing papers [...] the local news, which the London newspapers, of course, cannot give, and which is of the first importance to the working men of the town and district, will be fully reported... it is hoped that the working man after his week's labour will carry a copy home with him to his fireside [...].[66]

Working-class readers were increasingly targeted by another new publishing genre, the provincial evening paper, usually selling at a halfpenny. By the early twentieth century, in Middlesbrough, Bell found that the favourite reading matter of foundry workers' families

---

64   Smith, p. 149.

65   Graham Law, *Serializing Fiction in the Victorian Press* (Basingstoke: Palgrave, 2000), p. 142.

66   Announcement in *Birmingham Journal*, 21 November 1857, cited in Harold Richard Grant Whates, *The Birmingham Post, 1857–1957. A Centenary Retrospect* (Birmingham: Birmingham Post & Mail, 1957), pp. 47–48.

was the local halfpenny evening paper, the *North Eastern Daily Gazette*. In one home, 'The husband does not care to read more than the evening paper. Wife cannot read or write, but she gets her husband to read to her all that is going on in the world.'[67] Near St Helens, John Garrett Leigh found them equally popular, and in the oral history material, the local evening paper was the most popular type of newspaper in Preston and Barrow (Lancaster did not have its own evening title).[68]

In Preston's traditional weeklies, however, working-class readers were rarely allowed to speak for themselves. There are occasional letters, such as one from the village of Chipping near Preston, claiming to represent 'We, the poor [...]'[69] but only a tiny minority of the pseudonyms used by correspondents were avowedly working-class, and these tended to appear at particular times when workers were in the news, as when a textile strike loomed in 1880, and 'A Cotton Operative' or 'A Factory Lad' had their letters published. In Furness, less than ten per cent of letters to local papers could be identified as coming from working-class writers.[70] Like women correspondents, it seems that working-class letter-writers were discouraged from taking part in the public sphere of the correspondence column, unless in disguise.[71]

And yet, like women readers, working-class readers were more numerous than might appear from the texts of the newspapers. There are many references to poor people reading, and being read to, in pubs in the 1830s (see Chapter 2). During the 1853–54 Preston lockout (when sales of penny dreadfuls were unaffected and fewer books were left in pawn), Reverend John Clay, prison chaplain and campaigner, observed that 'reading is becoming necessary to the working-man'.[72]

---

67   Bell, pp. 44, 190.
68   John Garrett Leigh, 'What Do the Masses Read?' *Economic Review*, 4 (1904), 166–77 (p. 176).
69   *PH*, 25 September 1880, p. 6.
70   Lucas, 'First Furness Newspapers', p. 61.
71   See also Leah Price, *How to Do Things with Books in Victorian Britain* (Princeton, N.J.: Princeton University Press, 2012), p. 261, https://doi.org/10.23943/princeton/9780691114170.001.0001. Price follows the paper as object to reveal social differences hidden by the words printed on those pieces of paper.
72   Walter Lowe Clay, *The Prison Chaplain: A Memoir of the Rev. John Clay, B. D., with Selections from His Reports and Correspondence, and a Sketch of Prison Discipline in England* (Cambridge: Macmillan, 1861), pp. 545–47.

In 1864 a *Preston Chronicle* reporter found 'tidy, good, honest-looking men, with labour-hardened hands, and brave intelligent faces' reading the papers in the town's Central Working Men's Club, and a list of *Preston Herald* stockists in 1870 included shops in some of the poorest parts of Preston.[73] In the 1860s, the inmates of the workhouse read local newspapers and in the 1890s, when Preston's Harris free library opened, a reporter wrote of how he had 'often seen men with clogs on pattering away over the beautiful marble hall', while a photograph of the Harris reading room and news room (Fig. 1.5 below) shows some men without collars, in rumpled jackets and wearing flat caps.[74] Librarians and other observers believed that those who read newspapers in the news rooms of free libraries were more proletarian than those who borrowed books (although many commentators in other towns thought that libraries in general were little used by working men).[75]

Fig. 1.5. Men from different social classes together in the reading room and news room (at rear), Harris Free Library, Preston, 1895. By permission of the Harris Museum and Art Gallery, Preston, all rights reserved.

---

73 *PC*, 20 February 1864; 'Agents for the Sale of the "Herald', *PH*, 3 September 1870, p. 5.

74 *PG*, 30 January 1869, p. 2.

75 William Bramwell, *Reminiscences of a Public Librarian, a Retrospective View* (Preston: Ambler, 1916), p. 18; Martin Hewitt, 'Confronting the Modern City: The Manchester Free Public Library, 1850–80', *Urban History*, 27 (2000), 62–88 (p. 73), https://doi.org/10.1017/s0963926800000146; Leigh, p. 169; Bell, p. 163.

The newspapers reflected the interests of the local middle classes, despite the rhetoric of a unifying local identity that claimed to override class. These were the unspoken default readers of most local papers. In Preston, this implied readership harked back to the town's pre-industrial identity as a middle-class leisure town and legal/administrative headquarters. This era is captured in the 1822 painting of one of Preston's richest families, the Addisons, at breakfast (Fig. 1.6 below), in which John Addison Jr., aged 31, is reading the town's only newspaper at the time, the *Preston Chronicle*.[76] Middle-class readers, as the default, were not studied anthropologically like working-class readers, so there are fewer descriptions of them as a group. But we can pick up hints about some individual newspaper readers, such as two friends, Preston surgeon-dentist John Worsley and the vicar of Heskin near Chorley, Rev John Thomas Wilson. Worsley lived on Fishergate, Preston's main street, only yards away from the offices of all the local papers, and so it was easy for him to buy newspapers — local, regional and metropolitan — to send on to his friend in the country. Postcards sent by Wilson have survived, in which he often thanks his friend in town for gifts of newspapers.[77]

Some of Preston's wealthiest men read their newspapers at their gentlemen's club, the Winckley club. They had access to scores of publications in their news room in the elegant Georgian Winckley Square, and some of them bid successfully in the club's annual auctions of back copies, presumably to read at home or to leave in their waiting rooms (many were doctors or solicitors). Members of the club were mockingly described as

> members of the learned professions — men in cotton, with not less than twenty thousand spindles or four hundred looms — men with land or railway shares — men with cheek, and who are well dressed — men who have not kept a public house within four years, or in whose family there is not a mangle [...] young men in situations with prospects, or who having no ancestors, wish to get into society.[78]

---

76   The original painting, now lost, is described from earlier sources in Brian Lewis, *The Middlemost and the Milltowns: Bourgeois Culture and Politics in Early Industrial England* (Stanford University Press, 2002), pp. 104, 461.

77   Anne R. Bradford, *Drawn by Friendship: The Art and Wit of the Revd. John Thomas Wilson* (New Barnet: Anne R. Bradford, 1997).

78   'A Description of Preston and its People', reprinted from a 'north country magazine' in *PC*, 10 December 1870.

Fig. 1.6. Most local papers were aimed at middle-class readers in the first half of the century: 'The Addison Family at Breakfast', monochrome cabinet card reproduction of painting by Alexander Masses, Liverpool, 1822. By permission of Harris Museum, Preston, all rights reserved.

Biographical scraps for seventeen of the keenest Winckley Club readers give an impression of who they were: around half of them, eight, were local councillors, mostly Conservative, seven were magistrates, four were lawyers, three doctors, two dentists, four mill owners. Many were directors of local companies. Three of the seventeen were Roman Catholic. Two past and present owners of local papers were club members: Miles Myres, Preston coroner and solicitor, a Conservative councillor who served as mayor, a magistrate and a director of the joint stock company behind the *Preston Herald*, and Isaac Wilcockson, a retired printer and former owner of the Liberal *Preston Chronicle*, and a councillor and director of the town's gas and water companies. Other members were Rev T. Barton Spencer, vicar of St James's Anglican church and chaplain to the workhouse, and Colonel W. Martin, governor of Preston prison, a former soldier and policeman. Some of the club's younger members were described as 'cads' by one local magazine, which condemned the treatment they gave to journalist and explorer Henry Morton Stanley when he was invited to the club after giving a lecture in 1878. 'Some of the more juvenile members of the club [...] poked their guest about the ribs, called him by his surname, without a prefix, requested him to "stick to his point," and were altogether so free and easy that the discoverer of Livingstone declared he had never in his travels among the uncivilized come across such a jovial crew.'[79] The club's complaints book, and records of the second-hand newspaper auctions, show that this jovial crew, and their elders, were promiscuous in their newspaper reading, ranging across political, religious and geographical boundaries. They were much more complex than the implied readers suggested by each individual title they read.

Intensity

The readers of local newspapers at the Winckley Club, like readers elsewhere, differed in how they felt about each newspaper, and in how they used the local press. For some, newspaper-reading was a particularly important part of their lives, creating a more intense, invested reading experience. We can contrast these 'active readers', members of what Stanley Fish called an 'interpretive community', with the majority of readers discussed above, who were more emotionally distant from the newspaper, and more socially distant from those who produced the newspaper.[80] If we imagine a series of concentric circles (Fig. 1.7 below), with the newspaper, its publisher, editor and staff at the centre, the majority of readers were in the 'outer circle'. In the middle circle, forming an interpretive community around each newspaper, were active readers; they include members of the same social circles as local newspaper proprietors, editors and journalists; each paper also had scores, sometimes hundreds, of part-time correspondents and contributors, who sent in news items from outlying towns and villages, or wrote expertly on particular topics such as agriculture or local history, or had their poetry published in the paper regularly. There were news addicts, or 'quidnuncs' (Latin for 'what now?' or 'what's the news?'); habitual letter-writers, whose published correspondence reveals a close relationship with 'their' paper; public citizens who held office and liked

---

79 'Gossip Abroad', *The Wasp*, 7 December 1878, p. 7, Community History Library, Harris Library, Preston.

80 Stanley Eugene Fish, 'Interpreting the Variorum', *Critical Inquiry*, 2 (1976), 465–85, https://doi.org/10.1086/447852

to read about themselves, and readers active in local politics or church and chapel, and who saw particular local papers as supporters and allies of their causes.

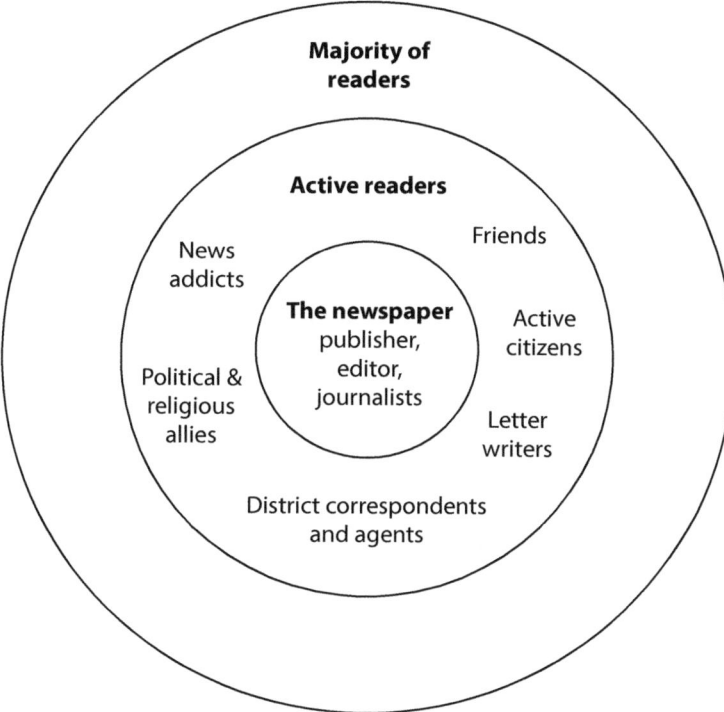

Fig. 1.7. Readers and the closeness of their relationship with a local newspaper. Diagram by the author, CC BY 4.0.

News addicts were typically male and working-class, for example the young James Ogden in Rochdale, whose thirst for reading was indulged by a local newsagent in the 1850s. He described himself as 'a studious and, in literature a ravenous lad' who was allowed to read the papers after the shop had closed.[81] Clitheroe weaver John O'Neil (b. 1810) revealed his news addiction in his diaries; the longest entry each week was usually a summary of what he had read in the newspaper each Saturday evening, taking precedence over the topics of family, friends or work. He had been a hand loom weaver in his native Carlisle, was probably self-educated, and had been active in two working-class

---

81   James Ogden, 'The Birth of the "Observer"', *Rochdale Observer*, 17 February 1906.

reading rooms and in local reform politics. He left Carlisle in search of work in 1854, settling in Low Moor, a factory village of about 1200 people, near Clitheroe in Lancashire, two years later. Here he worked as a power loom weaver at Garnett & Horsfall's factory. He was a widower with one daughter, renting a factory cottage and working sixty hours a week. He was able and popular, becoming president of his village reading room, and president of the Clitheroe Power Loom Weavers' Union. In the 1860s he was active in local Liberal politics as a member of Clitheroe Working Men's Reform Club and later the town's Liberal Club. He read local, regional and metropolitan newspapers in reading rooms, in pubs and at home, and discussed what he read with workmates and other users of public reading places. J. Barlow Brooks (b. 1874) worked as a half-timer in a cotton mill in Radcliffe near Bolton from the ages of ten to thirteen, before becoming a pupil teacher, and eventually a Methodist minister. He and his brother and mother bought local, regional and socialist newspapers every week, plus many other weeklies second-hand from the Co-operative reading room. They bought so many papers and magazines that the material filled a back bedroom and began to encroach on the stairs.[82]

Inveterate letter-writers, often signing themselves 'A Constant Reader', had a similarly intense relationship with particular titles, but were more active in responding to the content of the paper with a stream of correspondence. These readers are discussed in more detail in Chapter 6. They are similar to the minority of 'fans' of the Chicago community press identified by Janowitz in the mid-twentieth century, individuals who were emotionally involved with their weekly local paper.[83] These and other active readers who used a local newspaper in a public way, leaving historical traces, probably had more in common with the publishers and journalists than with the readership as a whole. With some exceptions, they tended to be middle-class and male, as confirmed by those who signed letters in their own names, or gave an occupation.

---

82   Joseph Barlow Brooks, *Lancashire Bred: An Autobiography* (Oxford: Church Army Press, 1951), pp. 169, 177.

83   'Fans' accounted for eleven per cent of survey respondents: M. Janowitz, *The Community Press in an Urban Setting* (Glencoe: Free Press, 1952), pp. 106–7.

While these news addicts and letter-writers read mainly for pleasure and interest, others who could be described as active citizens — business people, councillors, magistrates, trade union officials — liked to read about themselves and their public activities in the local press. One Preston editor claimed that 'nobody except Town Councillors and their wives or relatives will read through' a detailed report of a council meeting.[84] Another group, political activists, used rather than read the local paper, developing relationships with sympathetic newspaper owners who were politically active themselves, and writing letters and other articles in support of their causes. They read the paper for news of support or opposition to their party or campaign. Mary Smith, the Carlisle teacher, became friendly with radical editors of local papers, including Washington Wilks of the *Carlisle Journal* and then the *Carlisle Examiner* (and later the London *Morning Star*), a Mr Lonsdale, editor of the *Carlisle Observer*, and an unnamed editor of the *Carlisle Express*. These contacts enabled her to publish poems, articles and letters against capital punishment and in support of women's suffrage, or backing a radical election candidate, among other campaigns.[85] In Preston, Edward Ambler, a printer and prominent Liberal, Congregationalist and Oddfellow, read and wrote for Preston's Liberal papers in support of his party, his friendly society, his skirmishes as a Poor Law Guardian and his work for a free library.[86] Smith and Ambler were at the centre of the interpretive communities of readers built around their favoured local papers.

---

84 'Preston and Roundabout. Notions and Sketches [By "Atticus."]: Our Town Council and its Members', *PC*, 4 April 1868.

85 Smith, pp. 198, 204, 255, 260.

86 For example, letters from Ambler to George Melly, 23 and 30 March 1864, Liverpool Archives, George Melly Collection, 920 MEL 13 Vol. IX, 1990 and 1991; 'Death of a Preston printer', *PC*, 29 October 1887; H. A. Taylor, 'Politics in Famine Stricken Preston: An Examination of Liberal Party Management, 1861–65', *Transactions of the Historic Society of Lancashire & Cheshire*, 107 (1956), 121–39.

Conclusions

Studying the text of the local newspaper gives us some information about the type of readers being targeted. But the implied reader, usually a middle-class man, is only part of the picture. Other evidence reveals that the illiterate and semi-literate in particular were drawn to the local paper, that women and children were readers, and that working-class readers eavesdropped and 'poached' across newspapers created for middle-class purchasers. Literacy was a communal asset, particularly at mid-century, available to those who could read and those who could not; similarly, reading the local paper was usually a communal activity. Local newspapers were one part of the social revolution stimulated by the swift spread of literacy, in which children became the experts, better able to use the technology of print than their parents. The spread of literacy was even swifter in Preston, going from below the national average to above it in less than two generations. This demonstrates how reading is geographically and historically specific. However, even within one town, readers differed in their relationship to the local newspapers, some untouched by them, some on the fringes of their influence (such as the boys re-enacting the battles of the Franco-Prussian War), and some at the heart of interpretive communities clustered around each title. The latter group in particular left their mark on Preston, even creating or commandeering entire buildings in which to read newspapers, particularly local newspapers. These places are the subject of the next chapter.

2. Reading Places

We need to know *where* the local newspaper was read to understand *how* it was read, because the same texts take on different meanings in different places.[1] The same report of a Preston football victory over Blackburn has opposite meanings, of success or failure, in each town. To a reader far from home, missing familiar faces and places, a copy of their local paper takes on extra significance, as a physical reminder of who they are and where they are from. Equally, listening to a newspaper being read and interpreted by an ardent Chartist in a crowded pub becomes an intense and emotional act of political solidarity, a very different experience to reading the same paper in silence in a Church of England news room, under the eyes of the curate, or at home with one's family. We can see how newspaper buying, borrowing and reading was everywhere, by taking an imaginary stroll around Preston. The places of newspaper-reading, where 'media rituals' were enacted, are concrete evidence of the importance of newspapers, including local newspapers, in people's lives; they were willing to rent, repurpose and even erect purpose-built structures where newspapers could be produced, bought, read and discussed. Let us pretend that we are Victorian flaneurs, and visit the places, largely 'reading institutions', where newspapers were read. It is also a chance to get to know our case study town of Preston. An hour's leisurely walk, in 1855 and again in 1875 and 1900 will be enough to see the variety of such places, and how they changed over 45 years.

---

1   Robert Darnton, 'First Steps Towards a History of Reading', in *The Kiss of Lamourette: Reflections in Cultural History*, ed. by Robert Darnton (London: Faber & Faber, 1990), p. 167; see also James A. Secord, *Victorian Sensation: The Extraordinary Publication, Reception, and Secret Authorship of Vestiges of the Natural History of Creation* (Chicago: University of Chicago Press, 2003), p. 338.

   https://doi.org/10.11647/OBP.0152.02

1855

We will begin in the market square behind the town hall. On a Saturday evening in September 1855, an old, lame man, 'Uncle Ned', sings one of the broadside ballads he is selling.[2] One of the busiest shops lining the square is Dobson's at 17 Market Place, where a steady stream of people has been going in and out of this bookshop, printer's and newspaper publisher's, to pay 3½d for today's issue of the town's oldest surviving newspaper, the weekly *Preston Chronicle* (est. 1807). Men stand around outside the shop in groups, listening to others read aloud from the paper and commenting on what they hear, eager to learn the latest from the siege of Sebastopol, or any other news of the Crimean War. One man is reading the *Times*, which arrived in Preston in the early afternoon. We cross the square, past Henry Thomson's newsagent's shop and the general news room above 6 Friargate. Round the corner on the main street, Fishergate, there are more reading places — the Guild Hall news room inside the squat, boxy Georgian town hall, and, opposite, the Commercial News Room on Town Hall Corner, offering newspapers and telegrams. These rooms can become crowded if an exciting story breaks, with non-members bending the rules to keep abreast of the news. One member of the Commercial News Room complained that, during the American Civil War

> it is very annoying, these stirring times, to be unable to get near the telegrams, on account of some inveterate newsmonger, who does not subscribe, or be prevented reading the *Times*, through its being monopolised by one whose name does not figure in the list of subscribers.[3]

Across the road to the left, between the thatched Grey Horse Inn and the imposing four-storey Georgian Bull and Royal Hotel, is the *Preston Pilot* office (Fig. 2.1), with its own knots of readers and listeners standing outside. On either side, if we were to peep through the doors of the modest inn or the grander hotel, we would see men and the occasional woman reading newspapers provided by the house.

But we turn in the opposite direction, across Fishergate, past the groups of newspaper-readers outside the *Preston Guardian* office (busier

---

2   *Preston Guardian* (hereafter *PG*), 6 October 1860.

3   Letter from 'One Who Pays His Subscription', *Preston Chronicle* (hereafter *PC*), 6 July 1864.

Fig. 2.1. Office of *Preston Pilot*, Church Street, Preston. Detail from 'The Grey Horse', J. Ferguson, 1853. By permission of Harris Museum, Art Gallery & Library, Preston, England, all rights reserved.

than the other two newspaper offices), to Cannon Street, a steep, narrow sidestreet descending from Fishergate. On one corner is the Exchange Commercial News Room, opened in May. Like the others we have passed, this is a select establishment, charging one guinea per year, more than a week's wages for most cotton workers. Near the bottom of the street, on the left, is the old mechanics' institute, its rooms still used for education by various 'classical schools'. Until a few weeks ago, one room was let as Cowper's Penny News & Reading Room, for a poorer clientele than the other news rooms; in the tradition of previous working-class Preston news rooms, it was occasionally used for political lectures and discussions. Cowper's closed a few weeks before Stamp Duty became an optional postal charge rather than a compulsory tax in July 1855, leading to a reduction in newspaper prices, enabling more people to buy their own copy. A mill worker on a typical wage of fifteen shillings a week could earn a penny in twenty minutes, taking just over an hour to earn 3½d, the price of a local paper or a quart of beer (two pints). On the other side of the street is the first of three bookshops,

Charles Ambler's, Isaac Bland's, and Evan Buller's, the latter selling newspapers alongside books and all manner of crucifixes and Roman Catholic paraphernalia.

We turn left onto Cross Street, Syke Street then Avenham Lane. Further east are some of the poorest streets in Preston; there are no bookshops, newsagents or reading rooms in that district, only two schools, one of which, Grimshaw Street Independent Sunday School, boasts a circulating library. If we dared to go further we might find a newspaper or two in the many pubs and beerhouses, on sale in one or two corner grocer's shops, or in a rare home that can somehow obtain a newspaper and the light by which to read it. But instead, by the National School, with its Sunday School reading room, we cross the cobbled, winding lane, lined by terraced houses and shops, and walk up past Richard Alston's bookshop and newsagent's. Every pub we pass is also a reading place, of course.

On either side, in the streets off Avenham Lane, are at least eight small schools, mostly for girls, run from private houses — the local newspaper is probably among the reading material used at some of them. At the top of the hill, we are at the edge of Preston's wealthiest area — where each house can probably afford its own copy of a local paper and a London paper, and the gaslight to read them by. At the head of a tree-lined avenue is a solid, new neo-classical building fronted by steps and curling balustrades, the Institution for the Diffusion of Knowledge (Fig. 2.2 opposite), also known as the mechanics' institute, with its news room and reading room. The news room opened in 1850, and by last year had seventy-five members — although membership has fallen this year after the Stamp Duty became optional (within three years it will be 'well sustained by numerous subscribers' once again).[4] Round the corner is the wide Georgian splendour of Winckley Square, the epicentre of the town's wealth, these elegant villas home to the mill owners, merchants, lawyers and doctors who run Preston.

On the east side of the square, we come to the Literary and Philosophical Institute, an imposing building in the style of an Oxbridge college chapel, with its news room, reading room and circulating library, in front of the Grammar School. The institute's well-off members

---

4   Institution for the Diffusion of Knowledge, annual reports for 1855, p. 5; for 1858, p. 6, University of Central Lancashire, Livesey Collection, uncatalogued; *PC*, 30 June 1855.

Fig. 2.2. The Institution for the Diffusion of Knowledge (mechanics' institute),
Avenham, Preston, had a news room and a reading room. Engraving from
Charles Hardwick, *History of the Borough of Preston and its Environs, in the County
of Lancaster* (Preston: Worthington, 1857). Scan from Preston Digital Archive, CC
BY 4.0, https://www.flickr.com/photos/rpsmithbarney/5753101486/

seceded from the mechanics' institute after a 'slight misunderstanding'
in 1840. The next building, behind the same railings, sports similar
academic architecture, with its square tower and oriel window. This
is the Winckley Club, used as an HQ only a year ago by the town's
most powerful factory owners, as they co-ordinated their lock-out of
almost every cotton mill in Preston. The club opened in 1846, initiated
by members of the Gentlemen's News Room at the town hall. Besides
a billiards room and dining room, the Winckley Club boasts a 'large
and handsome news room on the ground floor, artistically decorated
and fitted', where 'the leading gentlemen of the town resort to read
newspapers and chat over the events of the day'.[5] For this, members
paid between £1 6s 6d and £2 12s 6d per year.

---

5   William Pollard, *A Hand Book and Guide to Preston* (Preston: H. Oakey, 1882), p. 142.
     Letter from 'A Working Man', *PC*, 14 February 1857.

The news room is the largest room in the club, with long tables, on which thirty to forty newspapers and magazines are scattered, and some higher tables with stands, for reading large broadsheet newspapers whilst standing. There are benches and comfortable chairs, writing desks, bookshelves full of reference books and bound copies of the most important papers (including some local titles), maps and pictures on the walls, a large fireplace, gas lamps, and a bell rope to summon the servants. This is not a quiet room generally, especially in the evening, with the sound of conversation, laughter, people reading an article aloud to their friends, the occasional argument, the clink of glasses, the sound of doors slamming elsewhere in the building, and the shouts of billiard and card players.

Fig. 2.3. Literary and Philosophical Institute (centre) and Winckley Club (left),
Winckley Square, Preston. Author's own copy, CC BY 4.0.

We continue up the square and back onto Fishergate, the busy high street. Almost opposite, down Fox Street, is the Catholic Institution with its reading room, but we turn back towards the town hall, past 97 Fishergate, Henry Barton's bookshop and printing office, from where he publishes his *Preston Illustrated General Advertiser* and the newly launched penny *Preston Herald* (2½d cheaper than Preston's three other papers). Further along is Ann Thomson's Catholic bookshop; next door but one is another bookseller, Edward Wilcock. Across the street is William Bailey's bookshop and printing office. Past the Shelley's Arms, a popular place to read the paper, like every other pub and beerhouse along this street, on past Henry Oakey's shop selling books and stationery, with its printing office at the back, on the corner of Guildhall Street. Mr Oakey also runs a circulating library, mainly of novels. We walk past the newly opened news room of the Young Men's Club on our right, frequented by clerks, book-keepers and the like, and back to the market square.

Our little walk has taken us past scores of places where newspaper-reading is an important activity — the street, the pub, bookshops and 'newsvendors', reading rooms and news rooms, printers' offices and newspaper publishers. Each of them offers different reading experiences, but in the 1850s most newspaper-reading was still communal, as papers were expensive and scarce. In the same way, twentieth-century film audiences gathered together in cinemas, and early TV viewers went to the one house in the street that had a set.

The street was an important reading place, full of signs and advertisements, shop windows, and walls plastered with posters and placards. People gathered outside newspaper offices to read the paper, but also in other public places, and under street lamps or shop lamps at night. Reading in the street was a communal activity, with one person reading aloud (adverts as well as editorial), interspersed with comment and discussion. It would have been unusual to see anyone reading a paper by themselves, and regardless of reading ability, anyone interested in the news could have picked up the main points by listening to the paper being read, or by asking someone in possession of a newspaper or leaving a news room. Reading places were sociable places.

Certain places were news hubs — the newspaper offices, larger reading rooms and, after the telegraph came to Preston in 1854, the telegraph company offices — the Magnetic Telegraph Company on Fishergate and the Electric and International Telegraph Company in the station at the far end of the street.[6] In 1857 the Magnetic Telegraph Company opened a subscription news room above its office. Before the telegraph, people probably waited at the station for news to arrive by train, as they did in Clitheroe in 1857, when O'Neil recorded in his diary:

---

6   Malcolm T. Mynott, *The Postal History of Preston, Garstang and the Fylde of Lancashire from the Civil War to 1902* (Preston: Preston & District Philatelic Society, 1987), p. 131.

I went up to Clitheroe in the evening and there was a great many
waiting for the train from Blackburn with the elections news as there
is no telegraph in Clitheroe. The first news I heard after the train came
in was that Cobden, Gibson and Bright were thrown out by large
majorities [...][7]

When Prince Albert died in 1861, the news was received by the
telegraph office at Preston station early on a Sunday morning, and
copies of the bulletin were posted at the town's main news hubs before
the town awoke — on the shutters of the four newspaper offices, at the
Winckley Club and outside the mechanics' institute.[8] Preston was one
of the first constituencies in the country to vote by secret ballot after
its introduction in 1872, but before then, voters and non-voters alike
would crowd around the windows of the town's newspaper offices to
see the current state of the poll, updated every hour.[9] Such excitement
could last for weeks during lengthy polls. James Vernon argues that the
earnest and private rationality of newspapers killed the inclusive drama
of public politics, but newspaper-reading actually increased the number
of places where public politics was performed.[10]

There were more than 400 pubs and beerhouses in Preston in the
1850s, and most of them probably provided at least one newspaper for
their customers.[11] The Victorian sign in the Liverpool pub in Fig. 2.4
shows that pubs saw newspapers as an attraction worth advertising in
their windows, even setting aside valuable space for their reading, as
with the 'reading room' of the Boar's Head Inn in Friargate, Preston or
the 'news room' of Blackburn's Alexandra Hotel (Fig. 2.5 below), whose
landlord even advertised the titles of the papers available (most of them
regional or local). Pubs were attractive, cheap and accessible reading
places for working-class people — warm, well-lit, with reading material

---

7   John O'Neil, *The Journals of a Lancashire Weaver: 1856–60, 1860–64, 1872–75*, ed. by
     Mary Brigg (Chester: Record Society of Lancashire and Cheshire, 1982), 28 March
     1857.

8   *PC*, 18 December 1861.

9   Tom Smith, 'Religion or Party? Attitudes of Catholic Electors in Mid-Victorian
     Preston', *North West Catholic History*, 33 (2006), 19–35 (p. 31).

10   James Vernon, *Politics and the People: A Study in English Political Culture, c. 1815–1867*
     (Cambridge: Cambridge University Press, 1993), pp. 142–43. Vernon is also mistaken
     in his assertion that 'provincial communities relied entirely on the national press for
     their news of important national events' before the 1860s (p. 143).

11   'Preston Annual Licensing Session Applications for more spirit licences. Opposition
     meeting in the temperance hall', *PC*, 18 August 1860.

sympathetic to their interests, unpoliced by middle-class reformers or evangelists, allowing free discussion, in a convivial atmosphere fuelled by alcohol.[12] In Clitheroe, O'Neil could obtain a newspaper to read at home, but he preferred to walk a mile into town to read the news in the Castle Inn every Saturday night.[13] However, it was impossible to read the paper if the pub was too busy or noisy, as during Clitheroe's fair, when the town was 'throng' with people. O'Neil wrote: 'I had a few glasses of ale but Public Houses was so throng and so noisy I could not read the newspaper [...]'[14] Neither could he read if he drank too much, as on New Year's Day 1859: 'I went up to Clitheroe and got my Christmas glass. It was the best whiskey I ever got in my life, it nearly made me drunk. It made me so that I could not read the newspaper, so I had to come home without any news.'

Fig. 2.4. News room sign in window of the Lion Tavern, Moorfields, Liverpool, built c.1841. Author's photo, CC BY 4.0.

12 Richard Altick, *The English Common Reader: A Social History of the Mass Reading Public, 1800–1900* (Chicago: University of Chicago Press, 1963), pp. 200–201; Arthur Aspinall, *Politics and the Press, c.1780–1850* (Brighton: Harvester Press, 1973), pp. 9, 29; Lionel Robinson, *Boston's Newspapers* (Boston: Richard Kay Publications, for the History of Boston Project, 1974), p. 8.

13 For example, 'I could not get up to Clitheroe it was so wet but I got a newspaper and read it' (Saturday 27 September 1856).

14 O'Neil diaries, Saturday 24 October 1857.

JOHN MAYSON,
A L E X A N D R A   H O T E L ,
DUKE'S-BROW, BLACKBURN.

PRIME Mild and Bitter ALES, PORTER, &c., on draught and in bottle. British and Foreign SPIRITS, WINES, Cigars, &c.

The NEWS ROOM is supplied with the following popular papers :— DAILY: *London Daily Times, Manchester Courier, Liverpool Mercury.* WEEKLY : *Preston Herald, Preston Guardian, Blackburn Times, Illustrated London News, Punch, and Fun.*

Fig. 2.5. Advertisement for Alexandra Hotel, Blackburn, listing newspapers available in its news room, *Preston Herald*, 10 November 1866. Transcription by the author, CC BY 4.0.

'Ask the landlord why he takes the newspaper. He'll tell you that it attracts people to his house, and in many cases its attractions are much stronger than those of the liquor there to be drunk', William Cobbett claimed in 1807.[15] In Preston, reading the paper aloud and discussing its contents had been a formalised event during the excitement of the 1830 election, at which the radical Henry Hunt defeated Lord Stanley:

> They flocked to the public-house on a Sunday evening as regularly as if it had been a place of worship, not for the set purpose of getting drunk, but to hear the newspaper read. The success of the landlord depended, not on the strength of his beer altogether, but on having a good reader for his paper [...] it was not the general custom to drink during the reading of the paper. Every one was expected to drink during the discussion of any topic, or pay before leaving for the good of the house.[16]

Like Sloppy 'who do the Police in different voices', these skilled public readers brought the newspaper alive in crowded pubs.

One Liverpool pub landlord, John McArdle, performed the paper himself, creating a very different experience from reading silently and alone. Irish nationalists came to his pub in Crosbie Street every Sunday night to hear him read the *Nation* (which cost sixpence in the 1840s).

---

15   *Cobbett's Political Register*, 26 September 1807, cited in Aspinall, p. 11.

16   William Pilkington, *The Makers of Wesleyan Methodism in Preston, and the Relation of Methodism to the Temperance and Teetotal Movements* (Preston: Published for the author, 1890), p. 183.

McArdle was a big, imposing looking man, with a voice to match, who gave the speeches of O'Connell and the other orators of Conciliation Hall with such effect that the applause was always given exactly in the right places, and with as much heartiness as if greeting the original speakers.[17]

The comments and interpretations of such 'local prophets' expounding upon the 'secular texts' of the newspaper, were considered dangerous by some commentators, who preferred the rule of silent reading found in many mechanics' institutes and free libraries.[18] There is evidence of reading the paper aloud in the pub as late as 1874, in Sheffield at least, and it seems likely that pubs continued to be significant places for reading and performing the newspaper well into the twentieth century.[19]

On our walk we passed many news rooms and reading rooms — places, spaces, businesses and institutions set aside specifically for the reading of newspapers and magazines. Members and customers preferred to read newspapers in these rooms than at home because it was cheaper to gain temporary access to many different titles than to have permanent ownership of a single copy at home; the penny admission to Cowper's Commercial News Room or the penny a week subscription for a church news room also paid for heat and light, scarce resources for many readers. These places also made newspaper-reading a sociable, convivial activity. There was no clear distinction between news rooms, reading rooms and libraries.[20] In the Institution for the Diffusion of Knowledge, these three functions occupied three separate spaces, in others, the library (a cupboard or a few shelves) may have been in the corner of a news room. Whatever their names, places devoted to the reading of newspapers were much more common than those dedicated to the reading of books, including novels.

O'Neil's news room career reveals the purposes and development of these institutions. In his native Carlisle he had been a member of that city's first working-class news room, opened in John Street, in the poor district of Botchergate, in 1847. Mechanics' institutes had been

---

17 John Denvir, *The Life Story of an Old Rebel* (Shannon: Irish University Press, 1972), pp. 15–16.

18 Richard Jefferies, 'The Future of Country Society', *New Quarterly Magazine*, 8 (1877), 379–409 (p. 399).

19 Lucy Brown, *Victorian News and Newspapers* (Oxford: Clarendon Press, 1985).

20 O'Neil used the terms 'club room', 'news room' and 'reading room' interchangeably, to describe Clitheroe Liberal Club's reading facilities.

established around the country for more than two decades by then, but were largely shunned by working-class men and women because they were controlled by middle-class philanthropists, like the York news room in Fig. 2.6 opposite. Working-class readers preferred to set up their own news rooms (as O'Neil explained in a letter to the *Carlisle Journal* in 1849), because they were cheaper, could be paid for weekly rather than in a hefty lump sum every quarter or every year, they had newspapers (many mechanics' institutes banned newspapers until the 1850s for fear of political discussions), and they were controlled by their users.[21] Despite occasional problems, as in one unnamed Lancashire news room of the 1840s where discussion 'led to confusion and bickering' and the room had to be closed,[22] conversation was integral to public newspaper-reading at mid-century, mixing oral and print cultures. Many news rooms were open on Sundays, working men's only day of rest. In 1851, O'Neil and his fellow newspaper-readers attracted national attention when they opened a new, purpose-built news room in Carlisle's Lord Street, of which O'Neil was secretary (Fig. 2.7).[23] By 1861, Carlisle had six working-class reading rooms, with a total membership of 800–1,000, twice as many as the mechanics' institute.[24] These rooms represented a huge amount of time, money and effort that working men were prepared to invest in creating their own places devoted primarily to reading and discussing the news.

In Preston there was a handful of small trades union and commercial news rooms at mid-century, but most were provided by middle-class religious or social reformers, like the York room in Fig. 2.6. Church-sponsored reading rooms aimed at working-class adults flourished in the 1850s and 1860s. In the 1850s, rooms in at least five Church of England

---

21   Mary Brigg, introduction to O'Neil diaries, pp. ix-xii.

22   *The Spectator*, quoted in 'Prosperous Lancashire', *PC*, 24 October 1891.

23   Henry Morley, 'The Labourer's Reading Room', *Household Words*, 3 (1851), 581–85 (p. 583 ff.). The image of the Carlisle room (Fig. 2.7) appears to be of the opening ceremony, with the mayor in the centre of the gallery, some men singing around an organ to the right, and women present, in their shawls and bonnets. The illustration tells us little about how the room was used, in contrast to the image of the York room (Fig. 2.6), which shows newspaper stands at the rear, maps on the wall to interpret the foreign news, and at least two conversations, on the left.

24   Robert Elliott, 'On Working Men's Reading Rooms, as Established since 1848 at Carlisle', *Transactions of the National Association for the Promotion of Social Science*, 1861, 676–79. The author, a doctor, was a friend of O'Neil's (Brigg, introduction to O'Neil diaries).

Fig. 2.6. Working men's reading and news room, York, set up by middle-class benefactors. *British Workman* 20, 1856, p. 78. Used with permission of the Nineteenth-Century Business, Labour, Temperance & Trade Periodicals project, www.blt19.co.uk, CC BY 4.0.

Fig. 2.7. Lord Street working men's news room, Carlisle, from *Illustrated London News*, 20 December 1851, p. 732. Used with permission of University of Central Lancashire Special Collections, CC BY 4.0.

parishes opened in connection with mutual improvement societies (it is not known whether the opening of five in five years was due to inter-parish competition or a diocesan or national initiative). The 250 members of St Peter's Young Men's Club paid 1d per week in 1861 for

> a reading room supplied with the leading papers; a library, containing 400 volumes; educational classes, three nights a week; a conversation room, where bagatelle, chess, draughts &c. are allowed; and an excellent refreshment room [...] The club [...] affords to the working man opportunities for spending his time rationally and instructively, without resort to the pot-house, where his money is wasted, and himself ultimately reduced to beggary.[25]

There were larger rooms such as the mechanics' institute (60 news room members in 1852, rising to 75 in 1854), the Winckley Club (150 members in 1861), and the Literary and Philosophical Institute. Paternalistic mill owners such as John Goodair provided workplace libraries.[26] As we saw on our walk, there was a mixed economy of news rooms in Preston at the start of the period.

News rooms were not only spaces in which to read, they also operated as sellers of second-hand newspapers and magazines. They recouped some of the cost of the publications by auctioning them to their members and the general public, in quarterly or yearly sales that functioned as a futures market in second-hand papers. Members bid for the right to take away daily papers the following day, weekly papers a few days after publication, and monthly and quarterly periodicals as soon as the next issue arrived.[27] Typically, a local auctioneer would ensure that these sales were entertaining and dramatic events, teasing successful bidders about their reading preferences, and poking fun at the relative popularity of each local paper, particularly if a publisher or editor was present. A newspaper might give a complete list of auction prices for each title if they could be made to show the paper's value to be higher than its competitors.[28]

---

25   *PC*, 31 October 1861. See similar descriptions of St Luke's Conservative Association, *Preston Herald* (hereafter *PH*) supplement, week ending 17 September 1870, p. 3, and Preston Temperance Society annual report for 1862, p. 7, University of Central Lancashire, Livesey Collection, LC M [Pre]).

26   [John Goodair], 'A Preston Manufacturer', *Strikes Prevented* (Manchester: Whittaker, 1854), cited in H. I. Dutton and John Edward King, *'Ten per Cent and No Surrender': The Preston Strike, 1853–1854* (Cambridge: Cambridge University Press, 1981), p. 85.

27   For example, 'Public sale of newspapers, Ripon', *Leeds Mercury*, 5 January 1839.

28   For example, *PC*, 6 January, 1872.

The proceeds provided a substantial proportion of news rooms' income, at least in the early part of the period. The Winckley Club spent £99 2s 5d on newspapers and periodicals in the year to April 1851 (the largest single item of expenditure), but recouped £24 7s 4½d from selling the back copies to members.[29] Members of Mudie's circulating library, the largest in the UK, could buy second-hand reviews and magazines by post.[30] The enduring value of used newspapers is shown by an appeal for reading material from the curate of St Paul's church, for a parish reading room: 'We would promise to send for the papers, keep them clean, and return them at any time that might be wished.'[31] Private ownership of newspapers and periodicals was thus available at reduced rates, through a recirculation system that challenges ideas of the newspaper as ephemeral.[32]

There were more news rooms than newsagents in Preston in the 1850s, if by newsagent we mean a shop mainly selling newspapers and periodicals. Buyers were more likely to get their paper from a bookshop, such as that of James Renshaw Cooper in Bridge Street, Manchester, where 'the doorway of the shop was garnished [...] with placards announcing the contents of the different local newspapers of the day'.[33] In Preston, Mr John Proffitt ran one of nine businesses described as newsagents around 1860. An advertisement (Fig. 2.8) for his shop on the main north-south route through Preston tells us a great deal about newsagents at the start of the period. Although most of the text is devoted to newspapers and periodicals, he describes himself as a 'hair dresser' first, 'news agent' second. This was a time when newsagents, more commonly known as news-vendors (also spelled 'venders') or newsmen, were starting to distinguish themselves from booksellers and grocers, but a shop devoted mainly to papers and magazines was still a rarity. As well as cutting hair and sharpening razors, Proffitt also offered printing, bookbinding,

---

29 Winckley Club minute book, Lancashire Archives LRO DDX 1895/1.

30 See an 1890 list reprinted in Laurel Brake, '"The Trepidation of the Spheres": The Serial and the Book in the 19th Century', in *Serials and Their Readers, 1620–1914*, ed. by Robin Myers and Michael Harris (Winchester: Oak Knoll Press, 1993), p. 82.

31 *PC*, 6 September 1856.

32 See also Laurel Brake, 'The Longevity of "Ephemera"', *Media History*, 18 (2012), 7–20, https://doi.org/10.1080/13688804.2011.632192. For the long lives of eighteenth-century newspapers, see Uriel Heyd, *Reading Newspapers: Press and Public in Eighteenth-Century Britain and America* (Oxford: Voltaire Foundation, 2012).

33 *Bolton Chronicle*, 30 June 1855.

picture-framing, stationery, second-hand books and a circulating library. At this time it was the norm for a purchaser to buy their paper in a grocer's or corner general store, a bookshop, stationer's, or tobacconist's, even fruit-shops, oyster-shops or lollypop-shops, as Wilkie Collins found in his survey of sellers of 'penny-novel Journals.'[34] Newspaper-selling was still only a part of other types of business, but the huge expansion in local papers (and national magazines) was about to change the shopping ecology of Preston and every other town in the country.

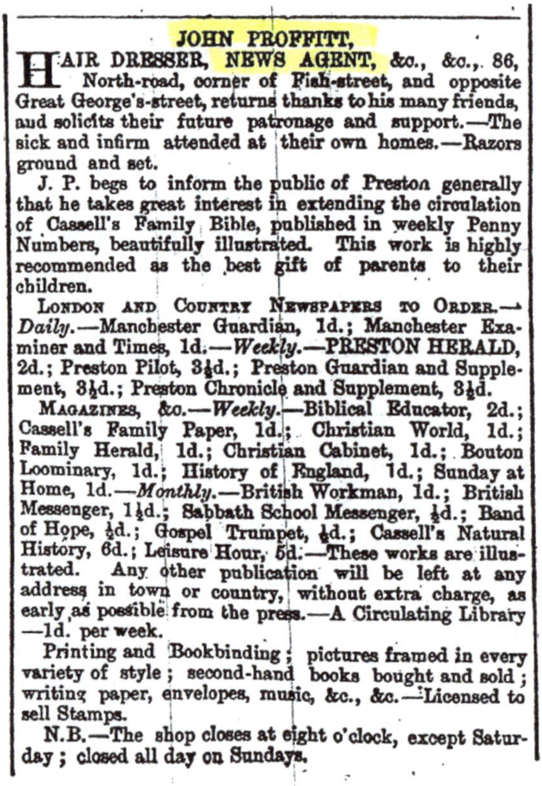

> **JOHN PROFFITT,**
> HAIR DRESSER, NEWS AGENT, &c., &c., 86, North-road, corner of Fish-street, and opposite Great George's-street, returns thanks to his many friends, and solicits their future patronage and support.—The sick and infirm attended at their own homes.—Razors ground and set.
>
> J. P. begs to inform the public of Preston generally that he takes great interest in extending the circulation of Cassell's Family Bible, published in weekly Penny Numbers, beautifully illustrated. This work is highly recommended as the best gift of parents to their children.
>
> LONDON AND COUNTRY NEWSPAPERS TO ORDER.— *Daily.*—Manchester Guardian, 1d.; Manchester Examiner and Times, 1d.—*Weekly.*—PRESTON HERALD, 2d.; Preston Pilot, 3½d.; Preston Guardian and Supplement, 3½d.; Preston Chronicle and Supplement, 3½d.
>
> MAGAZINES, &c.—*Weekly.*—Biblical Educator, 2d.; Cassell's Family Paper, 1d.; Christian World, 1d.; Family Herald, 1d.; Christian Cabinet, 1d.; Bouton Loominary, 1d.; History of England, 1d.; Sunday at Home, 1d.—*Monthly.*—British Workman, 1d.; British Messenger, 1½d.; Sabbath School Messenger, ½d.; Band of Hope, ½d.; Gospel Trumpet, ½d.; Cassell's Natural History, 6d.; Leisure Hour, 5d.—These works are illustrated. Any other publication will be left at any address in town or country, without extra charge, as early as possible from the press.—A Circulating Library —1d. per week.
>
> Printing and Bookbinding; pictures framed in every variety of style; second-hand books bought and sold; writing paper, envelopes, music, &c., &c.—Licensed to sell Stamps.
>
> N.B.—The shop closes at eight o'clock, except Saturday; closed all day on Sundays.

Fig. 2.8. Advertisement for John Proffitt, 'Hairdresser, news agent, &c &c'. *Preston Herald*, 1 September 1860, p. 4, British Library microfilm, MFM.M88490 [1860]. © The British Library Board, all rights reserved.

Ten miles away in Blackburn, the main agent for papers from Preston in 1849 was bookseller Edgar Riley

---

34   [Wilkie Collins], 'The Unknown Public', *Household Words*, 21 August (1858), 217–22.

whose shop [...] was the only news shop in the town that afforded elbow room, and elbow room was needed where many hundreds of large newspaper sheets had to be folded within an hour or so, before they could be sold singly to customers [...] Into his shop, about eight o'clock a.m. on Saturdays, were hauled three parcels of papers from Preston. The biggest was the parcel of *Guardians*. The *Chronicles* and *Pilots* likewise made good sized parcels. With deftness, Mr Riley, at the back of the shop, stood whipping the papers into their proper folds as fast as he was able, whilst the people poured in and out in a stream to buy their copies.[35]

Newsagents' shops could also serve as informal reading rooms, where reading and discussion was combined. In Clitheroe, Mr Fielding's shop became the 'rendezvous of professional men and others on their way to business, each of whom bought a paper to see how the world was wagging [...] Fielding's shop was the forum for the discussion of local and imperial politics [...]'.[36] In Rochdale in 1856, Joseph Lawton, shopkeeper and founder of the *Rochdale Observer*, allowed the young James Ogden to read without buying:

> to have the run of a newsagent's shop at that time, before reading rooms for young people and free libraries existed, was, to a studious and, in literature a ravenous lad, a perfect Godsend [...] when seated at his counter, I was immersed in the news of the day, the purchase of which was beyond my slender resources [...][37]

Just as news rooms acted as newsagents, so newsagents' shops became news rooms.

At mid-century, newspaper-readers were physically separated according to class and gender, at least in public. On our walk we passed different reading places for different classes. Even outside newspaper offices, middle-class men probably read the paper in their own groups, while working-class men who clubbed together to buy a shared copy would stand separately. If it was difficult for working-class men to gain access to a newspaper, it was even more so for working-class women, who were less likely to use pubs, while many public reading rooms

---

35 Recollections of William Abram, editor of the *Blackburn Times* and *Preston Guardian*, *PG* jubilee supplement, 17 February 1894, p. 12.

36 Hartley Aspden, *Fifty Years a Journalist. Reflections and Recollections of an Old Clitheronian* (Clitheroe: Advertiser & Times, 1930), p. 9.

37 James Ogden, 'The Birth of the "Observer", *Rochdale Observer*, 17 February 1906.

(including some church-sponsored ones) appear to have been male spaces. Women with a news addict such as O'Neil in their family may have seen or heard the paper at home if their menfolk paid a penny for one of the cheap weekly papers that launched in the late 1850s, or managed to get hold of a second-hand paper. Servants in middle-class houses probably had access to the newspapers and magazines bought by their employers, but in general, working-class readers had fewer opportunities to read or hear a newspaper.

1875

If we were to repeat our short tour past some of Preston's reading places a generation later, in 1875, we would find a changed town, unmistakably Victorian in its Gothic public buildings and its terraced streets laid out in grids, where newspapers are bought and read in different places, and in different ways. The population has increased by almost half in two decades, from around 70,000 to more than 100,000. The traditional lull of a Saturday afternoon has gone, as most of Preston's workers have been granted a Saturday half-day holiday in the last few years. Pubs such as the Cross Keys in the far corner of the market square still supply newspapers for customers. On the right of the Cross Keys is a passageway, Gin Bow Entry. Through the passageway and up the stairs is the Liberal Working Men's Club with its news room full of newspapers, read and argued over by reform-minded men.[38]

Back out on the square, Uncle Ned the ballad-seller looks older and frailer. He

> wore a battered shabby tall hat and a frock coat which was very shiny and decidedly the worse for wear. He held a long pole across the top of which was fixed a shorter pole at right angles in the form of the letter T. Over this was drawn through a corded loop a big bundle of long printed sheets illustrated with a crude picture at the top swung to and fro with the wind and the motion of the man's body. He sung the doggerel verse to some popular tune of the day [...][39]

---

38 *PC*, 20 October 1877.

39 This recollection, from 1889, is by J. H. Spencer, whose collection of broadside ballads is held at Preston's community history library: J. H. Spencer, 'A Preston Chap Book and its Printer,' *PH*, 21 January 1948.

Some of the ballads are traditional songs, but others celebrate more recent news. If we walked a few hundred yards down Church Street, we could visit the shop where his wares are printed by John Harkness, one of Lancashire's most prolific ballad publishers.

But instead we walk up the canopied steps of the town hall, into its cool marble corridors, to the Exchange Commercial News Room, which has been housed here since the new town hall opened in 1867, for the convenience of the town's businessmen. It is closed on a Saturday, but if we peep in we can see tidy piles of newspapers and magazines on the polished oak tables; there are some inkstands and a letter box, newspaper stands on other tables, chairs, two long benches with back-rails, a blackboard, a towel rail, a table with toilet materials, two umbrella stands, and dotted about the room, six spittoons. If it was a weekday we would hear the printing telegraph machine sporadically chattering out its market prices and news from the Press Association onto a narrow ribbon of paper.[40] Sometimes, when the window is open, members can hear the centuries-old songs of the ballad seller at the same time as the electro-mechanical chuntering of the telegraph machine. The list of rules on the wall stipulates no smoking and no dogs, and requests 'that no person detain a newspaper longer than fifteen minutes after its being asked for; and that no preference be shown by the exchange of papers.'[41] When the room is open, groups of friends and like-minded acquaintances cluster together to read and discuss the news, forming little 'interpretive communities':

> Occasionally on a very cold day there was only one fire the consequence being that all political creeds and set classes of theologians were pitched into one corner [...] when there was no doubt but that they desired being seated with their own fellows [...][42]

Membership has recently been reduced to £1 per year, since the news room is struggling for members.

Back outside, and onto Fishergate, the Magnetic Telegraph Company office with its own subscription news room has gone, closed when the

---

40   Thanks to Roger Neil Barton for background information on news room telegraph services.

41   Minutes of Preston Exchange & News Room committee, 24 June 1867, Lancashire Archives LRO CBP 53/4.

42   'Annual meeting of the subscribers to the Exchange Newsroom', *PC*, 19 November 1870.

telegraph companies were nationalised in 1870. The Liberal Working Men's Club had their own news room there for a while, but they too have moved. We pass Glover's Court, glimpsing David Longworth's printshop, where he produces his monthly *Preston Advertiser*, and walk down the busy main street and into Cannon Street, past two bookshops, James Robinson's and Isaac Bland's. The former mechanics' institute has recently been vacated by the printing department of the *Preston Guardian* and is now the printing office of the *Preston Chronicle*. On our way to Avenham Lane we can glimpse John Farnworth's newsagent's shop.

We are braver this time, and continue walking east, into some of the poorest parts of Preston. Twenty years on, there are more newspaper-reading and, in particular, newspaper-vending places to see. There is Bell's little shop, selling newspapers among its other necessities, up Oxford Street; on Hudson Street, two newsagents, Phillipson's and Pilkington's, past Syke Hill on our left, and Hannah Odlam's newsagent's. These paper shops are similar to those found in London and elsewhere:

> established for the sale of cheap periodicals and newspapers, bottles of ink, pencils, bill-files, account books, skeins of twine, little boxes of hard water colours, cards with very sharp steel pens and a holder sown to them, Pickwick cigars, peg-tops, and ginger-beer. Cheap literature is the staple commodity; and it is a question whether any printed sheet costing more than a penny ever passes through the hands of the owner of one of these temples of literature. One of the leading features in these second-rate newsvenders' windows [...] is always a great broadsheet of huge coarsely executed woodcuts [probably the front page of the *Illustrated Police News*].[43]

Now we turn off the busy, respectable Avenham Lane and into the shabbier Vauxhall Road. Straight ahead is St Augustine's Catholic church and its Men's Institute, with its reading room and library. Along Silver Street, past Wareing's grocer's shop, with its pile of Preston papers on the counter, into Duke Street, past Thomas Blezard's newsagent's shop, up Brewery Street past Wareing's little shop, which handles local papers along with everything else, and back along Queen Street.

---

43   'Nothing Like Example', *All the Year Round*, 30 (1868), 583–87 (p. 583).

We pause at a crossroads. On our left is the Weaver's Arms, whose meeting room is now the Conservative Reading Room, and facing the pub, across Queen Street, is St Saviour's new Anglican church. Beyond the church, one of the schoolrooms is used by the church's Mutual Improvement Society, for their reading room and library. We head back to the relative safety of Avenham Lane, up the hill past George Holland's newsagent's, and into a different world. The news room of the elegant Institution for the Diffusion of Knowledge is still busy, and now offers members the use of Mudie's circulating library, in addition to its own stock.

In Winckley Square, the Literary & Philosophical Institution (another branch of Mudie's) is quiet. Membership has fallen in recent years, and in 1867 they were forced to sell their huge building to the corporation. The more convivial Winckley Club next door, founded on less intellectual principles, is still thriving on billiards, newspapers and claret. Back on Fishergate we pass the shop of Chas Bond, bookseller, printer and fancy stationer, and Robinson's new and second-hand bookshop. Across the road is James Akeroyd's bookshop. Here are Cuff Bros' bookshop, Clarke's *Preston Pilot* office on the corner of Winckley Street, which also sells books and newspapers, then next door another printer and bookseller, Henry Oakey, whose shop is also a depot for the Society for the Promotion of Christian Knowledge (SPCK). Opposite is the YMCA, with its reading room 'well supplied with Papers and Periodicals', and a few doors along, the new post office, now doubling as a telegraph office, where crowds often gather to hear important news. There is Evan Buller's Catholic bookshop, also selling newspapers and magazines. A hundred yards further is a bookshop and newsagents' run by the *Chronicle*'s former owner, William Dobson, and almost opposite is the new home of the Central Working Men's Club, with its 'commodious newsroom, fronting Fishergate', available for a 1/6 quarterly membership fee. In one of the club's previous homes, in Lord Street, its news room presented a cosy picture, far preferable to the cramped, noisy and badly lit homes of its members:

> The fire was blazing cheerfully, the paper and pictures upon the walls were as beautiful as any artist could desire, and the general effect was decidedly one of comfort and quiet enjoyment. The library or reading

room, as the adjoining apartments were designated, was furnished in a similar manner, only books took the place of newspapers.[44]

In Barrow, some members of the Working Men's Club wanted somewhere more private than the reading room, but this was discouraged by the Reading Committee, who resolved in 1883 'that parties in habit of taking periodicals with them whilst in the water closet be requested by the steward to discontinue such practice'.[45]

Back in Preston, on the same side of the street the town's three main newspapers are clustered together; all three sell other newspapers, as well as their own. The *Herald*, next door to the working men's club, comes first, then the *Chronicle* five doors down. Next door but one, a bust of William Caxton perches atop the rather grand three-storey stone-fronted home of the *Preston Guardian* (Fig. 2.9, next page), the town's most successful paper, and the only one to have a purpose-built office. The local paper was changing the fabric of Preston's main street, as it was up and down the country.

There were significant shifts in the places of newspaper-reading between the 1850s and the 1870s — many more shops sold newspapers (and magazines), which means that many more people were buying their own copies to read at home. More schools had been built, in which more children were reading newspapers, and there were fewer news rooms, with those that survived tending to be run by political parties, clubs and societies, as a membership benefit. The number of newsagents increased steeply, from less than a dozen in the mid-1850s to more than fifty in the mid-1870s; one local trade directory, Mannex's, recorded a rise from thirty-four to fifty between 1874 and 1877. This is no doubt partly due to more shops being reclassified under the emergent category of newsagents rather than by the other goods they sold, but the trend is consistent across all trade directories, and also in the Census.

Other small shops seem to have sold newspapers as a sideline, and so were not classified as newsagents. For example, in 1870 there were sixty-six places in Preston selling the *Preston Herald* (and other newspapers

---

44   'Travels in Search of Recreation II, Central Working Men's Club', *PC*, 20 February 1864.

45   Barrow Working Men's Club Reading Committee minute book 1881–91, meeting of 27 July 1883, Cumbria Archive and Local Studies Centre, Barrow. One oral history interviewee remembered reading the *News of the World* in the outside toilet in the early twentieth century.

THE PRESTON GUARDIAN, SATURDAY, FEBRUARY 17, 1894.

GUARDIAN OFFICE, FISHERGATE.

Fig. 2.9. *Preston Guardian* offices, Fishergate, the town's first purpose-built
newspaper premises (Preston Guardian, 17 February 1894). British Library
MFM.M40487-8. © The British Library Board, all rights reserved.

too, probably), but only half of them were classified as newsagents in
the trade directories of the time.[46] The other stockists were confectioners,
a beershop, two beerhouses, grocers, a pork dealer, a pawnbroker, two
'furniture brokers', two chemists, and four milliners and hosiers. These

---

46 *PH*, 3 September, 1870, p. 5; the Mannex directories for Preston in 1873 and 1874 list
thirty-four 'newsagents and stationers'.

examples convey the variety of shops and offices where one might encounter reading matter for sale, and the types of businesses that developed into newsagents.[47] Further, there were no clear demarcations between new or second-hand bookshops, booksellers or newsagents, shops or libraries. W. H. Smith was not unusual in selling newspapers, new and second-hand books and periodicals, and operating a circulating library, which included 'the Quarterly Reviews and first-class Magazines' as well as books, like its rival, Mudie's.[48]

Newspapers of similar political persuasions sold each other's papers from their offices, such as the Conservative *Preston Pilot* and the *Herald*, even though they were commercial rivals. Political rivals, on the other hand, did not co-operate — the two Liberal papers did not sell the Tory *Herald*, nor did Clitheroe's Liberal, Quaker newsagent Mr Fielding, putting principle before profit.[49] Reading places, as well as reading matter, were differentiated by politics, and the distribution of news was influenced by principles as well as profit.

Supply and demand fed this growing army of newsagents. On the supply side, there were more newspaper and magazine titles, selling more copies, at lower prices. On the demand side, literacy was rising steeply, so that many people who had previously listened to a newspaper were now reading one themselves; wages had increased while working hours had fallen, creating more money and leisure time for reading — the Saturday half-holiday had become widespread in textile towns such as Preston by the early 1870s, for men as well as women and children.[50] Between 1853 and 1873 newsagents spread to districts outside the town centre in particular, which were populated by textile worker households whose relatively high disposable incomes drove the growth of music hall, the seaside tourism industry

---

47   This was a national phenomenon: Charles Mackeson, 'Curiosities of the Census. V.', *The Leisure Hour*, 20 June 1874, 390–92 (p. 390).

48   Stephen Colclough, '"A Larger Outlay than Any Return": The Library of W. H. Smith & Son, 1860–1873', *Publishing History*, 54 (2003), 67–93; Guinevere L. Griest, *Mudie's Circulating Library and the Victorian Novel* (Newton Abbot: David and Charles, 1970), pp. 18, 39. See list of 'second hand reviews and magazines' from Mudie's 1890 catalogue in Brake, 'Trepidation', p. 82.

49   Aspden, p. 9.

50   Gary Cross, *A Quest for Time: The Reduction of Work in Britain and France, 1840–1940* (Berkeley: University of California Press, 1992), p. 84; Mark Hampton, *Visions of the Press in Britain, 1850–1950* (Urbana: University of Illinois Press, 2004), p. 28.

and professional football. Did the reading habits of this culturally dynamic group shape the publishing industry in equally distinctive ways?[51]

More newspapers bought in shops meant more newspapers read at home. This was more convenient, but required heat and light, as O'Neil's diary entries emphasise: 'I have been sitting at a good fire reading the Carlisle paper' (received from his brother by post the day before), he noted in 1856.[52] In winter, reading at home became more difficult and expensive: in January 1860 he wrote that 'it was so dark I could not read unless I was standing at the window or door', and in December 1872 he noted that 'it has rained nearly all day and was so dark that I could not see to read very much.'[53] Practical and financial considerations such as these, and the desire for company and the comfort of a drink or two, led O'Neil to continue to do most of his reading in the Castle Inn or the Liberal Club news room in Clitheroe after it opened in 1872. In Preston, an advert for a town-centre pub, capitalising on interest in the Franco-Prussian War, was headed: 'The Latest News From The Seat of The War Can Be Read at Barry's Hoop and Crown, Friargate', showing the continued popularity of the pub as reading place.[54]

Increasingly, news rooms were provided by membership organisations, rather than operating as free-standing businesses or voluntary efforts. There was a burst of new reading rooms opened by political parties from the late 1860s, particularly around the time of the 1867 Reform Bill, which extended the franchise to working-class men in urban constituencies such as Preston. The local branch of the National Reform Union opened a reading room in March 1867, and in November 1869, within a week of each other, Preston's General Liberal

---

51 John K. Walton, *Lancashire: A Social History, 1558–1939* (Manchester: Manchester University Press, 1987), p. 190; Robert Poole, *Popular Leisure and the Music Hall in Nineteenth-Century Bolton* (Lancaster: Centre for North-West Regional Studies, University of Lancaster, 1982); Dave Russell, *Football and the English: A Social History of Association Football in England, 1863–1995* (Preston: Carnegie, 1997); John K. Walton, *The English Seaside Resort: A Social History, 1750–1914* (Leicester: Leicester University Press, 1983). For an explicit linking of these workers and new publishing genres, see Margaret Beetham, '"Oh! I Do like to Be beside the Seaside!": Lancashire Seaside Publications', *Victorian Periodicals Review*, 42 (2009), 24–36, https://doi.org/10.1353/vpr.0.0060

52 O'Neil diaries, 11 November 1856.

53 O'Neil diaries, 15 January 1860, 15 December 1872.

54 *PC*, 3 September 1870, p. 1.

Committee opened a reading room in Fishergate and the Central Conservative Club opened in Lord Street. By 1875 there were four Conservative and two Liberal news rooms in Preston. Trades union rooms multiplied in the 1860s, and all kinds of clubs and associations offered reading rooms as a benefit for their members, such as the 11th Lancashire Rifle Volunteers, the Preston Operative Powerloom Weavers' Association and the Spinners' and Minders' Institute in Church Street.[55] The national movement for working men's clubs (WMCs), launched by Rev Henry Solly in Lancaster, had some impact in Preston, with at least two set up in the town, the Central WMC in Fishergate and St Peter's Church of England WMC on Fylde Road. The creation of reading rooms above some branches of Co-operative grocery stores introduced a significant new player into Preston's public reading ecology. Preston Industrial Co-operative Society set up an educational department in 1875, and opened news rooms above its Ashton Street and Geoffrey Street shops the same year; in 1876 they opened two more, in Brackenbury Street and in Walton-le-Dale, two miles outside the town.[56] Co-op news rooms were more widespread in other towns — in 1879 the Rochdale Pioneers Co-operative Society had eighteen news rooms, Bury's had twelve, Oldham's seventeen.[57] These organisations all believed that offering a place to read and discuss the news would attract members.

More reading places meant more reading. O'Neil would typically read a paper once a week at the start of our period (for example in January 1861), but after the Mechanics' Institute and Reading Room re-opened in his village of Low Moor in 1861, he mentioned reading a paper fifteen times in January 1862, or every other day, and after the Liberal Club reading room opened in 1872 he sometimes mentioned reading papers there three times a week, in addition to his reading elsewhere.[58] Reading places must be factored into any calculation of how supply and demand affected developments in literacy, reading and publishing.

---

55   *PC*, 22 December 1861, 5 September 1863, 1 July 1871.

56   Anthony Hewitson, *Hewitson's Guild Guide and Visitors' Handbook: An Up-to-Date History of Preston, Its Guild, Public Buildings, Principal Objects of Interest* (Hewitson, 1902), p. 36.

57   Christopher M. Baggs, 'The Libraries of the Co-Operative Movement: A Forgotten Episode', *Journal of Librarianship and Information Science*, 23 (1991), 87–96 (pp. 90, 92).

58   O'Neil diaries, 28 September 1873.

Fig. 2.10. Tinted postcard c. 1900, showing Harris Free Library (left) and town hall (right). Preston Digital Archive, CC BY 4.0, https://www.flickr.com/photos/rpsmithbarney/5753101486/

1900

If we were to repeat our walk around Preston in 1900, one change would be highly visible, another hidden. A public library now dominates the town square, just as its news room dominates the town's ecology of public reading places. Less visibly, families are now reading their own copies of a halfpenny evening paper at home.

The market square has been transformed by the enormous neo-classical bulk of the Harris free library, taking up most of the eastern side of the square (Fig. 2.10). Before it opened in 1893, a council-funded 'free' library had operated since 1879 in the town hall on the south side of the square, in the room previously occupied by the declining Exchange and News Room (membership had fallen from 304 in 1869 to 97 when it closed in 1878).[59] The new purpose-built library features a news room and two reading rooms, one for ladies, one for men, with space for 276 people, and is more popular than the lending or reference

---

59   *PG*, 3 August 1878, p. 10; *PG*, 2 January 1878, p. 6.

departments.[60] In the photograph below, men sit reading magazines in the reading room in the foreground, while the newspaper readers in the news room at the back have a less comfortable experience, having to stand at the high, sloping reading desks (many libraries had standing accommodation only).[61] Light streams in from the large windows, bound file copies for reference are available on the windowsills in the middle, and a policeman keeps order to the right (visible in Fig. 1.5).

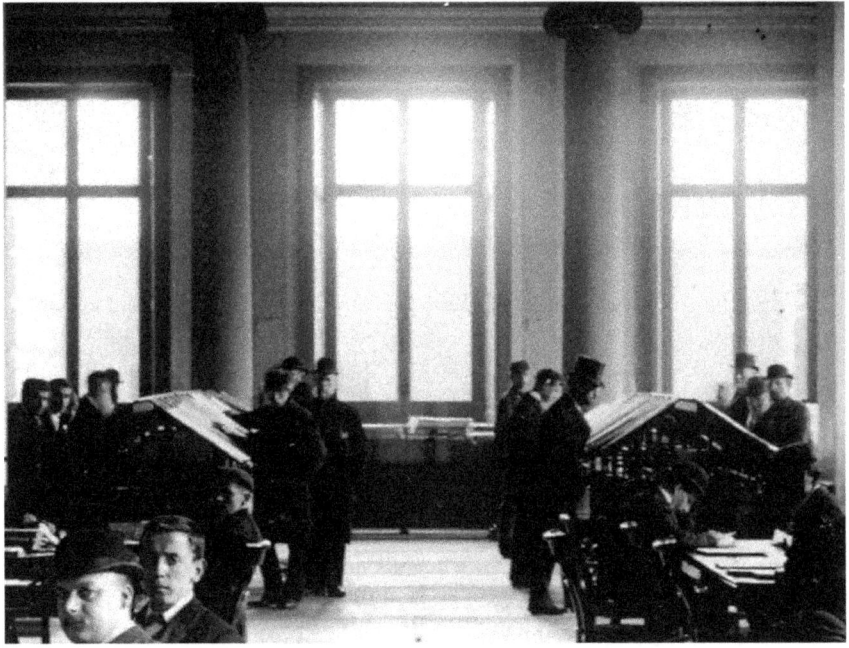

Fig. 2.11. Men standing to read newspapers in the news room of the Harris Free Library, Preston, 1895. Used by permission of the Harris Museum and Art Gallery, Preston, England, all rights reserved.

Elsewhere in the town centre, new reading rooms have opened, attached to party-political clubs — the purpose-built Conservative Working Men's Club on Church Street, the rather grander Central Conservative Club in Guildhall Street and the Reform Club in Chapel

---

60   John Convey, *The Harris Free Public Library and Museum, Preston 1893–1993* (Preston: Lancashire County Books, 1993), p. 20; William Bramwell, *Reminiscences of a Public Librarian, a Retrospective View* (Preston: Ambler, 1916).

61   Robert Snape, *Leisure and the Rise of the Public Library* (London: Library Association, 1995).

Street off Winckley Square. If we followed the same route into St
Saviour's parish as in 1875 we would notice even more newsagents
than before, each one offering a wider range of publications. Fishergate
and the whole of the town is now plagued by a new sight and sound,
hordes of newsboys, some of them as young as seven, noisily selling
evening papers from Preston, Blackburn, Manchester and Liverpool,
weekly papers and even magazines — boys from the St Vincent de
Paul orphanage in Fulwood are selling the Preston-based *Lancashire
Catholic* magazine.[62] As in previous times, there are a handful of older
disabled men selling papers.[63] Most are shouting the headlines from
the *Lancashire Daily Post*, as more arrive with the late special football
editions; they have bought three copies for a penny, to sell at a
halfpenny each.[64] In 1887 Hewitson described the techniques of these
news boys:

> Every afternoon, one of the streets contiguous to our leading
> thoroughfare is monopolised by a lad, who appears to have a special
> faculty for picking out and bawling out the grim, the astounding, and
> the dreadful in the papers he has for sale. His vociferations invariably
> refer to the serious, the alarming, or the awful — to fires, or murders, or
> embezzlements, or suicides, or executions, or disasters on land or sea.
> The other evening, by way of catching coin, a lad of this kind resorted
> to the bogus localising game. He walked along the main street, now and
> then went into shops, and shouted out, with much nerve, "Execution
> in Preston." [But] the execution related to the hanging of the Coventry
> murderer at Warwick![65]

If we were to go to the station at the end of Fishergate, on the platforms
we would see other boys running alongside the trains as they come in,
selling papers through the windows while they wait at the platform,
and then running again to finish their business as the trains pull away.

---

62   'Social and family life in Preston, 1890–1940', transcripts of recorded interviews,
      Elizabeth Roberts archive, Lancaster University Library (hereafter *ER*; the letters
      P, B or L at the end of the interviewee's identifier denotes whether the interviewee
      was from Preston, Barrow or Lancaster): Mr H6P (b. 1896). The transcripts are being
      digitised, with some available at www.regional-heritage-centre.org; *Lancashire
      Catholic*, August 1895, p. 163; *Cross Fleury's Journal*, November 1898, p. 2.

63   Mr C1P (b. 1884) and Mrs C5P (b. 1919), *ER*, both recalled the *Lancashire Evening
      Post* being sold or delivered by disabled old men.

64   Mr C1P (b. 1884), Mr G1P (b. 1907), *ER*. For street-selling in Middlesbrough, see
      Florence Eveleen Eleanore Olliffe Bell, *At the Works: A Study of a Manufacturing Town*
      (Middlesbrough: University of Teesside, 1907/1997), p. 144.

65   'Local Chit-Chat', *PC*, 10 December 1887.

Fig. 2.12. Paper boy on New Street station, Birmingham, detail from 'New Street
Station Going North', *Illustrated Midland News* 13 August 1870, p. 105, British
Library, EWS4150. © The British Library Board, all rights reserved.

Figure 2.12 shows a similar scene at Birmingham New Street station. W. H. Smith's station bookstall is busy. The growth of cheaper, smoother public transport has created new reading times and places, and national and local newsagents fed this new market.

The mechanics' institute has amalgamated its news room and reading room (membership fell after the free library opened). The news room at the Winckley Club still flourishes, despite membership fees of four guineas for 'town' subscribers (three guineas for shareholders, two for 'country' subscribers).[66]

On Fishergate, the crowds outside the *Lancashire Daily Post* offices (shared with its mother paper, the *Preston Guardian*) are larger and more frequent than in the 1870s, now that this evening paper publishes a new edition almost every hour from 10am onwards, each containing new sporting results. Since the rise of professional football in the early 1880s, Preston North End supporters almost block the street every Saturday of the football season, from September to May, to wait for news of the next goal from the newspaper office. In 1900, there is the additional excitement of the Boer War. Smaller crowds gather outside newsagents for football news.[67] Football has made some pubs more important as news hubs if they promote themselves as 'football houses' where fans and their teams gather. In Burnley, for example, the Cross Keys advertised itself as 'THE FOOTBALL HOUSE', where 'RESULTS OF ALL IMPORTANT MATCHES will be exhibited in the Smoke Room EVERY SATURDAY EVENING. Telegrams Regularly Received.'[68] The street is still a reading place, as seen in the 1906 postcard (Fig. 2.14) showing a wealthy-looking man in top hat and frock coat reading a newspaper as he walks down Fishergate. In Salford, groups of working-class men and boys read racing pages and comics on street corners into the early twentieth century.[69] Public transport such as the passing tram also became a popular reading place, the newspaper providing a barrier against the unwelcome looks of strangers, among other uses.

---

66   Winckley Club minutes of AGM, 17 May 1900, Lancashire Archives DDX 1895.
67   'Preston by gaslight', *PH*, 8 October 1890.
68   Advertisement, *Blackburn Standard*, 25 January 1890, p. 4.
69   Robert Roberts, *The Classic Slum: Salford Life in the First Quarter of the Century* (Harmondsworth: Penguin, 1973), pp. 127–28.

Fig. 2.13. Man reading newspaper in Fishergate (to left of tram), Preston, 1906, postcard. Used by permission of Preston Digital Archive, CC BY 4.0, https://www.flickr.com/photos/rpsmithbarney/3082785495/

If we knocked on doors in any part of Preston at the turn of the century, we would find newspapers being read at home, particularly the local evening paper. It is the paper mentioned most often by Elizabeth Roberts's working-class interviewees in Preston, where two-thirds of them recalled parents reading a newspaper at home, usually the *Post*. A photograph of Mrs Annie Stephenson, mother of countryside access campaigner Tom Stephenson (not reproduced here) illustrates the difficulties of reading at home, and explains why many still used more public, sociable reading places. Although probably taken in the early twentieth century, the scene would have been similar in the second half of the nineteenth century. She has tilted the newspaper flat to catch the light from the kitchen range, the only source of illumination.[70] Similarly, a candle can be seen on the mantelpiece of the man pausing from reading in Fig. 2.14. The spread of gas lighting made a huge difference, replacing the cost and danger of candles and rush lights and making reading at night easier and cheaper.[71]

---

70 Tom Stephenson, *Forbidden Land: The Struggle for Access to Mountain and Moorland* (Manchester: Manchester University Press, 1989), Fig. 1, 'Tom's mother, Annie Stephenson, nee Criddle' (frontispiece).

71 Altick, pp. 91–92.

ONE MAN ONE VOTE

(*From a Water-Colour by* WALTER LANGLEY, *R.I., in the possession of E. Atkinson, Esq.*)

Fig. 2.14 Man by fireside rests from reading *The Cornishman*. Reproduction of water colour painting by Walter Langley, 'One Man One Vote', *Cornish Magazine* 1 (1898), opp. p. 161. Author's copy, CC BY 4.0.

Many working-class people read newspapers sitting on their doorstep, a literally liminal space between the public and the domestic, as in the St Helens area, where 'in the summer the men sit akimbo on their door-steps, clad mostly in their shirt-sleeves, and they read their favourite organs with a thoroughness which puts to shame many of us who have fuller opportunities.'[72] Even if home was the workhouse, reading matter was still provided, with inmates having access to newspapers and magazines provided by well-wishers such as Mrs Cummings of the Old Dog Inn, presumably sending publications that had been read in her pub (most workhouses provided books, magazines and newspapers for inmates, according to surveys conducted by readers of the *Review of Reviews* in 1890).[73]

By 1901, home reading was supplied by seventy-odd newsagents in Preston, half as many again as in the mid-1870s (see Figs. 2.15 and 2.16), with similar growth in working-class districts of Blackburn.[74] The emergence of the newsagent as a distinct trade can be seen in the 'sedimented' signs of Fig. 2.16. 'Newsagent' has gone from secondary title in the older sign over the window ('stationer, newsagent, toy dealer, tobacconist, &c'), to primary title in the newer sign over the door ('newsagent & stationer &c'). Small grocers' shops that would not describe themselves as newsagents also continued to sell newspapers.[75] The population of Preston increased by roughly fifty per cent during the period, and the proportion of people able to read probably doubled, yet the number of paper shops increased tenfold, and the number of people working in such shops by even more (see graph below; the steeper rise in the number of 'newspaper agents' and 'news room keepers' recorded in the Census is probably explained by the growing staff of each shop). The development of newsagents, from a sideline of bookselling and grocery to a distinct type of shop, can be seen in the fact that all seven 'news-venders' identified in 1853 were also classified as booksellers.[76] But by 1901, only twelve newsagents out of seventy-six were also booksellers. They were serving not so much new audiences as new purchasers, helping to create a hugely expanding print market and becoming part of the physical and cultural landscape of urban areas.

---

72   John Garrett Leigh, 'What Do the Masses Read?', *Economic Review*, 4 (1904), 166–77 (p. 175).

73   *Preston Argus*, 24 September 1897, p. 1; *Review of Reviews*, 1 (April 1890), 269.

74   Michael Winstanley, *The Shopkeeper's World, 1830–1914* (Manchester: Manchester University Press, 1983), p. 42.

75   For such shops in Middlesbrough, see Bell, p. 144.

76   *Oakey's Commercial and Trade Directory of Preston* (Preston: Henry Oakey, 1853), Lancashire Archives.

Fig. 2.15. J. Smith, 'newsagent and stationer', Fylde Street, Preston, c.1909. A newsagent of this name on this street first appears in trade directories in 1869. Reproduced by permission of Mr William Smith, Preston, son of William Willson Smith (left) and grandson of shop owner Jane Smith, CC BY 4.0.

Fig. 2.16. Three rival Bristol newspapers are advertised outside the shop of newsagent Sarah A. Spiller in St Georges Road, Bristol, 1906. Postcard, Bristol Archives, 43207/35/1/50, CC BY 4.0, http://archives.bristol.gov.uk/GetImage.ashx ?db=Catalog&type=default&fname=43207-35-1-050.700x700.jpg

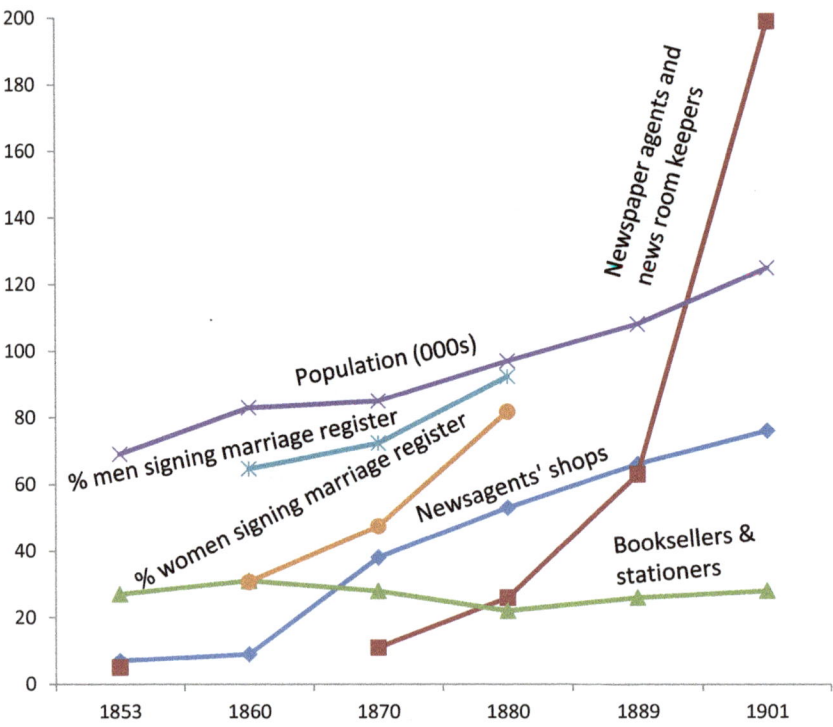

Fig. 2.17. Preston booksellers and newsagents, with indices of readership,
1853–1901, author's graph, CC BY 4.0.[77]

Preston's public library changed the town's news-reading ecology. On
the one hand it took away readers from small associative news rooms
and made the reading experience less social and sociable; on the other, it
provided easy access to a huge amount of serial print for all social classes.
It opened in 1879, after the peak of Preston's news room provision in
the 1850s and 1860s (Table 2.1 below), but this apparent decline may
be misleading. The news rooms of the last three decades of the century
were larger — pre-eminently the free library, the two Conservative
clubs and the Liberal club — so the actual numbers of readers using
public reading institutions may not have declined. Exceptions to this

---

77   Population figures from Censuses of 1851, 1861, 1871, 1881, 1891 and 1901. Figures
     for booksellers and newsagents from trade directories and searches of *Preston
     Chronicle*, literacy rates from Registrar General reports. 'Newspaper agents and
     news room keepers' is a Census occupational category.

trend towards fewer, larger news rooms were the six smaller reading rooms of the Co-op, the single biggest provider of reading rooms in the town from the 1880s to the early twentieth century. There was a decline in middle-class institutions and free-standing news rooms not connected to a club or organisation, but an increase in working-class ones, perhaps reflecting a middle-class shift from reading in public to reading in private.

Table 2.1. Approximate numbers of news rooms, reading rooms and libraries, Preston, 1850–1900.[78]

Pre-1850	1850s	1860s	1870s	1880s	1890s
5	27	27	24	16	16

However, many people still preferred to read or hear newspapers and periodicals in pubs and less formal news rooms, where they could also discuss the news with like-minded people, whilst drinking and smoking. Like curates 'who meet and converse, and write letters and postcards after consulting the clerical journals' at a London public library in the 1890s, the wealthy members of the Winckley Club were at odds with more 'respectable' middle-class readers who were migrating away from public reading places.[79] They still valued the convivial atmosphere of a club room, in which oral and print cultures were combined, even though they could afford to buy their own newspapers and magazines, and read them in their comfortable homes. Modern-day book groups and online 'social reading' behaviour are signs of a continuing desire to talk to other people about what we read, and a reminder of the corporeal and geographical realities of reading communities and interpretive communities.

There is some truth in the idea that news rooms and reading rooms, including public libraries, were intended by middle-class reformers to control working-class reading — particularly the mechanics' institute and the reading rooms set up by the churches in the 1850s and 1860s. The aim of keeping men away from the pub, to prevent drunkenness

---

78   *Sources*: Trade directories and searches of the digitised *Preston Chronicle*, using the search phrases 'reading room' and 'news room'.

79   'A Day at the London Free Libraries', *All the Year Round*, 26 March (1892), 305–9.

and poverty (and perhaps to limit political discussion) was behind reading rooms such as the Temperance Hall in the 1850s and 1860s, the Alexandra coffee tavern, opened in 1878, and reading and recreation rooms opened for dock workmen in 1886.[80] A similar impetus drove the campaign for a free library.

The public library quickly came to dominate reading room provision, especially for the less well-off. By 1884, an average of 1,492 visitors used the free library reading room every day.[81] When a member of Preston Co-op's Educational Committee suggested opening 'a grand central reading room equal to any political room in the town' in 1891, a voice from the floor of the meeting shouted 'The Free Library will do'.[82] Its arrival led to another fall in membership of the news room of the mechanics' institute, especially among less wealthy subscribers. The free library brought a significant proportion of public reading experiences under state control, however benevolent, as symbolised by the policeman in the photograph (Fig. 1.5), and its rule of silence influenced the style of reading, and began to break the old association between reading and discussing the news (note the 'No talking allowed' sign in the Sheffield news room of 1912, Fig. 2.18 opposite).[83] A writer in *All The Year Round* in 1892 noted 'the somewhat oppressive silence that pervades the free library in general':

> Everywhere you see posted up, 'Silence!' 'Silence is requested,' and so faithfully is the injunction carried out by the public, that after a round of free libraries one has an impression of belonging to a race that has lost its powers of speech. The silence really becomes oppressive, and one longs to hear a laugh or a whistle, or even a catcall, to break the solemn stillness of the scene.[84]

Within a year of opening, the free library had become Preston's best stocked and best used reading room. Hewitt's analysis of a similar change in Manchester's reading ecology leads him to conclude that

---

80   *PG*, 4 September 1886, p. 6.
81   Sixth annual report of the committee of the free public library and museum of the borough of Preston, 1884, Harris Library T251 PRE.
82   Report of quarterly meeting, *PC*, 18 April 1891.
83   Martin Hewitt, 'Confronting the Modern City: The Manchester Free Public Library, 1850–80', *Urban History*, 27 (2000), 62–88 (pp. 86–87), https://doi.org/10.1017/s0963926800000146
84   'Day at the London Free Libraries', p. 307.

Fig. 2.18. Silence ruled in Sheffield public library's news room. Detail from
'Everyday life in & around the city, no.14, The Free Library', *Yorkshire Telegraph
and Star* Saturday evening '*Green 'Un*', 13 April 1912, p. 4, British Library,
NEWS5890. © The British Library Board, all rights reserved.

the public library weakened the link between oral and print culture,
and undermined the disputational newspaper-reading of associational
news rooms. Its 'stress on the individual, private experience of print'
damaged Manchester's public sphere (see Figs. 2.19 and 2.20 below).[85]

However, the picture is more complex. The chronology of Preston's
reading places shows that the free library did not kill off a rich ecology
of associative reading places, as Hewitt describes in Manchester; most
of Preston's free-standing news rooms, unattached to any organisation,
devoted solely to the reading of newspapers, had already closed

---

85   Hewitt, 'Confronting', pp. 66, 86.

Fig. 2.19. Rochdale Road branch library reading room, Manchester, c.1899.
Allocated spaces for two copies of the *Manchester Evening Chronicle* are visible at
right, and spaces for the *Pall Mall Gazette, Illustrated London News* and *Graphic* on
the left. Flat caps and bowler hats are visible, worn by working-class and middle-
class men respectively, but no top hats, as in the Preston photograph. Photograph
by Robert Banks, from William Robert Credland, *The Manchester Public Free
Libraries; a History and Description, and Guide to Their Contents and Use* (Manchester:
Public Free Libraries Committee, 1899), p. 48. Author's copy, CC BY 4.0.

Fig. 2.20. Ancoats branch library reading room, Manchester, c.1899. Photograph
by Robert Banks, from Credland, p. 96. Author's copy, CC BY 4.0.

before the public library opened, and a major strand of associative reading places, sponsored by the Co-op, continued into the twentieth century.[86] Further, many working-class campaigners were involved in the movement for a public library, and any attempt to control reading material and behaviour had to be negotiated with the readers. In practice, Preston's chief librarian allowed a wide range of reading matter, and refused to censor betting news on principle. Some libraries attempted to retain the atmosphere of more relaxed reading places, as in Chorley with its smoking room, where readers could sit, smoke and read the papers, opened in 1899 as an alternative to the pub.[87] And, while limited social mixing had always taken place in inns and public houses, the free library was Preston's first reading institution not to discriminate by class, gender, politics or religion, a neglected aspect of these institutions.

O'Neil's reading habits remind us of the agency of the individual reader, who chose to read newspapers in many different places. O'Neil read at home, in a mechanics' institution, in the pub and in a Liberal club reading room, both public and private places with a range of rules and a tolerance of discussion. As the *All The Year Round* writer acknowledged, people had a choice, and many working-class people chose to stay away from the public library: 'The silence and good order are a little too much for them; they miss the freedom, the chaff, the jokes of out-of-doors and the full-flavoured hilarity of the public house.'[88] The proliferation of newsagents created a free trade in print, outside the control of any one group, so that purchasers were able to buy salacious Sunday newspapers, penny dreadfuls or radical and atheist magazines, according to taste, although most working-class readers were more conservative. Besides the pub and the street, the capitalist publishing market had given working-class people the freedom to create their own reading worlds — a democratisation of print.

The news room and reading rooms were the largest departments of Preston's public library, suggesting that newspapers and magazines were still seen as educational at the end of the century. An older perception of newspapers, as containing dangerous political information, to be kept out of the hands of working-class readers, had

---

86   Hewitt, 'Confronting', pp. 85–87.
87   Snape, p. 24.
88   'Day at the London Free Libraries', p. 308.

died out before the 1850s.[89] By 1869 the Vicar of Preston could defend the right of workhouse inmates to read the local newspapers, even on a Sunday.[90] At this time churches, middle-class reformers, some factory owners and both political parties in Preston were encouraging working-class news reading by opening news rooms. Previously, only Radicals had encouraged such behaviour. 'What was outspoken, radical and proscribed [...] became something close to the cultural and political orthodoxy.'[91] In the 1890s there was debate in Preston's co-operative movement over the value of their news rooms, but attempts to close them failed, with one supporter arguing that educational activities attracted new members, with news rooms a major factor.[92] There is little evidence here for the thesis that, from the 1880s, newspapers were no longer seen as educational or morally uplifting.[93]

Conclusions

The second half of the nineteenth century witnessed an exponential growth in the number of places where news was read and bought. On our tours of Preston at the beginning, middle and end of the period we saw news rooms appear around the town, for public reading and discussion of newspapers, followed by a new type of shop, the newsagent, meeting an exponentially growing demand for cheap newspapers and magazines; we saw the buyers of these publications take them to their homes, for individual and family reading. We saw new buildings erected and adapted by the local press, which attracted crowds of news-seekers who became a weekly fixture outside their offices. A public library was opened, and then a bigger one took its place at the centre of the town. This micro-geography of newspaper-reading

---

89 Abolition of newspaper taxes was resisted because of fears of losing market share and tax revenue, rather than fear of radicalism: Martin Hewitt, *The Dawn of the Cheap Press in Victorian Britain: The End of the 'Taxes on Knowledge', 1849–1869* (London: Bloomsbury Academic, 2014).

90 'A Library for the New Workhouse', *PG*, 30 January 1869, p. 2.

91 Brian E. Maidment, 'The Manchester Common Reader — Abel Heywood's "Evidence" and the Early Victorian Reading Public', in *Printing and the Book in Manchester, 1700–1850*, ed. by Eddie Cass and Morris Garratt (Manchester: Lancashire and Cheshire Antiquarian Society, 2001), pp. 99–120 (p. 119). Maidment is comparing the 1830s with the early 1850s.

92 *PC*, 18 April, 1891; *PC*, 15 April 1893.

93 See Hampton for a recent exposition of this view.

has highlighted a trend from sharing newspapers in public places, associated with discussion and conversation, to reading them silently or buying them for private consumption.[94] However, there was also continuity in newspaper-reading in the pub and on the street.

The greatest change was the growing number of places where working-class men, women and children could buy or read the local newspaper: until the opening of the free library and the Co-op reading rooms, poorer readers' access to reading material was limited, segregating them from middle-class readers.[95] By the end of the century, thanks to the Co-op, they had more of their own news rooms than ever before, they had access to a publicly funded central library news room, and newsagents' shops had spread to even the poorest parts of the town. Rapid changes in the content of newspapers, such as sport and serialised fiction (previously found mainly in magazines) reflected the growing power of working-class readers. Meanwhile, middle-class news rooms such as the Exchange, the Literary and Philosophical Institute and the mechanics' institute declined more than working-class ones, and there is no evidence that working-class readers stopped reading the news in pubs. The shift from public reading to domestic reading, akin to Raymond Williams's concept of 'mobile privatisation', was probably greater among the middle classes, whose use of public reading places declined.[96] Their homes were also more conducive to reading. The trend appears to be more complex among working-class readers: by the end of the century they could also afford to buy cheap reading matter from newsagents and read it at home, but many continued to read in pubs, in the free library and in their own public reading places, such as political clubs and Co-op reading rooms. Even at the end of the century, reading a newspaper alone, in silence, was not a preferred, 'natural' default.

Most of these reading places, whether news rooms or libraries, newsagents or bookshops, were devoted to newspapers and magazines rather than books, confirming the centrality of periodical print to

---

94 Aled Gruffydd Jones, *Press, Politics and Society: A History of Journalism in Wales* (Cardiff: University of Wales Press, 1993), p. 105.

95 See David Barton and Mary Hamilton, *Local Literacies: Reading and Writing in One Community* (London: Routledge, 1998), p. 17 on inequality of access to 'literary resources' in the late twentieth century.

96 Raymond Williams, *Television: Technology and Cultural Form* (London: Routledge, 1990), p. 26.

Victorian culture. Magazines and newspapers, particularly local papers (see Chapter 6), were central to the reading world of a provincial town in the second half of the nineteenth century. They physically changed the town. In the next chapter we will see how they changed the rhythms of readers' lives.

3. Reading Times

Time is part of the very name of 'newspaper', with its promise of something new, and of 'periodical', suggesting something published at regular intervals. Time is also part of their nature, their formal qualities, with their prominent dates and numbered series, demonstrating continuity and open-endedness.[1] Many theorists have sought meaning in the regularity of publication and a perceived acceleration in publishing frequency during the nineteenth century, linking these features to wider cultural changes in Victorian attitudes to time. Mark Turner boldly suggests that 'the media [...] provides the rhythm of modernity.'[2] Victor Goldgel-Carballo takes the same view, quoting nineteenth-century Argentine commentators on the popularity of magazines: 'Faster times [...] require faster media; and precisely because they were faster, and therefore seemed to mediate better, periodicals were considered more modern, that is, more appropriate to present times than previous media.'[3]

Time, like place, is socially constructed rather than 'natural', and so one might expect ideas of time to be influenced by cultural change.[4] But the prosaic evidence of local newspaper readers through the day, the week, the month and the year challenges many of these

---

1   Margaret Beetham, 'Open and Closed: The Periodical as a Publishing Genre', *Victorian Periodicals Review*, 22 (1989), 96–100 (p. 96).

2   Mark W. Turner, 'Periodical Time in the Nineteenth Century', *Media History*, 8 (2002), 183–96 (p. 185), https://doi.org/10.1080/1368880022000030540. See also D. Woolf, 'News, History and the Contraction of the Present in Early Modern England', in *The Politics of Information in Early Modern Europe*, ed. by Brendan Maurice Dooley and Sabrina A. Baron (London: Routledge, 2011), pp. 80–118.

3   Víctor Goldgel-Carballo, '"High-Speed Enlightenment"', *Media History*, 18 (2012), 129–41 (p. 133), https://doi.org/10.1080/13688804.2012.663865

4   Stuart Sherman, *Telling Time: Clocks, Diaries, And English Diurnal Form, 1660–1785* (Chicago: University of Chicago Press, 1997), pp. ix–x.

https://doi.org/10.11647/OBP.0152.03

theories, based as they are on an ahistorical, implied reader. And while the implied reader is singular, 'historical' readers are untidily plural, with differing attitudes and experiences of time, confirming that 'it makes sense to speak not of a culture's "time" but only of its several "times", precisely distinguished and carefully related, in their conflicts, their alignments, their convergences'.[5] While some readers did measure out their days and weeks in newspapers, the rhythms of their reading were often out of sync with the rhythms of publishing. And while the 'progress and pause' of Hughes and Lund's serials may fit a publishing schedule, reading schedules were often irregular: newspapers and magazines remained on the reading room tables to be read until the next issue arrived, up to a month later; and exhausted mill workers are unlikely to have experienced the sixty-hour working week between serial instalments as a 'pause'.[6] Weekly publishing schedules (the most common frequency) were not new, they were simply overlaid onto older rhythms of local market days and religious observance. Beyond pleasing symbolism, there may (or may not) be a correlation between change brought by industrial time-keeping and railway time on the one hand, and periodical time on the other. But correlation does not imply causation. Indeed, what would even count as evidence for one influencing the other? As Margaret Beetham notes, 'it is impossible to separate out the periodical from other structures in advanced industrial societies by which work and leisure have come to be regulated in time.'[7]

There is a disconnect between the linear, historical time of newspaper content, with its claims of advance, progression and change, and the cyclical, repetitive habits of historical newspaper readers, as they fitted these publications into their routines and rituals, domestic and public. This was a negotiation between the rigid times of publication and the more complex, messy times of access, leisure and sociability which enabled reading for the vast majority.

If time is socially constructed, periodical time is even more artificial, almost fictional. Publishers planned in advance a constructed 'now', a

---

5   Sherman, p. x. See also Linda K. Hughes and Michael Lund, *The Victorian Serial* (Charlottesville: University of Virginia Press, 1991), pp. 60–61 on competing views of time in the Victorian era.

6   Hughes and Lund, p. 63.

7   Beetham, 'Open and Closed: The Periodical as a Publishing Genre', p. 96.

present, that lasted until the next issue, while the date at the top of the newspaper, 'the single most important emblem on it' according to Benedict Anderson, was rarely the date on which it was published.[8] Morning newspapers were printed the night before, as were most weekly papers. Most editions of newspapers with 'evening' in their titles were published in the morning or afternoon. Bauman argues that time and space became separated in the modern era, but newspaper and periodical publishers united them in their fictional cover dates, which disguised the series of deadlines for multiple editions and the varying distances that these physical objects travelled from the printshop to the reader.[9]

James Mussell gives the example of the *Northern Star*, which carried Saturday's date on its front page, but some editions — those that had to travel the furthest from its place of publication, Leeds — were printed on a Thursday. Many readers across the country may have read copies of the paper, all labelled with the same day and date, simultaneously on a Saturday morning, but they were reading a variety of editions, each differing slightly in its content. And these were only the first readers of each copy. The majority of *Northern Star* readers probably read their copy on other days, as each copy was passed along a chain of readers. Equally, the morning papers of Manchester, Liverpool, Leeds, Birmingham and London reached readers at different times. So, while Anderson's idea of print creating imagined communities is useful, the element of synchronicity or simultaneity is also imagined.

Nineteenth-century publishers were more open about the conventions of publishing, reminding contributors of press times in their 'Notices to Correspondents' sections, or explaining that they were reprinting material omitted in some editions of the previous issue, but included in others.[10] Readers were aware of this — Clitheroe weaver

---

8   James Mussell, *Science, Time and Space in the Late Nineteenth-Century Periodical Press: Movable Types* (Aldershot: Ashgate, 2007), p. 94; Benedict Anderson, *Imagined Communities: Reflections on the Origin and Spread of Nationalism* (London: Verso, 2006), p. 33., paraphrased in Sherman, p. 112.

9   Zygmunt Bauman, *Liquid Modernity* (Cambridge: Polity Press, 2000); Mussell, pp. 15, 92 takes an opposite point of view.

10 'About half-past 1 o'clock on Saturday morning, as mentioned in a late edition of last week's Courier [...]' *Manchester Courier*, 28 September 1850 p. 9; 'To readers and writers. Cricket. We beg our Cricket contributors to send us their communications as early as possible in the week.' *Hastings and St Leonards Observer*, 12 June 1880, p. 7.

John O'Neil noted in his diary that 4 June 1856 was 'the day that Palmer was hanged. I have seen the fourth edition of the *Manchester Times and Examiner* which gives a full account of his execution at 8 o'clock this morning [...]' Readers were also aware of the distance between place of publication and place of reading, if this was not in the same town or city. This was the distance between core and periphery, a measure of the reader's distance from the centre of cultural power.[11] For the majority of magazines and a minority of newspapers, that centre was London, and one can only imagine the feelings of a reader in Preston waiting until lunchtime for a copy of the *Times* to arrive at the reading room, only to find that its contents reflected little about the reader's life in Preston. The local press challenged these relations of core and periphery, creating a network of widely distributed small centres of local cultural power, thereby subverting London's status as a centre, and positioning the capital as peripheral to life in the provinces.

This chapter is neatly divided into days, weeks, months and so on, but publishers sometimes stretched or blurred these categories. The bi-weekly *Preston Herald* pointed out that, on its two publishing days, it provided more up-to-date news than daily papers. But it was readers who were most likely to ignore the publishing calendar and clock. They fitted newspaper reading into their lives less tidily, regardless of the date on the front page or the frequency of publication. They read Saturday papers on Sundays, and weekly papers every day, such as readers of the *Preston Guardian* in the 1840s 'who were ready to pay 4½d or 3½d for their weekly journal, and who, bent on getting their money's worth out of it, read it in leisure minutes through the ensuing week.'[12] Equally, some readers' *weekly* reading was a daily, such as the *Manchester Guardian*, whose biggest sale in the 1850s and 1860s was on Saturday.[13] These practices were probably dictated by lack of leisure time, or lack of money. Reading rhythms were influenced, but not determined, by publishing rhythms. The next sections explore these reading rhythms, in Preston and other places, working from days through to the seasons of the year, and less regular rhythms dictated by unexpected events.

---

11   Margaret Beetham, 'Time: Periodicals and the Time of the Now', *Victorian Periodicals Review*, 48 (2015), 323–42 (p. 330), https://doi.org/10.1353/vpr.2015.0041

12   John Garrett Leigh, 'What Do the Masses Read?', *Economic Review*, 4 (1904), 166–77 (p. 175); *Preston Guardian* (hereafter *PG*) Jubilee supplement, 7 February 1894, p. 13.

13   David Ayerst, *Guardian: Biography of a Newspaper* (London: Collins, 1971), p. 129.

The Day

Reading did not occur uniformly around the clock in Preston, as elsewhere. There were clear reading rhythms to the day, starting at dawn with the arrival at the railway station of the morning papers from Manchester, Liverpool, Birmingham and Leeds (creations of the 1855 Stamp Duty changes), and the first editions of Preston's papers on Saturdays and Wednesdays, all soon to be read at middle-class breakfast tables. The commercial and middle-class reading rooms opened between 8am and 9am 'so that persons on their way to business can see the morning papers.'[14] Other reading places such as the YMCA in Fishergate (8am-10.30pm), Cowper's Penny News and Reading Room in Cannon Street (9am-10pm) and from 1879 the free library (9am-10pm) opened at similar times. The London and Scottish papers arrived before lunch, and on Wednesdays and Saturdays the last editions of the Preston papers came off the presses around midday.[15] In some workplaces, including those mills which provided libraries, lunchtime would be a chance to read.

By the end of the 1860s, late afternoon would see the arrival of evening papers from London such as the *Standard* and the *Echo*, and from Manchester, Liverpool, Bolton and other Lancashire towns.[16] Preston had its own evening paper during the Franco-Prussian War (1870–71) and continuously from 1886, with many copies sold outside factory gates as the hooters sounded at the end of the working day. They were probably scanned on the way home, and local autobiographies and oral history interviews record how in working-class and middle-class homes the man of the house (less often the woman) would relax in the evening by reading the paper. The local evening paper was part of a routine of leisure, particularly for men, but also for women:

---

14   Institution for the Diffusion of Knowledge, annual report, 1872, p. 2, Livesey Collection, University of Central Lancashire. 'Early frequenters of the News Room' at the Winckley Club, Preston, were anxious to see the Liverpool papers at 8.30am: Winckley Club suggestion book, 18 January 1879, LRO DDX 1895, Lancashire Archives.

15   'Earlier arrival at Preston (11.35 noon) of the Glasgow Herald', advertisement, *Preston Herald* (hereafter *PH*), 27 September 1873, p. 7.

16   For arrival times of Manchester evening papers, see Winckley Club suggestion and complaints book, 6 December 1872, 20 February 1885; for London morning papers, 15 December 1875, all LRO DDX 1895, Lancashire Archives.

Bert's slippers were warming by the fire. And by his chair were his packet of Woodbines, matches and the *Evening Gazette* [...] After his tea he would make himself comfortable in his own reserved chair and read the newspaper while puffing on his Woodbine.[17]

My grandmother [...] had a double-jointed gas pipe near so that she could pull the gas flame near to her *Lancashire Daily Post* in an evening.[18]

The same ritual was enacted in middle-class Preston homes, too, as described in this recollection of Dr Arthur Ernest Rayner from the early twentieth century, by his daughter:

[...] in front of the fire he would light his beloved cigar — Ramon Allone Corona — unfold the *Lancashire Daily Post,* and undo a waistcoat button. At last he was relaxed and we could breathe.[19]

'I should say nearly every home took the [*Lancashire Evening*] *Post'*, one interviewee said of Preston in the early decades of the twentieth century.[20] Whether they did or not, this reader imagined that they did — confirming Benedict Anderson's theory that an integral part of the private ritual of reading the local paper is the belief that thousands of others are performing the same act or 'ceremony' — thereby connecting them, in their imagination, to other readers.[21] However, contrary to Anderson and Hegel before him, simultaneity is not essential; indeed, the sense of simultaneity is often a fiction, evoked by the 'nowness', the sense of the present, in the selection and tone of address of the publication.[22] Others may read the paper at a different time of day, or even a different day of the week, but a sense of community comes from

---

17 Jean M. Shansky, *Yesterday's World* (Preston: Smiths, 2000), p. 21, describing the early 1900s.

18 'Social and family life in Preston, 1890–1940', transcripts of recorded interviews, Elizabeth Roberts archive, Lancaster University Library (hereafter *ER*; the letters P, B or L at the end of the interviewee's identifier denotes whether the interviewee was from Preston, Barrow or Lancaster): Mr Mr M2P (b. 1901), p. 3. The transcripts are being digitised, with some available at www.regional-heritage-centre.org

19 Phoebe Hesketh, *What Can the Matter Be?* (Penzance: United Writers, 1985), p. 111; see also '[My mother] always read the [*Evening*] Post at night, from beginning to end': Mrs J1P (b. 1911), *ER*.

20 Mr G1P (b. 1907), *ER*.

21 Anderson, pp. 35–36.

22 Brendan Maurice Dooley, 'Introduction', in *The Politics of Information in Early Modern Europe*, ed. by Brendan Maurice Dooley and Sabrina A. Baron (London: Routledge, 2011), p. 10; Mussell, p. 94, https://doi.org/10.4324/9780203991855

the belief that others are reading the same newspaper, issue by issue, for similar purposes, in other parts of the paper's sphere of influence, its circulation area. As we shall see, readers are also subjects of the local paper, actors in the continuous, continuing story of one place through time. Hegel and Anderson liken newspaper-reading to a religious ritual; here also, communities created by shared religious rituals do not require simultaneity, only similar practices for similar purposes.

As the working day ended, reading rooms for working men in church and school premises began to open in the early evening, and those that opened all day were at their busiest, while newsagents' shops were closing by 8pm, although reading matter could still be obtained at later hours in the smaller grocers' shops in the back streets. Between 9pm and 10pm the reading rooms in the town centre and on the outskirts of Preston closed their doors (except the Winckley Club, which stayed open until 11pm, possibly later), and the only remaining reading places would be homes and pubs.

The Week

The week was probably the most important newspaper-reading rhythm for most of the Victorian period, as weeklies outnumbered dailies significantly, even at the end of the century (see Introduction, Table 0.1). The local press in particular was part of the furniture of private and domestic life.[23] Reading the local paper was a ritual, woven into weekly routines, as seen in this effusive (and suspiciously well-written) letter in a Preston paper of 1852:

> I am an old man; and having, for [...] thirty years, been a devoted reader of the *Preston Chronicle*, that newspaper has become, as it were, a part and parcel of my very existence. I could as soon think of leaving Preston on the market-day *minus* my favourite old mare [...] as to leave the town without taking home with me a *Chronicle* [...] When the toils of the day are completed, and our substantial evening meal has been partaken of, it would gladden your heart to see how anxiously my family assemble, with eager ears, to listen to the events recorded in your columns.[24]

---

23   Lucy Brown, *Victorian News and Newspapers* (Oxford: Clarendon Press, 1985), p. 273.
24   'Rural Footpaths', letter from 'An Old Man', Correspondence, *Preston Chronicle* (hereafter *PC*), 11 September 1852, p. 6.

Whether this letter is genuine or not, such an attitude would have been credible to readers, as such habits are recorded in more reliable sources. Similar self-awareness by a purported reader about their ritual use of newspapers is seen in the 'old servant who has called "faar the news" at the market town once a week these fifty years, and the old master who has taken it in all his life, [who] speak of their constancy with a sort of pride.'[25]

The reading week had its rhythms, with long working hours limiting leisure time, including reading time, to the weekend for many people: textile workers gained the Saturday half-holiday from the 1860s onwards, so weaver John O'Neil read on Saturday afternoons, but mainly on Sundays.[26] For workers like O'Neil, reading was the chosen way to mark a pause in the work week.[27] Most of Preston's weekly and bi-weekly papers published on a Saturday, the main market day, with mid-week editions appearing on the second market day, Wednesday. This integration into the ancient routines of the local economy highlights the newspaper's economic role. The increasingly popular regional weekend news miscellanies such as the *Liverpool Weekly Post* and the *Manchester Weekly Times*, appearing from the late 1850s onwards, published on Fridays and Saturdays, ready for weekend reading.[28] Nationally, popular London Sunday newspapers had the highest circulations of any individual title throughout the period, yet they are rarely mentioned in the Preston sources until the end of the century, suggesting that their circulation may have been regionally concentrated, selling less in the North West; instead, local and regional weeklies are mentioned more frequently. In the early twentieth century, a Preston man made a Manchester Sunday paper part of his weekend routine while his children were at Sunday School:

> The absence of the children on Sunday afternoons gave an opportunity to father to have his weekly fireside bath and afterwards to relax in

---

25   Anon., 'A Chapter On Provincial Journalism', *Tait's Edinburgh Magazine*, July 1850, 424–27 (p. 424).

26   For half-holidays see Dave Russell, *Football and the English: A Social History of Association Football in England, 1863–1995* (Preston: Carnegie, 1997), p. 13.

27   Beetham, 'Open and Closed: The Periodical as a Publishing Genre', p. 96.

28   Richard Altick, *The English Common Reader: A Social History of the Mass Reading Public, 1800–1900* (Chicago: University of Chicago Press, 1963), pp. 86–87; Graham Law, *Serializing Fiction in the Victorian Press* (Basingstoke: Palgrave, 2000).

an armchair contentedly reading his favourite newspaper, the *Sunday Chronicle* [1885–1955].[29]

Such Sunday leisure was enjoyed less often by women, particularly those Preston wives and mothers who worked in the cotton mills, who had to cram much of the housework into the weekend. In St Helens, too, 'Saturday is not the women's reading day, and Sunday is their chiefest day of toil'.[30] In contrast, in Barrow, where fewer women worked, one mother set aside Sunday afternoons for reading:

> The only time my mother used to read was Sunday afternoon. She was always working, looking after the family, but Sundays, no work on Sundays, nothing had to be done. After Sunday dinner mother used to get those little books like *Home Chat* [1895–1959] and she'd read those and St Mark's church magazine.[31]

Men generally had more time, as well as more places, to read; in Middlesbrough, Bell's survey of working-class households notes many instances where 'wife no time for reading':[32] Few women would have been able to devote as much time to reading the paper as the Clitheroe weaver John O'Neil, a widower living with his daughter, who would sometimes spend the whole of Sunday reading a newspaper from his home town of Carlisle.

The publication day of a favourite magazine was a special event for some readers and listeners:

> My father used to read to [my mother], the newspaper, and he would read bits out of the newspaper and he used to read her the *John Bull* [1906–60] every Thursday, that was her highlight.[33]

Thus the different reading times of the Barrow woman on a Sunday afternoon, and the Preston woman listening to *John Bull* on a Thursday, were dictated by the publication days of their favourite periodicals, but also by the availability of leisure time.

Sunday newspaper reading was even found in the Preston workhouse, as reported by one of the Poor Law Guardians, William

---

29 Mr B10P, written account of life in Edwardian Preston, *ER*.
30 Leigh, p. 176.
31 Mr B1B (b. 1897), *ER*.
32 Florence Eveleen Eleanore Olliffe Bell, *At the Works: A Study of a Manufacturing Town* (Middlesbrough: University of Teesside, 1907/1997), pp. 146–62.
33 Mrs B1P (b. 1900), *ER*.

Howitt, a surgeon, who disapproved of this replacement of an older spiritual routine by a newer secular one:

> on Sunday morning last [...] instead of finding service being conducted there, as he expected, he found the men sitting reading the papers, spitting about the floor, and indulging in ribald and indecent talk. The women were also engaged in reading the papers.[34]

The papers in question were the Preston ones. 'Many persons believe it to be wrong to read newspapers and secular books on Sundays,' as one correspondent to the *Preston Chronicle* wrote in 1857.[35] The letter, from 'A Member of a Mechanics' Institute', supported the Sunday closure of Preston's institute; many of the town's other public reading places were also closed on Sundays, the chief exceptions being the pubs and the Winckley Club (of which Mr Howitt was a member), demonstrating how middle class readers had a greater choice of reading times than working-class readers; perhaps Mr Howitt believed that the middle classes were more resistant to possible harm from Sunday newspaper reading than the working classes. Clergymen such as Francis Orpen Morris, rector of Nunburnholme in Yorkshire, also complained that the weekend papers kept people away from church: 'the second-rate country penny press [...] many of them being published on a Saturday [...] furnish an attraction to the labouring men to keep them at home on a Sunday.'[36]

Oddly, monthly reading rhythms rarely appear in the Preston evidence. 'Magazine day' — variously dated to the last day of the month for publishers, the first day of the month for readers — was important to London periodical publishers and wholesalers, and to readers in Preston.[37] Monthlies were the most popular type of publication available in the reading rooms of the public library in 1880 (47 per cent of the 94 titles taken), but by 1900 they had been overtaken by weeklies (43 per cent of the 190 titles taken). The month was a metropolitan but not a local publishing rhythm, perhaps because of smaller local markets, most of them unable to sustain monthlies.

---

34 'A Library for the New Workhouse,' *PG*, 30 January 1869, p. 2.

35 *PC*, 7 February 1857.

36 'The pros and cons of church-going,' letter from F. O. Morris, *The Globe*, 3 December 1870, pp. 1–2.

37 Laurel Brake, 'Magazine Day', in *Dictionary of Nineteenth-Century Journalism in Great Britain and Ireland (DNCJ)*, ed. by Laurel Brake and Marysa Demoor (Ghent; London: Academia Press; British Library, 2009); Hughes and Lund, p. 10.

Fig. 3.1. Front page of Christmas supplement, *Manchester Weekly Express*, 22 December 1860. Courtesy of Manchester Libraries, Information and Archives, Manchester City Council, all rights reserved.

The Season and the Year

Reading had its seasons. Christmas annuals and supplements of monthly and weekly magazines (and magazine-newspapers such as the *Manchester Weekly Express*, Fig. 3.1, previous page) 'bulging with verse, stories and pictures', were popular then as now, such as *Owd Wisdom's Lankishire Awmenack for th' yer 1860, bein leop yer*, a dialect almanac published from Bolton but apparently printed and/or sold in many other Lancashire towns, including Preston.[38] Newspapers and magazines co-opted the ancient and popular time-focused print medium of the almanac, with the local press supplementing the circular time of prophecy and fulfilment, agricultural seasons, fairs and tides, with anniversaries of local notables and events, to create a linear continuity between past, present and future in one place.[39]

For other readers, seasonal holidays were an opportunity for more leisure, including reading. On Christmas Day 1877 the Winckley Club in Preston was open for business as usual, and in 1909–10 the Barrow public library was open on Christmas Day, Good Friday and Easter Monday.[40] Generally, newspaper sales fell in the summer, one reason given for the closure of the *Preston Evening News* in June 1871: 'Summer is upon us, when the proper out-door recreations of the season greatly modify the appetite for newspaper reading.'[41] Thirty-five years later James Haslam found the same seasonal decline in Manchester, noting how, 'in summer, the reading of newspapers and periodicals falls off. People go in for other things; they spend their money on holidays, on picnics and out-door life. The finer the weather, the less reading.' He quotes a Harpurhey newsagent explaining the best type

---

38 The almanac was edited and published by James T. Staton, 'editor oth "Bowton Loominary"', and the imprint includes J. Harkness of Church Street and J. Foster of Maudland-Bank in Preston, among others.

39 Brian E. Maidment, 'Beyond Usefulness and Ephemerality: The Discursive Almanac 1828–1860', in *British Literature and Print Culture*, ed. by Sandro Jung (Cambridge: D. S. Brewer, 2013), pp. 158–94; Brian E. Maidment, 'Almanac', in *DNCJ* online edition.

40 'No London papers at the Club on Christmas Day. It has not occurred before in my recollection', Winckley Club complaints book, 25 December 1877, Lancashire Archives, LRO DDX 1895; C. Baggs, 'More gleanings from public library annual reports', LIBHIST email discussion message, 6 January 2003, https://www.jiscmail.ac.uk/cgi-bin/webadmin?A0=lis-libhist

41 *Preston Evening News*, 7 June 1871, p. 2. The same seasonal dip in sales still holds true in the twenty-first-century, according to one Preston wholesale newsagent.

of weather for newspaper sales: 'I like [...] a wet Set'dy afternoon an' neet. There's a big rush for pappers then; I allus sell up!'[42] Conversely, some publications were designed specifically for summer reading, such as *Bright's Intelligencer*, the *Southport Visiter*, the *Morecambe Visitor* and other visitors' lists (directories of holidaymakers combined with local news and advertising, many of which became year-round local papers). They increased their publishing frequency during summer, appearing weekly during the tourist season and monthly the rest of the year.[43] Similarly, seaside and holiday annuals with a distinctive Lancashire flavour such as *Ben Brierley's Seaside Annual* (extant 1878) were popular in the late nineteenth and early twentieth centuries.[44] This seasonally adapted reading matter was waiting for the reader when they arrived at their holiday destination. These changes in place and frequency of publication are an example of the negotiation between demand and supply, publisher and reader.

These rhythms of reading — daily, weekly, monthly and seasonal — are examples of what Kristeva calls 'circular time'.[45] As we will see in Chapter 10, this is the dominant experience of time connected with reading the local paper, with its associations of ritual and reassurance. J. F. Nisbet noted this repetition in 1896:

> The great fault of the daily paper, however, is not so much its quantity of news as the essential sameness of its news from day to day. This, most people notice with regard to political speeches and leading articles on "the situation"; but is it not also true in relation to murders, divorces, breach of promise cases, suicides, swindles, robberies?[46]

But there is another type of reading time, a linear pattern, in which the uniqueness of now is foregrounded, a present that is different from the

---

42 J. Haslam, 'What Harpurhey Reads', *Manchester City News*, 7 July 1906.

43 For *Bright's Intelligencer*, see Andrew J. H. Jackson, 'Provincial Newspapers and the Development of Local Communities: The Creation of a Seaside Resort Newspaper for Ilfracombe, Devon, 1860–1', *Family & Community History*, 13 (2010), 101–13 (p. 102), https://doi.org/10.1179/146311810X12851639314110; John K. Walton, 'Visitors' Lists', in *DNCJ* online.

44 Margaret Beetham, '"Oh! I Do like to Be beside the Seaside!": Lancashire Seaside Publications', *Victorian Periodicals Review*, 42.1 (2009), 24–36, https://doi.org/10.1353/vpr.0.0060

45 Julia Kristeva, 'Women's Time', in *The Kristeva Reader*, ed. by Toril Moi (Oxford: Wiley-Blackwell, 1991), pp. 187–213.

46 J. F. Nisbet, 'The World, the Flesh and the Devil', *The Idler*, November 1896, p. 548.

past behind the reader and the future before them.[47] As Beetham notes, newspapers and magazines are read in both types of time; genres — of crime, spendthrift councillors or football results — are cyclical and repetitive, while their specific instances, issue by issue, are new and unique, part of linear time.[48] The experience of reading time differs according to the purpose of reading, so a reader looking for confirmation of their world-view experiences time in a ritual, repetitive way, while a businessman needing to know today's cotton prices in Manchester seeks new information in a linear way. In the next section, we see how readers experienced unexpected, exciting and frightening news, which disturbed cosy rituals and highlighted the uniqueness of the present and the uncertainty of the future.

Leisure for reading was sometimes unexpected and unwelcome, during trade slumps, strikes and lock-outs. During the Preston lock-out of 1853–54, enforced leisure increased reading, of books at least. Preston prison chaplain and social investigator Rev John Clay noted how

> the sale of the penny publications has scarcely diminished, though the demand for higher priced works has. The pawnbrokers, also, tell me of a fact, which points to the inference, that reading is becoming necessary to the working-man — viz., that the number of books in pawn is now very much less than it was during the time of full employment.[49]

In Barrow, the public library was busier during trade depressions; after one such slump ended, the librarian's annual report for 1889–90 records that

> the daily average number of books lent out from the Library is less than during the period covered by the last Report. This may be attributed, and the reason is a very satisfactory one, to the great improvement that has taken place in the trade of the town during the last year, thus affording less leisure for reading.[50]

---

47 Paddy Scannell, *Radio, Television, and Modern Life: A Phenomenological Approach* (Oxford: Blackwell, 1996), p. 149.

48 Beetham, 'Time', pp. 332–34.

49 Letter from John Clay to Lord Stanley, 25 January 1854, in Walter Lowe Clay, *The Prison Chaplain: A Memoir of the Rev. John Clay, B. D. with Selections from His Reports and Correspondence, and a Sketch of Prison Discipline in England* (Cambridge: Macmillan, 1861).

50 See also 1896–97 annual report, Cumbria Archive and Local Studies Centre, Barrow.

In Preston, too, there was an ebb and flow of ephemeral public reading places, organised by trade unions, churches and middle-class benefactors in response to similar crises. In 1862, during the 1861–65 Cotton Famine, the *Preston Chronicle* reported that 'The READING ROOM, established a few weeks ago in the Temperance hall, North-road, is well frequented. A good fire is constantly kept, and all unemployed operatives are welcomed.' A year later the Mechanics' and Engineers' Society of Preston started a reading room and school for unemployed members.[51]

Newsy Times

Wars, elections and other newsworthy events created less regular or predictable times when reading, particularly reading of news, became more important. Preston's Central Working Men's Club found its news room 'frequently crowded, especially during the meeting of Parliament, and when other questions of national interest are pending' while *Preston Chronicle* editor Anthony Hewitson noted in 1872 'a great run on London papers; yesterday being National Thanksgiving Day for recovery of Prince of Wales.'[52] Such stories, along with election or sporting results, attracted crowds to the newspaper offices, to read the telegrams and posters stuck on the windows or shutters, and to buy ad hoc supplements with verbatim reports of election speeches or special editions, the Victorian version of 'rolling news'.[53] Publishers also changed the frequency of papers to meet demand at happier times, such as the 1882 Preston Guild, the town's once-in-twenty-years civic festival, when for example the usually bi-weekly *Preston Herald* switched to daily publication during the Guild fortnight, with press times linked to train times in order to speed distribution. We have already seen how newspaper readers met

---

51 For trade union facilities, see Alison Andrew, 'The Working Class and Education in Preston 1830–1870: A Study of Social Relations' (doctoral thesis, University of Leicester, 1987), p. 114; *PC*, 15 November 1862, 28 November 1863.

52 *PC*, 24 January 1874; Diaries of Anthony Hewitson, Lancashire Archives DP512/1/5, 28 February 1872.

53 For election supplements in the *Warrington Examiner*, see Hartley Aspden, *Fifty Years a Journalist. Reflections and Recollections of an Old Clitheronian* (Clitheroe: Advertiser & Times, 1930), p. 21. For 'rolling news', see Tom Smith, 'Religion or Party? Attitudes of Catholic Electors in Mid-Victorian Preston', *North West Catholic History*, 33 (2006), 19–35 (p. 5); *PG*, 3 September 1870, p. 5; Mr B7P (b. 1904), *ER*.

in the pub on Sunday nights during the exciting 1830 Preston election. Publishers were good at adapting, at fitting messy, unpredictable events into the industrial processes and rhythms of printing and distribution. We can distinguish between reading and publishing rhythms, but at these newsy times they were particularly closely related through supply and demand (as during seasonal changes).

War has always been good for the news trade. Wars prompted the creation of reading institutions, such as the Lord Street Working Men's Reading Room in Carlisle, which began when fifty men, 'anxious to read about the European revolutions of 1848, clubbed together to buy newspapers'. A few years later the Crimean War motivated Hebden Bridge men to join a society in order to read the papers.[54] The Clitheroe weaver John O'Neil counted the days until he could hear more news of the Indian Mutiny in 1857, writing of how he 'heard today that Delhi has been taken but I could learn no particulars, so I must wait until Saturday when I will see the newspaper.'[55] He was gripped by reports of the battle that ended the second War of Italian Independence in 1859; on 2 July he 'got a newspaper and read the full account of the great battle of Solferino, fought on the 24th of June.' The next day, he wrote '[…] I have never been out of the house. I have been reading nearly all day different accounts of the great battle of Solferino.'[56] Publishers large and small responded to this intense, avid reading of war news, such as the unemployed London compositor, who compiled telegrams of the Ethiopian revolt and sold 10,000 copies of his '*Abyssinian Gazette Extraordinary*, at a profit to him, personally, of not less than £12'.[57] The circulation graph of the *Glasgow Herald* (Fig. 3.2) shows 'curious little spurts' in 1870, 1900 and 1914: 'There seems to be nothing like a war to improve the circulation position of the more expensive papers', as a later *Herald* editor noted.[58]

---

54   Jonathan Rose, *The Intellectual Life of the British Working Classes* (London: Yale University Press, 2001), pp. 65–66.

55   John O'Neil, *The Journals of a Lancashire Weaver: 1856–60, 1860–64, 1872–75*, ed. by Mary Brigg (Chester: Record Society of Lancashire and Cheshire, 1982), Thursday 6 August 1857.

56   O'Neil diaries, 3 July 1859.

57   *Printers' Register*, 6 July 1868, p. 171.

58   Letter including circulation figures from *Glasgow Herald* editor William Robinson to *Manchester Guardian* editor A. P. Wadsworth, 27 October 1954 (Manchester Guardian Archives 324/5A, John Rylands Library).

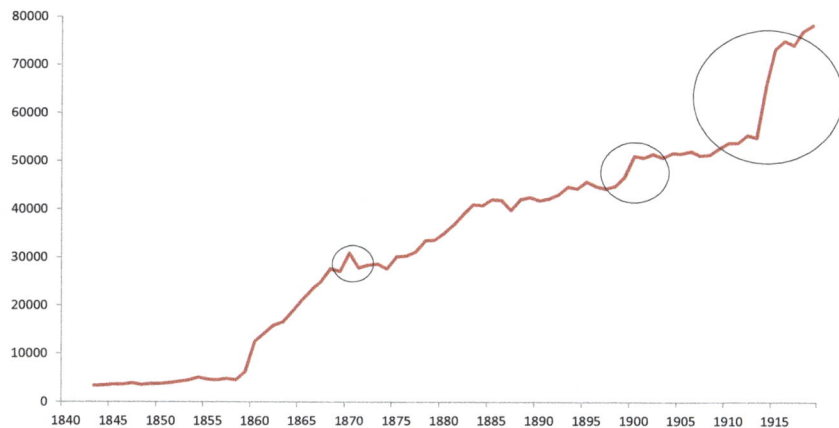

Fig. 3.2. *Glasgow Herald* sales, 1843–1919, showing rises during the Franco-Prussian War (1870–71), the Boer War (1899–1902) and the First World War (1914–18). Author's graph, CC BY 4.0.

There is a very small peak in 1855 during the Crimean War, but the Franco-Prussian War of 1870–71 was the first 'European war on a grand scale since the recent development of the cheap press and telegraphy,' as the *Printers' Register* noted, stimulating accelerated demand for war news among the mainly middle-class buyers of morning newspapers:

> Families which would a few years back expend a shilling in the course of a week will now spend three; and men who were content with their favourite morning paper formerly, must now indulge themselves with an evening paper as well, and occasionally with a second or third edition.[59]

A week later another trade paper reported that 'the war has been the means of increasing the sale of newspapers immensely, both London and Provincial.'[60] In Preston, too, the demand for news had an impact. The *Preston Guardian* boasted how 'a large crowd gathered on our special edition being published' to report the surrender of Emperor Napoleon III, causing 'great excitement in Preston'.[61] In 1870–71, the Winckley Club spent forty per cent more on newspapers, periodicals and stationery (from £53 8s 1½d to £74 4s 6d) than the year before. The minutes offer no explanation, but it is likely that the increase was due to the purchase

---

59 'The war and the newspapers', Supplement to *Printers' Register*, 6 August 1870, p. 186.

60 'Miscellaneous,' *London, Provincial, and Colonial Press News*, 15 August 1870, p. 18.

61 *PG*, 3 September 1870, p. 5.

of more titles and more editions to meet demand for war news. Even second-hand newspapers were in greater demand in 1870 — at the club's annual auction of second-hand papers and magazines that year, the resale value of newspapers such as the *Preston Chronicle, Liverpool Mercury* and *Manchester Guardian* rose, while those for magazines fell. Similarly, readers' scrapbooks show traces of a more intense connection to newspapers in wartime; Ellen Gruber Garvey argues that while some people kept up scrapbooks throughout their lives, others returned to them 'on occasions — such as war — that heightened their relationship to the newspaper'.[62]

War led to ad hoc changes in publishing and reading, which often had long-term effects. Formal outdoor newspaper reading was sometimes arranged at such times. In Hanley in north Staffordshire, during the Crimean War, the editor of the *Staffordshire Sentinel* and commercial traveller Samuel Taylor would read war reports from the *Times* in the market square, 'people flocking to the square in great numbers on the evenings when the readings took place.'[63] Demand for war news prompted the launch of three short-lived daily papers in Preston, and in 1871 the Conservative weekly the *Preston Herald* claimed that its circulation had 'more than trebled during the past twelve months', no doubt due to interest in war news. Pubs used war news to attract customers; an 1870 advert in the *Preston Chronicle* informed readers that 'the latest news from the seat of the war can be read at Barry's Hoop and Crown, Friargate', while the Cheetham's Arms, London Road, used the heading 'War News' to trick readers into looking at their advert in the same issue.[64] During the Russo-Turkish War (1877–78), newspapers (from Manchester and London) were mentioned more frequently in the postcard correspondence of the Vicar of Wrightington, Rev John Thomas Wilson.[65] The Boer War had the same effect (Fig. 3.3), boosting circulations of the *Lancashire Evening Post* and other provincial and

---

62   Ellen Gruber Garvey, *Writing with Scissors: American Scrapbooks from the Civil War to the Harlem Renaissance* (Oxford: Oxford University Press, 2012), p. 9, https://doi.org/10.1093/acprof:oso/9780195390346.001.0001

63   *Rendezvous with the Past: One Hundred Years' History of North Staffordshire and the Surrounding Area, as Reflected in the Columns of the Sentinel, Which Was Founded on January 7th, 1854* (Stoke-on-Trent: Staffordshire Sentinel Newspapers, 1954), p. 155.

64   *PC*, 3 September 1870, pp. 1, 4.

65   A. R. Bradford, *Drawn by Friendship: the Art and Wit of the Revd. John Thomas Wilson* (New Barnet: Anne R. Bradford, 1997).

London papers, particularly when news came through of events such as the Jameson raid (1895–96) or the relief of Mafeking (1900).[66] Just as the Crimean War created a demand for news among Carlisle working men, so the Franco-Prussian War and Boer War did the same in Preston and elsewhere, causing long-lasting changes in reading habits and therefore in publishing habits. The first two of these three wars helped to popularise new genres such as the provincial morning and evening paper (see Chapter 6 for details).

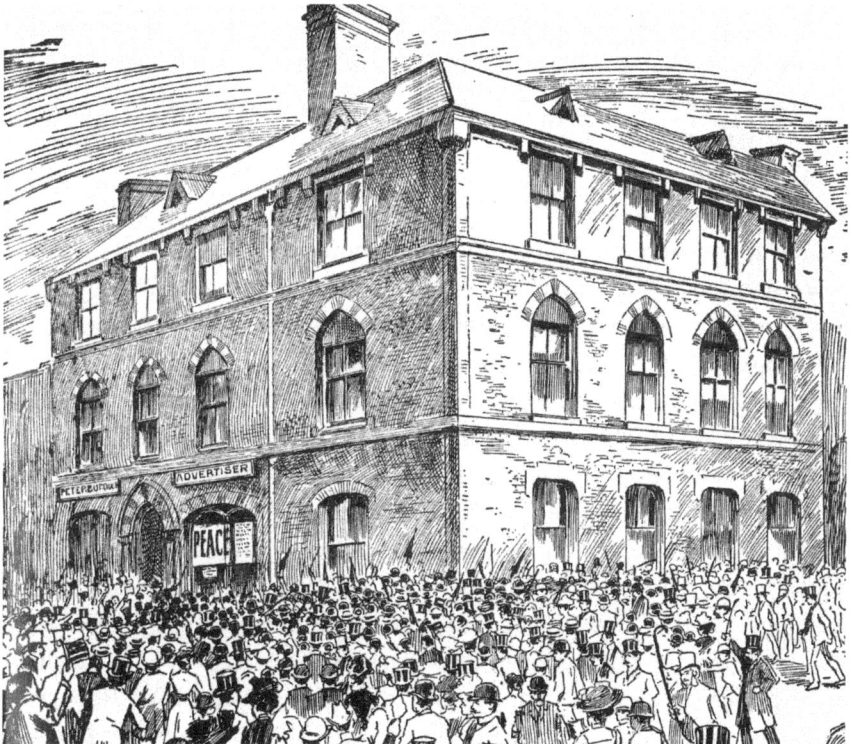

Fig. 3.3. Crowds gather outside the *Peterborough Advertiser* office at the end of the Boer War (the Second South African War), 1902. Courtesy of *Peterborough Telegraph*, CC BY.

If we imagine a continuum of reading times with circular/ritual at one end and linear/information-receiving at the other, then unexpected news events such as wars suspend normal rituals and move people's

66   J. B. Paterson, *'Western Evening Herald', Quadrat, a Periodical Bulletin of Research in Progress on the British Book Trade*, 12, 2001.

reading behaviour along the continuum towards a demand for new information, an orientation to linear time. A feeling of suspense is created, as readers wait for new developments. 'News stands on the cusp between past and future; it arouses recollection, anticipation, expectation, or apprehension.'[67]

Some editors recognised, and manipulated, the attractions of suspense and anticipation borrowed from serial fiction. As early as the 1830s, James Gordon Bennett eked out the details of a murder case day by day, greatly increasing the sales of his *New York Herald*.[68] On Wednesday 19 November 1856 O'Neil wrote of the suspense of waiting for the resolution of a running story: 'I can hear no news from the United States yet concerning the Presidential election.' He had to wait three days to hear that President Buchanan had been elected. Preston solicitor William Gilbertson was anxious to see the London papers as soon as they arrived before lunch at the Winckley Club, complaining three times in the suggestion and complaint book about their late arrival in 1877.[69] O'Neil often looked forward to further news of a continuing story, even predicting the days on which news would arrive by mail boat. On Saturday 12 September 1857 he summarised in his diary the latest news from India, adding 'the next mail will not be here before Monday, so next week we will be having some news.' Three months later, he noted that 'the newspaper [...] is full of the dispatches from India confirming all that had come by telegraph [...]'.[70] This knowledgeable newspaper-reader could differentiate between fast but brief telegraphed news and slower, more detailed reports arriving by mail boat, the first creating suspense in this case, the second closure and resolution of the story. Anticipation, of course, was also part of the ritual use of the local newspaper. In Wigton, Cumberland, an eight-year-old J. W. Robertson Scott would stay at home after school every Friday, waiting for his local paper to be delivered.[71]

---

67 Woolf, p. 81.
68 Joel H. Wiener, *The Americanization of the British Press, 1830s–1914: Speed in the Age of Transatlantic Journalism* (Basingstoke: Palgrave Macmillan, 2011), p. 38, https://doi.org/10.1057/9780230347953; see also Hughes and Lund, pp. 10–11; Scannell, p. 155.
69 Winckley Club Suggestion and Complaint Book, 1870–88, entries for 6 November, 25 December and 26 December 1877, Lancashire Archives DDX 1895 acc 6992, box 5.
70 O'Neil diaries, Saturday 5 December 1857.
71 John William Robertson Scott, *The Day Before Yesterday: Memories of an Uneducated Man* (London: Methuen, 1951), p. 86.

Short, Medium- and Long-Term Newspaper Lives

News, a report of what's new, is by definition ephemeral. Yet the long lives of some yellowing, crumbly papers complicate our ideas of news as here today, gone tomorrow. Three objects demonstrate this complexity: the pieces of torn newspaper hanging on a nail in an outside toilet; a bound volume of newspapers; and the rolled up copy of a newspaper in a time capsule buried beneath the foundation stones of a Victorian gas company office. These objects symbolise Uriel Heyd's three types of newspaper-reading time, short-, medium- and long-term.[72] News is indeed ephemeral, and during wartime or other newsy periods, only the freshest news had any value. In 1860, Manchester barber and part-time racing writer Richard Wright Procter described how 'news grows old in a few hours. Editions chase each other through the day like Indian runners, each one bearing a telegram. Consequently, many persons have become so finical in their purchases, that when the sixth edition is offered to them they decline to take it; it has been stale, they say, several minutes; they must have the impression just issued, or none.'[73] For most readers, a newspaper or magazine 'becomes obsolete as soon as the next one comes out'.[74] Of course, what is presented as news is not always new.

The torn pages of a newspaper used as toilet paper symbolise the worthlessness of old news and represent the majority of the copies printed. The material qualities of the paper become more valuable than what's printed on it.[75] However, some copies survived in the medium term — sold second-hand or bound into volumes for reference. These bound copies were kept, and heavily used, in reading rooms, news rooms, libraries and newspaper offices.[76] Publishers encouraged this,

---

72 Uriel Heyd, *Reading Newspapers: Press and Public in Eighteenth-Century Britain and America* (Oxford: Voltaire Foundation, 2012), p. 3.

73 Richard Wright Procter, *Literary Reminiscences and Gleanings* (Manchester: Thomas Dinham, 1860), p. 33.

74 Beetham, 'Open and Closed', p. 96; Mark W. Turner, 'Time, Periodicals, and Literary Studies', *Victorian Periodicals Review*, 39 (2006), 309–16 (p. 311), https://doi. org/10.1353/vpr.2007.0014

75 Leah Price, *How to Do Things with Books in Victorian Britain* (Princeton, N.J: Princeton University Press, 2012), Chapter 7, 'The book as waste', https://doi.org/10.23943/ princeton/9780691114170.001.0001

76 For a detailed analysis of the bound volume, see Laurel Brake, 'The Longevity of "Ephemera"', *Media History*, 18 (2012), 7–20, https://doi.org/10.1080/13688804.2011. 632192

and happily bound back copies into volumes. In the 1750s, *Boddely's Bath Journal* was numbered by volumes, and its bound volumes had ornate title pages printed in red, featuring the Bath city coat of arms.[77] At the Liverpool Lyceum, a third of the newspapers taken in the 1850s (thirty-two of ninety-three) were filed for reference (eleven Liverpool papers, eleven other provincial papers and ten London papers).[78] As late as 1920, a library management manual recommended keeping 'Permanent files of at least *The Times*, and all local newspapers; and temporary files of other newspapers most in demand.'[79] This demand for filed back copies of local papers needed to be emphasised in newspaper reports, to explain their absence from auctions in news rooms, in case anyone should think that the title in question was either not supplied there, or failed to sell in the auction.[80]

While publishers could make a few shillings from binding back copies, ephemerality — the appearance of built-in obsolescence — was more profitable in persuading readers to buy the next issue. Like the date on the cover, it is another fiction, something constructed to sell papers. As Michael Thompson argues in *Rubbish Theory*, ephemerality or transience is rarely 'natural', instead it is socially constructed in the interests of those with economic power.[81] When readers refuse to treat newspapers as ephemeral, saving them, collecting them and re-reading them, their timescales diverge from publishers' industrial timescales.

David and Deirdre Stam have explored a fascinating example of this medium-term reading time of newspapers and periodicals, by polar explorers such as W. Parker Snow, clerk on the Prince Albert, who went in search of Franklin's party in 1851 and wrote of how 'I have often, myself, when at sea, felt the greatest delight from perusing a journal, however old it might be'. Here, the freshness of the news is not important. Or French explorer Jean Charcot, on the Pourquoi Pas?

77   Bryan Little, 'Two Chronicles in a Fight to the Death'. *Bath Evening Chronicle*. June 1877, Centenary supplement marking one hundred years of daily publication.

78   John B. Hood, 'The Origin and Development of the Newsroom and Reading Room from 1650 to Date, with Some Consideration of Their Role in the Social History of the Period' (unpublished FLA dissertation, Library Association, 1978), pp. 355–57.

79   James Duff Brown and W. C. Berwick Sayers, *Manual of Library Economy*, 3rd edn (Grafton & Co., 1920), p. 385.

80   'Sale of newspapers at Avenham Institution', *PC*, 31 December 1881.

81   Michael Thompson, *Rubbish Theory: The Creation and Destruction of Value* (Oxford: Oxford University Press, 1979), pp. 7, 9, https://doi.org/10.2307/j.ctt1rfsn94

from 1908 to 1910, putting out copies of *Le Matin* and *Le Figaro* each day, exactly two years after their cover date: 'I await the next day's issue with impatience', he wrote, although he had read them on the day they first came out. Freshness is in the eye of the beholder, according to Roald Amundsen, another explorer, who met a ship in 1908 carrying old newspapers: 'Old! Yes to you! To us, they were absolutely fresh!'[82] The age of the news was equally irrelevant to John O'Neil when he received copies of the local paper from his home town of Carlisle.

The continuing but changeable value of old news can be seen in the practice of auctioning second-hand newspapers and magazines to members of news rooms (and to the general public). However, the relative values of different newspaper and magazine genres are impossible to interpret without knowing why each individual bought each individual title. The peaks and troughs of the graphs in Figs. 3.4 to 3.6, summarising auction prices at Preston's Winckley Club, reflect a title's value on a particular day among a particular group of men, and as with any auction, two keen bidders can distort the price; overall trends are more reliable.[83] At a more general level, there were big differences in the second-hand value of different genres and individual titles. The most valuable were *Punch* and the *Illustrated London News*, then the *Times*, the *Quarterly Review*, *Temple Bar*, then local weekly and bi-weekly newspapers, then at the bottom, morning daily newspapers (apart from the *Times*), with similar values for London and provincial big-city papers.

Second-hand, *Punch* was worth around seventy per cent of its cover price from the 1860s onwards, the *Illustrated London News* (*ILN*) slightly less at around sixty per cent. The *Times* sold for around fifty per cent of its cover price until the 1890s, significantly higher than the second-hand values of other dailies, London or provincial. Next in value were the serious literary and political *Quarterly Review* (around forty per cent until the 1880s, when there was a steep decline, after which it was no longer bought by the club), and *Temple Bar*, a shilling fiction monthly, also selling for around forty per cent of its cover price. Then the Preston papers, selling at between thirty and fifty per cent of cover price from the 1840s to the 1870s, followed by a steep decline. The *Preston Guardian*,

---

82   David H. Stam and Deirdre C. Stam, 'Bending Time: The Function of Periodicals in Nineteenth-Century Polar Naval Expeditions', *Victorian Periodicals Review*, 41 (2008), 301–22 (pp. 304, 309, 312), https://doi.org/10.1353/vpr.0.0054

83   Figures from Winckley Club minute books, Lancashire Archives DDX 1895.

the biggest-selling Preston paper, was often missing from the auctions, because it was bound and filed for reference, along with the *Times* and the *Manchester Guardian*, as a paper of record. The least valuable titles were the morning papers; the *Morning Post* fell in value from the 1860s onwards, and was worth only ten per cent of its original value in the 1880s and 1890s. Similarly, the *Manchester Guardian* and *Liverpool Mercury*, which both sold across the whole of North West England, declined steadily from forty to fifty per cent of cover price to less than ten per cent. The declining values mirror the growth of the periodical and newspaper market, as seen in the rise of the newsagent.

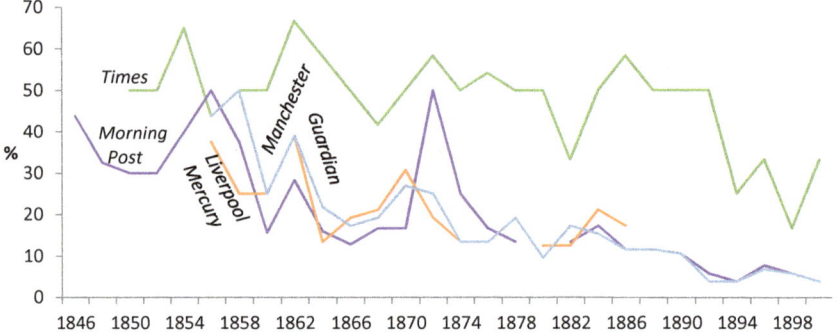

Fig. 3.4. Second-hand values (% of cover price) at Winckley Club, Preston 1846–1900: Morning newspapers. Author's graph, CC BY 4.0.

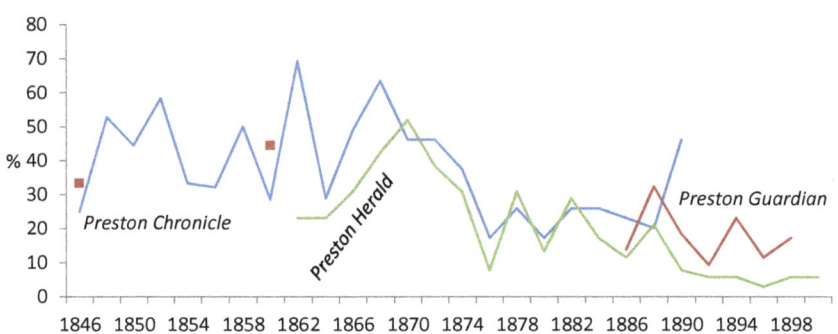

Fig. 3.5. Second-hand values (% of cover price) at Winckley Club, Preston, 1846–1900: Local weekly/bi-weekly newspapers. Author's graph, CC BY 4.0.[84]

84   The sharp rise in the value of the *Preston Guardian* in 1900 was caused by a member of the newspaper owner's family, Mr J. Toulmin, paying more than the original cover price; this could be an error in the minutes book, a joke or a blatant attempt to inflate its value for publicity purposes.

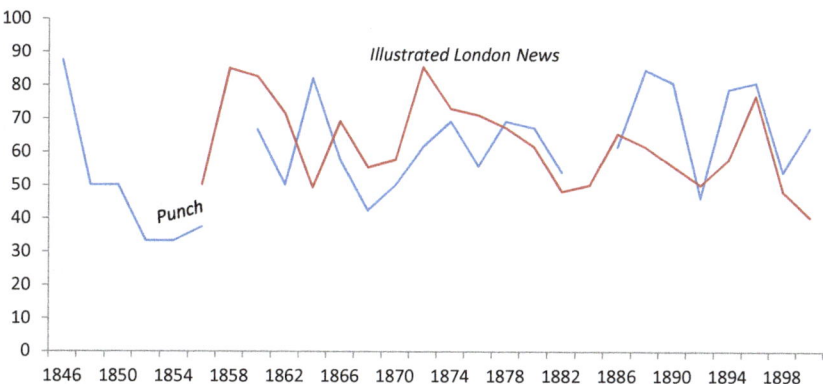

Fig. 3.6. Second-hand values (% of cover price) at Winckley Club, Preston, 1846–1900: *Punch, Illustrated London News*. Author's graph, CC BY 4.0.

There are likely to be many factors influencing the second-hand value of a publication, such as its 're-readability' and its availability elsewhere in Preston.[85] The *Times*, for example, sold far fewer copies in Preston than regional or local papers. From other sources we know that circulation figures for newspapers rose throughout the second half of the nineteenth century, so it seems likely that the increased affordability of papers depressed their second-hand value, as more people could afford to buy them new.[86] A fall in the cover price of a publication generally led to a depreciation in second-hand value, as with most newspapers between 1851 and 1856. While the trends in these auction records are suggestive, the bare names, titles and figures allow too many interpretations, divorced from the commentary and banter that no doubt was part of the annual sale. Crucially, while figures are safer at aggregate level, for any particular title there are at least two opposing explanations for a low resale value — either that it was so popular that most people preferred to buy it new, or that it was so *un*popular that it was unwanted both new and second-hand.

Heyd's third category of newspaper-reading time, the long term, is symbolised by the copy of the local paper in a time capsule, intended

85 Lee Erickson, *The Economy of Literary Form: English Literature and the Industrialization of Publishing, 1800–1850* (London: Johns Hopkins University Press, 1996), p. 9.

86 Arthur Aspinall, 'The Circulation of Newspapers in the Early Nineteenth Century', *The Review of English Studies*, 22 (1946), 29–43; Brown, pp. 52–53; Alan J. Lee, *The Origins of the Popular Press in England: 1855–1914* (London: Croom Helm, 1976) Tables 1–6, pp. 274–79.

to survive and fulfil its function a century or more after it was buried. For example, copies of Preston's three weekly papers, plus the latest edition of the *Times*, were placed in a bottle with some coins, inside the foundation stone of the new gas offices in Fishergate, Preston in 1872.[87] Members of St Jude's Anglican church followed the same custom when they laid the foundation stone of their church extension in 1890. Under the stone, in a bottle, they buried 'the Preston papers' and the parish magazine, among other commemorative items.[88] In Kendal, copies of the town's two papers, the *Kendal Mercury* and the *Westmorland Gazette*, were placed in a bottle, along with some coins and a commemorative document, in the hollow of a foundation stone below a new market hall in 1855 (Fig. 3.7 opposite).[89] These buried newspapers were simultaneously ephemeral and permanent, valuable because they were of their time, yet intended to survive far beyond that time. In Thompson's terms, most copies of a newspaper went from low-value to no value, treated as rubbish within a few days of being printed. However, those that survived eventually increased in value with time, as a look at the prices of Victorian newspapers on eBay can confirm.[90] Putting them in a bottle and ceremonially burying them guaranteed that they would go from low value to high value, without passing through the 'rubbish' phase.

Individual elements of the newspaper sometimes had long lives, for example when pasted into a scrapbook, even if the rest of the issue was discarded. Garvey has established the depth of scrapbooks as sources for the history of reading. So many people defied the supposed ephemerality of newspapers that stationers mass-produced scrapbooks for just this purpose (Fig. 3.7). Among other insights, Garvey uses scrapbooks to reveal *how* certain items were read:

> Saving clippings overcame the daily press's ephemerality and disposability with a claim that newspaper items might be worth the kind of intensive reading associated with the Bible. The iconic, intensively read newspaper item is the single clipping of advice or poetry treasured

---

87   *PC*, 19 October 1872.
88   *PH*, 29 October 1890, p. 5. For similar uses of local papers, see O'Neil diaries, 15 June 1861; *Rendezvous with the Past*, p. 15.
89   *Kendal Mercury*, 28 July 1855, p. 5.
90   Thompson, p. 7.

in a wallet; its worn and tattered state inspires readers to beg editors to reprint the item.[91]

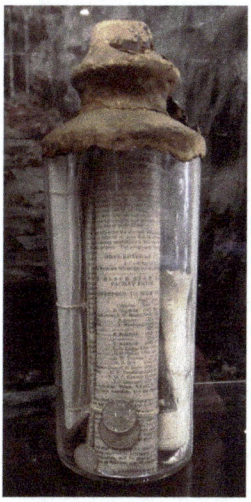

Fig. 3.7. A Victorian time capsule containing Kendal local newspapers, buried in 1855 under the 'new market house' and rediscovered in 1909 during the demolition of what had become the 'old Market Hall', now in Kendal Museum. Author's photo, CC BY 4.0.

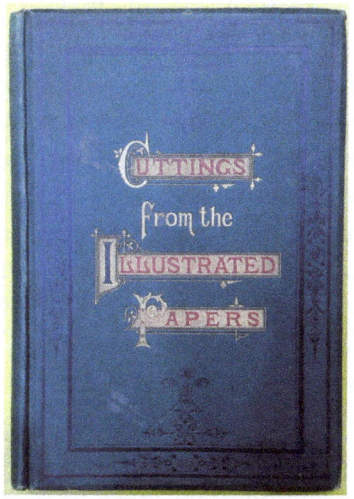

Fig. 3.8. Cover of Victorian scrapbook. Author's copy, CC BY 4.0.

91   Garvey, p. 36.

Newspaper items were preserved in other ways, besides being cut out and glued into scrapbooks. Local newspaper poetry, seen as throwaway, was sometimes collected and immortalised in group anthologies, such as Newcastle's *Songs of the Bards of the Tyne* (1849) or Manchester's *The Festive Wreath* (1842). Poems were sometimes collected and republished in volume form by the newspapers themselves, as with *The Poetry and Varieties of Berrow's Worcester Journal for the Year 1828*. However, such anthologies were less common in Britain than in the United States. These volumes challenge the alleged ephemerality of newspaper poetry, and exemplify how newspapers were part of the ecology of publishing; many Victorian volumes of prose also first appeared as newspaper series.

Changing Times

Enlarging our focus to cover the whole period, the times of newspaper-reading changed significantly. In larger towns and cities, daily *local* news became available from 1855 onwards thanks to new regional daily papers; in outlying towns such as Preston, these papers brought regional news from Manchester, Liverpool and Bolton. Daily local news appeared briefly in Preston in 1870–71, and continuously from 1886, when the *Lancashire Evening Post* was launched. Wiener argues that accelerating speed was the defining characteristic of the nineteenth-century newspaper press, and this 'discourse of speed' may have been 'the main measure of competitive success in the news industry', but this applies only to sudden, unexpected events, which make up the minority of content in any newspaper, particularly a local paper.[92] In peacetime at least, readers seemed prepared to wait for news. Even O'Neil the news addict was usually content to wait a few days, as on May 28 1856, when he wrote, '[...] we got word this morning that Palmer was found guilty for the murder of John Parsons Cooke, but I will have all the news on Saturday.'

This Preston case study foregrounds other changes more significant than speed, such as the move from public to domestic reading, from listening to reading, and (for the working-class majority) from the sense of eavesdropping on middle-class news to being addressed directly by more populist publications. As this last point suggests, change

---

92   Wiener; Mark Hampton, *Visions of the Press in Britain, 1850–1950* (Urbana: University of Illinois Press, 2004), pp. 89–92.

happened at different speeds in different reading places frequented by different classes. The value of second-hand reading matter fell by a half between the 1850s and 1900 at the upper-class Winckley Club, suggesting that new copies of the publications, for reading at home, were now more affordable or desirable for these gentlemen. However in a different reading community, at Preston's Central Working Men's Club, newspapers maintained their second-hand value of around a quarter of their face value for longer, presumably because members were less able to afford to buy new.[93]

Times of reading shifted and expanded. For most working people, newspapers were read or heard mainly on Sundays at the start of the period, but the Saturday half-day offered more reading time earlier in the weekend.[94] Morning and evening newspapers were fitted into new public and (increasingly) domestic rituals. Reading times became more plentiful and as each family began to buy their own paper, reading became more relaxed and less pressured by the demands of other readers. When one news room closed, among the items for auction was a ten-minute time glass (used to prevent readers hogging popular titles), now redundant — although some pubs still had notices requesting patrons not to monopolise the latest edition of the paper for more than five minutes.[95] There were also continuities. Even when 'national' London papers such as the *Daily Mail* became more affordable and available, the places where they were read affected how they were read and interpreted.

Periodical Time

Many readers were fine-tuned to the periodical-ness of newspapers and magazines, waiting for the next instalment of a novel or the detailed dispatches from a faraway battle to supplement the telegraphed headlines. John O'Neil used the latest issue of the local paper in the same way as polar explorers used two-year-old newspapers, to mark

---

93   The Central Working Men's Club spent £33 11s 10d on 'newspapers, &c' in 1873 and recouped £8 8s 5d from their sale: *PC*, 24 January 1874.

94   On Sunday reading in the pub, see William Cooke Taylor, *Notes of a Tour in the Manufacturing Districts of Lancashire: In a Series of Letters to His Grace the Archbishop of Dublin* (London: Duncan and Malcolm, 1842), p. 136.

95   [J. F. Wilson], *A Few Personal Recollections, by an Old Printer* (London: Printed for private circulation, 1896), p. 11; Lionel Robinson, *Boston's Newspapers* (Boston: Richard Kay Publications, for the History of Boston Project, 1974), p. 3.

time and create rituals. He also had a sophisticated understanding of the temporal nature of news-gathering and publishing practices. The processes of publishing a paper or magazine developed so as to require regularity, yet neither the world that newspapers claimed to report, nor the world of readers in particular places at particular times, were regular. Publishing schedules turned the chaotic flow of events into a regular pulse, a new issue or edition. This untamability was seen in the 'unpredictable ebb and flow of news' at the different telegraph offices throughout the country, creating a staffing nightmare for the telegraph companies in the days before zero-hours contracts.[96] Publishers imposed a fiction of order and regularity on this flow of chaos, and readers recognised its constructedness, as seen in the old jest that there is always just enough news to fill a paper every day.[97] Sommerville has argued that 'Periodicity is about economics. There can be news without its being daily, but if it were not daily a news industry could never develop' because of the need to fully utilise expensive printing machinery.[98] However, the rhythms of newspaper publication often left machines idle. More broadly, even in the twenty-first century, with rolling news and live Tweeting, news periodicity continues: electronic news publishers have adapted to modern consumers' habits, releasing their best material during commuting times, lunchtime and evenings.[99]

Conclusions

Newspaper-reading happened at particular times, negotiated between publishers and readers. Readers understood that publishing conventions such as the date on the title page, or the claim of novelty, were fictions and

---

96 Jonathan Silberstein-Loeb, 'The Structure of the News Market in Britain, 1870–1914', *Business History Review*, 83 (2009), 759–88 (p. 781).

97 Versions of this joke are found in seventeenth-century critiques of the emergent newspaper, in Henry Fielding's novel *Tom Jones* (1749) and, for example, in the *Ladies' Repository* 18, 1858 ('New York Literary Correspondence', p. 505): 'The rustic wondered how it happened that there was always just enough news to fill up the village weekly sheet'.

98 Charles John Sommerville, *The News Revolution in England: Cultural Dynamics of Daily Information* (Oxford: Oxford University Press, 1996), p. 4.

99 Deborah Robinson and Andrew Hobbs, 'How the Audience Saved UK Broadcast Journalism', in *The Future of Quality News Journalism: A Cross-Continental Analysis*, ed. by Peter J. Anderson, George Ogola, and Michael Williams (New York: Routledge, 2014), pp. 162–83 (p. 165), https://doi.org/10.4324/9780203382707

constructions. In a regional market centre like Preston, most newspapers began by publishing on Saturday, the main market day, and the three papers that published bi-weekly all chose the second most important market day, Wednesday, for their mid-week edition. Regional and metropolitan papers also worked around readers' routines, publishing at weekends when there was more leisure time for reading. News-reading declined in the summer, and increased in the autumn and winter when Parliament was in session and, in later years, when the football season was running and outdoor pursuits reduced. The move from weekly to bi-weekly and eventually to daily publishing rhythms enabled a significant change in reading habits for people in Preston (but changes happened more slowly for working-class readers, particularly women). The halfpenny evening paper, for example, allowed many to read news at home in the evening for the first time, and was probably more significant than the provincial morning paper for most readers. Times of news-reading were also dictated by less predictable events, such as the death of a statesman, a famous boxing match, strikes or wars. Telegrams posted in windows, special editions and new wartime publications catered for readers' demands in these situations. Readers became accustomed to receiving the latest news, and publishers were happy to respond to this growing demand.

The next two chapters interrupt this case study of newspaper-reading in one town, to introduce the local press as a national phenomenon. We then return to the readers, most of whom preferred the local newspaper.

4. What They Read:
The Production of the Local Press in the 1860s

We know who the readers of local newspapers were, we know where they read them, and when. But *what* exactly were they reading? This chapter explores the content of the mid-Victorian newspaper, how it was written, assembled and distributed, and by whom. We will follow a typical Victorian journalist, Anthony Hewitson, working in the provinces (Preston), on the most popular type of paper, a weekly, during one week in the 1860s (the following chapter moves forward to the 1880s). Structuring these two chapters around two weeks in Hewitson's working life brings alive the working methods and organisation of local newspapers and the distinctive routines, networks and attitudes of their personnel. This is a complex world of distinctive but connected local print cultures, peopled by a surprising variety of newspaper contributors, producing content that was significantly different from that of the smaller market of London dailies like the *Times* and the local newspapers of the twenty-first century. After a short biographical sketch of the journalist, Anthony Hewitson, he is placed within the national and local ecologies of periodicals at that time, before we follow him through a typical working week.

Anthony Hewitson (1836–1912), a printer who became a journalist and newspaper proprietor, frames this chapter. His diaries, covering nineteen of the forty-eight years between 1865, when he was a reporter on the *Preston Guardian*, and his death in 1912, are the only known diaries of a provincial Victorian journalist. 'The transition from the

     https://doi.org/10.11647/OBP.0152.04

composing room to the reporters' office, and thence to the editor's chair, has been frequently achieved', so Hewitson's career was not unusual, moving from a printing apprenticeship to ten years of reporting, twenty-two years as owner-editor of the *Preston Chronicle* and fifteen as owner of the *Wakefield Herald*.[1] Hewitson was born in Blackburn, Lancashire, on 13 August 1836, the eldest son of a stonecutter. He attended the village school at Ingleton in Yorkshire, and in 1850 began a printing apprenticeship on the *Lancaster Gazette*. While an apprentice he continued to educate himself, learning shorthand and attending essay classes, where he mixed with political and theological radicals, including the poet Goodwyn Barmby, then minister of the Free Mormon Church in Lancaster (where he held the title of Revolutionary Pontifarch of the Communist Church).[2] Hewitson's reporting week is a good introduction to the people and processes involved in the production of the provincial press in the second half of the nineteenth century, and supports the idea that producers and readers of the local press were often members of the same interpretive communities.

Like most mid-Victorian journalists, Anthony Hewitson lived and worked outside London (Fig. 4.2). In September 1865 he was chief reporter of the *Preston Guardian*, a major bi-weekly newspaper covering North and East Lancashire, an area larger than most English counties. Compulsory Newspaper Stamp Duty had been repealed in 1855, two years before Hewitson finished his apprenticeship, greatly increasing the opportunities for an able and hard-working young man. His printing and composing (typesetting) background was not unusual for a mid-nineteenth-century reporter, nor his rapid job moves: in the year after July 1857, when he finished his apprenticeship, he worked in Kendal, Brierley Hill in Staffordshire, Wolverhampton and Preston.[3] He settled

---

1   'Reporting and Reporters', *Printers' Register*, 6 April 1870, p. 80.

2   Anthony Hewitson, 'Recollections of earlier life', Lancashire Archives DP512/2; brief family history and autobiography at end of 1873 diary, DP512/1/6. These are referred to as the Hewitson Diaries hereafter.

3   Compositor and reporter, *Kendal Mercury*, July-August 1857 (Hewitson, 'Recollections'; Hewitson Diaries 1873); compositor, reporter and editor, *Brierley Hill Advertiser*, September?–November? 1857; compositor, reporter and editor, *Wolverhampton Spirit of the Times*, December 1857?–May 1858 (Hewitson Diaries 1873, back pages); compositor and reporter, *Preston Guardian* May? 1858-late 1858. A contemporary, Harry Findlater Bussey, worked on sixteen papers in twelve towns between 1844 and 1858, from Carlisle to Plymouth: H. F. Bussey, *Sixty Years of Journalism: Anecdotes and Reminiscences* (Bristol: J. W. Arrowsmith, 1906).

in Preston, on the Radical *Preston Guardian* initially, as compositor and reporter, then on the Whig *Preston Chronicle* as reporter, at 28/- a week. By September 1861, if not before, he was earning a comfortable £2 6s a week on the Conservative *Preston Herald*, where he became 'manager'. He may have returned to the *Chronicle* before rejoining the *Preston Guardian* as a reporter in December 1864, and by June 1865 was chief reporter. By now he had mastered news reporting, descriptive writing and some leader-writing, and adopted the pen-name of 'Atticus', for a series of irreverent sketches of local officials and institutions, in which he developed a distinctive style that made him Preston's best-known writer for the rest of the century.[4]

Fig. 4.1. Anthony Hewitson, Preston reporter, editor and newspaper proprietor. Carte de visite, photo by C Sanderson, Commercial Buildings, 130A Castle St., Preston, used with permission of Hewitson's great-grandson Martin Duesbury, CC BY 4.0.

---

4   Atticus was a celebrated Roman editor, banker and patron of literature, and the best friend of the orator and philosopher Cicero.

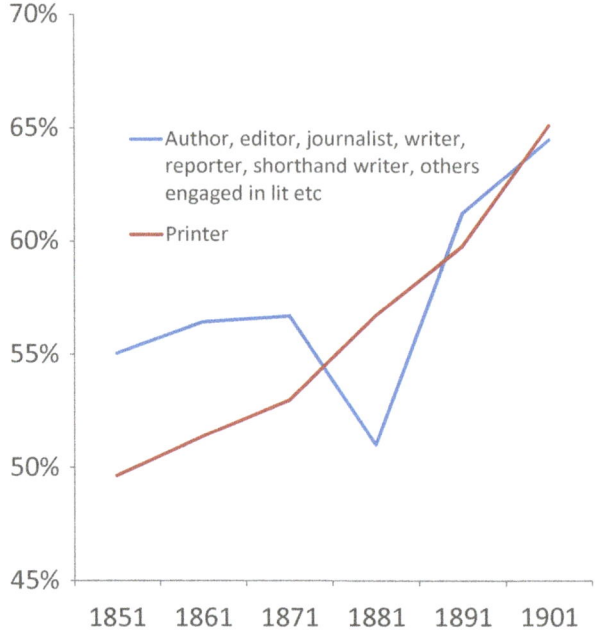

Fig. 4.2. Print personnel in England and Wales, 1851–1901, showing the
proportion outside London.[5] Author's graph, CC BY 4.0.

National Periodicals Ecology

Hewitson was chief reporter of the *Preston Guardian*. This bi-weekly
paper, published every Saturday and Wednesday, was part of an
ecology of London and provincial papers worth sketching briefly here.
London morning newspapers such as the *Times* and the *Daily Telegraph*
are the most well-known type of Victorian paper. These two titles have
survived, but other London dailies such as the *Daily News* (1846–1960),
Morning Chronicle (1770–1865), *Morning Advertiser* (1793–1965) and
Morning Post (1772–1937) were also current. These broadsheets, full of
classified advertisements (on some days more than half of the *Times* was
advertising), high politics, diplomacy and commercial news focused
their coverage on national institutions and events in south-east England,

---

5   The 1881 figures have been checked, and are probably an error in the original.
     Sources: 1851 Census (1852–53, 1691 [parts 1 & 2]); 1861 Census (1863, 3221); 1871
     Census (1873, C.872); 1881 Census (1883, C.3722); 1891 Census (1893–94, C.7058);
     1901 Census (1904, Cd. 2174).

where they sold most copies.[6] London evening papers included the *Standard* (est. 1827), the *Pall Mall Gazette* (1865–1923) and the *Globe* (1803–1923); from 1868 the more downmarket halfpenny *Echo* became popular. Traditionally, London evenings took most of their news from the morning papers, supplemented by original articles of commentary and analysis, and reviews. Small numbers of these London papers (with the possible exception of the *Echo*, which had higher sales) could be found in reading rooms and middle-class homes in the provinces. The abolition of the compulsory penny stamp in 1855 ended cheap postal distribution of London papers, leading to a significant decline in their provincial circulation.[7]

The popular London Sunday papers were less reliant on postal distribution and were aimed at a different readership, the lower middle classes. The *News of the World* (1843–2011) sold nearly 110,000 in 1855, *Lloyd's Weekly Newspaper* (1842–1931) some 2–3,000 fewer and *Reynolds's Newspaper* (1851–1967) nearly 50,000 by 1855, the latter particularly popular in the old Chartist strongholds of Lancashire and the West Riding.[8] These Sunday newspapers featured sensational, titillating crime reports, literary/humorous tit-bits, gossip and practical advice via 'Notices to Correspondents', alongside political and foreign news; they introduced fiction from the 1880s, led by the *News of the World*, and more sport.[9] Other popular London weeklies included the *Illustrated London News* (1842–2003), the *Illustrated Police News* (1864–1938) and specialist sporting and religious papers. The weeklies had more varied, magazine-like content than the London dailies.

---

6   For a more detailed comparison of the *Times* and other newspapers, see Andrew Hobbs, 'The Deleterious Dominance of *The Times* in Nineteenth-Century Scholarship', *Journal of Victorian Culture* 18 (2013), https://doi.org/10.1080/13555502. 2013.854519

7   Anon., 'The Modern Newspaper', *British Quarterly Review*, 110 (1872), 348–80 (p. 371).

8   H. R. Fox Bourne, *English Newspapers: Chapters in the History of Journalism, Vol. II* (London: Routledge/Thoemmes Press, 1887); Virginia Berridge, 'Popular Sunday Newspapers and Mid-Victorian Society', in *Newspaper History from the Seventeenth Century to the Present Day*, ed. David George Boyce et al. (London: Constable, 1978), pp. 247–64.

9   Berridge; Laurel Brake and Mark W. Turner, 'Rebranding the News of the World: 1856–90', in *The News of the World and the British Press, 1843–2011*, ed. Laurel Brake, Chandrika Kaul, and Mark W. Turner (Basingstoke: Palgrave Macmillan, 2015), 27–42, https://doi.org/10.1057/9781137392053_3

Regional morning newspapers were creations of the post-Stamp Duty era, and had a status second only to the London dailies, on which they were modelled.[10] In their circulation areas, they probably outsold all London dailies (see Table 7.11). Many Victorian commentators acknowledged that the provincial dailies, when treated as a body rather than as individual titles, were as significant as the London press:

> The provincial morning newspapers [...] have, as a whole, a greater weight in the conduct of the affairs of the Empire than the morning papers of London [...] the district served by the London press [...] does not contain more than six or seven million persons, and to the remaining thirty millions the London press, with the exception of a few of the more widely circulating dailies, is little more than a name.[11]

The *Manchester Guardian* (1821–) and the *Leeds Mercury* (1718–1939) were particularly close in style to the *Times*. These two papers were already well-established as weekly and bi-weekly papers, while other successful provincial dailies were new titles, such as Liverpool's *Daily Post* (1855–) and Sheffield's *Daily Telegraph* (1855–). Most sold at a penny by the mid-1860s, with advertising providing most of the income. They were expensive to run, requiring costly telegraphic news and 'original matter', and overtime payments for printers working at night.[12] Some of these titles set up weekly companion news miscellanies, which became more popular — and profitable — than their daily stablemates, although the genre had largely died out by the 1930s. Early titles included the *Glasgow Times* (1855–69) and the *Manchester Weekly Times* (1855–1922), with the Dundee-based *People's Journal* (1858–1990) selling more than 100,000 by the late 1860s. They were published on Saturday, and aimed mainly at working-class readers, priced at a penny or twopence. They featured a summary of the week's regional, national and international news, slanted towards the more sensational stories, plus middle-brow magazine-style material aimed at a family audience, including serial fiction.[13] In the 1870s and 1880s they became

---

10   Maurice Milne, *The Newspapers of Northumberland and Durham: A Study of Their Progress during the 'Golden Age' of the Provincial Press* (Newcastle upon Tyne: Graham, 1971), p. 19.

11   Arnot Reid, 'How a Provincial Paper Is Managed', *Nineteenth Century* 20 (1886), p. 391.

12   *Printers' Register* supplement, 6 August 1870, p. 169.

13   Graham Law, 'Weekly News Miscellany', in *Dictionary of Nineteenth Century Journalism (DNCJ)*, ed. Laurel Brake and Marysa Demoor, online, C19: The Nineteenth Century Index (ProQuest).

the main publishing platform for new novels (Thomas Hardy's *Tess of the D'Urbervilles*, for example, was commissioned by the publisher of the *Bolton Journal*).[14] As Graham Law has noted, they published many journalistic genres later identified with the 'New Journalism' of the 1880s and 1890s.

While the provincial morning and weekly papers covered whole regions, most (but not all) of the traditional weeklies and bi-weeklies tended to be more local in their coverage and circulation. They were the oldest type of provincial newspaper, dating back to the early eighteenth century, with the *Norwich Post* (1701–13) and the *Bristol Post-Boy* (1702–15) some of the first. The local newspaper market expanded in the 1830s after advertising duty and paper duty were halved, and stamp duty was reduced from 4d to 1d, between 1833 and 1836. (Stamp duty was both a tax — bad for newspapers — and a postage fee — good value for those titles needing postal distribution, particularly London papers.) The highest-circulation papers went from weekly to bi-weekly, and new titles entered the market. The content tended towards a newspaper-magazine hybrid, mixing news and features. Weeklies with good circulations and plenty of advertising could be very profitable — by the 1840s the *Hampshire Advertiser* made £2,000 a year and the *Birmingham Journal* £5,000.[15] In rural areas, weeklies were typically published from the market town and circulated in all the areas oriented to that market, whilst in more urban areas such as Manchester or Liverpool, they sold across a smaller but much more densely populated territory. There were also some county papers, such as the *Westmorland Gazette*, published from the county town of Kendal, with an editorial remit to cover the whole shire.

The abolition of the three main newspaper taxes between 1853 and 1861 profoundly altered the economics of newspaper publishing, enabling publishers to reduce their cover prices to as little as a halfpenny, increase their circulations and therefore charge more for advertising, their main source of income (as it had been since the eighteenth century; accurate figures are scarce, but by 1849 the *Buckinghamshire Herald* received three or four times as much income from advertising as

---

14   Commissioned by Tillotsons, the manuscript was rejected on grounds of taste.

15   F. David Roberts, 'Still More Early Victorian Newspaper Editors', *Victorian Periodicals Newsletter*, 18 (1972), 12–26.

from sales, for example).[16] The number of local weekly papers roughly doubled, from 363 in 1856 to 698 in 1866, according to Mitchell's *Newspaper Press Directory* (Introduction, Table 0.1). Weeklies were at the centre of this golden age of the local press.[17]

However, the late 1850s and the first half of the 1860s were a volatile time for local newspapers, as many new entrants joined — and left — the market and experimented with new formats and publishing models. Throughout the nineteenth century, but particularly at this time, the most common business model for a newspaper was to launch with too little capital, lose a great deal of money and then fold in a matter of weeks.[18]

Magazines accounted for only thirty per cent of the periodicals market in the 1860s, newspapers around seventy per cent.[19] In contrast to newspapers, most magazines were published in London, with the most popular featuring serial fiction, alongside 'humour, fiction, poetry, gossip [...] general interest articles and answers to correspondents'. These included *Cassell's Illustrated Family Paper* (1853–1932), *Chambers's Journal* (1832–1956), the *Family Herald* (1842–1940), *London Journal* (1845–1928) and *All The Year Round* (1859–95).[20] One of the only provincial magazine genres to be successful was the satirical and comic periodical of the late 1860s to the mid-1890s, often named after small but annoying creatures. Notable examples included Liverpool's *Porcupine* (1860–1915) and Manchester's *City Jackdaw* (1874–84).[21]

---

16 Martin Hewitt, *The Dawn of the Cheap Press in Victorian Britain: The End of the 'Taxes on Knowledge', 1849–1869* (London: Bloomsbury Academic, 2014), p. 23.

17 For more details see Andrew Hobbs, 'Provincial Periodicals', in *The Routledge Handbook to Nineteenth-Century British Periodicals and Newspapers*, ed. by Andrew King, Alexis Easley, and John Morton (Abingdon: Routledge, 2016), pp. 221–33, https://doi.org/10.4324/9781315613345; Hobbs, 'Deleterious Dominance'.

18 Hewitt, p. 14.

19 Simon Eliot, *Some Patterns and Trends in British Publishing, 1800–1919* (London: Bibliographical Society, 1994), p. 83.

20 Laurel Brake, 'Markets, Genres, Iterations', in *Routledge Handbook to Nineteenth-Century British Periodicals and Newspapers*, pp. 237–48 (p. 242).

21 Simon Gunn, *The Public Culture of the Victorian Middle Class: Ritual and Authority in the English Industrial City, 1840–1914* (Manchester: Manchester University Press, 2000); Patrick Joyce, *The Rule of Freedom: Liberalism and the Modern City* (London: Verso, 2003).

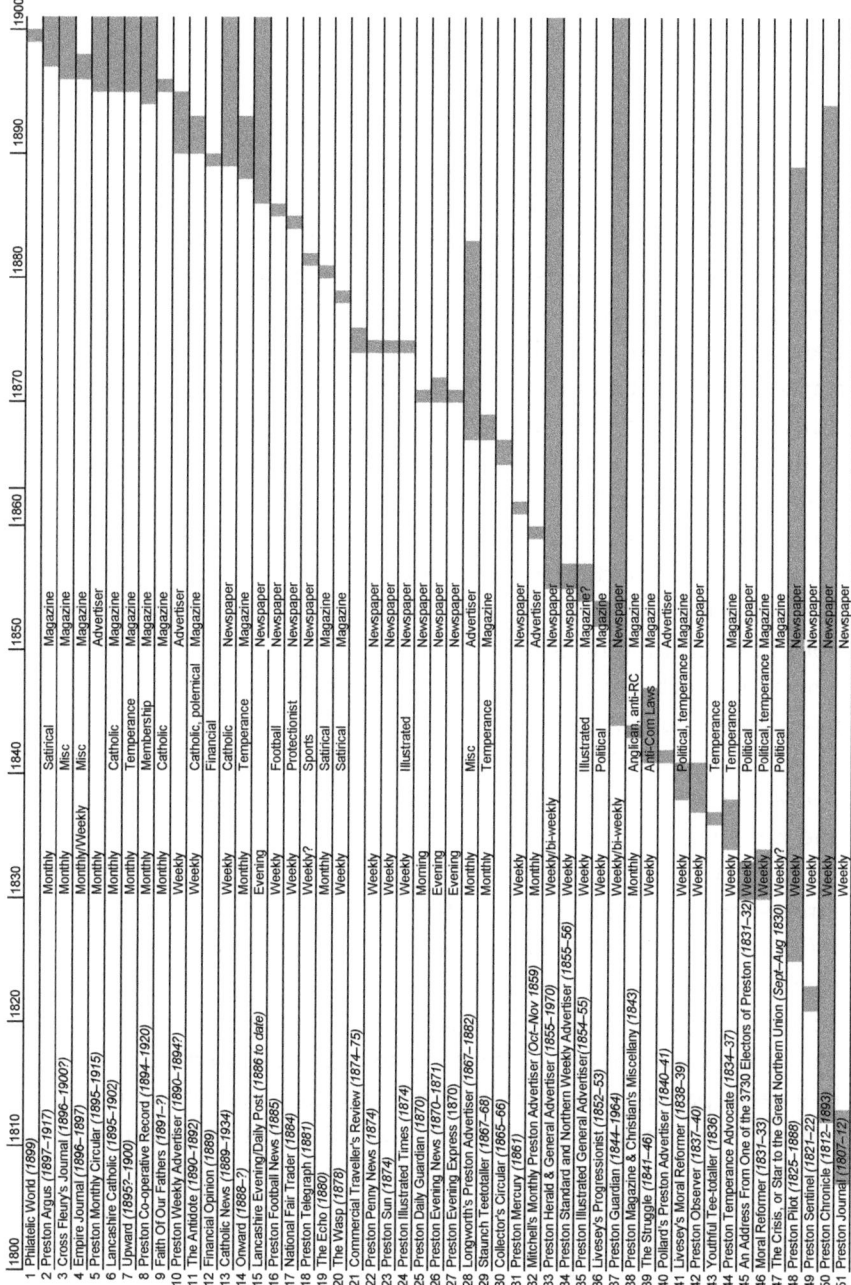

Table 4.1. Newspapers and periodicals published in Preston, Lancashire 1800–1900.[22] Author's diagram, CC BY 4.0.

22   Sources: British Library catalogue, John S. North, ed., *The Waterloo Directory of English Newspapers and Periodicals, 1800–1900* (North Waterloo Academic Press); Anthony Hewitson, *History of Preston* (Wakefield: S. R. Publishers [first published 1883], 1969), pp. 341–44.

Local Periodical Ecology: Preston

The case study of Preston, one node in the national network constituted by the local press, reveals the number, local distinctiveness, diversity, dynamism, even instability, of local newspapers and magazines. 'The transformation of Victorian Britain and Ireland brought into being unprecedented, self-authenticating local cultures that operated under different aesthetic laws and created their own traditions,' according to Brian Maidment, and this included local print cultures.[23] Preston's distinctive print ecology was influenced by its geographical position, economy and culture. Its newspapers had a wider circulation than titles in most towns, reflecting its status as a market and administrative centre, and possibly its sub-regional importance as a rail hub. But Preston was not unusual in the number and variety of its papers and periodicals, many of which are not listed in the British Library catalogue, and have left no surviving copies. The main titles each had their distinct histories, moulded by their founders and subsequent owners, the periods in which they were published, and by their competitors, local and non-local.

Preston's newspaper history began in the 1740s, with the first of three short-lived titles published in the eighteenth century, and from 1807 onwards was served continuously by one or more paper of at least weekly frequency, sometimes by as many as eight rival publications. At least fifty-one titles were published during the nineteenth century (Table 4.1 above). Three of Preston's four longest-running weekly and bi-weekly papers were established in the first half of the nineteenth century. The *Preston Journal* (1807–12) became the *Preston Chronicle* (1812–93) when it changed hands in 1812, and was a Liberal paper for all but the last three years of its existence. After the *Guardian* launched in 1844, the *Chronicle*'s sub-regional circulation area shrank to Preston and a dozen miles around. Its style was more literary and magazine-like than other Preston papers. In 1854, the last year in which government Stamp Duty figures provide reliable circulation figures, the *Chronicle* sold 1,769

---

23   Fiona J. Stafford, *Local Attachments: The Province of Poetry* (Oxford: Oxford University Press, 2010), pp. 295–96.

copies per week.[24] A second long-running weekly, the Conservative *Preston Pilot* (1825–88), was launched in 1825, although by the 1860s it had transmogrified into a Lytham paper, despite its name. As in Charles Dickens's fictional town of Eatanswill in *The Pickwick Papers*, Preston's newspapers often traded insults. In 1847 the *Chronicle* described the *Pilot* as 'a pilot […] whose dead-weight and unskillfulness would blunder a cork boat to the bottom and contrive to wreck a buoy of India-rubber […] our dear old doting grandmamma […] we shall be obliged to give our ancient relative a cold bath in the [river] Ribble, for the benefit of her delirious fever […]'[25] The *Pilot* was of poor journalistic quality, patrician Tory in tone, and increasingly out of step with local Conservatives and in fact any readers at all. In 1854 it sold a mere 933 copies per week.

The staid world of Preston's newspapers was disrupted in 1844, with the launch of the *Preston Guardian* (1844–1964), the town's most successful paper, in terms of circulation, profits and reputation. It was set up by teetotaller and anti-corn-law campaigner Joseph Livesey, a wealthy, self-made cheesemonger who had already published half-a-dozen polemical weeklies, and was involved in most of Preston's progressive causes.[26] The *Guardian* was a sub-regional paper from its inception; its strength was its comprehensive, relatively balanced news reporting and its accessible style under Livesey and his sons. The *Guardian* was better in form and content than its two Preston rivals, achieving a circulation in its first year higher than their combined sales. Hewitson claimed it was subsidised by a national pressure group, the

---

24   1854–55 (83) 'Return of Number of Stamps issued at One Penny to Newspapers'. These government newspaper taxation statistics have been used to characterise Preston's press at the start of the period despite their limitations, noted in H. Whorlow, *The Provincial Newspaper Society. 1836–1886. A Jubilee Retrospect* (London: Page, Pratt & Co., 1886), p. 12; Aled Gruffydd Jones, *Press, Politics and Society: A History of Journalism in Wales* (Cardiff: University of Wales Press, 1993), p. 90; Alfred Powell Wadsworth, 'Newspaper Circulations, 1800–1954', *Transactions of the Manchester Statistical Society*, 9 (1955), 1–40 (p. 33). They can provide a rough guide to aggregate copies printed (not sold), and comparative circulations of different papers. For a more sceptical view, see Marie-Louise Legg, *Newspapers and Nationalism: The Irish Provincial Press, 1850–1892* (Dublin: Four Courts Press, 1999), p. 30.

25   'Grandmamma's Arithmetic', *Preston Chronicle* (hereafter *PC*), 27 November 1847. Note the local reference to the River Ribble.

26   Ian Levitt, ed., *Joseph Livesey of Preston: Business, Temperance and Moral Reform* (Preston: University of Central Lancashire, 1996); Andrew Hobbs, 'Preston Guardian', in *DNCJ* online.

Anti-Corn Law League, at its launch, and Livesey admitted that it did not make a profit until its fourth year.[27] By 1854 it was the tenth best-selling provincial paper in the country (7,288 copies per week, less than the *Manchester Guardian*'s 9,677, but more than the *Sunday Times*'s 7,154). The repeal of compulsory Stamp Duty in 1855 encouraged the *Guardian* to go from weekly to bi-weekly, and in 1859 Livesey sold the booming paper to his protégé, George Toulmin, for £6,600, the equivalent of around £1 million today, suggesting high profitability. Toulmin, a Radical, had trained as a printer in Preston, before working on a Conservative newspaper, the *Bolton Chronicle* (which he continued to manage until 1882). Such 'switching sides' was not unusual among printers and journalists. Toulmin brought a sterner, less populist tone to the *Guardian*, but nevertheless made a great success of it. By 1866 the *Preston Guardian* was selling 13,600 copies a week.[28] The local market for weeklies was mature even before mid-century in Preston, and the *Guardian* had probably only succeeded in breaking into it because of Livesey's exceptional journalistic ability, good business sense and the help of an Anti-Corn-Law League subsidy, against two unremarkable competitors.

The *Preston Guardian* was unusual among the town's papers in being enmeshed in a national political network of middle-class radical Nonconformist individuals and organisations, as shown by some of its editors and staff. John Hamilton was a *Preston Guardian* reporter who went on to edit the radical London daily the *Morning Star*; he was due to become editor of the *Preston Guardian* in 1860 but became fatally ill.[29] John Baxter Langley (editor, 1861–63), also associated with the *Morning Star*, was a Chartist and radical campaigner and lecturer in support of free libraries, mechanics' institutes and co-operation.[30] Washington Wilks, co-editor of the *Morning Star* and proprietor of the *Carlisle Examiner*, wrote leaders for the *Preston Guardian*, and Thomas Wemyss Reid (editor 1864–66) went on to edit the *Leeds Mercury* and

27   Letter from Anthony Hewitson, *Preston Guardian* (hereafter *PG*), 8 June 1912, pasted into back of Hewitson Diary 1912; *PG*, 14 December 1872, p. 6.
28   Jubilee supplement, *PG*, 17 February 1894.
29   *PG*, 20 October 1860.
30   For Langley, *PC*, 4 August 1861; 31 January 1863; for Reid, Stuart Johnson Reid, *Memoirs of Sir Wemyss Reid, 1842–1885* (London: Cassell, 1905).

was friendly with the Liberal leadership at national level. The *Guardian* even had a future Fenian on its staff, John Boyle O'Reilly (1844–90), an Irish schoolmaster's son who joined the paper as a printer in 1859 before moving into reporting, so would have been a contemporary of Hewitson. He joined the local militia, the 11th Lancashire Rifle Volunteers and became an NCO, able to afford the five-guinea yearly subscription for officers. He left the *Guardian* in 1863 to return to Ireland, where he was active in the Irish Republican Brotherhood (the 'Fenians') by 1865. In 1866 he was arrested and sentenced to death, commuted to life imprisonment; he eventually escaped to the US, where he became a leader of the Irish-American community, editing the *Boston Pilot*.[31]

The Conservative *Preston Herald* (1855–1971) became the only serious competitor to the *Preston Guardian*, which described it as 'a subsidised Tory organ [...] a journal in which so many outrages upon decency have been tolerated, in the supposed interest of a political party [...] vulgar diatribes [...] putrescent slime [...] gross stupidity or determined mendacity [...]'.[32] It was launched in 1855 by printer Henry Barton, using partly printed sheets (pre-printed pages produced in London, to be supplemented by local advertising and editorial, a common publication method for smaller newspapers).[33] The *Herald* struggled until it was indeed subsidised by the Tories, on its purchase by the local Conservative association in 1860.[34] Its editor in 1860–61, Sidney Laman Blanchard, was probably the most cosmopolitan journalist to pass through Preston. The eldest son of Samuel Laman Blanchard (author, Liberal Party journalist and friend of Dickens),

---

31   I am grateful to Ian Kenneally for this information. See Ian Kenneally, *From the Earth, A Cry: The Story of John Boyle O'Reilly* (Cork: Collins Press, 2011).

32   Leading article, *PG*, 24 October 1868; obituary of *Preston Herald* company chairman Miles Myres, *PG*, 17 December 1873.

33   Charles Hardwick, *History of the Borough of Preston and Its Environs, in the County of Lancaster* (Preston: Worthington, 1857), p. 456; Andrew Hobbs, 'Partly Printed Sheets', in *DNCJ* online. Larger provincial publishers also produced partly printed sheets, such as the Toulmins, publishers of the *Preston Guardian*. From 1871 to 1876 they sold 1,000 partly printed copies per week of their *Blackburn Times*, with pages 3 and 4 printed and pages 1 and 2 blank, to a Colne printer, E. J. Taylor. Taylor filled the blank pages with Colne news and advertisements, and sold it as the *Colne and Nelson Guardian* ('County Court', *Blackburn Standard*, 18 August 1877).

34   Obituary of Miles Myres, *Preston Herald* (hereafter *PH*), 17 December 1873, p. 3.

he began his career as Disraeli's private secretary.[35] He studied in Paris in the early 1850s, and edited the *Bengali Hurkaru* in India in the mid-1850s, resigning in 1857 after his attacks on Lord Canning led to the paper's suspension.[36] On the *Herald's* Conservative takeover, it strove to imitate the Radical *Guardian* in its sub-regional reach and comprehensive news service (with some success, although at a financial loss), but was more populist in content. In the early twentieth century it was subsidised by the Earl of Derby's family (such political subsidy was not unusual, particularly for Conservative papers).[37] By the 1860s the only other nineteenth-century Preston titles that had survived for more than a year were Joseph Livesey's anti-Corn-Law and temperance publications, and the *Preston Observer* (1837–40), one of seven short-lived weekly newspapers.[38]

The births, long lives, failures to thrive, forced marriages and deaths of Preston's publications largely confirm other studies of the provincial press and the complex set of factors necessary (but rarely sufficient) for success in this dynamic, unstable period of newspaper history.[39] This is the world in which Anthony Hewitson went about his business as a reporter in Preston in 1865.

---

35 Benjamin Disraeli, *Benjamin Disraeli Letters 1848–51*, ed. J. B. Conacher and M. G. Wiebe, vol. V (Toronto: University of Toronto Press, 1982), p. 357, letter 2046, note 1.

36 Mitchell's *Newspaper Press Directory*, 1861; Jitendra Nath Basu, *Romance of Indian Journalism* (Calcutta: Calcutta University, 1979), p. 155. Basu says that Laman Blanchard returned to England in 1864, three years after Mitchell's directory names him as *Preston Herald* editor. He became a barrister in 1866 and returned to Indian journalism from 1873 to 1880. A frequent contributor to London periodicals, he was credited with the quip 'Let us start a comic *Punch*': *Times*, 7 June 1866; Dyke Rhode, 'Round the London Press, XI. Turveydrop and Weller in Type', *New Century Review*, January 1899.

37 Colin Buckley, 'The Search for "a Really Smart Sheet": The Conservative Evening Newspaper Project in Edwardian Manchester', *Manchester Region History Review*, 8 (1994), 21–28.

38 For more detailed histories of Preston's newspapers and magazines, see Andrew Hobbs, 'Reading the Local Paper: Social and Cultural Functions of the Local Press in Preston, Lancashire, 1855–1900' (unpublished PhD dissertation, University of Central Lancashire, 2010); for temperance periodicals, see Annemarie McAllister, 'Temperance Periodicals', in *Routledge Handbook to Nineteenth-Century British Periodicals and Newspapers*, pp. 342–54.

39 M. Milne, 'Survival of the Fittest? Sunderland Newspapers in the Nineteenth Century', in *The Victorian Periodical Press: Samplings and Soundings*, ed. J. Shattock and M. Wolff (Leicester: Leicester University Press, 1982), 214–17.

A Week in the Life of
a Provincial Newspaper Reporter, 1865

Friday 22 September 1865[40]

Got up at six; had a shower bath; wrote till eight; went to office at nine;
more writing; got two columns about Exhibition into <u>The Times</u>; went to
a dinner at Theatre in evening given by Lieutenant Colonel Birchall and
Major Wilson to members & friends of Artillery Corps of Preston. Got
home after two in morning.

This extract from Anthony Hewitson's diary begins on a Friday, the
busiest day of the week, when the main edition of the paper went to
press for Saturday publication. He worked at home before breakfast,
arriving at the office on Fishergate, the main street, at nine. For most
of the previous week he had been reporting the opening of the Preston
Exhibition of Art and Industry (Fig. 4.3) for the *Guardian*. Hewitson
was also a local correspondent for other newspapers, including the
Times, for whom he wrote a two-column report of the exhibition.[41] He
was part of a national network of local correspondents, some of them
'moonlighting' staff journalists, others freelance, who supplied news
to regional dailies in other places, and to metropolitan papers such as
the *Times*.

In the evening Hewitson attended a dinner for the local artillery
volunteers, taking a shorthand note and writing an article of almost
2,000 words, which was published early the following morning, while
the speakers were still asleep. Hewitson's shorthand enabled him to
capture the atmosphere and bon mots of the speakers — the invention
of shorthand added new descriptive power to journalism from the
1830s onwards, and was almost as significant as the leap from silent
film to 'talkies' a century later.[42] The dinner, attended by mill owners,
solicitors, doctors and the volunteers themselves, was typical of the

---

40   Hewitson Diary 1865, Lancashire Archives DP512/1/1.

41   'Preston Art And Industrial Exhibition', *Times* 22 September 1865, p. 10; an image
     can be seen in the *Illustrated London News*, 14 October 1865, p. 365.

42   Nancy P. Lopatin, 'Refining the Limits of Political Reporting: The Provincial Press,
     Political Unions, and The Great Reform Act', *Victorian Periodicals Newsletter*, 31
     (1998), 337–55 (p. 340); Donald Read, 'John Harland, Father of Provincial Reporting',
     Manchester Review, 8 (1958), 205–12 (p. 211).

type of event covered by a local newspaper, which was far better at reporting the lives of its middle-class readers than those further down the social scale. 'Newspapers were, in a sense, free publicity for a town's ruling classes'.[43] Twenty hours after he woke up, Hewitson went to bed in the early hours of Saturday morning, not unusual on press day. As Hewitson slept, the printers worked through the night, to ensure that the first edition of the Saturday *Preston Guardian* came out before breakfast, ready for delivery by train and horse-drawn cart across its wide circulation area.

Fig. 4.3. Opening ceremony of the Preston Exhibition of Art and Industry in the Corn Exchange, 21 September 1865. Hewitson is probably at the reporters' table, below the chairman's table in front of the stage. Copyright Harris Museum, Art Gallery & Library, Preston, England, all rights reserved.

---

43   Peter Brett, 'Early Nineteenth-Century Reform Newspapers in the Provinces: The Newcastle Chronicle and Bristol Mercury', in *Studies in Newspaper and Periodical History: 1995 Annual*, ed. by Tom O'Malley and Michael Harris (London: Greenwood, 1997), p. 51.

Saturday 23 September 1865

Went to a most ridiculous meeting about Cattle Plague in afternoon at Bull Hotel. R C Richards of Kirkham wanted to be the propounder of some fine theory involving the raising of a fund of £5000. He failed & meeting ended in nothing.

Saturday was publishing day for the *Preston Guardian's* main edition. That day's paper, an 8-page broadsheet with 7 columns per page, sold for 2d. At 2,000 words a column, it contained approximately 112,000 words, about two-thirds the length of an average Victorian novel. Advertisements made up a quarter of the paper (14½ columns), Preston news almost a half (23 columns, although the proportion of local news was unusually high, including 17 columns about the town's exhibition of art and industry). Hewitson probably wrote most of the exhibition report, more than 30,000 words, or more than a third of the paper's editorial content.

Local and regional content was the single most significant type of material in papers like the *Guardian*. 'Trumpery as it may seem to those uninterested in the district, the local news is the bone and muscle of a country paper', claimed Frederick George Carrington, editor of the *Gloucestershire Chronicle*.[44] A later commentator, T. Artemus Jones, agreed on the priority of local news: 'The most piquant of parliamentary proceedings and the most gruesome of murders are condensed to find room for local matters'.[45] And not just news: local advertisers worked hard to make their adverts attractive, such as J. S. Walker, the tailor, capitalising on interest in the exhibition with his strapline, 'Preston exhibition of fashionable clothing'. Local Preston editorial and advertising accounted for between a third and a half of the paper in the 1860s, but there was plenty of national and international news and non-local, non-news material — the 'localness' of the local press was not a simple matter.

The remaining editorial matter consisted of six and a half columns of news from other parts of Lancashire, about five columns of UK and Irish news (including arrests of Fenians, crime, accidents, a

---

44 Frederic Carrington, 'Country Newspapers and Their Editors', *New Monthly Magazine* 105 (1855), 147.

45 Artemus T. Jones, 'Our Network of News: The Press Association and Reuter', *Windsor Magazine*, July 1896, p. 521, British Periodicals.

ladies' swimming race at Llandudno and 'Mr Ruskin on servants'),
two columns of foreign news, one and a quarter of business news and
three columns of features. This non-news content, seen more often
in provincial weeklies than London dailies, included history, births,
marriages and deaths, train times and a column of 'Varieties'. Here
were jokes from *Punch*, facts about Baden-Baden extracted from Sir
Lascelles Wraxall's new book, *Scraps and Sketches Gathered Together*,
and an anonymous poem, 'September', from *Harper's*, an American
magazine (in fact written by George Arnold [1834–65], an American
poet). The same poem appeared in the *Preston Herald* a week later.
As Bob Nicholson has established, American print culture, in the
form of poetry, jokes and other material grew increasingly popular in
Victorian Britain, half a century before Hollywood.[46] The book extract
and poem are also examples of a significant function of the local press,
printing and reprinting literary material.[47] The sheer number of local
papers probably makes this the leading publishing platform for such
material, ahead of books and magazines.[48]

Hewitson was not working towards a typical issue this week, instead
focusing largely on the exhibition and the cattle plague, but then no
newspaper issue is typical, because the balance of newspaper content
reflects the news agenda of the time. The paper usually carried reviews
of books and magazines, and literary extracts. There was no sport in
this issue, but the following Wednesday's paper devoted two thirds
of a column to a cricket match between the gentlemen and players of
Lancashire County Cricket Club, and the next Saturday edition (30
September) had three quarters of a column about a Blackpool race
meeting. The *Guardian's* main rival, the Tory *Preston Herald*, printed
much of the same news, but there were differences: while one of the

---

46 Bob Nicholson, 'Looming Large: America and the Late-Victorian Press, 1865–1902' (unpublished PhD dissertation, Manchester University, 2012).

47 Such extracts, from fiction and non-fiction, were sometimes made by publishers themselves, such as Cassell and Longman, and inserted into their own partly-printed newspapers, for provincial publication. Publishers and authors saw extracting as free advertising, raising doubts over Mary Hammond's metaphors of piracy and abducted orphans for such material: Mary Hammond, 'Wayward Orphans and Lonesome Places: The Regional Reception of Elizabeth Gaskell's Mary Barton and North and South', *Victorian Studies*, 60 (2018), 390–411.

48 Andrew Hobbs and Claire Januszewski, 'How Local Newspapers Came to Dominate Victorian Poetry Publishing', *Victorian Poetry*, 52 (2014), https://doi.org/10.1353/vp.2014.0008

Guardian's leading articles discusses a local topic, the exhibition, the *Herald* comments only on national and international politics — John Bright, and the French press's attitude to Fenianism. The *Herald* had more church news, mainly Anglican, and a list of where army regiments were stationed, reflecting its support of both the established church and a strong army. There were other political differences, too — the following Saturday's *Preston Guardian* devoted one column to the marriage of Lady Louisa Cavendish, daughter of a prominent Liberal family; this story received less coverage in the Tory *Herald*. In the same edition, both papers covered the revision of Preston voters' lists and both made direct appeals to voters of their favoured party, to ensure their registration.

While Saturday's paper was still on sale, Hewitson began reporting stories for the Wednesday edition. He attended a meeting about the cattle plague, which is reported soberly, objectively and verbatim across one and a half columns in Wednesday's paper, but dismissed as 'ridiculous' in his diary. The *Preston Guardian*'s owner, George Toulmin, prided himself on such objectivity, particularly in party politics. Toulmin was an active Gladstonian Liberal, but was part-owner of a profitable Tory paper, the *Bolton Chronicle*, where he had learnt the commercial value of political balance in the 1850s. He later recalled how

> previously [...] the reports inserted were generally written out with a view to influence the political situation in the borough, especially as respects the length at which they were published, those meetings of the same politics as the paper being given at great length, while those held by the opposite party were rarely represented by more than a short travesty. The reforms which I effected in this department, combined with attention to all matters of local interest [...] largely increased the circulation and influence of the paper, so that [...] it became a valuable property.[49]

Toulmin applied this technique to the *Preston Guardian*, making the paper attractive even to readers who disagreed with its politics.[50] Those politics were made clear in its leader and comment columns, less so in

---

49   'Seventieth birthday of Councillor Toulmin JP — presentation', *PG*, 5 January 1884, p. 11.

50   *Printers' Register*, 6 February 1873, p. 474. For the view that Liberal papers were more balanced, see Aled Gruffydd Jones, *Powers of the Press: Newspapers, Power and the Public in Nineteenth-Century England* (Aldershot: Scolar Press, 1996), p. 146; Buckley, p. 22.

the selection and slant of its news. This openly commercial basis for objectivity contrasts with the rhetorical smokescreen of professionalism and balance seen in early-twentieth-century American journalism. Toulmin (like many other provincial publishers) had promoted objectivity on an avowedly political paper, funded by the Bolton Conservatives, before the liberalisation of the market, contradicting Jean Chalaby's simple dichotomy of pre-1855 repeal 'publicists' and post-1855 journalists.[51] Such balance is more important in smaller local markets than in metropolitan or later 'national' markets; the latter are large enough to be segmented profitably along political lines.

Sunday 24 September 1865

Sorted apples in forenoon; in afternoon went to Cemetery to see graves of my two dear children. At night read Watson's evidences of Christianity.

In 1865 Hewitson was renting 48 Fishergate Hill, a modest terraced house ten minutes' walk from the *Preston Guardian* office. He was probably earning more than the substantial £2 6s per week he was on in his previous job as 'manager' of the *Preston Herald*, and the following year he bought his house, making him one of only ten per cent of the population to own their own home.[52] Hewitson was leaving behind his skilled working-class origins as a compositor (typesetter) and moving into the middle class.[53] He probably earned more than most provincial reporters, and his relative wealth and respectability would have differentiated him from other less respectable reporters.

His daughters Madge and Ethelind had died, both aged three, in 1863 and in March 1865 respectively (Ethelind had died six months before

---

51 Michael Schudson, 'The Objectivity Norm in American Journalism', *Journalism* 2 (2001), 149–70, https://doi.org/10.1177/146488490100200201. For a differing view on the history of objectivity, see Jean Chalaby, *The Invention of Journalism* (Basingstoke: Macmillan, 1998), p. 13; Stuart Allan, 'News and the Public Sphere: Towards a History of Objectivity and Impartiality', in *A Journalism Reader*, ed. by Michael Bromley and Tom O'Malley (London: Routledge, 1997), pp. 296–329.

52 Stephen Merrett and Fred Gray, *Owner Occupation in Britain* (London: Routledge & Kegan Paul, 1982), p. 1.

53 However, the craft of compositor was seen as a literary job, part of a 'labour aristocracy', and apprenticeships required parents to pay a substantial bond to the employer: Patrick Duffy, *The Skilled Compositor, 1850–1914: An Aristocrat Among Working Men* (Aldershot: Ashgate, 2000), pp. 121, 53, 54.

this diary entry). Preston was the birthplace of all his children; three of their graves were in this town (another daughter, Ada, died in 1873 and was buried in the same grave); he was rooted here. He lived and worked in or near Preston, on and off, until his death, and he wrote about it as an insider. Charles Dickens may have been a better writer, but he wrote about Preston as an outsider.[54] Hewitson's emotional geography was centred on Preston, in contrast to the places he had passed through on his way up the professional ladder as a young compositor and reporter.

On Sundays Hewitson tended to read, and note in his diary, devotional books; this one was probably Richard Watson's *Theological Institutes: Or, A View of the Evidences, Doctrines, Morals, and Institutions of Christianity*.[55] There is some self-conscious parading of cultural capital here (there are hints in other entries that Hewitson hoped his diaries would be read, if not published), but he read many other books of theology, a legacy of his childhood schooling and theologically liberal mutual improvement classes in Lancaster. He had the confidence, and learning, to talk theology with priests and bishops, and his liberalism could be seen in his writing, particularly when he began to edit his own newspaper, the *Preston Chronicle*. In 1868 he was attacked for his defence of Roman Catholics, and he reported 'heterodox' Unitarian sermons.[56] At this time, in 1865, he attended a Congregational chapel.[57]

Monday 25 September 1865

Went to Leyland with sister-in-law (Sarah Rodgett) & my child. Ran over our dog & got bitten when starting. Better luck further on. Attended a cattle plague meeting at Leyland; then had dinner; then went on in conveyance to Tarleton where there was a similar meeting. Very pleasant 'out' & hardly anything to do. Farmers are very obtuse & don't talk much worth reporting. Got home about 8 o'cl[ock]& found dog mending. It had got ~~part of~~ its tail cut off and a bit of its ~~leg~~ foot or toe.

---

54 Charles Dickens, 'On strike', *Household Words*, 11 February 1854, pp. 553–59. *Hard Times* was inspired by the lock-out (not a strike), but Coketown is not Preston.

55 An eighth edition was published by Mason in 1864.

56 Hewitson diary, 11 April 1875.

57 For the links between provincial newspapers and Nonconformity, see Simon Goldsworthy, 'English Nonconconformity and the Pioneering of the Modern Newspaper Campaign', *Journalism Studies* 7 (2006), 387–402, https://doi.org/10.1080/14616700600680690

Hewitson mixed business and pleasure, presumably using the *Preston Guardian*'s horse and cart for his 'out' to the countryside south and west of Preston. He reported two meetings about the rinderpest outbreak that was devastating the whole country, with the reports appearing in Wednesday's paper; his stories included verbatim quotes, while a report of another cattle plague meeting at Bretherton, a village in the same area, is only a summary without verbatim quotes, and probably supplied by a part-time local correspondent who had no shorthand.

'Every village, however remote, has its newspaper representative in the person of the village schoolmaster, bookseller, shopkeeper, or barber.'[58] These district correspondents collected news and advertising, in towns and villages on the periphery of their circulation area, while events at the core, where the newspaper was based, were covered by staff reporters.[59] At mid-century the *Manchester Guardian* spent more on its district correspondents (Hewitson was one) than on its reporting staff, revealing their number and importance, and their value in gathering 'original' local news, for which readers were prepared to pay.[60] In 1889 the *Preston Guardian* boasted that 'the appointment of local correspondents in nearly every Town and Hamlet, keep the Guardian in the vanguard of Lancashire Newspapers [...]'[61] Half-way between readers and full-time reporters, these people were significant creators of newspaper content across the UK. Hewitson's former teacher in Ingleton, Robert Danson, was one such node in the reporting network, acting as a debt collector and Ingleton district correspondent for the *Lancaster Gazette*. He was also the village postmaster, an ideal occupation for a district correspondent in search of local news and gossip. It may be that Danson inspired Hewitson to become a journalist, and facilitated his apprenticeship on the paper for which Danson was correspondent. In the 1830s and '40s Edwin Butterworth had been Oldham's registrar

58   Alfred Arthur Reade, *Literary Success: Being a Guide to Practical Journalism*, 2d ed. (London: Wyman & Sons, 1855), https://catalog.hathitrust.org/Record/100571156

59   The most detailed analysis of this neglected journalistic figure is Michael Winstanley, 'News from Oldham: Edwin Butterworth and the Manchester Press, 1829–1848', *Manchester Region History Review* 4 (1990), 3–10.

60   In the first half of 1856 'District & Provincial reporting' cost £514 1s, while reporters' salaries totalled £422 8s 2d ('Summary of expenses for the year ending 30 June', 1856, TS in box of miscellaneous notes on history of *Manchester Guardian*, ref: 324/5A, *Manchester Guardian* archive, Manchester University.

61   Advertisement, *Sell's Dictionary of the Press* 1889, p. 1206.

for births and deaths whilst also serving as the town's correspondent for Manchester newspapers, while Hartley Aspden entered a full-time journalism career after sending Clitheroe news to the *Preston Guardian* whilst working as a solicitor's clerk.[62] John Wilson, the Ambleside correspondent for the *Kendal Mercury*, earned around five shillings per column of 'correspondence and literary matter' in the 1880s and 1890s.[63] Some part-time correspondents, particularly those from working-class backgrounds, went on to full-time journalistic careers, but most continued in other jobs. They were core members of the interpretive communities around each newspaper, although they might perform the same service for rival publications.[64] Together they formed a local news network which connected with the national network of newspaper titles. Their snippets of news and gossip were pieced together by a sub-editor at the newspaper office to create a mosaic of detailed, intensely local news. Some traditional newspapers still retain district correspondents today.

Tuesday 26 September 1865

Paragraphing. Nothing extra. Weather warm. News slack.

By 'paragraphing', Hewitson means actively seeking out and recording original anecdote and gossip, ideally in witty and well turned phrases. The following Saturday's paper includes one such 'paragraph' which could have been written by Hewitson, entitled 'A FENIAN IN TROUBLE'. It tells of 'a tradesman, a true type of John Bull' discussing the Fenians in 'a noted hostelry' in Preston, when 'one of the Emerald Isle' spoke in support of the Fenians. The Irishman was knocked to the floor and left shortly afterwards.[65] Paragraphing was a recognised journalistic skill, included in job adverts such as one in the *Leeds Mercury* of 28 January 1860:

---

62   Winstanley, 'News from Oldham'; Hartley Aspden, *Fifty Years a Journalist. Reflections and Recollections of an Old Clitheronian* (Clitheroe: Advertiser & Times, 1930), pp. 7, 8.
63   *Lancaster Observer*, 3 March 1893, p. 6.
64   The village correspondent for Audlem in Cheshire acted for five weeklies in the late twentieth century: Geoffrey Nulty, *Guardian Country 1853–1978: Being the Story of the First 125 Years of Cheshire County Newspapers Limited* (Warrington: Cheshire County Newspapers Ltd, 1978), p. 56.
65   *PG*, 30 September 1865, p. 5.

TO REPORTERS — WANTED, on an Established Weekly Journal, a REPORTER qualified to take a verbatim note. He must also be a good paragraphist.

This ad from *The Journalist* of 30 March 1888 makes clear the gossipy element:

Gossip. — Experienced Journalist wishes to contribute a column or so of racy paragraphs to Provincial Papers [...]

By the 1880s, 'how-to' books on journalism were devoting whole chapters to the art of paragraphing.[66] Elsewhere in Hewitson's diaries he describes paragraphing as 'rambling about' and '"boring" stupid people for news'.[67] This active news-gathering contradicts Lucy Brown's assertion that Victorian reporters were little more than stenographers, and crosses the professional boundaries of London journalism, which distinguished between journalists and mere reporters. A writer in the *St James's Magazine* explained:

it is the leader-writer's business to comment upon facts, the reporter's to collect them; the one puts his own thoughts into type, the other simply takes down the thoughts of others.[68]

But the same article acknowledges that things are different 'in the country', where journalists were often required to do both.[69] Paragraphs could also be supplied by non-journalists, or district correspondents such as Will Durham, a Blackburn Poor Law Guardian and innkeeper:

"Will." Durham was not a regular staff reporter. He had no training for such duties. He was retained by the *Preston Guardian* as a paragraphist, correspondent, and contributor of original notes, in the Blackburn district, and this sort of work he could do in a readable style. He had the

---

66   Reade, *Literary Success*, ch. IV, 'On Paragraph-Writing'; John Dawson, *Practical Journalism, How to Enter Thereon and Succeed. A Manual for Beginners and Amateurs* (London: Upton Gill, 1885), ch. 2, 'Paragraph-writing and reporting'. I am grateful to Dr Steve Tate for information on paragraphing.

67   Hewitson Diaries, 9 August 1865; 29 November 1866, for example. See also Bussey, pp. 73, 179–80; Carrington, p. 148.

68   Lucy Brown, *Victorian News and Newspapers* (Oxford: Clarendon Press, 1985), p. 103; Hewitson also reported many sermons, contra Brown, pp. 99–100; 'Gentlemen of the Press. IV. The Reporter', *St. James's Magazine*, February 1882, 173–79, British Periodicals.

69   'Gentlemen of the Press. IV. The Reporter', 174.

advantage of an accurate inkling of everything that was transpiring or about to happen.[70]

Wednesday 27 September 1865

Today went to Great Eccleston agricultural show in a conveyance. Had to pass Lea Road railway station where there had been a railway collision between an excursion train & a goods train. Twenty injured — some seriously. Just got to place in time to obtain particulars which I sent off to 14 newspapers. Afterwards went on to Eccleston Show — dull affair. Had dinner & paid for my own beer. Returned in evening & telegraphed half a column about accident to <u>The Times</u>.

Hewitson reported the train crash in great detail, obtaining the names of most of the injured, their place of origin and their injuries. Presumably he carried stationery with him, enabling him to make copies of his report and post them to the fourteen newspapers. The higher fees paid by the *Times* made it worthwhile to telegraph his report to them; it appeared on page nine as 'Disastrous Railway Collision' the following morning, and made half a column in Saturday's *Preston Guardian.* Hewitson was North Lancashire correspondent for the *Times*, a district correspondent on the same model of core and periphery as district correspondents for local papers.

Using the digital *British Newspaper Archive (BNA)*, we can track the train crash story as it spread around the country. Almost identical story structure and wording suggests that all the stories originated from Hewitson — he had an 'exclusive'. Only a minority of newspapers are digitally available via the *BNA*, but we can still gain an impression of how news spread at this time. By Wednesday evening Hewitson's posted reports should have reached their fourteen destinations (probably the provincial dailies mentioned elsewhere in his diaries for whom he acted as correspondent); this would explain the full reports in Thursday morning's editions of the *Manchester Guardian, Leeds Mercury, Liverpool Daily Post, Sheffield Daily Telegraph* and *Dundee Advertiser* (the last two labelled as 'From Our Correspondent' and 'From Our Preston Correspondent' respectively). The reports in Thursday's London morning papers, such as the *Daily News* and the *Morning Post,*

---

70 William Alexander Abram, *Blackburn Characters of a Past Generation* (Blackburn: Toulmin, 1894), p. 322.

and evening papers such as the *Evening Standard* and the *Globe*, were probably taken from the *Times*. The story was now public property and Hewitson would have earned no more money from it.

London-based freelance reporters may have summarised the *Times* story and telegraphed it to provincial papers on Thursday morning, and at least one London publisher of partly printed sheets or stereotyped pages (metal printing plates sent by train) included it in one of their pages; this page then appeared in smaller local newspapers (on Friday in the *South Buckinghamshire Free Press* 'London supplement', on Saturday in the *Bury Free Press* and the *Kentish Independent*, for example, Fig. 4.4). The Central Press news agency (established in 1863) probably took the story from Thursday's *Times* and sent it to its client newspapers, including the *Western Morning News* (which carried the story in full on Friday). By Thursday afternoon the *Times* would have reached all parts of Britain and Ireland, enabling more remote papers to take the *Times* version, ready for Friday's papers; some may have taken the story from their nearest provincial daily. The story appears in eight dailies and seven weeklies in the *BNA* on the Friday, and in more than forty *BNA* weeklies on Saturday, either in full, as a long summary including all names, or an abbreviated summary of twelve lines or so. It was carried in full in Sunday papers such as *Reynolds's Newspaper* and *Lloyd's Weekly Newspaper*, and was still appearing in some weeklies up to seven days after it happened, depending on their day of publication.

Provincial and metropolitan papers were part of the same systems and networks, originating, publishing and republishing news from around the UK and from overseas. In the mid-1860s news came from the staff of each paper, from London newspapers, but also from provincial newspapers and reporters around the UK, and — before international telegraph cables were laid beneath the oceans — from UK ports. News from America usually came via American newspapers carried on boats to Liverpool, from France and the Continent via ships docking at Dover and Portsmouth, and so on. Hewitson's train crash story spread as an individual item, but stories were also collated and transmitted together: in newspapers themselves, which became sources of news for other papers; from the 'intelligence departments' (news departments) of the private telegraph companies, in partly printed sheets or stereotyped pages and columns, usually produced in

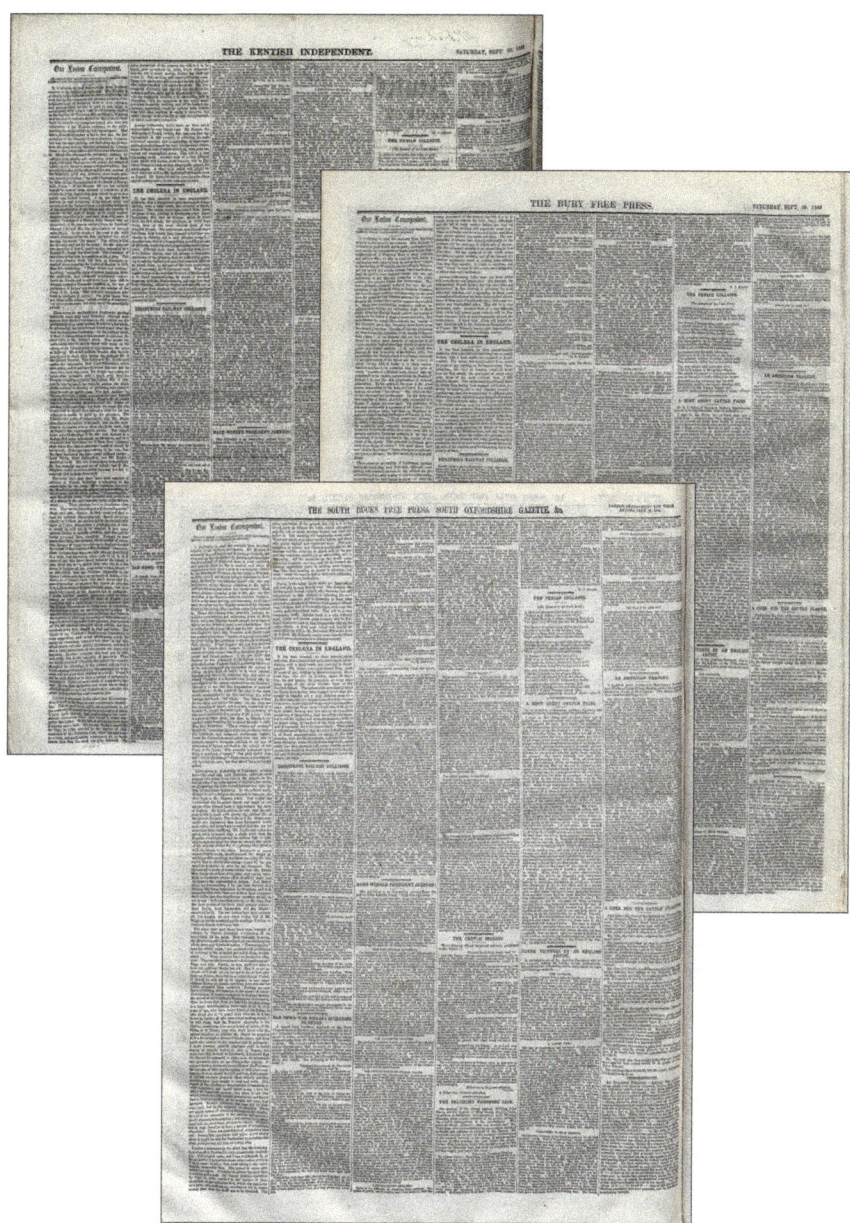

Fig. 4.4. Identical pages (either from partly printed sheets or page stereotypes) carrying Hewitson's train crash story half-way down the second column, in three weekly newspapers, *Kentish Independent* (British Library NEWS2740), *Bury Free Press* (British Library NEWS4711) and *South Bucks Free Press* (MFM.M22733), Saturday 30 September 1865. © The British Library Board, all rights reserved.

London; and from news agencies such as Reuters (established in 1851) and Central Press.[71]

Paul Fyfe argues that Hewitson's sale of the train crash story was no accident — in fact, he says, accidents were a popular type of news, because they symbolised the 'paradoxes of urban modernity' and appealed to a mid-Victorian sense that towns and cities were changing, no longer controllable or designable, before more modern ideas of probability and emergent systems. 'Accident news brings into focus how the Victorian newspaper fashioned itself into a periodical encounter with uncertainty', he believes.[72] While Fyfe's larger argument has merit, Hewitson's story-mongering does not support it. He, and other provincial 'stringers' (retained freelance correspondents) for metropolitan papers, sold all types of stories, not just accidents — besides the staple of crime, political speeches were particularly lucrative, whilst five days earlier, Hewitson had sold a two-column report of the Preston Exhibition of Works of Art and Industry to the *Times*.[73] As Fyfe acknowledges, uncertainty, chance and the unexpected had always been the stock in trade of the newspaper.[74]

Hewitson's use of the telegraph to send his story to the *Times* demonstrates how this recent technology was used to move news from where it originated to a central processing point (newspapers or news agencies). From that centre, it was broadcast out again to newspapers like the *Preston Guardian* (which published telegraphic news from Reuters and the British and Irish Magnetic Telegraph Company),

---

71 For the Central Press, see Andrew Hobbs, 'William Saunders and the Industrial Supply of News in the Late Nineteenth Century', in *The Edinburgh History of the British and Irish Press*, vol. 2: *Expansion and Evolution, 1800–1900*, ed. by David Finkelstein (Edinburgh: Edinburgh University Press, 2019).

72 Paul Fyfe, *By Accident or Design: Writing the Victorian Metropolis* (New York: Oxford University Press, 2015), p. 33, https://doi.org/10.1093/acprof:oso/9780198732334.001.0001

73 For the trade in reports of speeches, see H. C. G. Matthew, 'Gladstone, Rhetoric and Politics', in *Gladstone*, ed. Peter John Jagger (London: Hambledon, 1998); Hewitson diaries, 22 September 1865.

74 Fyfe's discussion of the 'Accidents and Offences' column (p. 44) is based on the small minority of weekly London newspapers, ignoring London dailies and the majority of the press published in the provinces. A quick search of the rare instances of such columns in provincial papers between 1830 and 1870 finds that they were dominated by distinctly unmodern stories, often from rural areas, of drownings, suicides, domestic fires, and people falling off horses and horse-drawn vehicles; only three of the thirty-one stories were rail accidents.

and directly to news rooms and reading rooms, such as the Exchange news room in Preston, where a telegraph machine was installed for members.[75]

Before Hewitson left the office that morning, he would already have skimmed through Wednesday's *Preston Guardian*. The mid-week edition was only four pages in 1865, half the size of the Saturday edition. That day's paper included general news from around the UK, with two-and-a-half columns on the arrest of Fenians in Liverpool, news of the cattle plague, and foreign news (mainly from America, where the civil war had ended four months earlier, in May 1865), as well as suicides, elopements, and murders, much of this news taken from other papers. Local news focused on Preston's exhibition of art and industry, the cattle plague, accidents, court cases, speeches given at dinners, and a report of a meeting of the Board of Guardians (administrators of the Poor Law and the workhouse), a cricket match report and cricket results. There were short sections of news from surrounding towns and villages such as Blackburn, Clitheroe, Burnley, Ulverston and the Lakes; market and trade reports; and letters from readers. Besides news from provincial and London papers, this edition reprinted gardening notes from the *Gardener's Chronicle*, a review of the corn trade from the *Mark Lane Express* (a farming newspaper named after the address of London's corn exchange) and what would now be called a news backgrounder on anti-colonial resistance in New Zealand, 'How the Maories were supplied with ammunition' from the *Hawkes Bay Times*, New Zealand. Advertising accounted for one third of the paper.

As usual, the paper's 'Manchester Trade Report' on the prices of cotton and other commodities was labelled 'From our own Correspondent'. This is an example of another type of non-journalistic contributor, the specialist or expert. The *Lancaster Guardian*, for example, could call on Mr Housman of Skerton who was 'a leading authority' on shorthorn cattle, or two brothers, Dr James and Mr Christopher Johnson, the former an expert on 'the suitability of various manures for particular soils' the

---

75   The use of telegraphs for sending news to newspapers was an afterthought by the private telegraph companies, who had hoped to make money from transmitting news directly to 'telegraphic news rooms' — so much for technological determinism: Roger Neil Barton, 'New Media: The Birth of Telegraphic News in Britain 1847–1868', *Media History* 16 (2010), 379–406, https://doi.org/10.1080/13688804.2010.507475

latter a specialist 'on scientific and professional subjects'.[76] It was not unusual for leader columns to be written by individuals other than the editor and, although Hewitson probably wrote most of the *Chronicle*'s, on at least one occasion he used two by William Livesey on the game laws and Plimsoll's ship safety recommendations, and some leaders in the Conservative *Preston Herald* were probably written by the vicar of Preston in the late 1860s.[77] The Congregational ministers Rev W. Hope Davison and Rev John Mills wrote leaders for the *Bolton Evening News* and the *Staffordshire Sentinel* respectively, and the sermons of the Bishop of Liverpool, Alexander Goss (after he had proof-read and augmented them) occasionally served as leaders in the *Catholic Times*.[78]

Hewitson's one-and-a-half-column report of the Great Eccleston agricultural show and dinner in the following Saturday's paper would enable scores of participants to read about what they already knew, that they had won a prize or been highly commended in one competition class or another. The whole report includes more than sixty names, all of whom would be proud to read of their successes. Small achievements were celebrated, lives were recorded, and distinctive local identities were evoked by the list of competition categories, revealing local farming practices, climatic conditions, customs, crafts such as the creation of 'ropes' of onions, and food cultures such as oatcakes.

Thursday 28 September 1865

> To Town Council meeting at 11 o'cl[ock]. Nothing transpired of any moment. In afternoon gave an order for 2600 envelopes to be printed — for newspapers, also a circular head. Aft[erwar]ds got particulars of 16 cows being seized in cattle plague. Wrote it out for 20 papers. In evening went to distribution of prizes at Preston School of Science.

---

76   *The Lancaster Guardian. History of the Paper, And Reminiscences by 'Old Hands', Published in Connection with Its Diamond Jubilee* (Lancaster: E & J Milner, 1897), Lancaster Library, pp. 27–28.

77   Hewitson Diaries, 7 and 8 March 1873; Frank Singleton, *Tillotsons, 1850–1950: Centenary of a Family Business* (Bolton: Tillotson, 1950), p. 9; *Rendezvous with the Past: One Hundred Years' History of North Staffordshire and the Surrounding Area, as Reflected in the Columns of the Sentinel, Which Was Founded on January 7th, 1854* (Stoke-on-Trent: Staffordshire Sentinel Newspapers, 1954), pp. 14–15; John Denvir, *The Life Story of an Old Rebel* (Shannon: Irish University Press, 1972), pp. 157–58.

78   'The Irish Church', letter from 'A Looker-On', *PC*, 23 May 1868.

The council meeting made one-fifth of a column in the following Saturday's paper, the prize-giving one column, again full of names — the commodity that local papers sold back to the bearers of the names, immortalised in Times 8pt type.

Hewitson's stationery order was probably for his sideline as a 'moonlighting' correspondent for other newspapers, prompted by the success of his train crash story the day before. From the publisher's point of view, 'stringers' such as Hewitson were expensive, so they were always looking for other ways to gather and publish news as cheaply and as profitably as possible. Partly printed sheets and telegraphic news agencies are two examples, but there were others. William Saunders, owner of the Central Press news agency, also owned daily newspapers around the UK, and used some of the same material — including leading articles — in all his papers.[79] Some regional publishers set up series of local titles, such as Alexander Mackie's *Warrington Guardian* series of seven papers, established in the 1850s or W. E. Baxter's *Sussex Agricultural Express* series (twenty-four titles by 1870). Titles usually shared some content between them, and produced their own unique local news in addition. In Preston, the Toulmins developed a minor empire of Lancashire newspapers, and the rival *Preston Herald* was linked to the *Blackburn Standard*, sharing material and personnel. These non-local connections were usually played down, because localism was a selling point.

More ambitious publishers experimented with national publishing structures, raising intriguing questions over whether they were producing national or local media, or more likely a hybrid, as with local newspapers using partly printed sheets. Publishers of Anglican parish magazines used the same model, selling national insets, which were supplemented by local parishes to create 'local' publications.[80] In the early 1880s, the Carnegie-Storey syndicate of American millionaire Andrew Carnegie and Radical Sunderland MP Samuel Storey was a loose, decentralised group of radical halfpenny papers aimed at working-class readers, sharing some material, but also producing their own unique local content.[81] Charles Diamond used similar methods,

---

79   Hobbs, 'William Saunders'.
80   Jane Platt, *Subscribing to Faith? The Anglican Parish Magazine 1859–1929* (Basingstoke: Palgrave Macmillan, 2015), https://doi.org/10.1057/9781137362445
81   Andrew Hobbs, 'Carnegie-Storey Syndicate', in *DNCJ* online.

with his *Catholic Herald* series, launched in 1888. It was headquartered in London, and shared some content with dozens of local editions (forty-two separate titles across England and Scotland by his death in 1934), each with some unique local material — 'a national publishing structure based on local variation'.[82] The most successful experiment was Alfred Harmsworth's simultaneous publication of the *Daily Mail* in London and (from 1900) Manchester. But was the northern edition of the *Mail* a national or regional newspaper? Perhaps it was a combination of the two, as suggested by this boast from 1912, describing how the paper publishes

> from its offices in London and Manchester no fewer than eight separate and distinct local editions, each of which contains the complete London edition with two pages of additional local news — eight separate local newspapers, in fact, which are supplied to our readers in the various districts for the price charged for the London *Daily Mail*.[83]

The publishers of the *Mail* clearly believed that the paper became more national by becoming more local. Complex publishing structures lay behind the misleadingly simple idea of a 'local newspaper'.

This week in the life of a provincial reporter of the 1860s reveals many aspects of the Victorian newspaper press. Every local paper was part of national networks (decentred, distributed) and national systems (usually but not always centred on London), through their changing personnel, the personal, business and political networks of their proprietors, and the methods by which they gathered and distributed editorial and advertising material. London and provincial newspapers were part of the same systems and networks. The occupation of reporter was becoming increasingly important, but a significant proportion of editorial content was produced by non-journalists, such as part-time district correspondents and local experts. They, and many other local newspaper personnel, had a stake in their locality and produced material that celebrated the deeply meaningful banality of local life. There were hundreds of local papers, churning out thousands of pages, full of tens

---

82 A. Hilliard Atteridge, 'Catholic Periodical Literature', *Catholic Encyclopedia*, Vol. 11 (New York: Robert Appleton, 1911); Joan Allen, 'Diamond, Charles', in *DNCJ* online.

83 *Daily Mail* promotional article, 13 May 1912, cited in Robert Waterhouse, *The Other Fleet Street: How Manchester Made Newspapers National* (Altrincham: First Edition, 2004), pp. 27–28.

of thousands of editorial items, every day. How these many different journalistic and literary genres, such as the paragraph or the market report, were created, and how they moved about the country — and the world — reveals the complexity of this borderland between the creative and the industrial. This eco-system, comprising many species of papers and magazines, was constantly evolving. The next chapter, based on another week from Hewitson's diaries, in 1884, shows how quickly this occurred.

5. What They Read:
The Production of the Local Press in the 1880s

In 1867 Preston newspaper reporter Anthony Hewitson was sacked from his job as chief reporter on the *Preston Guardian*, possibly because his employer, George Toulmin, wrongly believed that Hewitson was planning a rival paper.[1] The following year he bought the *Preston Chronicle*, running this smaller Liberal newspaper from 1868 to 1890. Another week of diary entries, from 1884, introduces further aspects of the provincial press, and reveals how journalism, including provincial journalism, was changing. Some of those changes require some background first.

Changes, 1865–84

Hewitson's diary entry for 23 March 1868 reads: 'Started as proprietor of the Preston Chronicle today. How will matters end? I am anxious.' However, he made a success of it. His diary describes how he made the paper more profitable, invested in property, rented larger houses, employed more servants and began to enjoy foreign holidays. In 1872

---

1   'This forenoon got notice to leave Preston Guardian as reporter. No specific cause could be assigned. I asked the proprietor and he said he could not lay his finger on anything in particular. He also gave me to understand that he had been informed I was going to start a general newspaper reporting agency and that he should be glad to employ me especially in that capacity when necessary' (Hewitson Diaries, Lancashire Archives DP512/1/3, 30 November 1867).

    https://doi.org/10.11647/OBP.0152.05

the paper was making £12 profit per week, and by the following year it may have had the highest sale in Preston itself (while its two larger competitors, the *Herald* and the *Guardian*, probably sold more in other parts of their wider circulation areas).[2] He bought the *Chronicle* by instalments over five years; the initial capital probably came from his freelance earnings, savings from his salary and possibly an inheritance.[3]

As an owner-editor, Hewitson made three important decisions, which differentiated him and his paper from his rivals. First, he made the *Chronicle* more local and Preston-focused; second, he performed local identity in print, making the paper more personal in its writing style and subject matter; and third, he performed local identity in person by taking an active and very visible part in the commercial, cultural and political life of Preston. The concept of performing local identity is used in two ways here: first, in print, the style and content of Hewitson's writing was more local, and was intended to identify his paper and himself as committed to Preston; second, he made a virtue of his business and his residence in the town centre and his involvement in local life, presenting himself personally as at the heart of local affairs. He greatly increased the amount of local content in the *Chronicle* as soon as he bought the paper, differentiating himself from the *Preston Guardian*'s wider geographical coverage. Local advertising increased, and the leader columns — traditionally on national topics, even in the local press — became locally focused. Hewitson sustained this localism throughout the 1870s, but after that the *Chronicle*'s coverage became less distinctive, although it retained Hewitson's more personal tone of voice. By 1880 the *Chronicle*'s Preston coverage had declined to levels below those before he bought it; and the columns of district news from outlying towns and villages, which had been fewer in the first decade under Hewitson, now outnumbered those for Preston.[4]

Hewitson, born in Blackburn, ten miles from Preston, became the first non-native to own a significant Preston paper. Previously, papers had

---

2   Hewitson Diaries, 15 May 1872. For speculation on the three papers' circulations, see 'A fine farce — the two Preston papers "gone to the wall", Correspondence, *Preston Chronicle* (hereafter *PC*) 8 November 1873, p. 6.

3   John Leng was able to save half his £2 weekly salary as chief reporter and sub-editor, amassing 'a couple of hundreds of pounds' by 1851: 'Journalistic Autobiographies. I. Sir John Leng, MP, DL, Etc.', *Bookman*, February 1901, p. 157.

4   Andrew Hobbs, 'Reading the Local Paper: Social and Cultural Functions of the Local Press in Preston, Lancashire, 1855–1900' (unpublished PhD dissertation, University of Central Lancashire, 2010).

been handed on to sons or former apprentices, but the economy of the provincial press was changing. Before, the publishers of most of Preston's newspapers had been local men, closely connected with one another. All but one of Preston's main titles (with the exception of the *Herald*) could trace their lineage to one printer, Thomas Walker (d. 1812), who had unusual abilities as a trainer of newspapermen, numbering among his apprentices future proprietors Edward Baines of the *Leeds Mercury*, Thomas Rogerson of the *Liverpool Mercury* and Thomas Thompson of the *Leicester Chronicle*. Other Walker apprentices launched the *Preston Journal* (which became the *Preston Chronicle* when it was sold to another of his protégés, Isaac Wilcockson), and the *Preston Pilot*. Thomas Walker's son John trained George Toulmin, who later bought the *Preston Guardian*, the town's most successful newspaper.[5] Most papers were started by printers, with Joseph Livesey, a cheesemonger, the only exception. When papers were sold, they were usually sold to other printers, or to men who had begun their careers as printers — and usually to a purchaser well known to the seller. Most Preston printers associated with newspapers were Liberal, with the Clarkes and their *Pilot* the exception. Many wrote and published works of local history, and in Preston and elsewhere, some printers showed their local patriotism by giving their technical inventions local names, such as Bond's 'Prestonian' web printing machine, Soulby's 'Ulverstonian' machine and the 'Wharfedale' press, invented in that valley in Otley in 1858.[6]

As well as their connections to each other, many of Preston's printers were also involved in a wider local print culture, involving news publishing, news retailing, libraries and news rooms. Livesey set up reading rooms, while his successor, George Toulmin, was active in establishing the Reform Union reading room. In neighbouring Blackburn, the town's first librarian, William Abram, resigned after five years in 1867 to become editor of the *Blackburn Times* (owned by the Toulmins, publishers of the *Preston Guardian*). He became a councillor, a member of the library committee and then its chairman.[7] Publishers

---

5   Hobbs PhD, Fig. 6: Some newspaper publishing connections, Preston, 1793–1893, p. 75.

6   Frederick G. Kilgour, *The Evolution of the Book* (Oxford University Press, 1998), p. 117.

7   *PC*, 23 December 1871. Robert Snape, *Leisure and the Rise of the Public Library* (London: Library Association, 1995), p. 83; For eighteenth-century newspaper proprietors and reading rooms, see Victoria E. M. Gardner, 'The Communications Broker and the Public Sphere: John Ware and the *Cumberland Pacquet*', *Cultural and Social History* 10 (2013), 533–57, https://doi.org/10.2752/147800413X13727009732164

gave copies of newspapers and books to libraries and reading rooms, perhaps partly out of commercial considerations, but also from a belief in the power of the press, and perhaps an emotional attachment to print. Among those who gave books to the free library in Preston town hall between 1879 and 1881 were William Dobson (local historian and former owner of the *Preston Chronicle*), Hewitson (owner of the *Chronicle*), Livesey, Toulmin and the librarian himself.[8] Liberal newspapermen appeared to give greater support than their Conservative colleagues, although all the local papers were in favour of a free library.[9]

The year 1870, two years after Hewitson took over the *Chronicle*, was momentous for British journalism. The nationalisation of the private telegraph companies, 'the first major government purchase of private enterprise in modern British history', was structured in a way that favoured provincial newspapers over metropolitan ones.[10] It came fifteen years after the abolition of cheap postal distribution, which disproportionately affected the provincial circulation of London papers, and Jonathan Silberstein-Loeb believes that this rigging of the market accounts for the success of the provincial press in the second half of the nineteenth century. However, provincial circulations were growing before 1870, and later chapters will argue that readers' desire to see their lives validated in print was also part of local papers' success.

Lobbying by newspaper proprietors about the expense and inefficiency of the private telegraph companies led to their nationalisation, which came into effect in 1870. Cheap telegraphed news benefited the provincial press more than the London press, because they had greater need of the material to supplement the little news gathered by their smaller staffs, and were far from Parliament and other centralised news sources. Provincial publishers, acting through their trade body, the Provincial Newspaper Society, were also more dynamic in seizing the legal and commercial opportunities of nationalisation by creating their own co-operatively owned news agency, the Press Association. PA, as it became known, charged higher prices to London papers, and struck a

---

8   Free Public Library report and accounts, 1879–1887, Harris Library T251 PRE.

9   See leader column, *Preston Guardian* (hereafter *PG*), 5 January 1878, p. 10, for example.

10 Jonathan Silberstein-Loeb, *The International Distribution of News: The Associated Press, Press Association, and Reuters, 1848–1947* (New York: Cambridge University Press, 2014), p. 92, https://doi.org/10.1017/cbo9781139522489

deal with Reuters for cheap foreign news. It went into operation within days of the nationalisation of the telegraphs.[11]

By lucky coincidence (from a journalistic point of view), the Franco-Prussian War broke out in July 1870, a few months after PA's launch. Interest in the war, and fear of invasion, created a huge demand for foreign news, which local papers could supply cheaply thanks to the Reuters deal. A new type of publication, the provincial evening newspaper, came into its own. Now many more provincial evenings were launched, full of the latest telegrams from the continent. Looking back from 1900, one commentator argued:

> The Franco-Prussian war may be said to have begotten the evening newspaper in England. Many of the best-established and most flourishing newspapers in England and Scotland at the present day [...] had their origin in miserable little productions which were published in order that an impatient public might have the earliest news of the fate of the French and German forces.[12]

In 1870 nine new evening papers were launched in Lancashire alone — two of them in Preston, one by Hewitson and one by his former employer, George Toulmin. Thus began a brief but rancorous newspaper war between the two Preston Liberal newspaper publishers. On 25 July 1870, a week after war was declared, Hewitson launched the *Preston Evening Express* and, on the other side of Fishergate, Toulmin launched the *Preston Evening News*, both priced at a halfpenny. Hewitson had moved first, but Toulmin was ruthless in protecting his market (by 1870 the Toulmins dominated North Lancashire, with the *Preston Guardian*, *Blackburn Times*, *Accrington Reporter* and the *Warrington Examiner* series, and George Toulmin still managed the *Bolton Chronicle*). Two weeks later Toulmin increased the pressure by launching a morning paper, the penny *Preston Daily Guardian*. Two weeks after that, Hewitson admitted defeat and closed his *Evening Express*. Toulmin's deeper pockets had ensured victory.[13] The threat gone, Toulmin closed his new morning and evening

---

11 Silberstein-Loeb, pp. 100–01.

12 *The Journalist*, 24 February 1900.

13 His evening paper had almost certainly lost money — it took another evening paper, the *Sunderland Echo*, eight years to go into profit: Maurice Milne, 'Survival of the Fittest? Sunderland Newspapers in the Nineteenth Century', in *The Victorian Periodical Press: Samplings and Soundings*, ed. by Joanne Shattock and Michael Wolff (Leicester: Leicester University Press, 1982), pp. 193–223 (p. 204).

papers soon afterwards.[14] Across the country, however, the number of provincial evenings grew from thirteen in 1870 to sixty-eight in 1880.[15]

Hewitson was both owner and editor of his newspaper. In contrast, the Toulmins employed editors for their papers, an increasingly common approach as more capital, and management ability, was required to buy and run a paper. The number of newspaper chains such as the Toulmins' grew, as owners sought economies of scale. Table 5.1 below uses the presidents of the Provincial Newspaper Society as a sample of proprietors, and reveals a steep decline in the proportion who edited their own papers.

Table 5.1. Owner-editors as a proportion of Provincial Newspaper Society presidents, 1836–86[16]

Years	%
1836–39	75
1840–49	20
1850–59	60
1860–69	30
1870–79	20
1880–86	28.6

Sales of all types of newspaper grew, but the increase was greater for provincial titles than metropolitan ones. Innovations in London distribution such as slightly earlier 'newspaper trains' (see Fig. 5.1) from the capital in the 1870s had little impact. These trains, carrying early editions of morning papers, captured the imagination of metropolitan writers, who saw it as a symbol of the influence of London newspapers:

> that centrifugal action by which London flings abroad the tidings and thoughts which had reached it since [the reader] last went to bed. The

---

14 Andrew Hobbs, 'Preston's Nineteenth-Century Newspaper Wars', *Bulletin of Local and Family History*, 5 (2012), 41–47.

15 Alan J. Lee, *The Origins of the Popular Press in England: 1855–1914* (London: Croom Helm, 1976), p. 122.

16 Based on 43 presidents for whom information is available. Source: Henry Whorlow, *The Provincial Newspaper Society. 1836–1886. A Jubilee Retrospect* (London: Page, Pratt & Co., 1886).

Fig. 5.1. 'Notes in an early newspaper train', *The Graphic*, 15 May 1875, p. 472, showing the national distribution of London newspapers by special trains. British Library, HS.74/1099. © The British Library Board, all rights reserved.

newspaper trains start at five o'clock for their daily sowing of the land with type, handfuls of which are hurled out at stations far and near [...][17]

However, there is little evidence that these newspaper trains increased sales of London dailies in provincial markets served by locally published dailies.

One of the most successful newspaper formats by the 1880s was the regional news miscellany, which spread around the country, out-selling Sunday newspapers within their regional territories. In 1873 the various editions of the Dundee *People's Journal* were selling 125,000 copies per week; the *Newcastle Weekly Chronicle* sold 45,000 in 1875, and the *Manchester Weekly Times* sold 60,000 by 1884.[18] For comparison, by 1886 the Sunday newspapers *Lloyd's Weekly Newspaper* sold 612,000 and *Reynolds's* sold 300,000, across the whole country. The success of the weekly news miscellanies, and their 'literary supplements', full of magazine-style material, influenced traditional local and regional weeklies like the *Preston Guardian* and *Preston Herald*, which introduced 'literary supplements' in the 1870s, while the main body of the paper continued to provide more sober news from North Lancashire and further afield. Preston's most popular paper was the *Preston Guardian*, selling 15,500 in 1870 and 20,000 in 1887.[19] Hewitson's *Chronicle* probably sold less than half these figures.

Nationally, magazines were growing in popularity, from 480 titles in 1861 to 930 by the end of the 1870s, although they were still a smaller part of the periodicals market than newspapers by the 1880s in numbers of titles available.[20] From the 1870s magazines catered more for niche readerships such as men, women, boys, girls and other interest groups.[21] The most significant periodical to launch between these two weeks

---

17   *Morning Post*, 29 March 1875.

18   Graham Law, *Serializing Fiction in the Victorian Press* (Basingstoke: Palgrave, 2000), p. 42; Owen R. Ashton, *W. E. Adams: Chartist, Radical and Journalist (1832–1906): 'An Honour to the Fourth Estate'* (Whitley Bay : Bewick Press, 1991), p. 128.

19   J. H. Spencer, 'Preston's Newspapers: The Preston Guardian (continued)', *Preston Herald* (hereafter *PH*), 18 June 1943; *PG*, 9 February 1887.

20   Howard Cox and Simon Mowatt, *Revolutions from Grub Street: A History of Magazine Publishing in Britain* (Oxford: Oxford University Press, 2014), p. 18; Simon Eliot, *Some Patterns and Trends in British Publishing, 1800–1919* (London: Bibliographical Society, 1994), p. 83.

21   Jennifer Phegley, 'Family Magazines', in *The Routledge Handbook to Nineteenth-Century British Periodicals and Newspapers*, ed. by Andrew King, Alexis Easley, and John Morton (Abingdon: Routledge, 2016), pp. 276–92, https://doi.org/10.4324/9781315613345

from Hewitson's diaries was George Newnes's *Tit-Bits*, first published in Manchester in 1881; its content — cuttings and 'tit-bits' from other publications — was less innovative than its promotional and distribution techniques, and its reader involvement through submission of material and prize competitions.[22]

Local markets were generally too small, certainly in a town the size of Preston, to attract enough readers to make a local magazine viable; low circulation meant low advertising charges. For those produced by 'pressure groups', such as temperance and Roman Catholic publications, this was less important. A rare Preston magazine in this period was *Longworth's Preston Advertiser, Railway Time Table, and Literary Miscellany* (1867–82), a free-distribution sideline to David Longworth's printing business.[23] Longworth is the only Preston journalist known to have written in Lancashire dialect, reprinting some of his prose as pamphlets after their publication in the *Advertiser*.[24] None of the six newspapers and two magazines launched in Preston in the 1870s lasted more than a year, most running for a matter of weeks. Of two attempts at satirical magazines, the longest-lasting, the *Wasp*, ran for thirteen weeks in 1878. In the 1880s there were two short-lived sports titles, the *Preston Telegraph* (1881) and *Preston Football News* (1885), of which no copies survive.[25] These unsuccessful attempts to meet the growing demand for football news too early, before the market was big enough to make a local sports paper viable, show how the success or failure of any title was always a negotiation between publishers and readers.

Within Preston's main newspapers, local and regional content was the single most significant type of subject matter, but there was plenty of non-local material too in 'local' papers. Figure 5.2 below shows the trends in different types of geographical coverage. (The increases in international news in 1870 and 1900 are due to the Franco-Prussian War and the Boer War, respectively.) The three main papers have roughly similar proportions of geographical content, and follow similar trends. They can be differentiated, however. The *Guardian* and the *Herald*

---

22   Cox and Mowatt, p. 23.

23   'Death of Mr David Longworth', *PC*, 13 October 1877.

24   For example, 'Owd Bill Piper' (1873), 'Doses for the Dumps: A Series of Short Humorous Pieces' (n.d.).

25   Anthony Hewitson, *History of Preston* (Wakefield: S. R. Publishers [first published 1883], 1969), pp. 343–44, pp. 343–44; *Barrett's Preston Directory*, 1885.

had the most county material, reflecting their wider circulation areas, attempting to be county papers for North Lancashire. The *Chronicle* was the most local paper, with around forty per cent of its content concerning Preston. The percentages mask the growth in number of pages and columns, so that in fact there was more of everything by the end of the century — more local and Lancashire news, and even more non-local news, from other parts of the British Isles, Parliamentary news and foreign news. But the biggest increase was in non-local features, including serial fiction, women's columns and general interest articles. The New Journalism was on its way.

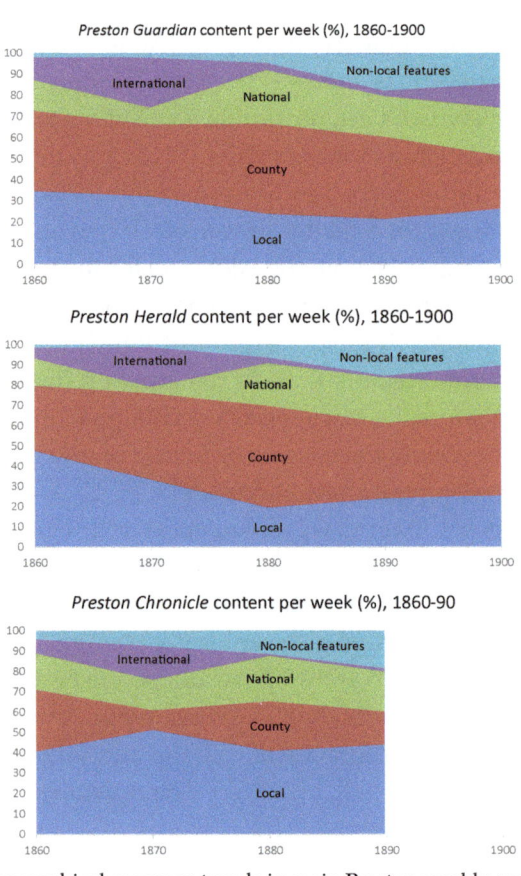

Fig. 5.2. Geographical coverage trends in main Preston weekly papers, 1860–1900. Author's graphs, CC BY 4.0.[26]

---

26 The *Preston Chronicle* ceased publication in 1893; for details of content analysis, see Hobbs PhD, appendices, Tables A4, A7, A9.

A Week in the Life of
a Provincial Newspaper Owner-editor, 1884

Saturday 5 January 1884

Had a fairly easy day as to work. In the evening a blustering, blackguardly fellow — Alderman Walmsley assaulted me in Fishergate — struck at me several times with a folded newspaper on account of some paragraphs in the Chronicle. I did not retaliate and decided to summon him before the magistrates.

Anthony Hewitson was now the owner-editor of the *Preston Chronicle*, published every Saturday. 'Work' on publication day would involve overseeing distribution, selling newspapers from his shop counter on Preston's main street, Fishergate, and chatting to customers. At five o'clock, Hewitson was in the shop with his wife, gossiping with auctioneer Henry Walton, another man, Henry Nightingale, and the errand boy, when Benjamin Walmsley, a mill owner and senior Conservative on the town council, burst in. He bought a *Chronicle*, had angry words with Hewitson about a 'paragraph' in the paper, refused to leave, and followed Hewitson onto the street, slapping the editor about the face with a folded-up copy of Hewitson's own paper.[27]

Hewitson had been mocking Walmsley in print for more than a decade, using a personal writing style later associated with the 'New Journalism'. He had previously insinuated that Walmsley had not one slate missing but the whole of his roof, and was an ass and a brainless fool. Today's paper included a twenty-line story, 'The Reason', mocking an unnamed alderman (in fact Walmsley) who stayed away from a club for fear of being attacked by another member.[28]

The incident is a physical manifestation of many aspects of Victorian print culture. Unlike the anonymous editors of London papers and periodicals, Hewitson was physically present to his readers, and performing local identity.[29] In contrast, Hewitson's rival and former

---

27   The subsequent court case is reported in gleeful detail in a rival newspaper: 'The fracas between an alderman and an editor: Charge of assault', *PH*, 19 January 1884, p. 6.

28   *PC*, 5 January 1884, p. 5.

29   Victoria E. M. Gardner, *The Business of News in England, 1760–1820* (Basingstoke: Palgrave, 2016), p. 163, https://doi.org/10.1057/9781137336392

employer, George Toulmin, was less approachable, cutting himself off from large sections of Preston society through his teetotalism, while his business was large enough to employ others to sell newspapers at his front counter. Hewitson was at the centre of a physical, local community.[30]

Further, the editor and the reader — and the editor's wife and friends — were all part of the same 'interpretive community', decoding the paragraph in the way intended by the writer (not Hewitson, incidentally), using their cultural capital to draw shared meaning from the scrap of gossip. Walmsley responded to the text emotionally, as did many newspaper readers. A similar dramatic incident occurred in Leith in 1870, when plumber and gas-fitter John Fulton Maccallum had tried to throw the editor of the *Leith Herald*, Ebenezer Drummond, into a bath full of water, 'telling him that he would teach him not to write against him in the papers and say that his singing at the Choral Union Concert last week was "execrable," and that he had neither "voice feeling, nor training."'[31] However, most readers responded less violently. Hewitson and Walmsley were part of the same geographical community, even part of the same local elite, but community is not necessarily harmonious.[32]

Hewitson was at the counter, selling copies of his paper, a very direct form of distribution, but there were many other ways in which newspapers reached the hands of readers. We have seen the importance of newsagents, news rooms and pubs in Chapter 2. Postal distribution was used less after 1855, but did continue, especially for papers with large sales territories. In the 1840s 'a large proportion' of the *Lancaster Guardian*'s copies were sent by post; the same printed stamp allowed re-delivery at no extra charge, so that in 1851 the wholesale newsagent W. H. Smith reckoned that 'every daily paper published in London is read

---

30   'The provincial journalists [...] were somebodies in the town [...] They were members of a community, and scribbled in our midst': J. B. Priestley, 'An Outpost', in *The Book of Fleet Street*, ed. T. Michael Pope (London: Cassell, 1930), p. 179; see also Matthew Engel, 'Local Papers: An Obituary', *British Journalism Review*, 20 (2009), 55–58, https://doi.org/10.1177/0956474809106672 (p. 56) describing David Armstrong MBE, who edited the *Portadown Times* for forty years: 'He knew every second person we passed, no, two in three probably.'

31   *London, Provincial, and Colonial Press News*, 16 May 1870, p. 25.

32   Kristy Hess and Lisa Waller, *Local Journalism in a Digital World* (London: Palgrave, 2017), pp. 8, 54, https://doi.org/10.1057/978-1-137-50478-4

by three or four distinct persons.'[33] In evidence to the Newspaper Stamp Committee, Smith gave the example of a clergyman whose *Times* (cover price 5d) only cost him a penny because he was part of a chain of readers including a Norwich news-room, an individual reader in Norwich and a nearby village, followed by two or three other places.[34] Some copies of local papers passed through similar chains of readers, for example those sent to Clitheroe weaver John O'Neil by friends and relatives.[35] Second-hand papers were sold by news rooms and newsagents.[36]

Papers were distributed to homes by newsagents such as Preston's John Proffitt, who offered free delivery to 'any address in town or country'.[37] Newspaper publishers offered the same service themselves, such as the team of 'newsmen' employed by the *Warrington Advertiser* for that town's outlying areas in 1863, who had 'districts assigned to them for regular perambulation'.[38] This system dated back to the eighteenth century, and has similarities to the work of chapmen.[39] J. Barlow Brooks remembered a young door-to-door newsagent in his home town of Radcliffe near Bolton, who brought weekly papers, most of them local and regional titles, every Saturday afternoon.[40] In 1840s Lancaster, however, Mr Milner, the owner of the *Lancaster Guardian*, preferred to cut out the middle-man, believing that 'townspeople who wanted a copy of

---

33 *The Lancaster Guardian. History of the Paper, And Reminiscences by "Old Hands", Published in Connection with Its Diamond Jubilee* (Lancaster: E. & J. Milner, 1897), pp. 24–25, Lancaster Library.

34 W. H. Smith evidence to House of Commons, 'Report from the Select Committee on Newspaper Stamps; Together with the Proceedings of the Committee, Minutes of Evidence, Appendix, and Index', 1851 (558) XVII. 1., paras 2830, 2832–33.

35 John O'Neil, *The Journals of a Lancashire Weaver: 1856–60, 1860–64, 1872–75*, ed. by Mary Brigg (Chester: Record Society of Lancashire and Cheshire, 1982), 23 April 1859, 8 July 1861, for example.

36 For example, 'The *Daily Telegraph* may be had at half price the morning after publication, at [Lytham] *Times* office': advertisement, *Preston Pilot*, 18 November 1885, p. 4; 'Newspapers at half-price [...] the day after Publication, punctually posted from a News Room,' Liverpool advertisement listing some of the titles available, *PC*, 23 December 1865, p. 1.

37 Advertisement for John Proffitt, 'hairdresser, news agent, &c &c', *PH*, 1 September 1860, p. 4.

38 Geoffrey Nulty, *Guardian Country 1853–1978: Being the Story of the First 125 Years of Cheshire County Newspapers Limited* (Warrington: Cheshire County Newspapers Ltd, 1978), p. 9.

39 C. Y. Ferdinand, *Benjamin Collins and the Provincial Newspaper Trade in the Eighteenth Century* (Oxford: Clarendon Press, 1997), p. 208.

40 Joseph Barlow Brooks, *Lancashire Bred: An Autobiography* (Oxford: Church Army Press, 1951), pp. 169–70.

the "Guardian" ought to go to the office for it. No would-be newspaper agent need apply.' Only the town's bellman and bill-poster was allowed to vend them away from the office, selling around 200 copies a week, mainly among farmers coming into town on Saturday.[41]

Inside Saturday's *Chronicle*, besides the paragraph of gossip that so incensed Alderman Walmsley, were many 'feature'-style articles, reflecting the Christmas and New Year period during which the paper was prepared, traditionally a quiet time for news. Consequently, two columns listing the current stations of the army and navy, and a full-column advert listing titles of sheet music available at the *Chronicle* office, were probably filler, to make up for the lack of news. Cotton workers were still on strike in East Lancashire and the county magistrates had held their quarter sessions, producing two columns of short crime stories. There were reports of Christmas tea parties at local churches, district news from outlying areas, including a horse sale at Cockerham, and two and a half columns of readers' letters. International news and stories from the rest of the UK took up less than a column. Features included 'varieties' culled from books, magazines and newspapers, two columns of agricultural news, one column on the poet Oliver Goldsmith (part of a series by a local writer), reminiscences of Goosnargh, half a column on the coin collection at the town's museum, poems, an instalment of a serial novel, 'Some Lasses of Andernesse, an original story by a Lancashire Lass', and 'Our Ladies' Column, by one of themselves'. There were reviews, of the visiting Carl Rosa Opera Company, a local pantomime, and half a column of 'Literary Notices', including reviews of two almanacs and a round-up of the January magazines and part-works. Titles reviewed (probably by Hewitson himself), included *Longman's Magazine*, *English Illustrated Magazine*, *Science Monthly*, *Magazine of Art*, *The Atlantic*, *Arabian Nights' Entertainment*, *Amateur Work*, *Universal Instructor*, *History of the World*, *Magazine of Art*, *Picturesque Europe*, *Practical Dictionary of Mechanics*, *World of Wonders*, *Royal Shakespere*, *Popular Educator*, *The Sea: Its Stirring Story of Adventure*, *Little Folks*, *Quiver* and *Cassell's Magazine*.

The *Chronicle* of 1884 had increased only slightly in size since Hewitson took it over, adding 1 column per page in 1875 but maintaining 8 pages and 1 issue per week. If he had been slapped in the face with a

---

41   *Lancaster Guardian History*, p. 25.

Saturday *Preston Herald* or *Preston Guardian*, it would have stung a little more. The Saturday *Herald* of 1884 was 12 pages (7 columns in the main part, with a 4-page supplement of 6 columns); it had widened its pages since 1868, and doubled the size of its Wednesday edition from 4 to 8 pages. As Dallas Liddle has remarked, this growth in the material size of newspapers, and therefore in the amount of material they published, is one of the most striking, yet neglected, aspects of nineteenth-century newspaper history.[42] Hewitson's *Chronicle* was unusual in growing by only 16 per cent between 1868 and 1884; more typical was the *Preston Herald's* growth, from publishing around 170,000 words per week to 300,000. Looking back further, the *Preston Guardian* of 1884 reckoned to publish in a month the same amount of material as a Preston paper of 1829 published in a year.[43] And it was more for less, with prices falling by a third in the last 3 decades of the century: in 1868 the Liverpool Lyceum had spent £335 per year on supplying 218 individual copies of newspapers and magazines; by 1900, they bought 236 for £237.[44]

Sunday 6 January 1884

> In bed till nearly noon. In afternoon Mr Standen, a young naturalist from Goosnargh came to my house, had tea and then went with me and my wife to St George's church. Good music. He afterwards for upwards of an hour was at my house. A very nice intelligent young fellow.

Hewitson's visitor Robert Standen is an example of the experts, litterateurs and activists who were part of the reading community of each local paper; these individuals were usually part of professional, political and learned networks, whose activities were bolstered by their contributions to, and appearances in, the local press. The networks would probably have existed without the help of the local newspaper, but it could act as a catalyst and amplifier. Standen (1854–1925), an expert on molluscs, went on to work at the zoology department of Owens College, Manchester (forerunner of Manchester University) and at the Manchester Museum. Hewitson reprinted some of Standen's articles about Lancashire wildlife

---

42   Dallas Liddle, 'The News Machine: Textual Form and Information Function in the London *Times*, 1785–1885', *Book History* 19 (2017), 132–68, https://doi.org/10.1353/bh.2016.0003

43   *PG*, 4 October 1884, p. 5.

44   Liverpool Lyceum annual reports, Liverpool Archives 027 LYC/17.

from the *Field Naturalist* magazine, an example of the local paper's role in curating material relevant to its local readership.[45]

But the local newspaper did more than curate content from elsewhere. It was a major publishing platform for literary and learned material. For certain genres, such as fiction, poetry or history, for example, more material was published in weekly local and regional newspapers than was published in magazines or in books. As Graham Law has established for fiction, this requires us to rethink nineteenth-century publishing history.[46] This non-news material, produced mainly by non-journalists and amateurs, was one factor in the failure of journalists to establish themselves as truly professional (anyone could write for the newspapers), and raises doubts about any decline in a public sphere in this period.

Two examples, of poetry and history published in the local press, challenge conventional perceptions that the local newspaper was a minor part of Victorian print culture; that few non-professional writers were published; and that literary culture was situated largely in London. Alongside the work of other amateur contributors, the output of local poets and historians shows that the local newspaper was a porous, culturally democratic and broadly inclusive publishing platform, encouraging popular participation — the local hub of a geographically distributed, truly national print culture.

In the previous day's paper Hewitson had published three poems, the anonymous 'New Year's Eve', 'A Hymn for New Year's Day, 1884' by the established poet Martin Tupper, and 'Ghost Stories' by local poet J. V. Caffrie. All across the nation local papers published similar numbers of poems, so that, during the 1880s, more than 100,000 poems were published in the English local press each year; I estimate that more than 4 million poems were published on this platform during Victoria's reign in England, meaning that most Victorian poetry was published and — from the 1860s — read in the local newspaper.[47] This challenges claims that poetry became marginalised and neglected, particularly

---

45 'A visit to a Lancashire heronry', *PC*, 22 July 1882; 'Notes On The Smaller Mammalia Observed Near Goosnargh', *PC*, 9 December 1882; Standen obituary, *Manchester Guardian*, 18 March 1925, p. 11.

46 Law, *Serializing*.

47 Andrew Hobbs and Claire Januszewski, 'How Local Newspapers Came to Dominate Victorian Poetry Publishing', *Victorian Poetry*, 52 (2014), https://doi.org/10.1353/vp.2014.0008

among working-class readers.[48] Thackeray's eponymous character Arther Pendennis 'broke out in the Poets' Corner of the County Chronicle', as did the young Thackeray himself, in Exeter's *Western Luminary*; Branwell Brontë published his first poem in the *Halifax Guardian*, but these well-known writers were a minority. Most were like Hewitson's friend Caffrie, a local doctor, their poetic careers climaxing with an appearance in the local paper. Nonetheless, their verse can be seen as a journalistic form that added an emotional dimension to the news.[49] In the previous week's *Chronicle* Hewitson had published an anonymous poem, 'The Ideal', from the *Atlantic* magazine, an example of how the local press, as an aggregate, provided a national distribution system for poetry first published in books and periodicals, reprinting verse for readers who never saw it in its original form.

Similarly, the local weekly newspaper was probably the most popular platform for the publishing of history in the nineteenth century, including chronologies, news of archaeological finds, dedicated 'Notes and Queries'-style columns, folklore, dialect and wholesale scholarly transcription of historical sources.[50] While historical topics from across the world were covered, the focus was on local history. This huge mass of history writing was produced mainly by gentleman amateurs, local newspaper editors, and readers, all part of what Alan Kidd describes as a 'local history community'.[51] These individuals also wrote books and articles for transactions of learned societies and for popular magazines. Local history material often moved from the columns of local newspapers into books, usually published from the same newspaper office.

---

48   Lee Erickson, 'The Market', in *A Companion to Victorian Poetry*, ed. Richard Cronin, Alison Chapman, and Antony H. Harrison (Malden, Mass.: Blackwell, 2002), pp. 345–60; Sabine Haas, 'Victorian Poetry Anthologies: Their Role and Success in the Nineteenth Century Book Market', *Publishing History* 17 (1985), 51–64, http://dx.doi.org/10.1002/9780470693537

49   Natalie M. Houston, 'Newspaper Poems: Material Texts in the Public Sphere', *Victorian Studies* 50 (2008), 233–42, https://doi.org/10.2979/vic.2008.50.2.233

50   Andrew Hobbs, 'History as Journalistic Discourse in 19th-Century British Local Newspapers', *Academia.edu* (blog), 2016, https://www.academia.edu/27138940/History_as_journalistic_discourse_in_19_th_century_British_local_newspapers

51   Alan J. Kidd, 'Between Antiquary and Academic: Local History in the Nineteenth Century', *Local Historian*, 26 (1996), 3–14; Alan J Kidd, '"Local History" and the Culture of the Middle Classes in North-West England, c. 1840–1900', *Transactions of the Historic Society of Lancashire and Cheshire*, 147 (1998), 115–38.

Like many newspaper editors, Hewitson was a keen historian. A member of the Historic Society of Lancashire and Cheshire, he wrote or edited four history books. He took over the *Chronicle* from another historian-editor, William Dobson, a member of the scholarly Chetham's Society and author of nine books on Preston. A study of provincial editors of the 1840s found that, of forty-nine who wrote books, thirty-one wrote histories. It was predominantly 'local history which was full of intense pride of locality'.[52] These journalist-historians were members of local and regional networks of scholars — five of the founding members of the Historic Society of Lancashire and Cheshire were newspaper editors.[53]

In 1871 Hewitson and a local Roman Catholic historian, Joseph Gillow, transcribed and annotated a manuscript diary written from 1712 to 1714 by Thomas Tyldesley, a Roman Catholic officer in the rebel Jacobite army. Hewitson published their edition of the diary, in weekly instalments of 2–3,000-word annotated entries, from 2 December 1871 to 10 August 1872. In 1873, he republished the diary in book form, using the same type, which had been composed, unusually, across two columns in the newspaper, for this very purpose.[54] Gillow, his co-editor, was a gentleman amateur (a common type of Victorian local historian), described as 'the Plutarch of the English Catholics', who went on to compile the five-volume *Biographical and Bibliographical Dictionary of the English Catholics*, still in use today. Before republishing the diaries in volume form, Gillow and Hewitson revised their edition, added an introduction and index, and Hewitson circulated the proofs for informal peer review to four other members of his region's local history community.[55]

Some very rough calculations suggest that more words of historical writing were published in local newspapers than in book form, or in magazines, at least in the sample year of 1890, when the boom in history publishing via the local press was almost at its peak. Multiplying the

---

52   F. David Roberts, 'Still More Early Victorian Newspaper Editors', *Victorian Periodicals Newsletter*, 18 (1972), 12–26 (p. 23).

53   V. I. Tomlinson, 'The Lancashire and Cheshire Antiquarian Society 1883–1983', *Transactions of the Lancashire & Cheshire Antiquarian Society*, 83 (1985), 1–39.

54   *The Tyldesley Diary: Personal Records of Thomas Tyldesley* (*Grandson of Sir Thomas Tyldesley, the Royalist*) *during the Years 1712–13–14*, ed. by Joseph Gillow and Anthony Hewitson (Preston: A. Hewitson, 1873), https://archive.org/details/tyldesleydiaryp00attigoog

55   Hewitson Diaries, 22 February 1872.

number of words in a typical history book of 1890 (224,000) by the number of books published for the year (430, according to the COPAC catalogue), produces a figure of 96 million words of history published in book form during 1890.[56] For magazines, extrapolating from two weekly titles publishing a significant amount of history — the *Academy*, a learned review, and the *Girl's Own Paper*, an earnest, improving but well-written magazine for girls — produced a figure of 106 million words of historical writing in 1890. For newspapers, a fairly typical local bi-weekly, the *Lancaster Gazette*, published around 225,000 words of history in 1890. Multiplying by 1000 (the approximate number of weekly and bi-weekly newspaper titles published that year, excluding morning and evening newspapers) produces a figure of 225 million words of history in local weekly newspapers. Obviously, these figures can be disputed (the figure of 430 history books seems low, and probably omits many local history books published outside London). However, the figures are of a similar order of magnitude, and suggest that at least as much, if not more, history was published in local weekly newspapers than in books or magazines. The high sales of local newspapers across the country means that historical writing, often of a high scholarly standing, reached all levels of society, regardless of class, gender or literacy. The volume of history (and many other genres) disseminated in this way places the weekly local newspaper at the centre of nineteenth-century writing and publishing.

Amateur local poets and historians were part of a hidden army of district correspondents, campaigners, experts, inveterate letter-writers and dialect aficionados, and officers of clubs, societies and local institutions. The uniform columns of print disguise the number and variety of amateur authors, comprising men, women and children from all classes. Their writings and their lives take us beyond the 'canonical fraction' of journalism and literature, and reveal a thriving cultural public sphere, a space in which private citizens could join public debate.[57] I estimate that between a quarter and a third of editorial texts were produced by such non-journalists. They are sidelined by anachronistic assumptions that journalism is produced by journalists, despite general scholarly agreement that journalism was not and is still

---

56   The COPAC catalogue includes the British Library, the national libraries of Scotland and Wales, and the libraries of most UK research universities.

57   Franco Moretti, 'Conjectures on World Literature', *New Left Review*, 1 (2000), 54–68.

not a profession along the lines of medicine or the law. Indeed, one reason that journalists failed to establish themselves as a profession was that they were not able to differentiate themselves from these amateurs, dilettantes and dabblers.[58]

Monday 7 January 1884

Bothering about the Walmsley job.

Tuesday 8 January 1884

Working. In afternoon took out a summons against the blustering blackguard.

The case went to court, Hewitson won and Walmsley was fined twenty shillings plus costs. More significant is the word, 'Working', which opens Hewitson's diary entry for Tuesday, and provides an opportunity to examine the most common type of Victorian editor, the local newspaper editor.[59]

Editing a weekly or bi-weekly local paper was not a demanding job: in the 1840s, the editor of the weekly *Preston Pilot*, a Mr Higgins, was also an actuary at the town's Savings Bank; in the 1860s Wemyss Reid found that two-and-a-half days a week was enough to edit the bi-weekly *Preston Guardian*, leaving him 'ample leisure' for reading Carlyle, Browning and Thackeray, and long walks in the countryside.[60] In 1855 it was said that 'the life of a country newspaper editor consists in doing a day's work in three days at the beginning of the week, and three days' work in one day at the end of the week.'[61] This captures the

---

58   For another approach to this issue, see Mark Hampton, 'Journalists and the "Professional Ideal" in Britain: The Institute of Journalists, 1884–1907', *Historical Research*, 72 (1999), 183–201, https://doi.org/10.1111/1468-2281.00080

59   There is no survey for this period equivalent to the excellent Roberts, 'Still More', but see Derek Fraser, 'The Editor as Activist: Editors and Urban Politics in Early Victorian England', in *Innovators and Preachers: The Role of the Editor in Victorian England*, ed. by Joel H. Wiener (Westport, Conn: Greenwood Press, 1985).

60   'History of Chess in Preston', *PC*, 21 January 1893; Stuart Johnson Reid, *Memoirs of Sir Wemyss Reid, 1842–1885* (London: Cassell, 1905), p. 81; see also William Donaldson, *Popular Literature in Victorian Scotland: Language, Fiction, and the Press* (Aberdeen: Aberdeen University Press, 1986), pp. 5–6.

61   Frederic Carrington, 'Country Newspapers and Their Editors', *New Monthly Magazine*, 105 (1855), 142–52 (p. 149).

rhythm of Hewitson's week as an editor. Friday, before press day, was the busiest:

> Laid in bed till 8.30 this morning. Looked through letters; sub-edited; then proceeded with writing remainder of description of Newhouse Catholic Chapel, which I began last night. Next proceeded with a leader, on Municipal Corporation, which I wrote in three hours. Subsequently read proofs; and then wrote a column of Stray Notes. Had three glasses of beer during the night. Finished work at 2 o'clock in morning.[62]

The work involved directing reporters and contributors and sub-editing (copy editing) their work, some of the more prestigious writing, and liaising with compositors and printers. Local newspaper editors were not held in high esteem, at least in 1850, when a writer in *Tait's Edinburgh Magazine* claimed that

> there is always at hand some unfledged poet, some incomparable, because uncompared, local genius to fan the flame of discontent and in the fullness of his pride, to say nothing of his love of pelf [money], willing to undertake the Sisyphian labour of conducting a new journal.[63]

Edward Dicey believed that provincial editors were generally journalists who had tried and failed to make a career in London, but this neglects the many reasons why ambitious and able journalist such as Hewitson chose not to live and work in London.[64]

Editors were not very powerful. Many, particularly on smaller papers, were little more than reporters with a title. In 1857–58 Hewitson, for example, was 'compositor, reporter and editor' of two small Midlands papers in succession, staying less than six months at each; he was then twenty-one years old, and had completed his printing apprenticeship only months before. In 1868, Hewitson claimed that he was the only resident editor of a Preston paper, suggesting that on the town's other papers, the job was done from London.[65] However, in earlier decades other Preston newspaper proprietors had also edited their papers, including Wilcockson in the early years of the *Chronicle*, Joseph Livesey

---

62 Hewitson Diaries, 5 January 1872.

63 Anon., 'A Chapter On Provincial Journalism', *Tait's Edinburgh Magazine*, July 1850, 424–27.

64 [Edward Dicey], 'Provincial Journalism', *Saint Pauls Magazine*, 3 (1868), 61–73.

65 Handbill announcing Hewitson's ownership of the *Preston Chronicle*, Community History Library, Preston.

in the early years of the *Guardian*, and William Dobson throughout his ownership of the *Chronicle*. But by the 1880s Hewitson's rivals, George Toulmin & Sons, had a more typical arrangement in which they as owners hired and fired editors, as the *Preston Herald* had done from its purchase by a limited liability company in 1860.[66]

Editors who did not own their papers had far less power than Hewitson did in 1884, of course, and it is significant that the best known provincial editors, such as C. P. Scott and Edward Russell, also had a stake in their publications.[67] Otherwise, there was the danger of humiliation and interference from the owner, as when the editor of the *Lancashire Daily Post* was forced to publish a statement in 1900, dissociating his employer, George Toulmin, from the previous day's leader column, which had attacked Labour leader Keir Hardie, then a Preston Parliamentary candidate.[68] Those who were also 'conductors' or 'managers', even without a share in the ownership, may have held more sway.

However, it was more common for owners to employ editors. It was a job with a high turnover, as Hewitson's early experience in the Midlands suggests. Preston's four bi-weeklies and one evening paper had thirty different editors in forty-five years, the *Lancashire Evening Post* with at least six between 1890 and 1900 alone.[69] Few editors of Preston papers had traditional Lancashire surnames, suggesting that their brief time in Preston was part of an itinerant journalistic career. Former printers were more likely to become editors of smaller papers, whilst graduates and literary men were found on more prestigious papers, such as 'poet and mystic' Henry Rose, editor of the *Lancashire Evening Post* in 1890, the novelist A. W. Marchmont BA, editor of the *Preston Guardian* and the *Evening Post* in 1894, and J. B. Frith BA, editor of the *Evening Post* in 1897. An 1894 picture of the editor's room at the *Preston*

---

66   Ivon Asquith, 'The Structure, Ownership and Control of the Press, 1780–1855', in *Newspaper History from the Seventeenth Century to the Present Day*, ed. by David George Boyce, James Curran, and Pauline Wingate (London: Constable, 1978), p. 114.

67   Christopher Kent, 'The Editor and the Law', in *Innovators and Preachers: The Role of the Editor in Victorian England*, ed. by J. H. Wiener (Westport, Conn: Greenwood Press, 1985), p. 101; A Conservative Journalist, 'The Establishment of Newspapers', *National Review*, 5 (1885), 818–28.

68   'Mr George Toulmin and the Preston Election', *Lancashire Daily Post*, 2 October 1900, p. 2.

69   Hobbs PhD, appendices, pp. 15–28.

Guardian and *Lancashire Evening Post* (Fig. 5.3 below) suggests that, by the 1890s at least, a provincial newspaper editor in a large town was a literary gentleman. It could almost be the study of an academic or an author, with its books, paintings and writing desk, very different from the workspace Hewitson would have occupied as compositor, reporter and editor of the *Brierley Hill Advertiser* in 1857.

Fig. 5.3. The editor's room, *Preston Guardian* and *Lancashire Evening Post*, 1894. Source: *Preston Guardian* jubilee supplement, 17 February 1894, p. 2 (British Library MFM.M40487-8). © The British Library Board, all rights reserved.

The writer in *Tait's Edinburgh Magazine* of 1850 believed that editors of provincial papers could not take 'high social rank' because they were usually ex-printers, 'deficient in education, breeding, and position', while Edward Dicey, writing in 1868, thought that 'the very indefiniteness of his social standing tells unfavourably upon him'.[70] Hewitson does not fit this stereotype, partly because as a newspaper proprietor he ranked above a

---

70   Anon., 'Chapter', p. 425; Dicey, p. 66.

mere editor, but also because of his education. His personal qualities, too, probably enabled him to move between the different ranks of society, as evidenced by a request from a coal agent for marital advice in 1872, and an invitation to mediate in a dispute between grocery magnate E. H. Booth and Alderman James Burrows in 1896.[71] His best friends, when he lived in town, were a shoemaker and a slightly bohemian photographer. His church-going career ascended the social scale from the Nonconformist Cannon Street chapel to the socially exclusive St George's Anglican chapel.[72] From 1885, he rented two country villas in succession, rearing livestock and socialising with local gentry. During Hewitson's court case against Walmsley, his solicitor argued that as 'a gentleman holding the position he did, he could not submit with impunity to such an indignity in a public thoroughfare'.[73] Yet his wife managed a stationery shop, and he spent most Saturdays standing at his shop counter, taking tuppences for the newspaper he owned.[74]

Hewitson's uncertain social status differentiated him from anonymous London owners and editors. He was a public figure, active in local life — many provincial owner-editors had their names emblazoned above their doors on the main street of their town.[75] 'There is nothing of the anonymous about provincial journalism', as Dicey noted.[76] Hewitson also built a reputation as an author, producing fourteen books, including eight of local interest, four of local history and one of travel. Dicey believed that this lack of anonymity made provincial journalism timid. Those like Hewitson who imitated the bolder style

71　Hewitson Diaries, 23 April 1872; 9 April 1868; 27 June 1896.

72　His choice of church was partly dictated by commercial considerations (he left the Unitarians in disgust after they gave their printing work to a Methodist, despite Hewitson having published their 'very heterodox' sermons in his paper), and perhaps also because Preston's Nonconformists lacked political clout: Hewitson Diaries, 11 April 1875; 1881 passim; Paul T. Phillips, *The Sectarian Spirit: Sectarianism, Society, and Politics in Victorian Cotton Towns* (Toronto: University of Toronto Press, 1982), p. 46.

73　'The fracas between an alderman and an editor: Charge of assault', *PH*, 19 January 1884, p. 6.

74　Hewitson Diaries, 10 February 1872; 4 December 1872.

75　Roberts, 'Still More', p. 12; Mortimer Collins, 'Country Newspapers', *Temple Bar*, 10 (1863), p. 136; Joseph Hatton, *Journalistic London: Being a Series of Sketches of Famous Pens and Papers of the Day* (London: Routledge/Thoemmes, 1882), p. 28; Maurice Milne, 'Periodical Publishing in the Provinces: The Mitchell Family of Newcastle-Upon-Tyne', *Victorian Periodicals Newsletter*, 10 (1977), 174–82.

76　Dicey, p. 66.

of the London press were at risk of assault with a folded newspaper or worse. Indeed, W. T. Stead's dislike of journalistic anonymity as 'impersonal' and 'effete' may have stemmed from his experience as a provincial editor.[77] But there were advantages in being known: greater accountability to readers, and a greater understanding of them. For a journalist with Hewitson's evident social ease, standing at a shop counter Saturday after Saturday, selling papers and gossiping, was time well spent. It would have enabled him to gauge responses to what he published and to develop personal relationships with many of his 'constant readers', giving physical reality to an interpretive community. Newspaper proprietors like Hewitson were 'communications brokers' marshalling a local public sphere, 'for whom the imagined community of readers was a real community of friends and business associates.'[78]

Wednesday 9 January 1884

At work all day. Today Richard Cookson 73 years of age married a woman aged 71 after 50 years courting. He lives at Goosnargh.

Thursday 10 January 1884

Working all day. Wrote my first article about my American tour today.

Hewitson mentions two stories in these two diary entries, both signalling major changes in British journalism that coalesced in the 'New Journalism' of the 1880s. The amusing, touching tale of the fifty-year courtship, which made a paragraph in the following Saturday's paper, was typical of a more popular, light, 'human interest' journalism, while Hewitson's trip to America symbolised the view that most of the changes in British journalism came from the United States. Joel Wiener argues that a more democratic American society produced a more demotic style of journalism, focusing on 'human interest' stories such as crime rather than high politics, inventing the newspaper interview,

---

77   James Mussell, '"Characters of Blood and Flame": Stead and the Tabloid Campaign', in *W. T. Stead, Newspaper Revolutionary*, ed. by Laurel Brake and others (London: British Library, 2012).

78   Victoria E. M. Gardner, 'The Communications Broker and the Public Sphere: John Ware and the *Cumberland Pacquet*', *Cultural and Social History*, 10 (2013), 533–57, https://doi.org/10.2752/147800413X13727009732164

deifying speed in reporting and publishing, and presenting this news in a more visually attractive way, with illustrations and bold headlines. This more populist style reached mainstream newspaper journalism much earlier in the US than in Britain.[79] However, in his earlier and more sophisticated work on the New Journalism, Wiener placed more emphasis on British journalistic genres from the radical unstamped press, Sunday newspapers, provincial papers, and magazines, alongside such American innovations as interviewing and investigative journalism.[80]

'New Journalism', a phrase probably coined by W. T. Stead,[81] is best seen as a constellation of journalistic techniques, which moved between different types of publication in different places. This alternative explanation is supported by a study of Hewitson and other innovative provincial journalists such as Stead, and builds on Wiener's original insights. Stead was not unique in bringing innovation from the provinces to the metropolis, and exemplifies a bigger point, that the provincial and London press were part of the same system. British journalism was more networked and less centralised than most accounts suggest.

Table 5.2 below attempts to list the main elements of 'New Journalism'. Hewitson's *Preston Chronicle* of 5 January 1884 includes some of these elements: his characteristically personal style, the item of gossip about the fifty-year courtship, a women's column, and a serial novel. Similarly, the *Preston Herald* of the same date had a column of 'London gossip', a first-person flaneur's account of 'Going to the Races' '(by the "Herald" Wanderer)', a rather wooden 'Open Secrets' gossip column, also written in the first person singular, and 'The Ladies' Column' ('By a Lady'). Of course, Hewitson had been writing 'articles and paragraphs of a spicy character' (as a barrister described his personal, gossipy style, in a libel case against him), since the 1860s.[82] In 1872 he had used investigative techniques on a sensational story about a fourteen-year secret marriage

---

79   Joel H. Wiener, *The Americanization of the British Press, 1830s-1914: Speed in the Age of Transatlantic Journalism* (Basingstoke: Palgrave Macmillan, 2011), p. 4, https://doi.org/10.1057/9780230347953

80   Joel H. Wiener, 'How New Was the New Journalism?', in *Papers for the Millions: The New Journalism in Britain, 1850s to 1914*, ed. Joel H. Wiener (London: Greenwood, 1988), pp. 47–72.

81   Tony Nicholson, 'The Provincial Stead', in *W. T. Stead: Newspaper Revolutionary*, ed. by Roger Luckhurst and others (London: British Library, 2012), pp. 7–21.

82   'Alleged libel case', *PC*, 14 March 1874, p. 3.

between the vicar of Preston, Rev John Owen Parr, then in his seventies, and his thirty-five-year-old housekeeper.

Table 5.2. Some elements of the New Journalism

Address	Direct
	Chatty
	Personal (journalist as protagonist)
	Sensational/melodramatic
Genres	Gossip
	'London letter'
	Answers to correspondents
	Women's and children's columns
	Serial fiction
Working practices	Interviewing
	Investigative journalism
	Campaigning
Layout and design	Illustration
	Headlines and cross-heads (subtitles breaking up the text)
Reader involvement	Reader-generated content
	Competitions

Few individual elements in the table above were new by the 1880s. As Wiener, Laurel Brake and John Tulloch have pointed out, most had appeared in other types of newspaper or in magazines aimed at women and children, decades earlier.[83] What was new was their combination in a critical mass, and their appearance in prestigious London morning and evening newspapers. For example, some of the unstamped radical newspapers of the 1830s were written in a sensational or chatty style,

---

83   Wiener, 'How New?'; Laurel Brake, 'The Old Journalism and the New: Forms of Cultural Production in London in the 1880s', in *Papers for the Millions*; John Tulloch, 'The Eternal Recurrence of New Journalism', in *Tabloid Tales: Global Debates over Media Standards*, ed. by Colin Sparks and John Tulloch (Oxford: Rowman & Littlefield, 2000), pp. 131–46.

and included illustrations, answers to correspondents, campaigns, and reader-contributed material. The provincial weekly news miscellanies studied by Graham Law — significant 'carriers' for these New Journalism elements from the world of magazines into the world of newspapers — contained a slightly different combination of elements, such as gossipy London letters, illustrations, serial fiction, bigger headlines, children's columns, answers to correspondents, competitions and reader-generated content.

The 'New Journalism' was not the result of a linear progression, rather a recombination of journalistic elements. Many of these elements had previously been associated with particular types of publications or audiences, generally of lower status, so what was shocking to commentators in the 1880s was their appearance in the higher status form of the London morning newspaper. Dallas Liddle, in his application of the ideas of Bakhtin to Victorian journalistic genres, explains that 'genres contain and encode meaning [...] working to make the text they contain reflect the genre's own worldview.'[84] Tracing the paths of any of these New Journalism elements, as they jump from one type of publication to another, reveals the complexity and interconnectedness of journalism, by nature derivative or mimetic. Some of these elements could be found, at various times, in American, Scottish, Irish or English provincial newspapers; in disreputable Regency gossip sheets or the society newspapers of the 1870s, in mid-century improving and family magazines. Two brief examples will suffice, but as Liddle argues, a more systematic analysis is overdue.[85]

To take the example of interviewing, the first known journalistic interview was published in 1836, by expatriate Scottish journalist James Gordon Bennett in the *New York Herald*. It was another twenty years before an interview was published in a British paper, by Henry Mayhew, in the *Illustrated Times* in 1856.[86] Around the same time, another British journalist, Edmund Yates, ran a series of interviews with 'Men of Mark' in his *Train* magazine.[87] Interviewing was considered shockingly bad

---

84   Dallas Liddle, *The Dynamics of Genre: Journalism and the Practice of Literature in Mid-Victorian Britain* (Charlottesville: University of Virginia Press, 2009), p. 5.

85   Liddle, *Dynamics*, p. 2.

86   "Our Interview with Dr. Alfred Taylor," *Illustrated Times* Supplement, 2 February 1856, p. 91.

87   Wiener, *Americanization*, p. 149.

manners, an invasion of privacy, on both sides of the Atlantic, until about the 1860s in the US, and the early twentieth century in the UK.[88] W. T. Stead published some interviews on the Darlington *Northern Echo* in the 1870s and on the London evening paper the *Pall Mall Gazette* in the 1880s; other London evenings also carried interviews. The technique began to appear in London morning papers from the 1880s.

A second example, the 'London letter', combining political, literary, artistic and society gossip, developed from London correspondence sent to provincial papers in the late eighteenth and early nineteenth centuries. A more scurrilous version could be found in disreputable London weekly papers of the 1820s and 1830s such as *The Satirist* and *Town*. When large provincial weeklies switched to daily publication in the 1850s they adopted the London letter, which also appeared in the new weekly news miscellanies from the 1860s, and provincial evening papers in the following decades. Some of the same London hacks who gave the impression that they lounged in every club and dined with every earl and actress wrote similar material for the new weekly London 'society' papers such as the *World* and *Truth*. Meanwhile, London correspondents of provincial papers invented 'Lobby' reporting from Parliament, supplementing their London letters with exclusive political gossip not available to metropolitan papers. Eventually, in the 1890s, columns such as 'London day by day' appeared in the *Daily Telegraph* and other London morning papers. The provincial tail had wagged the metropolitan dog, challenging simplistic ideas of the diffusion of innovations from the centre.[89] These two examples show that the relationships between metropolitan and provincial press, and American and British journalism, were more complex, and dialogic, than simply one of core and periphery.

These techniques and genres were spread by journalists such as Edward James Whitty, owner-editor of the *Liverpool Journal*, and agent and correspondent for American papers, reading exchange copies of newspapers and magazines sent within and between countries.[90] They

---

88   Frank Luther Mott, *A History of American Magazines, Vol. 3: 1865–85* (Cambridge, Mass: Harvard University Press, 1938), p. 272.

89   Andrew Hobbs, 'The Provincial Nature of the London Letter', in *The Edinburgh History of the British and Irish Press, Vol. 2: Expansion and Evolution, 1800–1900*, ed. by David Finkelstein (Edinburgh: Edinburgh University Press, 2018).

90   1851 Newspaper Stamp Committee, Q613.

were also spread by journalists changing jobs and taking successful techniques with them, and by journalists travelling between Britain and America — American journalists working as London correspondents, British expatriates coming back to visit (such as Hewitson's friend Ernest King, former editor of the *Blackburn Times*, now editor of the *Middletown Sentinel*, Connecticut) or British journalists such as Hewitson visiting the United States for business and pleasure. Many others made the same journey as Hewitson and his daughter: William Haly, in preparation for the launch of the *Morning Star* in 1856; Hewitson's former employer, George Toulmin, in 1865; George Rippon of the *Oxford Times* as a youth in 1868; W. E. Adams of the *Newcastle Weekly Chronicle* in 1882 (the success of his travelogue, *Our American Cousins*, may have inspired Hewitson), and William Tillotson of the *Bolton Evening News* in 1884 (to open an American office of his fiction syndication bureau).[91] Other provincial journalists such as W. T. Stead were fascinated by America, and its journalism, long before they ever travelled there.[92] English local newspapers, like other parts of their communities, were 'engaged in a dialogic relationship with other localities and global flows of media and capital.'[93]

Once we reject the idea of a linear progression towards the New Journalism, it is harder to tell the pessimistic story of decline of the public sphere, or a deterioration from the educational ideal of the press at mid-century to a more consumerist, representative ideal at the end, typically symbolised by a decline in Parliamentary reporting.[94] It is true that a more populist, less improving tone of voice took hold in some Conservative provincial miscellanies such as the *Sheffield Weekly Telegraph* and later the *Daily Mail*, but the older, more democratic,

---

91 Martin Hewitt, *The Dawn of the Cheap Press in Victorian Britain: The End of the 'Taxes on Knowledge', 1849–1869* (London: Bloomsbury Academic, 2014), p. 130; Owen R. Ashton, *W. E. Adams: Chartist, Radical and Journalist (1832–1906): 'An Honour to the Fourth Estate'* (Whitley Bay: Bewick Press, 1991), p. 148; Law, *Serializing*, p. 73.

92 Helena Goodwyn, 'A "New" Journalist: The Americanization of W. T. Stead', *Journal of Victorian Culture*, 23 (2018), 405–20, https://doi.org/10.1093/jvcult/vcy038

93 Christopher Ali, *Media Localism: The Policies of Place* (Urbana: University of Illinois Press, 2017), p. 47, https://doi.org/10.5406/illinois/9780252040726.001.0001

94 Jurgen Habermas, *The Structural Transformation of the Public Sphere: An Inquiry into a Category of Bourgeois Society* (Oxford: Polity, 1992); Mark Hampton, *Visions of the Press in Britain, 1850–1950* (Urbana: University of Illinois Press, 2004). For other critiques of Hampton, see Liddle, *Dynamics*, Chapter 6; James Thompson, *British Political Culture and the Idea of 'Public Opinion', 1867–1914* (Cambridge: Cambridge University Press, 2013), pp. 7–8, https://doi.org/10.1017/cbo9781139208611

improving Liberal ideal survived, and even flourished (in newspapers, and notably in the British Broadcasting Company, from 1922).[95] Some Liberal newspaper publishers squared their principles with aspects of the New Journalism, notably in Scotland, but also in Ireland and on Gladstonian evening papers such as those at Middlesbrough and Blackburn, and in many of the weekly news miscellanies.[96]

It was not either/or, but both/and. There was more of everything — more publications, more editions, more pages, more columns, more journalism. The content of Preston's newspapers changed during the period, but they provide little evidence that 'serious' news was being *replaced* by 'feather-brained' features or sensational reporting.[97] Instead it was being *augmented* by new types of content, with an increase in non-local content such as fiction and syndicated women's columns. There were also political differences, as Law suggests. The Liberal *Preston Guardian* had more coverage of Parliament, national politics and economics in 1900 than it did in 1860 (two columns for the sampled September weeks in 1900, 1.7 columns in 1860), although the growth in the size of the paper meant that this coverage declined as a proportion of the issue, from 2.5% to 2.3%. The *Lancashire Evening Post*, also Liberal, had more than 11 columns of Parliamentary and other political and economic news in 1900, a substantial amount, although this was a decline from 17 columns in 1890. The *Chronicle* (Liberal) had about the same quantity in 1890 as it did in 1860 (a slight decline from 9/10 of a column to 4/5). In contrast the Tory *Herald* had no Parliamentary coverage in 1900, possibly because of its more populist approach, possibly because Parliamentary news had been squeezed out by 13 columns of foreign news, mostly about the Boer War.

The Liberal educational ideal of the press continued alongside the New Journalism in England and Scotland, often emanating from the same provincial publisher. From the 1850s onwards, they segmented their local markets, offering different types of newspaper to different

---

95   Law believes this Liberal idea was the road not taken: *Serializing*, pp. 150–51.

96   Deian Hopkin, 'The Left-Wing Press and the New Journalism', in *Papers for the Millions*, pp. 226–28; see also Felix M. Larkin, '"Green Shoots" of the New Journalism in the Freeman's Journal, 1877–1890', in *Ireland and the New Journalism*, ed. by Karen Steele and Michael de Nie (New York: Palgrave Macmillan, 2014), pp. 35–55, https://doi.org/10.1057/9781137428714_3.2014

97   Contra Hampton, *Visions*, p. 130; see also Jean Chalaby, *The Invention of Journalism* (Basingstoke: Macmillan, 1998), p. 4.

readerships, as with the Toulmins' *Preston Guardian* and *Lancashire Evening Post*. In Liverpool, Edward James Whitty and his successors published a traditional weekly, the *Liverpool Journal* (1830–85), then in 1855 Whitty launched the *Daily Post*, a morning paper aimed at middle-class readers, followed in 1878 by a weekly news miscellany, the *Liverpool Weekly Post*, for a working-class family readership, and in 1879, the *Liverpool Echo*, aimed mainly at working-class men. The provincial morning papers continued to imitate the *Times*, whilst weekly news miscellanies (and the new 'literary supplements' of the traditional county journals) and evening papers offered New Journalism. The national picture, incorporating metropolitan and provincial developments, is very different from the narrow London view.

Friday 11 January 1885

> Hard at work from 9.30 in morning till 1.45 on Saturday morning.

Hewitson worked a 16-hour day to prepare the paper for printing. It included the first instalment of 'Westward Ho! America: There and Back Again, Scenes and Sights on Sea and Land, Particulars of a Recent Trip', by "Atticus" (evidence, apart from anything else, that local newspapers could be profitable businesses, enabling owners to travel the world). The travelogue continued weekly until September, and then — like his serialisation of the Tyldesley diary — reappeared as a 281-page book in April 1885, printed and published at Hewitson's *Chronicle* office.

Provincial booksellers and publishers had been the progenitors of provincial newspaper publishing in the eighteenth century. The book trade may have been concentrated in London, but as with newspapers, almost every town and city became a publishing centre. Much work has been done on the connections and contrasts between supposedly ephemeral periodicals and apparently permanent bound volumes (often containing material first published in the paper), revealing a fluidity behind the implicit cultural hierarchies of different publication formats.[98] But these scholars have focused on London publishing; a study of book production by local newspaper publishers is needed.

---

98   See, for example, Laurel Brake, 'Writing, Cultural Production, and the Periodical Press in the Nineteenth Century', in *Writing and Victorianism*, ed. by J. B. Bullen (London: Longman, 1997), pp. 54–72; Catherine Delafield, *Serialization and the Novel in Mid-Victorian Magazines* (Routledge, 2016), https://doi.org/10.4324/9781315608440

After 1884

Hewitson continued to run the *Chronicle* until 1890, when he sold it to two local journalists. Three years later it was up for sale again, and this time Hewitson's rivals, the Toulmins, bought the title and closed it down. No diary survives for 1893, so we can only imagine Hewitson's feelings. But the economic structure of provincial newspaper publishing was changing, and under-capitalised owner-editors like Hewitson were being squeezed out, especially in local markets like Preston, dominated by much more powerful publishers. The Toulmins showed their might in 1886, when they were goaded into launching a pro-Gladstone halfpenny evening paper, the *Lancashire Evening Post*, in response to a paper of identical politics set up ten miles away in Blackburn (traditional Toulmin territory), by interlopers from Middlesbrough. Both these new evening newspapers carried plenty of sports news, particularly football news. But Hewitson's personal dislike of the game, and his press campaign against rates-funded expansion of Preston's docks, were both out of step with the public mood, and probably cost him sales.

The Conservative *Preston Herald* continued its competition with the Liberal *Preston Guardian*, but probably lost money and required continued party subsidy. While the *Guardian* boasted 'A Staff of over Twenty Reporters — the largest in the Kingdom' in 1889 (this may have included *Evening Post* staff), the *Herald* had only seven.[99] The Tory paper, which had been offered to Hewitson in 1874, changed hands in 1890, valued at £4,357.[100] Other Preston publications came and went, but nothing to challenge the Toulmins. Four Roman Catholic titles were launched in the 1880s and 1890s, plus at least one parish magazine, issued by the parish church (1898–99), with some local content. The *Catholic News* (1889–1934) was the first Preston publication to appeal directly to the town's large Catholic minority, but struggled until it was incorporated into Charles Diamond's syndicate of local Catholic papers. The temperance publishing tradition continued after Joseph Livesey's death in 1884 (an example of membership publications

---

99 Advertisement, *Sell's Dictionary of the Press 1889*, p. 1206; *PC*, 10 December 1892.

100 Letter from J. H. Buxton, manager, *Manchester Guardian*, to the Proprietors of the *Preston Herald*, 17 February 1890, *Manchester Guardian* archives, John Rylands Library, letter book 1886–91, ref. 264, pp. 687–88.

immune to market forces) and there were a number of magazines, both satirical and general local interest.[101] Five new periodicals with local content were published in the late 1890s, three of them surviving into the twentieth century. One, the *Empire Journal* (1896–97) had a short and peculiar career, beginning in December 1896 as a free-distribution magazine for 'Preston and District', before attempting to go national and even international, presumably on the model of *Tit-Bits* and *Answers*, whose style it followed. It was gone within a year. More dynamic developments were happening in Manchester, where Edward Hulton was building a popular newspaper empire based on sport, before he was eclipsed by Alfred Harmsworth, who successfully transferred magazine-style journalism into a London evening paper and then the hugely successful *Daily Mail.*

Hewitson's career began before the repeal of the newspaper taxes; he became the owner of a weekly paper when owner-editors were common. As a reporter and a publisher of newspapers and books, he was part of important national networks. The strategies he pursued to defend his paper's market share were very successful in the late 1860s and early 1870s, although even then he was only in third place in Preston's press pecking order, after the commercially powerful Toulmins and the politically subsidised *Herald.* However, Preston's print culture changed significantly in the late 1880s; the Toulmins' capital and investment in distribution and news-gathering enabled them to launch a successful evening paper, meeting a new demand for more up-to-date news, and football coverage. The *Lancashire Evening Post* took advertising revenue from other newspapers, and Hewitson's *Chronicle*, without the political subsidy enjoyed by the *Herald*, began to struggle. An individual journalist could make an impact until the third quarter of the nineteenth century, but after that, capital became more important.

At mid-century, as populations and reading ability expanded, the local market was able to support more titles, while for newspapers particularly, the average number of pages, physical dimensions, frequency, and copies sold all increased. The local print market continued to expand into the early twentieth century, but consolidation

---

101 Annemarie McAllister, 'Temperance Periodicals', in *The Routledge Handbook to Nineteenth-Century British Periodicals and Newspapers*, pp. 342–54.

made it harder to enter. By the end of the century there were fewer titles of any consequence in Preston, but they each sold more copies. However, Preston's local press, for the most part, continued to be produced by local people who were deeply involved in the political, cultural and economic life of their area. The corps of correspondents who fed snippets to each paper were mainly local people; only the reporters and editors were likely to be from elsewhere.

The abolition of the compulsory Newspaper Stamp, and the nationalisation of the telegraphs, both helped the provincial press, but continuities and changes of longer duration were also important. These might include the rapid growth in literacy and expanding populations, which may have had more impact in the provinces, where reading ability caught up with London and where growing populations created newly viable local and regional newspaper markets. There was continuity in the demand for local content, an unmet demand which could only be answered when cover prices fell to a penny or a halfpenny after 1855.

So the provincial press expanded more than the metropolitan after 1855 for many reasons, which combined in complex and often unforeseen ways. All these factors — pricing, distribution methods and costs, news costs, print times, proportion of income from advertising versus copy sales, distance between publishing office and market, size of market, literacy, disposable income and a constant thirst for publications that reflected readers' local lives — deserve more study.

New types of content were added to the local paper, as literacy continued to spread, prices came down, and newspapers worked to turn communal readers into individual purchasers, using the techniques of New Journalism. The cultural work of the local press continued, as a major, nationally networked publishing outlet for all kinds of literary and journalistic material. The political role of local newspapers and their proprietors has been passed over in these two chapters, largely because it has been dealt with so fully elsewhere.[102] However, Hewitson was active in local and constituency politics for the Liberal party, and the political allegiance of each paper was important to their economic

---

102 Aled Gruffydd Jones, *Powers of the Press: Newspapers, Power and the Public in Nineteenth-Century England* (Aldershot: Scolar Press, 1996); Lee, *Origins*; Stephen Koss, *The Rise and Fall of the Political Press in Britain, Vol. 1, The Nineteenth Century* (London: Hamish Hamilton, 1981).

success. The local newspaper continued to be self-consciously three things at once – a commercial, cultural and political product. In the next chapter we will discover who read this apparently simple, but deeply complicated, artefact.

6. Who Read What

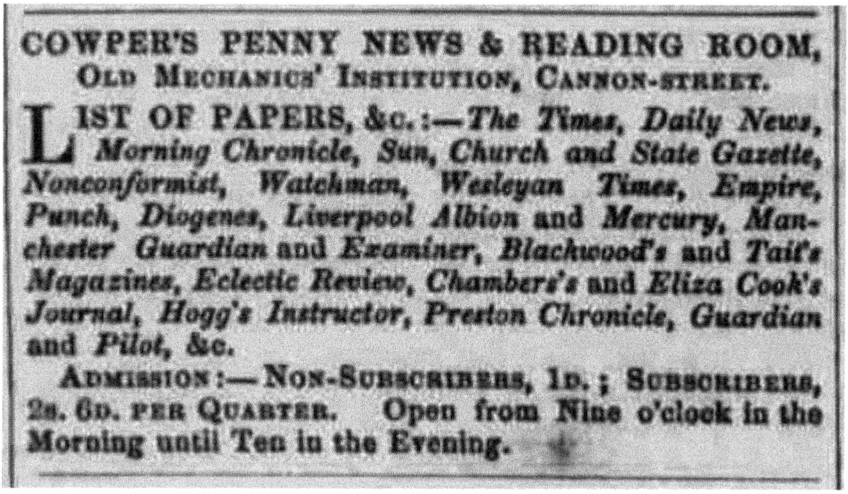

COWPER'S PENNY NEWS & READING ROOM,
OLD MECHANICS' INSTITUTION, CANNON-STREET.

LIST OF PAPERS, &c.:—*The Times, Daily News, Morning Chronicle, Sun, Church and State Gazette, Nonconformist, Watchman, Wesleyan Times, Empire, Punch, Diogenes, Liverpool Albion* and *Mercury, Manchester Guardian* and *Examiner, Blackwood's* and *Tait's Magazines, Eclectic Review, Chambers's* and *Eliza Cook's Journal, Hogg's Instructor, Preston Chronicle, Guardian* and *Pilot*, &c.

ADMISSION:—NON-SUBSCRIBERS, 1D.; SUBSCRIBERS, 2s. 6D. PER QUARTER. Open from Nine o'clock in the Morning until Ten in the Evening.

Fig. 6.1. Advertisement for Cowper's Penny News & Reading Room, Preston (*Preston Chronicle*, 30 September 1854, p. 1, from 19th-Century British Library Newspapers database). © The British Library Board.

In 1854, the local newspaper was too expensive for most people in Preston. The three local papers each cost 4½d. But people could still read them — or listen to them being read — without buying them, in pubs, commercial news rooms like Cowper's in Preston (Fig. 6.1 above) and mutual improvement society reading rooms. This chapter brings together the evidence used in previous chapters to argue that, cheap family magazines aside, local and regional newspapers were more widely read and purchased than those produced in London, with the local weekly the most popular type of Victorian newspaper. It also

https://doi.org/10.11647/OBP.0152.06

investigates the influence of social class and gender on preference for local papers. Discovering what the majority of Victorians read helps us to discover who they were.[1]

The local newspaper was popular, but national magazines were more popular. Half of the population of Britain read penny weekly magazines like the *London Journal, Family Herald, Reynolds's Miscellany* or *Cassell's Illustrated Family Newspaper* in the first half of the 1850s.[2] In Preston, these penny magazines topped the list of reading matter for 'factory hands' in two bookshops in 1854, investigated by the Rev John Clay, the Preston prison chaplain and social reformer lampooned by Charles Dickens in *Hard Times*.[3] The numbers of magazines and 'penny dreadfuls' sold from these two shops alone were greater than the combined circulation of two Preston papers put together (one shop was a wholesaler, but its territory was unlikely to have been as wide as that of the local papers). This balance between magazines and newspapers changed rapidly as the end of newspaper taxation brought down their prices.

The nature of public reading places like Cowper's penny reading room exposed readers to a large number of publications, and to a wide range of political and religious viewpoints. As Thomas Wright, the 'Journeyman Engineer', wrote in 1876:

> At present a working man with a taste for reading will in the course of a week glance through a score of papers — not to speak of periodicals — lying on the tables of the "Institution" to which he belongs [...] [Previously] he would probably have had to be content with a single weekly paper, for which he would have to pay treble the amount of his weekly subscription to a modern institution.[4]

---

1   Linda K. Hughes, 'On New Monthly Magazines, 1859–60', in *BRANCH: Britain, Representation and Nineteenth-Century History*, ed. by Dino Franco Felluga, http://www.branchcollective.org/?ps_articles=on-new-monthly-magazines-1859–60

2   Andrew King, *The London Journal, 1845–1883: Periodicals, Production, and Gender* (Aldershot: Ashgate, 2004), pp. 88–89, https://doi.org/10.4324/9781315238555

3   Letter from John Clay to Lord Stanley, 25 January 1854, in Walter Lowe Clay, *The Prison Chaplain: A Memoir of the Rev. John Clay, B. D., with Selections from His Reports and Correspondence, and a Sketch of Prison Discipline in England* (Cambridge: Macmillan, 1861); Charles Dickens, *Hard Times*, ed. by Fred Kaplan (New York: Norton, 2016), p. 16, n. 3. For full list, see online supplementary material, Table 1.

4   Thomas Wright [The 'Journeyman Engineer'], 'Readers and Reading', *Good Words*, 17 December (1876), 315–20 (pp. 316–17).

Cowper's penny news room listed 24 titles in the advert above (Fig. 6.1) in 1854, while the 'free' (public) library in Barrow-in-Furness provided a staggering 195 titles in 1888.[5] Preston's free library stocked 48 publications plus 'local papers' in 1879, rising to 81 titles the following year and 171 by 1900. In virtually all public reading rooms and news rooms, the number of publications increased, a sign of growing demand, growing literacy, and growing supply. More working-class rooms carried more local titles, such as Newcastle Mechanics' Institute, which offered 13 regional or local newspapers and eight London papers. By contrast, in 1869 the more middle-class Preston mechanic's institute, known as the Institution for the Diffusion of Knowledge, offered 49 magazines, 11 London papers, 10 regional or local papers and 9 trade or technical titles. Church reading rooms offered only a small selection of papers and magazines, such as 'the London and Manchester daily and weekly papers, the local papers, *Household Words*, the *Leisure Hour*, *Family Economist*, &c &c.' intended for a reading room at St Paul's CE school, Preston in 1856.[6] Public libraries such as Preston's had the greatest number and variety of titles, from the *Anti-Vivesectionist* to the *Westminster Review*, the academic philosophy journal *Mind* to the women's magazine *Madame*.

The readers who created and used each news room decided (directly or indirectly) the titles taken there. Cowper's advert in Fig. 6.1 suggests a Nonconformist and Radical clientele; some pubs probably had particular political, cultural or religious affiliations, which might dictate the newspapers available. The reading matter was usually chosen by the members, although publications in rooms with clear religious or political agendas may have been selected by clergymen and ward committees rather than the readers, and local authority library committees controlled public libraries. In 1853 James Hole claimed that working-class news rooms' selection of papers did not give both sides of the argument, unlike middle-class mechanics' institutes.[7] A speaker at the opening of a reading room established by

---

5   Barrow Library annual report 1887–89, Cumbria Archive and Local Studies Centre, Barrow, Ba/L/1/1-1/5.

6   *Preston Chronicle* (hereafter *PC*), 6 September 1856. See also Fig. 6.1 above; 'Travels In Search Of Recreation II, Central Working Men's Club', *PC*, 20 February 1864; report of St Peter's Working Men's Club, *PC*, 22 October 1864, p. 4.

7   James Hole, *An Essay on the History and Management of Literary, Scientific, & Mechanics' Institutions* (London: Longman/Society of Arts, 1853), pp. 72–73.

the Preston Branch of the National Reform Union (Liberal party) in 1867 hoped that the Liberal *Times* and the Tory *Standard* would both be available, 'as he was always desirous of seeing both sides of the question.'[8] Nevertheless, in most public rooms, readers would be confronted by newspapers and magazines of opposing viewpoints. Birmingham librarian J. D. Mullins, writing in 1869, believed that the range of opinions available in free library news rooms was educational, and that 'the opinion of a man of one newspaper —who gets all his information from one side — is not worth much.'[9] A significant proportion of readers' letters to local papers were responding to other newspapers, usually of opposing politics, suggesting that many readers were exposed to a range of opinion (see Chapter 10). However, for many, papers with disagreeable politics may have been read only reluctantly. For example, a letter to the *Preston Chronicle* in 1869 complained that there were thirteen Liberal newspapers and only one Conservative title in the Exchange and Newsroom. Worse, 'most of the Radical journals are in duplicate, so that if one enters the room tired, and desirous of reading a paper while seated, nothing but a red-hot Radical effusion is get-at-able' (an exaggeration but in 1868 there were indeed twice as many Liberal as Tory titles available there).[10]

It is not easy to answer the question, 'who read what?' particularly at the level of the individual. The lack of evidence means that most of this chapter makes generalisations about broad groups of people, but occasionally there are glimpses of individual readers. John O'Neil (b. 1810), the Clitheroe weaver, recorded in his diary the news he read in the papers, but, without thought for twenty-first-century newspaper historians, he rarely mentioned the name of the paper.[11] From 1856 to 1861 he walked a mile into Clitheroe every Saturday evening to read the newspaper(s) at the Castle Inn. From occasional references to local news, these were probably weekly papers from Blackburn, Burnley and Preston, the nearest publishing centres (Clitheroe's first newspaper only launched in 1884). Occasionally he saw a daily paper,

---

8   *PC* March 9, 1867.
9   J. D. Mullins, *Free Libraries and Newsrooms: Their Formation and Management*, 3rd edn (London, 1879), p. 4.
10   Correspondence, *PC*, 2 October 1869, p. 6.
11   John O'Neil, *The Journals of a Lancashire Weaver: 1856–60, 1860–64, 1872–75*, ed. by Mary Brigg (Chester: Record Society of Lancashire and Cheshire, 1982).

such as the *Manchester Times and Examiner* of 14 June 1856, with news of that morning's execution of William Palmer, the Rugeley poisoner. He sometimes received local papers from his home town of Carlisle, sent by his brother. He never mentions London newspapers. In 1861 his reading habits changed: 'I have joined the Low Moor Mechanics' Institute and Reading-room. It is a penny per week, so I will see a daily paper regular' (2 December 1861). Unfortunately he does not give the names of any papers taken at the Mechanics' Institute, and no records survive, although by 1866 the reading room took four daily and three weekly papers, 'besides other periodicals', according to the *Preston Herald*.[12] Naturally, O'Neil began to read newspapers more often, and when a Liberal club and news room opened in Clitheroe in 1872, he was soon walking there almost every other day to read newspapers. He occasionally read at home — either a paper sent to him from Carlisle or a Lancashire one he bought himself — but did most of his reading in pubs and reading rooms. O'Neil's reading matter was mainly local and regional — we can reasonably surmise that in the 1850s he read local weeklies, and from the 1860s onwards he saw regional dailies more often.

The Rev John Thomas Wilson (1837?–1910), vicar of Wrightington near Wigan, was less avid in his newspaper reading, and less radical in his politics. Between 1876 and 1883 his friend John Worsley of Fishergate, Preston, a surgeon-dentist, sent him newspapers, sometimes every day. These included the *Manchester Evening News* (Liberal) and *Manchester Evening Mail* (Conservative), the Tory London *Standard*, the *Graphic* illustrated weekly paper and the *Liverpool Mercury* (Liberal), all of which the vicar appreciated, particularly for their news of the Russo-Turkish War (1877–78).[13] Wilson also bought papers himself, at least when they reported his parish activities, including the *Chorley Guardian*, an unnamed Wigan paper and other local papers.[14] He asked his dentist friend to send a copy of the *Manchester Courier* when it mentioned his parish. Wilson was not local — he was born at Windermere in the Lake District (where his father had been a friend of Wordsworth), and studied

---

12 *Preston Herald* (hereafter *PH*), 14 July 1866.
13 Anne R. Bradford, *Drawn by Friendship: The Art and Wit of the Revd. John Thomas Wilson* (New Barnet: Anne R. Bradford, 1997).
14 Bradford, 22 September 1877; see also 10 January 1879.

at Durham University, although he must have had some attachment to his rural Lancashire parish, staying there for forty-three years.[15] However, this non-native professional middle-class graduate read local and regional newspapers.

Joseph Barlow Brooks (1874–1952) was another working-class reader with radical views. He began work as a half-time weaver in Radcliffe near Bolton, Lancashire, at ten, advancing to cashier in the same mill before entering the Methodist ministry at twenty-one. His autobiography describes a house full of newspapers and magazines in his teenage years and early twenties, during the 1880s and 1890s, when he, his brother and mother bought the *Radcliffe Times* and the *Bury Times* (two local papers); the *Manchester Weekly Times* (a regional news miscellany), the *Cotton Factory Times* (also a news miscellany, known for its dialect writing, aimed at cotton workers), and the *Clarion* (Robert Blatchford's populist socialist weekly, 'crammed full of fearless, vivacious and well-written articles on books, men and things') — all three published in the Manchester area (the *Clarion* moved to London in 1895). In answer to his mother's grumbles about the amount of reading, his brother would say:

> "But mother, th' *Clarion* gives yo' some good stuff. Blatchford's writin's literature, an' Bloggs an' Bounder an' th' others are fine. An' yo' wouldn't miss th' *Cotton Facthery Times* for anythin', especially Professor Spoopendike an' 'is Club!" Sam would argue. It was Professor Spoopendike's request that brother So-and-so should remove his feet from off the stove and allow the heat to circulate round the room that served as a stock joke in the family for several years.[16]

There was also the Liberal, Nonconformist, middle-brow *British Weekly*. All were delivered to their house every Saturday. Brooks bought second-hand copies of the *Review of Reviews* (which 'gave us something of a world outlook') and other weeklies from the Co-op reading room, delivered every quarter for 'a shilling or so'.[17] Local and regional newspapers are highlighted in the memoir of this working-class man, some with a Liberal or socialist slant.

---

15   'Late Vicar of Wrightington', *Wigan Observer*, 3 December 1910, p. 5.

16   Joseph Barlow Brooks, *Lancashire Bred: An Autobiography* (Oxford: Church Army Press, 1951), p. 169.

17   Brooks, pp. 169, 177. This memoir, written in old age, may be slightly innacurate in the details of the publications; the *Radcliffe Times*, for example, was only launched in 1899, by which time Brooks had left home.

Before we examine the readership of each type of newspaper, a word on sources and methods. Evidence of individual readers such as the three men above is rare, but valuable in helping us to tie together the partial evidence of reading on the one hand, and buying on the other. Total sales of any publication tell us little about sales or readership in one place. Sales or availability of particular titles in one shop tell us nothing about sales in another shop, serving a different part of town, or run by a newsagent with opposing politics, nor about postal subscriptions nor distribution through membership organisations such as the co-operative movement or churches; the titles available in public reading places are strongly influenced by the particular locale, clientele and policies of those who control that reading space.

This chapter uses lists of publications available in news rooms and reading rooms (from annual reports and committee minutes), sales figures gathered by investigators during the period, the record of one retail newsagent, oral history interviews with people born in the 1880s and later (conducted in the 1970s and 1980s), marketing claims by newspaper publishers, contemporary comment by writers and journalists, newspaper reports of discussions of newspapers, and other less circular evidence. All are partial and problematic in their own ways, but most tell the same story, of the wide readership of the local paper. Lists of titles in news rooms have been tabulated and classified according to type of publication. I started from the categories of Alvar Ellegard in his ground-breaking 1957 study of mid-Victorian newspaper and periodical readership, but split some of his categories, for example London general weekly newspapers and London Sunday papers, and combined others, such as 'fortnightly/ quarterly reviews' and 'weekly reviews/newspapers of review type'; 'religious quarterly reviews' and 'religious periodicals', and monthly and weekly magazines. I created new categories of trade/business/ technical/scientific magazines, local weekly newspapers, local evening newspapers, regional weekly newspapers and regional morning newspapers.[18] The disputed borderlands between newspaper,

---

18 Henrik Alvar Ellegard, 'The Readership of the Periodical Press in Mid-Victorian Britain', *Göteborgs Universitets Arsskrift*, 63 (1957). Part II was republished as Alvar Ellegard, 'The Readership of the Periodical Press in Mid-Victorian Britain II. Directory', *Victorian Periodicals Newsletter*, 13 (1971), 3–22.

magazine and periodical have been left unmapped in this project of examining the geographical origins of what was read.[19]

The surviving lists are sporadic, and not always recorded in the same way. Some publications were given to public library news rooms by publishers, particularly those promoting minority political and religious views; local publications were also sometimes 'presented' in this way, rather than purchased, but numbers of titles and copies of local papers remained the same regardless of whether they were bought by the news room or presented by the publisher, suggesting that this practice has not distorted the evidence.[20] However, the wide variation between the titles available in different news rooms at different times shows how distinctive reading communities could be, in different places and times — with location more significant than era.

Provincial Preference

A handful of London newspaper titles had always sold more than the hundreds of provincial titles put together, but this situation was reversed in less than a decade after the Newspaper Stamp became an optional postage charge (rather than a compulsory tax) in 1855. In 1854 roughly twice as many London papers were sold as all the English provincial papers put together, according to the government's Stamp Duty returns, with 64.7 million stamps issued to London papers and 25.4 million issued to provincial papers.[21] But by 1864, papers published outside London were outselling London papers, according to figures gathered by Edward Baines, MP and publisher of the *Leeds Mercury* (Table 6.1 below). Baines's rhetorical purpose was to argue that these readers deserved the vote, rather than any comparison between provincial and metropolitan newspaper sales; this, and his information sources, make the figures fairly reliable.

---

19 Laurel Brake, 'Nineteenth-Century Newspaper Press Directories: The National Gallery of the British Press', *Victorian Periodicals Review*, 48 (2016), 569–90 (pp. 578–86), https://doi.org/10.1353/vpr.2015.0055

20 Full lists from public libraries in Preston and Barrow-in-Furness, showing my categories, are available as supplementary online material.

21 Return of Number of Stamps issued at One Penny to Newspapers in United Kingdom, 1854–55 (83), 1854.

Table 6.1. Metropolitan versus provincial newspaper sales, 1864, United Kingdom and Ireland.[22]

London weeklies	2,263,200 per week
Provincial weeklies	3,907,500 per week
London dailies	248,000 per day
Provincial dailies	439,000 per day

Ten years later in Manchester, sales of Manchester newspapers outstripped London titles, according to wholesale newsagent Abel Heywood and author John Nodal. Their figures suggest that the city's own publications (both newspapers and magazines) sold thirty-nine million copies per year in the city and its environs. While no directly comparable figure is given for non-Manchester publications, they sold substantially less, with a total of seventeen million copies per year for cheap weekly papers, higher-class magazines, family magazines, penny miscellanies, shilling magazines, *Chambers's Journal*, *All The Year Round*, children's magazines and penny dreadfuls.[23] No figures are given for London daily papers, but Heywood believed that, despite their increased sales, if the numbers of London papers sold in Manchester in 1851 were doubled or trebled, 'they will not approach the numbers of the London dailies now circulated here, and are a mere nothing compared with the present circulation of the Manchester papers'.[24]

---

22 Edward Baines, *Extension of the Franchise: Speech of Edward Baines on Moving the Second Reading of the Borough Franchise Bill, in the House of Commons, on the 11th May, 1864* (London, 1864), pp. 13, 14. Baines gathered his figures from John Francis, publisher of the Athenaeum, who in turn got them from 'Messrs. Mitchell, publishers of the Newspaper Press Directory, and [...] the principal publishers of periodical and serial literature in London'.

23 John H. Nodal, 'Newspapers and Periodicals: Their Circulation in Manchester, I', *Manchester Literary Club Papers II*, 1876, 33–38; Abel Heywood, 'Newspapers and Periodicals: Their Circulation in Manchester, II', *Manchester Literary Club Papers II*, 1876, 39–58.

24 Heywood, p. 41. See supplementary online material, Table 2, for full interpretation of Nodal and Heywood figures. Margaret Beetham draws the opposite conclusion from these reports: Margaret Beetham, '"Oh! I Do like to Be beside the Seaside!": Lancashire Seaside Publications', *Victorian Periodicals Review*, 42 (2009), 24–36 (p. 24), https://doi.org/10.1353/vpr.0.0060. Oddly, Haslam, in his 1906 surveys of reading in various districts of Manchester, omits the local press, not even mentioning his own paper, the *Manchester City News*. Perhaps they were not part of his project of criticising working-class reading habits: James Haslam, *The Press and the People: An Estimate of Reading in Working-Class Districts, Reprinted from the 'Manchester City News'* (Manchester, 1906).

Newspaper sales are one thing, numbers of readers another, yet both types of evidence agree after 1855. Lists of newspapers taken in news rooms and reading rooms around the country also find a preference for local and regional newspapers rather than London newspapers — even before 1855, suggesting that provincial papers may have had more readers per copy than London papers. Table 6.2 opposite shows the proportions of different types of publication in different news rooms. In every news room, more regional or local papers are available than London papers, suggesting they were more popular. Even in middle-class mercantile rooms like the Liverpool Lyceum, regional and local newspapers were more popular than London papers for most of the last three decades of the century (apart from some years in the 1880s). Fig. 6.2 below summarises the lists of newspapers and magazines from annual reports. These subscription or membership news rooms could only survive financially if they were in tune with members' preferences. The Lincoln Co-op room is the only exception, but even in Co-op reading rooms, it is likely that ideology or an 'improving' mission had to compromise with reader preference. In the Halifax Working Men's Club and two mechanics' institutes (Bury Athenaeum and Preston Institute) magazines outnumbered newspapers, but everywhere else, newspapers were more popular. The growing popularity of magazines can be seen in the two 1898 lists and in the records of the Liverpool Lyceum (Fig. 6.2).

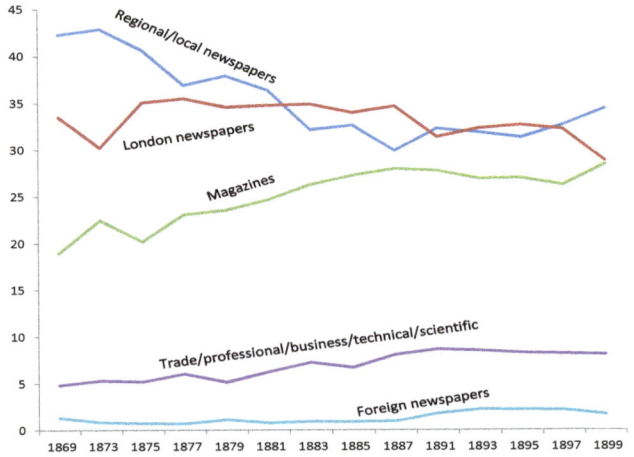

Fig. 6.2. Type of publication as percentage of copies available at Liverpool Lyceum, 1869–99.[25]

---

25   Local satirical magazines have been grouped with local bi/weeklies. The 1871 and 1889 annual reports are missing from Liverpool Archives.

Table 6.2. Type of publication in selected news rooms as percentage of
titles available, 1854–98.[26]

	Regional / local newspaper	London newspaper	Magazine	Trade / professional / business / technical / scientific
1854 Colne Mechanics' Institute	43	21	36	
1856 Liverpool Lyceum	55	25	16	4
1864 Halifax Working Men's Club	19	14	52	14
1868 Preston Exchange Newsroom	33	18	30	18
1869 Preston Institution	14	12	61	12
1870 Darlington Telegraphic Newsroom	53	27	13	7
1874 Preston Exchange Newsroom	39	28	22	11
1870s Newcastle Mechanics' Institute	62	33	5	
1898 Bury Athenaeum	18	12	55	15
1898 Lincoln Industrial Co-operative Society	28	25	37	11
Total	**364**	**215**	**327**	**92**

26   John B. Hood, 'The Origin and Development of the Newsroom and Reading Room from 1650 to Date, with Some Consideration of Their Role in the Social History of the Period' (unpublished FLA dissertation, Library Association, 1978); minutes of Preston Exchange Newsroom, Lancashire Archives, CBP 53/4; annual reports of Insitution for the Diffusion of Knowledge, Livesey Collection, University of Central Lancashire (multiples copies included in figures).

Almost all Preston reading rooms preferred provincial papers to London papers. Magazines were more popular than newspapers in the Institution for the Diffusion of Knowledge (a largely middle-class mechanics' institute which admitted women and men) in the 1850s and 1860s, but local and regional newspapers outnumbered London papers by sixty-two to fifty-one titles. The businessmen of Preston's Exchange Newsroom preferred newspapers to magazines (Table 6.2) and provincial papers to London papers in the late 1860s and early 1870s (one member reported that the uncut pages of the *Athenaeum* showed that it was 'not appreciated' and it was no longer taken in 1874.[27] But the more working-class and mixed-sex readership at the town's free (public) library preferred magazines to newspapers, both general leisure magazines and specialist trade, professional, business, technical and scientific titles (Fig. 6.3). Here again, local and regional newspapers were more popular than London papers. In the Barrow-in-Furness public library reading room in north Lancashire, leisure magazines featuring fiction were also the most popular type of reading material, but again provincial papers were far more popular than London papers (Fig. 6.4).

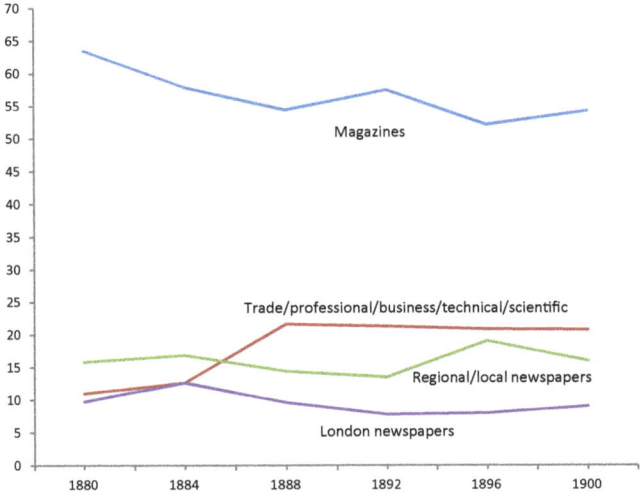

Fig. 6.3. Type of publication in Preston Free Library reading room as percentage of publications available, 1880–1900.

---

27   'Annual meeting of the subscribers to the Exchange Newsroom', *PC*, 19 November 1870.

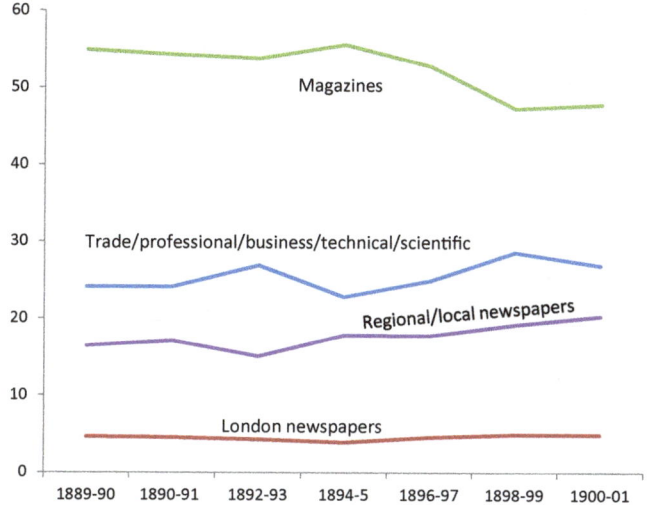

Fig. 6.4. Type of publication in Barrow Free Library reading room as percentage of titles available, 1889/90–1900/01.

Magazines and newspapers took precedence over books in the nineteenth-century public library. Free news rooms were specifically mentioned in the 1850 Public Libraries Act, revealing their importance to the free library ethos, and in Manchester, 'the newsroom was generally more popular than the book rooms by a ratio of two or even three to one'.[28] Newspapers were still central to public libraries in 1902, when Fulham librarian Arnold G. Burt wrote that 'the popularity of a Public Library depends to a very large extent upon its news-room'.[29] News rooms were given separate billing in the title of the standard work *Free Libraries and Newsrooms: Their Formation and Management*, first published in 1869. Its author, John Davies Mullins, head of Birmingham's public library, suggested how to arrange a single-floor library, giving half of the public area to newspapers, the same space as for books and periodicals

28   Alan J. Lee, *The Origins of the Popular Press in England: 1855–1914* (London: Croom Helm, 1976), p. 36; William Robert Credland, *The Manchester Public Free Libraries; a History and Description, and Guide to Their Contents and Use* (Manchester: Public Free Libraries Committee, 1899), p. 216, cited in Michael Powell and Terry Wyke, 'Manchester Men and Manchester Magazines: Publishing. Periodicals in the Provinces in the Nineteenth Century', in *Periodicals and Publishers: The Newspaper and Journal Trade 1740–1914*, ed. by John Hinks, Catherine Armstrong, and Matthew Day (London: British Library and Oak Knoll Press, 2009), p. 2.

29   Arnold G. Burt, 'Newsroom Arrangement', *Library World*, 1902, 256–64 (p. 256).

combined. While newspapers take up more table space, this still shows their importance to public library users.[30] The newspapers, magazines and reference books were public attractions, while the lending library sent its users back to domestic spaces, according to Thomas Wright, the 'Journeyman Engineer':

> The reading of the current newspapers and periodicals is of necessity carried on in the reading-rooms of institutions; but the reading of books, the more standard reading, is for the most part home-work — a labour of love in which each man indulges by his ain fireside.[31]

Three years after Wright's comment, in 1879, Preston's first public library opened in a room in the town hall. The advertisement in Fig. 6.5 does not mention books, suggesting that newspapers and periodicals were the main attraction. In 1892 a visit to some of London's local public libraries still found news rooms well used, and more popular than other parts of the libraries. One small library was operating from 'three or four rooms in an ordinary house, and affording an adequate supply of newspapers and periodicals, but with only a limited store of books.' Newspapers were also foregrounded in Kensington library, and in Hammersmith, where a 'handsome room, pleasantly overlooking lawns and flower-beds, is devoted to newspapers, and is well filled with readers at whatever hour it may be visited.'[32]

The 1879 edition of Mullins's guide to running a public library listed the newspapers that every library news room should offer, beginning with the London dailies: '*Times, Pall Mall Gazette, Daily News, Standard, Daily Telegraph*; and the Local Papers of course [...]' Those two words 'of course' (which often appear in oral history interviews) tell us that the local paper was ubiquitous, almost necessary.[33] And among local papers, the most popular type was the weekly.

---

30   Mullins, frontispiece.
31   Wright, p. 316.
32   'A Day at the London Free Libraries', *All the Year Round*, 7 (1892), 305–9 (pp. 305–6).
33   Mullins, p. 6.

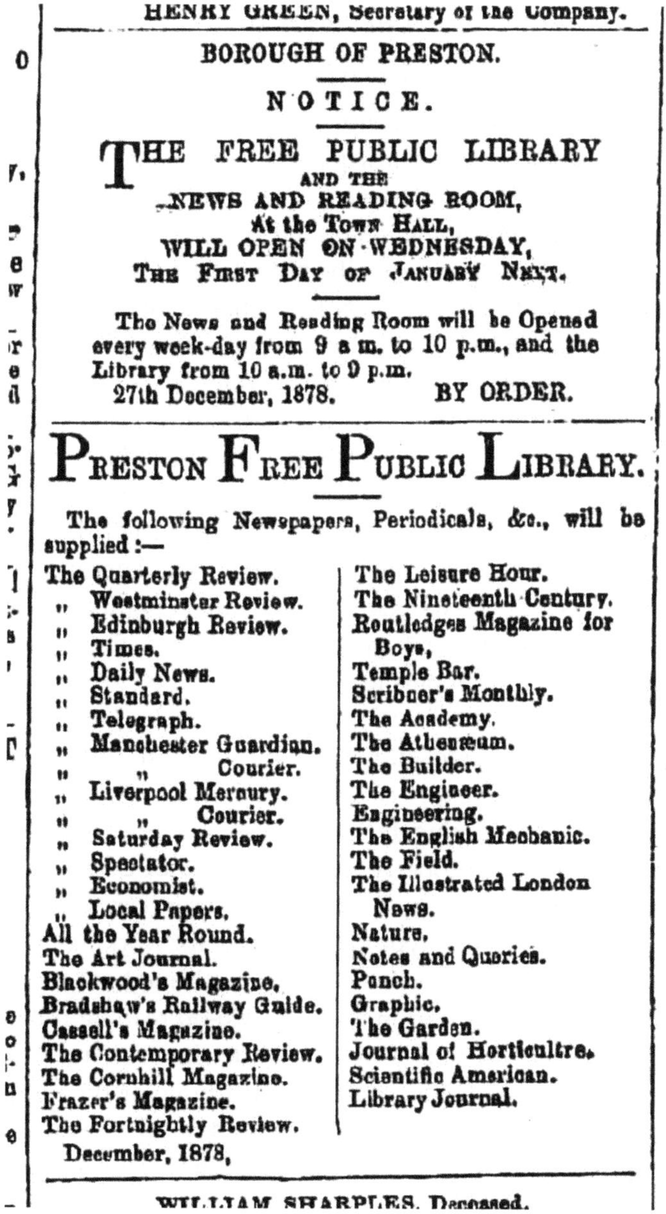

HENRY GREEN, Secretary of the Company.

BOROUGH OF PRESTON.

NOTICE.

THE FREE PUBLIC LIBRARY
AND THE
NEWS AND READING ROOM,
At the Town Hall,
WILL OPEN ON WEDNESDAY,
THE FIRST DAY OF JANUARY NEXT.

The News and Reading Room will be Opened
every week-day from 9 a.m. to 10 p.m., and the
Library from 10 a.m. to 9 p.m.
27th December, 1878.   BY ORDER.

PRESTON FREE PUBLIC LIBRARY.

The following Newspapers, Periodicals, &c., will be
supplied :—

The Quarterly Review.
 „ Westminster Review.
 „ Edinburgh Review.
 „ Times.
 „ Daily News.
 „ Standard.
 „ Telegraph.
 „ Manchester Guardian.
 „   „   Courier.
 „ Liverpool Mercury.
 „   „   Courier.
 „ Saturday Review.
 „ Spectator.
 „ Economist.
 „ Local Papers.
All the Year Round.
The Art Journal.
Blackwood's Magazine.
Bradshaw's Railway Guide.
Cassell's Magazine.
The Contemporary Review.
The Cornhill Magazine.
Frazer's Magazine.
The Fortnightly Review.
  December, 1878,

The Leisure Hour.
The Nineteenth Century.
Routledges Magazine for
  Boys,
Temple Bar.
Scribner's Monthly.
The Academy.
The Athenæum.
The Builder.
The Engineer.
Engineering.
The English Mechanic.
The Field.
The Illustrated London
  News.
Nature,
Notes and Queries.
Punch.
Graphic,
The Garden.
Journal of Horticultre,
Scientific American.
Library Journal.

WILLIAM SHARPLES, Deceased.

Fig. 6.5. Advertisement announcing opening of Preston Free Public Library,
1879 (*PC*, 28 December, 1878, from 19th-Century British Library Newspapers
database). © The British Library Board, all rights reserved.

Local weeklies

'It has been a great mistake [...] to suppose that the daily papers are the papers most interesting to those who are permanently resident in distant local districts,' *Westminster Review* editor and social reformer William Edward Hickson told the 1851 Newspaper Stamp Committee. 'I find even with myself coming to London occasionally only as I do now, that I really take more interest in the "Maidstone Gazette" than I do in the "Times" paper, though I read both.'[34] Hickson was a partial witness who opposed newspaper taxes, but the defence of the local press was not part of his agenda. His point, that working-class readers tended to read local weeklies like the *Maidstone Gazette* more than London dailies like the *Times*, is borne out by other evidence, before and after the abolition of the newspaper taxes. Hickson's comment was made when weeklies and bi-weeklies were the only type of provincial newspaper, but even after the creation of regional dailies and, later in the century, local evening papers, the weekly paper remained popular.

Like the provincial merchants of earlier times, the users of these business-oriented news rooms may have subscribed to one or two local papers at home, but this news room supplied the latest commercial information from scores of different sources — information that was not available in such detail via London papers. This information was found in lists, tables, commentaries, analysis and news reports, but also in advertisements, for property, auctions, sales of cargo, arrivals and departures of ships, and tenders for goods and services.[35] Local weeklies were also the most popular type of newspaper for working-class readers in the public libraries of Preston and Barrow throughout the 1880s and 1890s (Figs. 6.5 and 6.6), and in Lincoln's Co-op reading room in 1898. Lincoln contrasts with Bury's more middle-class Athenaeum reading room, where London dailies were the most popular type of paper. In the working-class Halifax news room in 1864, local weeklies vied with morning newspapers from London and provincial cities, while in the

---

34   Evidence of William Edward Hickson Esq, House of Commons, 'Report from the Select Committee on Newspaper Stamps; Together with the Proceedings of the Committee, Minutes of Evidence, Appendix, and Index 1851 (558) XVII. 1', para. 3201.

35   For the commercial importance of the eighteenth-century provincial press, see Victoria E. M. Gardner, *The Business of News in England, 1760–1820* (Basingstoke: Palgrave, 2016), https://doi.org/10.1057/9781137336392

Table 6.3: Type of newspaper in selected news rooms as percentage of newspapers available, 1854-98.

	London daily	Local bi / weekly	Regional morning	Regional bi / weekly	London weekly	Local evening	London Sunday
1854 Colne Mechanics' Institute	22			67	11		
1856 Liverpool Lyceum	22	57	6	6	6	2	2
1864 Halifax Working Men's Club	29	29	29		14		
1868 Preston Exchange	25	25	36		14		
1869 Preston Institution for the Diffusion of Knowledge	25	20	25	5	25		
1870 Darlington Telegraphic Newsroom	25	33	33		8		
1874 Preston Exchange	31	17	43		9		
1876–79 Newcastle Mechanics' Institute	35	10	40			15	
1898 Bury Athenaeum	26	18	18	15	15	9	
1898 Lincoln Industrial Co-operative Society	24	15	12	15	18	12	6

commercial news room at Darlington in 1870, local weeklies were equal in popularity to provincial morning papers, probably for the same business reasons as in Liverpool in 1856.

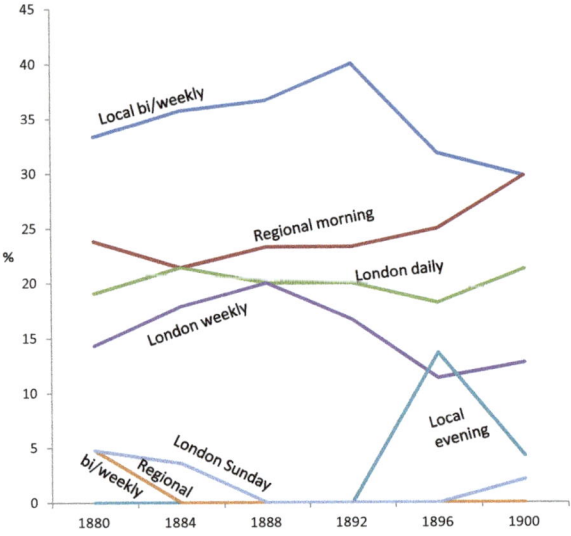

Fig. 6.6. Types of newspaper available in Preston Free Library reading room, 1880–1900, as percentage of all newspapers available in each year.

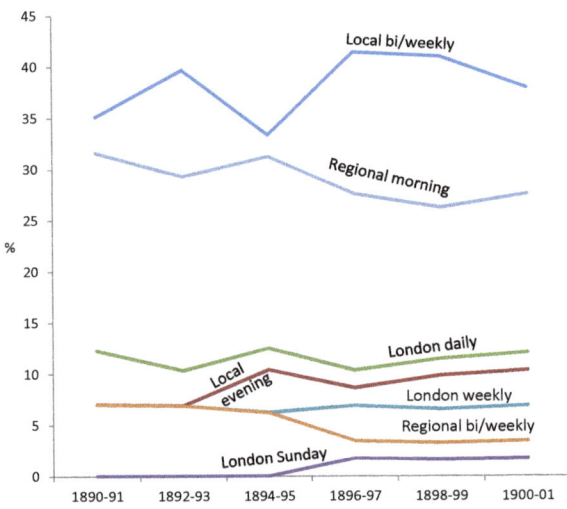

Fig. 6.7. Types of newspaper available in Barrow Free Library, 1888/89–1900/01, as percentage of all newspapers available in each year.

A rare glimpse of a newsagent's weekly newspaper sales in the East Lancashire town of Bacup in 1860 confirms that the local weekly was the most popular type of paper, particularly for working-class readers. No newspaper was published in Bacup in 1860 (1861 Census population 24,000), so residents relied on the 'district news' columns of papers produced in nearby towns. The *Bury Times*, published twelve miles away, provided the best Bacup news service, even though other papers were published in nearer towns, such as Todmorden, Rochdale and Burnley. The *Bury Times* published a list of the weekly newspapers sold the previous Saturday by a Bacup news agent, purportedly in response to a reader's query (Table 6.4 below).[36] This is very partial evidence; its main purpose is to persuade readers that this paper, the *Bury Times*, out-sells its rival, the *Bury Guardian*. This was almost certainly true, but whether the difference in sales (286 copies versus 8 copies in this particular shop) was so extreme is uncertain. The list is partial in other ways, excluding magazines and daily newspapers, and covering only one day. Some weekly papers may have sold more copies on other days of the week, or have been sent by post. However, the titles and quantities sold probably have some basis in fact.[37] The list claims that almost half of all weekly newspaper sales are accounted for by one title, the *Bury Times*, as in the twenty-first century, when the local paper is usually sold from a pile on the counter, whilst less popular papers are displayed on shelves, in smaller numbers. Three quarters of the weekly newspapers sold in this shop are local or regional titles (Table 6.5 below). The list has a Liberal, even Radical flavour, with the only two Conservative titles, the *Bury Guardian* and the *Manchester Courier*, selling in small quantities. It was probably the shop of either Thomas Brown or Thomas Leach, booksellers and newsagents, both of whom were active in Parliamentary reform, and later became publishers in succession of the *Bacup Times*.[38] There were four or five booksellers and 'news-agents'

---

36   *Bury Times*, 24 November 1860, p. 2. See Table 3 in supplementary online material for more information on each title.

37   For more reliable sales records of a newsagent and circulating library in Castlebar, Co. Mayo, see Marie-Louise Legg, *Newspapers and Nationalism: The Irish Provincial Press, 1850–1892* (Dublin: Four Courts Press, 1999), chap. 11.

38   'Reform meeting at Bacup', *Rochdale Observer*, 12 March 1859, p. 3; 'Parliamentary Reform', *Rochdale Observer*, 13 May 1865, p. 6; Mannex *Directory of North & East Lancashire* (1868); Mannex *Directory of North-East Lancashire with Bury and District* (1876).

in Bacup in 1860, and others may have sold more Conservative papers.[39] However, Bacup was a radical town, with a history of Luddism and Chartism, and this is reflected in the list of papers — most notably in the *National Reformer*, a newly launched republican, atheist journal of the National Secular Society, edited by Charles Bradlaugh.

Table 6.4. Weekly newspapers sold by a Bacup newsagent, Saturday 17 November, 1860.

Newspapers	Copies sold
Illustrated London News	1
Illustrated News of the World	1
Liverpool Weekly Mercury	1
Irishman	1
Lloyd's Newspaper	2
Builder	3
Illustrated Times	4
Weekly Times	6
Bell's Life	6
Manchester Weekly Express	6
Todmorden Post	6
Weekly Dial	7
Bury Guardian	8
Manchester Courier	12
Alliance Weekly News	13
Reynolds's Newspaper	14
News of the World	16
Sporting Life	19
Penny Newsman	19
Halifax Courier	24
National Reformer	24
Rochdale Observer	28
Manchester Weekly Times	34
Preston Guardian	45
Bury Times	286

---

39   *Slater's Directory of Manchester, Liverpool and the manufacturing towns of Lancashire* (1858); *Kelly's Post Office Directory of Lancashire* (1864), pt. 1; advertisement for Edward Cockrill, 'news-agent', *Bury Times*, 7 January 1860, p. 1.

When we classify these newspapers geographically (Table 6.5 below), we can see the dominance of the local weekly even more clearly. The top five titles, apart from the *National Reformer*, were all Radical papers which reported favourably on respectable working-class political and cultural activities, and therefore appealed to readers of that bent. The *Bury Times* and the *Rochdale Observer* both cost a penny, while the other three were twopence. The high sales of the second most popular weekly, the *Preston Guardian*, published twenty-eight miles away, confirm its status as a regional newspaper for the whole of North Lancashire. The *Manchester Weekly Times* was more populist and less radical than the Preston paper by 1860. The *Rochdale Observer* was a penny Radical local paper, like the *Bury Times*, but carried less Bacup news even though it was three miles closer. The *Halifax Courier*, published eighteen miles away in Yorkshire, may have been popular with Yorkshire 'immigrants' who had moved to Bacup, and for its news of the woollen trade.

Table 6.5. Type of weekly newspaper sold in Bacup newsagent, 1860.

Type of weekly newspaper	Copies sold
Local	352
Regional	111
London Sunday	81
London, other	38
Trade / professional / business / technical / scientific	3
Total (excluding 1 Irish paper)	585

Multiple copies of the same title, presumably to meet demand, confirm that the local weekly was important to middle-class business readers. Table 6.6 below shows the titles requiring multiple copies in Preston's Exchange Newsroom in 1868 and 1874. The three main Preston papers (*Guardian*, *Herald* and *Chronicle*) were the most popular when the news room opened in October 1868, with three copies each. However, only two copies each of the Preston titles were required in 1874, whilst the number of copies of papers from elsewhere was largely unchanged. This may be because of falling membership. The businessmen who used this room could afford to take one or two papers at home, but to keep abreast of prices, markets, tenders, auctions and other commercial news, they needed to see a wide range of papers. The three Preston weeklies were probably in particular demand on Saturday mornings, as soon as they were published.

Table 6.6. Publications with multiple copies, Exchange Newsroom, Preston, 1868 and 1874.[40]

Publications	1868	1874
Preston Herald	3	2
Preston Guardian	3	2
Preston Chronicle	3	2
Liverpool Courier	2	1
Liverpool Daily Post	2	1
Liverpool Mercury	2	2
Manchester Courier	2	2
Manchester Examiner	2	2
Manchester Guardian	1	3
Daily News	2	2
Daily Telegraph	2	2
Standard	2	2
Times	2	2

Magazines were the most popular *genre*, but at the level of the individual *publication*, it was the local paper. Some economic theory can assist here. In the relatively small Preston periodical market, the choice of local papers was limited by the number of possible purchasers; the local paper as a product had a limited geographical market, and could not easily be traded across markets.[41] The small number of local papers in any one market made each one an 'independent good', which could not be substituted by a similar product. For a national magazine,

---

40   Minutes of Exchange & News Room committee, Lancashire Archives CBP 53/4.

41   Lisa M. George and Joel Waldfogel, 'The *New York Times* and the Market for Local Newspapers', *American Economic Review* 96 (2006), 435–47, https://doi.org/10.1257/000282806776157551

on the other hand, Preston was just one small part of a much bigger national market, with millions more possible purchasers. The larger market supported more competitor titles, creating more consumer choice; this made a national magazine a 'substitute good'. In a Preston reading room, Reader A may want to read the *Family Herald* but Reader B already has it; however, Reader A will probably make do with a substitute title such as the *London Journal*, *Reynolds's Miscellany*, the *Leisure Hour* or *Household Words* (although there is no substitute for the next episode of a serial novel!). But if Reader A wants a local Tory perspective on the local and wider world, there is probably only one substitute title, if that. Multiple copies are perhaps a clue to *intensity* or *quality* of demand, rather than *quantity* of demand. Of course multiple copies in a public reading place tell us nothing about private and family reading behaviour in the home, nor about purchasing behaviour. Paying money for one's favourite newspaper or magazine, for which there is no substitute, is very different from reading in a public place, where one cannot expect to immediately lay hands on a favourite publication.

Local weeklies were the most popular individual titles in the free libraries of Preston and Barrow in the 1880s and 1890s, using numbers of multiple copies as a guide. Preston free library, opened in 1879, had in the order of ten times as many users as other news rooms in the town, and the widest social range of readers, so we can give more weight to this evidence of the reading tastes of the town as a whole. Here, whilst local papers were insignificant as a genre, accounting for around six per cent of serial publications available, they were the most popular individual titles, requiring up to six copies to meet reader demand (Table 6.7 below; single copies of the *Preston Guardian* were presented to the library free 1880–84, and single copies of the *Preston Herald* were given 1882–84, but this does not alter the ranking). In Barrow's free library, the Barrow weeklies and evening paper also required the greatest number of multiple copies (Table 6.8).

Table 6.7. Publications with multiple copies, Preston Free Library, 1880–1900.[42]

Publications	1880	1884	1888	1892	1896	1900
Preston Guardian	2	2	3	3	6	5
Preston Herald	1	2	3	3	5	5
Preston Chronicle	1	1	1	3		
Lancashire Evening Post					4	1
Liverpool Daily Post		1	1	1	2	2
Manchester Guardian	1	1	1	1	2	2
Manchester Evening Mail					2	1
Punch	1	2	2	2	2	2
Illustrated London News	1	2	2	2	2	2
Graphic	1	1	2	2	2	2
Queen	1	1	1		2	2
Lady's Pictorial					2	2

Table 6.8. Publications with multiple copies, Barrow Free Library, 1889/90–1900/01.[43]

Publications	1889–1890	1890–1891	1892–1893	1894–1895	1896–1897	1898–1899	1900–1901
Barrow Herald	3	3	4	1	4	4	4
Barrow News	3	3	3	1	4	4	4
Barrow Journal					2	2	
North Western Daily Mail						3	3

---

42 Preston Free Library annual reports, 1880–1900, Harris Library.

43 Some titles were given free: *Barrow Herald* and *Barrow News* (1890/91 and 1896/97), *Barrow Journal* (1896/97), *Co-operative News* (1890/91), *War Cry* and *Young Soldier* (both Salvation Army publications, 1889/90 and 1894/95), *All The World* (1890), *Liberal Unionist* (1889/90), and *Son of Temperance* (1889/90).
Barrow Library annual reports, Cumbria Archive and Local Studies Centre, Barrow, Ba/L/1/1-1/5.

Manchester Courier	2	2	2	2	2	2	2
Manchester Guardian	2	2	2	2	2	2	2
Liverpool Echo	2	2	1	1	1		
Lancashire Evening Post			1	2	2	1	1
Manchester Examiner	2	2	2				
Fun	2	2	2	2	2	2	2
Graphic	2	2	2	2	2	2	2
Punch	2	2	2	2	2	2	2
Illustrated London News	2	2	2	1	2	2	2
Illustrated Sporting & Dramatic News	2	2	2	2	2		
Judy	2	2		2	2	2	2
Co-operative News	2	2	2	2	2		
All The World	1	2	1	1	1		1
Awake			3	1	1	1	1
Young Soldier	3	3	3	3	3	2	2
War Cry	3	3	3	3	2	2	2
Liberal Unionist	3	3					
Son of Temperance	2	1	1	1			

Many readers had an emotional attachment to the local weekly, more than for other types of paper. A discussion, 'The Blackburn Weeklies: Which is the best general newspaper?' took place over three weeks at the Regent Hotel in Blackburn in August 1888; by comparison, a similar debate, on the local evening papers, lasted only a week. It was standing-room only and 'the debate on the weeklies [...] was declared one of the most popular and interesting subjects ever discussed at the Regent debates.'[44] A Mr Stout argued that 'the public to-day read the evening papers, got all the political news they wanted each night, and as a little interesting refreshment wanted the weekly papers to be journals of literature — social articles and local tales.'[45] Other speakers agreed that this local non-news content marked out their favourite weekly, with a Mr Walton arguing in support of the *Blackburn Weekly Express* that 'its original matter was unequalled in the district'.[46] Similarly, Mr Moorfield said: 'I have always found Lancashire people to be particularly jealous of their folklore and everything creditable to the [county] palatine, ranging from Pendle Hill to Tim Bobbin, and from Edwin Waugh's poems to the ancient milk stone, situate at the boundary of the borough of Rochdale [...] surely the "Local History" to be found in the *Weekly Express* must be most interesting and instructive to the majority of its readers.'[47] In 1950, looking back at the success of the series of south-east Lancashire weeklies published from Bolton from the 1870s onwards, a company history made the same distinction between evening and weekly papers: 'The Tillotson newspapers first secured entrance to the homes of the people by being a complete mirror of local life and events — industrial, religious, political, civic, social, sporting — in a way and to a degree which no evening paper could attempt.'[48]

The local weekly was still the most popular type of newspaper in towns without well-established evening papers, even at the end of the century, although the halfpenny local evening paper was spreading rapidly at this time. We know this from oral history interviews with

---

44 *Blackburn Evening Express*, 25 August 1888; *Blackburn Standard*, 1 September 1888.
45 *Blackburn Standard*, 25 August 1888.
46 *Blackburn Evening Express*, 20 August 1888.
47 *Blackburn Evening Express*, 27 August 1888.
48 Frank Singleton, *Tillotsons, 1850–1950: Centenary of a Family Business* (Bolton: Tillotson, 1950), p. 19.

people born in Barrow, Lancaster and Preston in the 1880s and later, all of whom were asked about reading matter in their childhood homes (Table 6.9 below).[49] Local newspapers were the single most popular reading matter, as a genre and as individual titles, with two-fifths of Preston interviewees (twenty-four out of sixty) recalling a local paper being read at home, a third of Barrow interviewees (twenty-two of sixty-seven) and a quarter of Lancaster interviewees (fourteen of fifty-six). In the early twentieth century, Lancaster was the only one of the three towns not to have its own evening paper (although the Preston-based *Lancashire Evening Post* published a Lancaster edition). Consequently, almost equal numbers of Lancaster interviewees recalled a weekly or an evening paper (seven and six mentions respectively). We can only rely on broader trends in this oral history, rather than detail. The titles of publications mentioned in interviews reveal the chronological vagueness of oral history evidence. Although the tenor of the questioning was about childhood, some interviewees mentioned titles only published in their adulthood (although they may be using later titles to refer to earlier incarnations of papers whose names changed through amalgamations). These responses have been omitted from the analysis, but they show the complexity of what is happening during an oral history interview, and the consequent dangers of mining such material for factual information without 'triangulation' against other sources. It is likely that titles that survived were mentioned more often than those that were no longer published at the time of the interviews. Equally, the questioning reflects twentieth-century assumptions about newspaper reading — that it took place in the home rather than in public reading rooms — and limited knowledge of newspaper genres, for example the now-extinct regional news miscellany. The interview schedule included a question specifically about newspaper-reading, but there was no equivalent question about magazine-reading, which probably explains their under-representation.

---

49   'Social and family life in Preston, 1890–1940', transcripts of recorded interviews, Elizabeth Roberts archive, Lancaster University Library (hereafter *ER*; the letters P, B or L at the end of the interviewee's identifier denotes whether the interviewee was from Preston, Barrow or Lancaster). The transcripts are being digitised, with some available at www.regional-heritage-centre.org

Table 6.9. Working-class periodical reading material in Preston, Barrow and Lancaster, 1880s to 1920s.[50]

Category	Preston	Barrow	Lancaster	
Local evening	19	13	6	
Local weekly	2	8	7	
Local other	2	2	1	
Regional weekly	1	3	1	
Manchester daily	1	5	3	
Manchester Sunday	4	3	6	
London Sunday	6	4	2	
Sunday, unknown	1	1	5	
All Sundays				**32**
Scottish papers	1	4		
London daily	4	8	3	
London weekly	5	6	4	
Comic/children's publication	9	3	6	
Religious	3	4	2	

Evening Newspapers

The huge growth in readership of the local evening newspaper, with its football scores and betting tips, was an unintended result of the high-minded abolition of newspaper taxes, the nationalisation of the telegraphs in favour of the provincial press, and free, compulsory education.[51] By the end of the century, many halfpenny local evenings sold more copies in their town or city alone than the *Times* did across the whole nation. Bourgeois commentators deplored their popularity, but when working-class voices can be heard through the noise of

---

50   Replies mentioning 'Morning newspaper' and 'national newspaper' have been included under London dailies, which probably under-represents Liverpool and Manchester papers. Fuller version in additional online material.

51   David Vincent, *Literacy and Popular Culture: England 1750–1914* (Cambridge: Cambridge University Press, 1989), pp. 194–95, https://doi.org/10.1017/cbo9780511560880

middle-class judgments, they show a strong preference for this type of newspaper — cheap, local and (by the end of the century) in tune with popular working-class culture.

The first provincial halfpenny evening newspaper was probably Liverpool's *The Events* (1855–57), closely followed by the *South Shields Gazette* (although the latter was merely a telegraphic sheet from 1855 until 1864).[52] Other early titles, which survive to this day, included the *Bolton Evening News* (1867–), *Manchester Evening News* (1868–) and the Middlesbrough *Daily Gazette* (1869–). In London, Cassell & Co., keen watchers of the provincial newspaper market, launched the first London halfpenny evening paper, *The Echo*, in 1868. The first editions of these 'evening' papers appeared as early as 11am, with updated editions until early evening (Barrow public library provided three separate editions of the town's evening paper, the *North Western Daily Mail*). They were usually four pages, of smaller dimensions than a morning paper. Before the 1880s, they contained telegraphed national and international news, items reprinted from other provincial papers, local news and adverts, some business news and occasional paragraphs of racing news. Some evening papers of the 1870s and early 1880s, such as the *Aberdeen Evening Express* or the Norwich *Eastern Evening News*, sometimes contained no sport at all. Instead, they were read for the latest news, especially during the Franco-Prussian War (1870–71) and the Russo-Turkish War (1877–78). The Rev Wilson, vicar of Wrightington, thanks his friend for copies of the *Manchester Evening News* and *Manchester Evening Mail* during the Russo-Turkish War and mentions the war news in particular.[53]

In Lancashire, most evening papers were launched in the 1870s, but this newspaper genre came into its own in the 1880s (Table 6.10). Many did not survive, despite the availability of cheap telegraphed news via the Central Press news agency from 1868 and the Press Association from 1870 onwards, and demand for war news. In 1876 Abel Heywood estimated that Manchester's 2 evening newspapers sold a combined 45–50,000 copies each day.[54] This figure probably rose sharply in the 1880s, when developments in sport stimulated — and benefited

---

52   Lee, p. 136.
53   Postcard dated 24 July 1877, in Bradford.
54   Heywood, p. 40.

from — higher sales: more regular racing meetings, and the creation of the Football League, leading to frequent, scheduled sporting events which could be previewed beforehand and reported afterwards.[55] In Blackburn, an early football centre, the *Northern Daily Telegraph* doubled its circulation from 20,000 to 40,000 between 1887 and 1888, with football news a big attraction.[56] In Preston, perhaps less football-mad than Blackburn, the *Lancashire Daily Post* sold less — 38,000 copies per day by 1900.[57]

Table 6.10. Evening newspaper launches in Lancashire, by decade, 1855–98.

	No of evening newspaper launches
1850–59	2
1860–69	5
1870–79	15
1880–89	7
1890–99	4

A halfpenny newspaper covering sport appealed mainly to working-class readers, perhaps particularly to working-class Conservatives.[58] The favourite newspaper among Middlesbrough steel workers in 1905 was the 'local halfpenny evening paper [the *Evening Gazette*], which seems to be in the hands of every man and woman, and almost every child,' according to the social investigator Lady Bell, who interviewed workers employed by her husband.[59] Bell was unlikely to exaggerate the ubiquity of the Liberal *Evening Gazette*, as it had defeated her husband's attempted rival Conservative paper, the *Middlesbrough &*

---

55 Tony Mason, 'All the Winners and the Half-Times', *The Sports Historian*, 13 (1993), 3–13 (p. 4), https://doi.org/10.1080/17460269309446373

56 *Journalist*, 18 March 1887, 16 March 1888, cited in Lee, Table 30, p. 292.

57 Colin Buckley, 'The Search for "a Really Smart Sheet": The Conservative Evening Newspaper Project in Edwardian Manchester', *Manchester Region History Review*, 8 (1994), 21–28 (p. 22).

58 Matthew Roberts, 'Constructing a Tory World-View: Popular Politics and the Conservative Press in Late-Victorian Leeds', *Historical Research*, 79 (2006), 115–43, https://doi.org/10.1111/j.1468-2281.2006.00367.x

59 Florence Eveleen Eleanore Olliffe Bell, *At the Works: A Study of a Manufacturing Town* (Middlesbrough: University of Teesside, 1907/1997), p. 144.

Stockton Sporting Telegraph five years earlier.[60] The evening paper was the only reading matter for many families, Bell believed. Preston's *Lancashire Daily Post* is mentioned more than any other single title in the oral history interviews in Preston, Lancaster and Barrow (nineteen mentions, compared to three for the next most popular title, the *News of the World*), while the most popular genre was the evening paper (thirty-eight mentions, see Table 6, additional online material). The story was the same in the St Helens area in 1904, where 'evening papers are bought largely [...] and it is to be feared that it is in respect to sport that they are most attractive',[61] and in 1880s London, where two evening papers, the *Echo* and the *Evening News*, 'exclusively appeal to and are almost exclusively bought by the man who earns his livelihood by manual toil'.[62] Evening papers begin to appear in the records of reading rooms from the 1870s onwards (Table 6.3 above), particularly in working-class rooms such as Lincoln and Newcastle. Their popularity can be seen in the multiple copies required in the Preston and Barrow public libraries (Tables 6.7 and 6.8). However, while the majority of evening newspaper readers were working-class, these papers also appealed to other readers — they grew as a proportion of the newspapers taken at the middle-class Liverpool Lyceum from two per cent in 1869 to ten per cent in 1899 (Fig. 6.8 below). Liverpool evening papers were in greater demand at the Lyceum than the *Times* by the late 1890s (twelve copies each in 1897 and 1899, compared to ten of the *Times*).

Regional News Miscellanies

The two most popular types of regional newspaper were weekly news miscellanies such as the *Manchester Weekly Times* or the *Liverpool Weekly Mercury*, aimed at working-class readers, and morning newspapers

---

60 Diana Dixon, 'New Town, New Newspapers: The Development of the Newspaper Press in Nineteenth-Century Middlesbrough', in *The Moving Market: Continuity and Change in the Book Trade*, ed. by Peter C. G. Isaac and Barrie McKay (New Castle, DE: Oak Knoll Press, 2001), pp. 107–16 (p. 113).

61 John Garrett Leigh, 'What Do the Masses Read?', *Economic Review*, 4 (1904), 166–77 (p. 176); see also Alexander Paterson, 'Provincial Newspapers', in *Progress of British Newspapers in the Nineteenth Century* (London: Simpkin, Marshall, Hamilton, Kent & Co., 1901), p. 79.

62 Edward G. Salmon, 'What the Working Classes Read', *Nineteenth Century* (July 1886), 108–17.

such as the *Manchester Guardian* and the Liverpool *Daily Post*, aimed at middle-class readers.

Graham Law's superb work has established that the weekly news miscellany was one of the most popular types of newspaper from the 1860s until the First World War.[63] It has received little scholarly attention, apart from Law, probably because it was provincial, is now extinct, and was a newspaper-magazine hybrid rather than a 'serious' political newspaper. This type of paper, described by Leigh in 1904 as 'the weekly edition of daily papers published in large provincial cities', was the most popular in the small town near St Helens (probably Sutton or Thatto Heath) that he surveyed:

> One house in two takes at least one of these weeklies, and a strangely considerable number take two, owing to the curious fact that the man and wife, or the man and his eldest son, are not altogether in accord as to the preferable journal [...] in spite of the existence of Sunday newspapers which add sport of all kinds to their contents, these Saturday weeklies continue to hold their own. Asked to state in a word what is the widest influence on the lives of artisan Lancashire, I should at once reply, "The weekly newspaper."[64]

The Bacup newsagent's list from forty-four years earlier, in 1860, confirms this preference for the Saturday news miscellanies over Sunday papers. The *Manchester Weekly Times* was the third most popular title sold in the Bacup shop, far ahead of London Sundays (early editions available on a Saturday in Lancashire) such as *Lloyd's Weekly Newspaper*, *Reynold's News* and the *News of the World*. As with evening papers, only low numbers of regional news miscellanies appear in the reading room records (one, the *Liverpool Weekly Mercury*, was auctioned at Barrow Working Men's Club in 1870; only one Sunday paper, the *News of the World*, was auctioned that year); it may be that these cheap working-class titles were so ubiquitous in the home that there was little demand for them in public reading rooms, particularly by the end of the century. In the oral history memories from Preston, Barrow and Lancaster, mainly from the early twentieth century, Sunday papers were mentioned more often than regional Saturday miscellanies (five mentions for the miscellanies, thirty-one for Sunday

---

63   Graham Law, *Serializing Fiction in the Victorian Press* (Basingstoke: Palgrave, 2000), p. 32.
64   Leigh, p. 175.

papers, Table 6.9 above). Even here, regional preference was apparent, with Manchester titles such as the *Sunday Chronicle* recalled more often than London Sundays (thirteen to eleven). A Preston man's brief memoir recalls his father 'reading his favourite newspaper, the *Sunday Chronicle*. He loved to read aloud the most telling and eloquent passages of articles by a popular journalist of the period, Robert Blatchford.'[65] The regional miscellanies' rare mentions in the oral history interviews may be because interviewees had forgotten this extinct genre (one man, 'S1P', born in 1900, required two prompts before recalling an example, the *Liverpool Weekly Post*), while a copy of the local evening newspaper, the most common type of publication mentioned, was probably in the room during some of the interviews in the 1970s and 1980s. All the evidence suggests that the regional news miscellany was read mainly by working-class men and women, and was often their only paper. An 1871 appeal to advertisers for the *Liverpool Weekly Mercury* described it as 'the *best medium* [...] for Advertisers wishing to reach a vast number of readers who rarely see a daily newspaper, and who therefore peruse a weekly one all the more thoroughly.'[66]

Morning Newspapers

The regional morning newspaper was invented shortly before the abolition of compulsory newspaper stamp duty in 1855. Some, such as the *Manchester War Telegraph* and the de facto daily publication of the *Manchester Examiner and Times* in 1854, began in response to demand for Crimean War news. Others, such as the Liverpool *Daily Post*, launched as soon as the compulsory stamp duty was abolished in July 1855, making a penny daily an economic possibility. The *Manchester Guardian* went from bi-weekly to daily publication in 1855, the *Liverpool Mercury* in 1858 and the *Leeds Mercury* in 1861. These Liberal papers were followed by Conservative dailies such as the *Liverpool Daily Courier* (1863) and the *Manchester Courier* (1864).

Regional dailies quickly became more popular than London dailies. In 1864 Baines claimed that provincial dailies sold almost twice as many copies as London dailies. In Bradford in 1868, records from a W. H. Smith bookstall show that, as soon as two dailies were launched

---

65   Mr B10P, written account of life in Edwardian Preston, Elizabeth Roberts archive.
66   *Liverpool Mercury*, 3 January 1871, p. 1.

in the city, sales of provincial dailies (including those from Leeds and Manchester) overtook those of London dailies (Table 6.11 below). The *Bradford Daily Telegraph* launched on 16 July, probably causing the rise in provincial sales by September, and the *Bradford Observer* switched from weekly to daily publication on 5 October, leading to the further increase in provincial daily sales in December.

Table 6.11. Average monthly sales of London versus provincial newspapers, W. H. Smith bookstall, Bradford 1868.[67]

	March	June	September	December
London dailies	218	254	218	225
Provincial dailies	213	208	277	345

These papers were more popular than London papers because they contained more regional and local news, they reached the provincial breakfast table four or five hours earlier (until train times improved towards the end of the period), and their news was more recent, thanks to later press times made possible by their shorter distribution journeys. In 1872, an anonymous writer in the *Quarterly Review* explained that

> [r]eaders who can get the *Manchester Guardian*, *Leeds Mercury*, or *Birmingham Post* at eight o'clock in the morning, with all the local news, in addition to everything of interest in the way of general intelligence, are not likely to care much for the *Times* or *Telegraph* at one o'clock in the afternoon.[68]

Most reading rooms provided provincial dailies from their own region only, with occasional exceptions (such as the *Manchester Examiner* taken in the Newcastle Mechanics' Institute), suggesting that they provided something — unique material, perhaps, or a unique regional selection of material — unavailable in other papers.

As more regional dailies launched, their readership increased, largely among the middle classes, as seen in Preston's public reading places. The *Liverpool Daily Post* and the *Manchester Examiner*, two of

---

67 Lucy Brown, *Victorian News and Newspapers* (Oxford: Clarendon Press, 1985), p. 41, Table 2.3.

68 Anon., 'The Modern Newspaper', *British Quarterly Review*, 110 (1872), 348–80 (p. 371).

the first penny provincial morning papers, were staples of the Preston news rooms, alongside the *Manchester Guardian*, the *Liverpool Mercury* and the *Leeds Mercury*. Regional dailies were the most popular type of paper in all but the most exclusive reading places: at the mechanics' institute (the Institution for the Diffusion of Knowledge) they were the most common type of newspaper, more popular than London or even local papers (but less popular than literary and technical magazines). At the Preston businessmen's Exchange and Newsroom, provincial dailies were the most popular type of publication (seven titles in 1868, rising to nine in 1874), and two copies each of three Liverpool dailies (the *Courier*, *Daily Post* and *Mercury*) and two Manchester dailies (the *Courier* and the *Examiner*) were needed to meet demand. By 1874, the *Manchester Guardian* required three copies (one of them the second edition). At the free library, the number of provincial dailies rose from five in 1880 to thirteen in 1900, most of them from Manchester and Liverpool, and always outnumbering the London dailies. Regional dailies were equal in popularity to London dailies in the Halifax Working Men's Club in 1864, and were the most popular type of newspaper in the Darlington Telegraphic Newsroom in 1870 and the Newcastle Mechanics' Institute in the late 1870s.

Working-class people may have read regional morning papers in news rooms, but few bought them. O'Neil's diary mentions reading a daily paper (almost certainly from Manchester) only occasionally in the 1850s, but by the 1870s he read one almost every day, in the Clitheroe Liberal club — but he did not buy a copy. In 1892 the *Newcastle Daily Chronicle* recalled its support for the region's coal miners in the past, when they had 'no spokesman but ourselves outside of their own class', an admission that the newspaper was not a working-class paper. Even by the early twentieth century, Leigh found that near St Helens, 'not one in a hundred of this vast community read a morning paper, even a halfpenny morning.'[69]

At the most exclusive news rooms, the Liverpool Lyceum and Preston's Winckley Club, regional morning papers were less popular for most of the period. At the Lyceum, Liverpool dailies were at their most popular in the 1870s, when they required more multiple copies

---

69 Leigh, p. 176; see also *The Spectator* quoted in 'Prosperous Lancashire', *PC*, 24 October 1891.

than London dailies — the *Mercury*, *Courier* and *Daily Post* all needed a dozen copies each, but the numbers of multiple copies fell by a half by the 1890s. Generally, they were less popular than magazines, London dailies or London weeklies, and declined as a proportion of all publications available at the Lyceum from seventeen per cent in 1869 to ten per cent in 1899. At Preston's Winckley Club, the most significant change in the list of titles auctioned each year was the growth in the number of big-city provincial newspapers, from none in 1851 to five in 1856, after which the number stayed roughly constant. However, these penny provincial dailies supplemented but did not supplant the London dailies at the club.

Gentlemen preferred London dailies to regional dailies. At the Liverpool Lyceum, they accounted for fifteen to twenty per cent of all publications available, more than regional morning papers, which declined from twenty-one per cent of publications in 1869 to less than fourteen per cent in 1899 (Fig. 6.8 below). At Preston's Winckley Club, 'that mystic department of eau de cologne and exclusiveness',[70] they were the single most popular type of publications, increasing from eight to twelve copies in the second half of the century. An upper middle-class preference for London papers can also be seen in the correspondence of the Vicar of Wrightington, who mentions metropolitan titles nine times, compared to four mentions each for regional dailies and local weeklies.[71] By the 1890s, London dailies were preferred in some less exclusive reading places, including the Bury Athenaeum and the Lincoln Co-op reading rooms (Table 6.3 above). In the same decade, London dailies, including the *Daily Mail* and the illustrated *Daily Graphic*, became more popular at the Liverpool Lyceum (Fig. 6.8), possibly because provincial papers such as the Liverpool *Daily Post* and *Manchester Guardian* were slower to adopt the 'New Journalism', preferring to follow the traditional *Times* model.

Old-fashioned or not, the *Times* was the most popular London paper in all reading places except pubs. In smaller rooms such as Colne Mechanic's Institute (1854) and the Darlington Telegraphic Newsroom (1870), only two London titles were taken, the *Times* and the Radical *Daily News*. In medium-sized rooms such as the Preston

---

70   'Stray Notes', *PC*, 13 May 1876, p. 4.
71   Bradford.

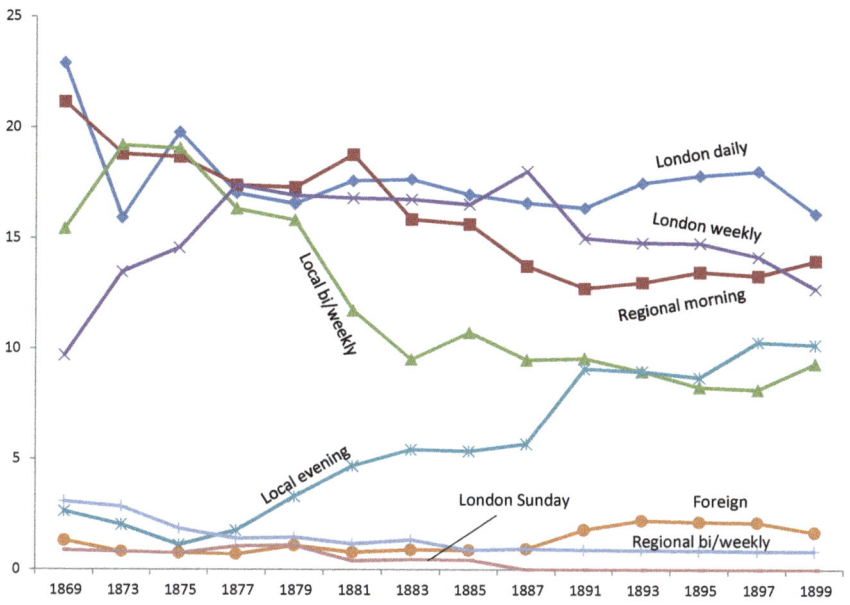

Fig. 6.8. Type of newspaper as proportion of all titles available,
Liverpool Lyceum, 1869–99.[72]

Exchange (1860s–70s) and Newcastle Mechanics' Institute (1870s) these two titles were supplemented by the *Daily Telegraph* and the *Standard* (a morning edition was launched in 1857), and the *Daily Mail* and *Daily Graphic* at the end of the century. Larger, more select news rooms such as the Winckley Club also took the higher-priced, smaller-circulation *Morning Chronicle* and *Morning Herald* (until their closure in 1865 and 1869 respectively), the *Morning Post* and the *Morning Advertiser*. In the Liverpool Lyceum, eighteen copies of the *Times* were needed to meet demand in 1869, falling to ten copies by the 1890s. One might expect members of a club like the Lyceum to have their own copy of the *Times* at home, which raises unanswerable questions about whether members would read the same paper at home and at their club, and the relative importance of the sociable atmosphere of the club and the reading matter. Many news room records remind us of the decentred Victorian newspaper map, on which London papers were not the default — even in the Winckley Club, the 'London *Times*' and the 'London *Daily Mail*' required a place name when recorded in

---

72 The 1871 and 1889 annual reports are missing from Liverpool Archives.

the minutes in 1900, to avoid confusion with provincial papers with similar titles.[73]

The *Times* was less prominent in cross-class reading places such as the public library and the public house. Mullins, in his library management guide, recommended that free libraries should take the *Times, Daily News, Standard, Daily Telegraph* and *Pall Mall Gazette* (the latter, a London evening paper, was available in many news rooms, along with the *Globe* and the *Echo*).[74] Mullins believed that these papers were read by 'tradesmen and persons of small [private] income'[75] in his Birmingham library, probably a similar readership to the Preston and Barrow public libraries. In Preston's public library, London titles were always a minority of the daily papers available, even though they increased from four to ten between 1880 and 1900. No multiple copies of London dailies were required in Preston, nor in Barrow, in contrast to the multiple copies of three Manchester dailies, local weekly papers, evening papers from Barrow, Preston and Liverpool, and London magazines such as the *Illustrated London News, Punch, Judy* and *Fun*. Preston's church and working-class news rooms always took 'the London papers' or included them among the 'leading' and 'best' papers. In the pub, it was the norm for at least one newspaper to be provided by the landlord even in smaller establishments, perhaps the *Morning Advertiser*, organ of the Licensed Victuallers Association ('intensely respectable [...] one of the few newspapers ever seen across the "bar"'), or a sporting paper such as *Bell's Life in London*, while larger commercial hotels advertised the number of titles available.[76] In the working-class home, London dailies hardly featured at all in the memories of oral history interviewees — they are mentioned four times by Preston interviewees, compared to twenty-one mentions of local papers.

---

73   Minutes of AGM, 17 May 1900, Lancashire Archives, DDX 1895.

74   The *Echo* (1868–1905), the first London halfpenny evening paper, deserves more scholarly attention, as an attempt at a popular daily newspaper with national circulation, three decades before the *Daily Mail*. By 1870 it was received in Preston on the day of publication.

75   Mullins, p. 5.

76   Richard Altick, *The English Common Reader: A Social History of the Mass Reading Public, 1800–1900* (Chicago: University of Chicago Press, 1963), pp. 200–01.

Magazines and Specialist Publications

As with newspapers, the number of magazines, specialist publications and reviews taken in public reading places grew enormously. At Preston's Winckley Club, magazines and reviews grew steadily from nine auctioned in 1851 to thirty-one in 1900, with growth particularly in comic, sporting and fiction-related titles. At Preston's free library, magazines and reviews made up around eighty per cent of the serial reading matter between 1880 and 1900. As a genre, London magazines were mentioned nineteen times by Preston oral history interviewees, almost as often as local papers (twenty-one instances), but no title was mentioned more than once. Children's comics and magazines were over-represented, revealing another limitation of these interviews, with their focus on childhood memories. When the Barrow and Lancaster interviews are included, only two individual magazine titles were remembered more than twice — *John Bull*, a conservative general-interest news miscellany, and the *Catholic Fireside*, a religious and general-interest magazine aimed at women and children, including serial fiction, and originally published in Liverpool.

The most popular non-news publications in all public reading rooms were the *Illustrated London News* and *Punch*, with the *Punch* imitators *Judy* and *Fun* close runners-up. In some places, such as the Darlington Telegraphic Newsroom, these were the only titles that were not newspapers (although where there were both news rooms and reading rooms, for newspapers and magazines respectively, records of only one of the two rooms can mislead). These titles were found across the social scale, from Barrow Working Men's Club to Preston's high-class Winckley Club; however, the single copy of the *Illustrated London News* sold in the Bacup newsagent's in 1860 (Table 6.4 above) might suggest that, although such titles were widely read, they were actually purchased only by the middle classes. Working-class readers preferred the *ILN*'s cheaper illustrated rivals, the *Illustrated Times* (four copies sold at the Bacup shop) or the the *Illustrated Police News* (launched in 1864, so not recorded in the Bacup list). Richard Jefferies, writing in 1877, reported that this sensational paper, 'with its cuts of savage murder, or awful explosions, finds its way largely even into the most outlying hamlets.'[77] By the early twentieth century,

---

77　Richard Jefferies, 'The Future of Country Society', *New Quarterly Magazine* (July 1877), 379–409 (p. 399).

newspapers with prize competitions and 'periodicals filled with "snips and snaps"' (probably the *Daily Mail, Answers* and *Tit-Bits*) were very popular in working-class areas of Manchester.[78]

The popularity of particular magazine genres and titles depended on the social class, occupations and gender of the reading room clientele. Public libraries, catering to everyone, supplied everything (so their records are therefore less revealing of individual reading behaviour). Shilling monthly magazines containing fiction, particularly *Macmillan's Magazine, Cornhill* and *Temple Bar*, were available at mixed-gender middle-class institutions such as mechanics' institutes, public libraries (mixed gender and mixed social class) and at exclusive gentlemen's clubs. Dickens's light and improving magazines and similar publications were popular with working-class readers such as the members of Preston's Central Working Men's Club, where *Once a Week* 'and other good and healthy periodicals' were available in 1864.[79] In 1892 *All The Year Round* reported that 'those who have been at work all day wade patiently through the monthly magazines and illustrated papers' at an unnamed London public library.[80] *Chambers's Journal* and *Cassell's Magazine* were the most popular penny weeklies containing fiction; *Chambers's* had wide appeal, from male and mixed working-class rooms to the superior, men-only Liverpool Lyceum; *Cassell's* appealed to working-class men and middle-class men and women, but not to the upper middle-class men of the Liverpool Lyceum and Preston's Winckley Club (the Winckley Club had no penny weeklies at all). Temperance magazines and newspapers were widely available (in the public libraries of Preston and Barrow, in Barrow Working Men's Club and in Halifax and Preston mechanics' institutes), although some were supplied free.[81] The most popular were the *Alliance News* and the beautifully illustrated *British Workman*. Even in the more sophisticated Liverpool Lyceum, one temperance title, the *Alliance News*, was available in the 1870s (not a single temperance publication was available in the

---

78   James Haslam, 'What Harpurhey Reads', *Manchester City News*, July 7 (1906).

79   'Travels In Search Of Recreation II, Central Working Men's Club', *PC*, 20 February 1864.

80   'A Day at the London Free Libraries'.

81   Annemarie McAllister, 'Temperance Periodicals', in *The Routledge Handbook to Nineteenth-Century British Periodicals and Newspapers*, ed. by Andrew King, Alexis Easley, and John Morton (London: Routledge, 2016), pp. 342–54.

rakish Winckley Club). Literary reviews were available in all but the working-class rooms, although some working men read them at the public library; about a dozen were observed taking 'a hurried glance at the monthly reviews' in a branch library near St Helens, their only use of the library.[82]

Public libraries supplied more women's titles, and more specialist and technical publications, than other public reading places (in fact, more of everything). In 1880 Preston library stocked one women's magazine, by 1900 there were twelve. The most popular titles aimed exclusively at women were the *Lady's Pictorial* (taken in the working-class Lincoln Co-op and middle-class Bury Athenaeum, as well as the Barrow and Preston public libraries), *Gentlewoman* (Bury Athenaeum and the two public libraries) and *Queen* (Bury Athenaeum, Lincoln Co-op and Preston library). Two feminist titles, the *Woman's Signal* and the *Women's Suffrage Journal*, were available in Preston and Barrow public libraries. Exclusive news rooms offered some professional, scientific and technical titles, as did working-class news rooms (with fewer professional publications), but the widest selection was available in the public libraries, differentiated to suit local trades and industries. In Preston library, business titles grew from one to eight and scientific and technical publications from five to twenty.

Sporting newspapers were most popular in upper-class news rooms, less so in working-class rooms and hardly at all in improving middle-class rooms such as mechanic's institutes. One of the oldest established sporting papers, *Bell's Life in London*, was available from the 1860s at the upper-class Liverpool Lyceum and Preston's Winckley Club; in 1870 *Sporting Life* was available at Barrow Working Men's Club. Other sporting titles at the two exclusive clubs were the *Illustrated Sporting and Dramatic News*, *The Field*, *Land and Water*, *Country Life*, *Fishing Gazette* and the *Sportsman* (the latter was the only sports title in a mechanic's institute, Newcastle, in the late 1870s). Organised sport and the sporting press grew in tandem from the 1870s onwards, so that by 1898 the middle-class Bury Athenaeum took the daily *Sporting Chronicle* and the weekly *Athletic News* (the leading football paper, and both published by Hulton in Manchester), the *Wheeler*, the *Cyclist* and *Sports*. In contrast, Lincoln's working-class Co-op reading room supplied no sports papers at all in

---

82   Leigh, p. 169.

1898. This must have been a policy decision because readership surveys at the turn of the twentieth century bemoaned the popularity of sporting papers (but without naming the titles, annoyingly). In Middlesbrough, Bell estimated that about a quarter of the foundry workers read nothing but a sporting paper ('that hardly comes under the head of reading'), but in the St Helens area Leigh reported that 'Easily first comes the sporting paper [...] On one evening weekly football claims attention, but day by day throughout the year [horse] racing is dominant [...] The only daily paper which is at all widely read is the sporting daily.'[83] He could be referring to the *Sporting Chronicle*, the *Sporting Life* or the *Sportsman*, or the racing 'tissues', flimsy sheets of results and tips. Racing papers were popular in Salford and working-class areas of Manchester, according to Haslam in 1906.[84]

Who Read Which Section?

The question 'who read what?' can be asked at the level of publication genre and individual titles, but also within each publication — 'marriages for the maids, christenings for married ladies, deaths for undertakers, accidents for doctors, trials for lawyers, cutting-up for butchers, and amusements for every body', as one wag put it in 1829.[85] But there is some truth in this — the mother of Preston oral history interviewee Mr G2P (b. 1903) would 'occasionally [...] go through the deaths', the mother of Mrs C2B (b. 1887) 'had [the *North Western Evening Mail*] to see who was dead and born' and in the interwar years of the twentieth century the husband of Mrs W1P (b. 1899) 'used to have the [*Lancashire Evening*] *Post* and he would give me my column, the Deaths column.' Clitheroe weaver and news addict John O'Neil liked to read about foreign diplomatic news, wars and battles; he was interested in Parliamentary news if it concerned working people, in market prices, and news of emigration prospects, such as accounts of the Australian goldfields.[86]

Sensational news was popular with all classes. In 1877 Richard Jefferies (a Tory) claimed that the farm labourer enjoyed three types

---

83   Bell, p. 145; Leigh, pp. 171, 176.
84   Haslam, *Press and the People*.
85   'The Newspaper Club', *Sheffield Independent*, 23 May 1829.
86   O'Neil diaries, Saturday 17 May 1856, Sunday 3 July 1859.

of article in particular: 'First, the most sensational topics of the week, as murders, fires, startling discoveries in California. Secondly, local intelligence, village gossip from places he knows. Thirdly, leaders, or articles of a somewhat violent character attacking the powers that be [...]'[87] At the other end of the social scale, the leading article was less popular; a doctor at a fictional gentlemen's club in 1829 offers to read the paper aloud to other members warning that 'I never read anything but accidents and offences; one good accident is worth twenty leading articles.' Betting men (and some betting women) turned to the racing columns. In public libraries at the end of the century this became controversial, and some libraries blacked out those parts of the paper.[88] William Bramwell, Preston's chief librarian from 1879 to 1916, was against such censorship. In a newspaper interview, he described how betting men

> used to crowd round the [newspaper] stands to the exclusion of other people. Then they got to talking as well. The way to meet that thing was not to black out the sporting items, which I think is a most abominable, a most un-English thing to do. Well, when it reaches the point I have just indicated they have either to cease altogether or go out. They choose the former, and there I consider my jurisdiction ended.[89]

Adverts, especially small ads, were probably as popular as editorial, with different types of reader interested in different types of ad. The *All The Year Round* writer noted that some of the first newspaper readers of the day at a London branch library in 1892 were youths, young men and young women, looking at the 'situations vacant' columns.[90] Some adverts, however, were read less willingly. The fictional doctor at the club begins to read aloud from the accidents column:

---

87   Jefferies, p. 399.

88   Robert Snape, *Leisure and the Rise of the Public Library* (London: Library Association, 1995), p. 24. The practice was adopted by Stockton Town Council, for example, in 1895, despite objections that 'Stock Exchange gambling was as pernicious as turf betting, and Exchange quotations should also be obliterated': 'The "Blacking-Out" Question At Stockton', *The Journalist*, 8 June 1895, p. 190.

89   William Bramwell, *Reminiscences of a Public Librarian, a Retrospective View* (Preston: Ambler, 1916), p. 18. But six years after Bramwell's retirement, the free library committee agreed to 'expunge racing news', a practice that continued until the1950s: John Convey, *The Harris Free Public Library and Museum, Preston 1893–1993* (Preston: Lancashire County Books, 1993).

90   'A Day at the London Free Libraries', p. 305.

"During the dreadful storm, last Thursday, a lamplighter, lighting one of the gas lamps on Holborn-hill, was blown off his ladder and carried to the amazing distance of Hatton-garden. He fell at the door of No. 60, where Macassar Oil continues to be sold." — Throwing down the paper in a passion. "Pshaw! A puff — a vile puff — of all things I hate a puff — I was never taken in so before, and never, never, will again."[91]

Class and Gender

Each reader and listener had their own preferences for genre, title and type of content. But it is still possible to generalise about preferred newspapers and magazines, according to the demographic variables of class and gender. Working-class readers preferred publications specifically targeted at them, such as halfpenny evening newspapers and regional news miscellanies. Local weeklies varied in their appeal to working-class readers — the *Ulverston Advertiser* of the 1860s prided itself on appealing to 'the nobility and landed gentry, the professional gentlemen, the yeomen, the tradesmen, and the farmers', in contrast to the greater working-class appeal of the rival *Ulverston Mirror*.[92] In the next town, Barrow, the *Barrow Pilot* probably had a more working-class readership, as it had the most advertisements for domestic service of the town's three weeklies; in contrast, the *Barrow Times* had most of the ads for foremen and managerial jobs.[93] Class differences in readership were partly related to the topics covered in the paper, the editorial attitude to working-class readers and its related political stance. However, the political views of readers were related to, but not entirely determined by, their social class. While the titles available in news rooms differed according to the class of the clientele, individual readers had their own preferences. One former paper boy from Whitehaven recalled

that at one house of call where the master was a Conservative, he was ordered to leave 'The Pacquet'. Invariably, his wife asked to see THE WHITEHAVEN NEWS [Liberal] and, to keep the waiting boy quiet while she enjoyed herself for twenty minutes or more, she gave him what

---

91   'The Newspaper Club', *Sheffield Independent*, 23 May 1829, p. 2.
92   Peter J. Lucas, 'The First Furness Newspapers: The History of the Furness Press from 1846 to c.1880' (unpublished M.Litt, University of Lancaster, 1971), p. 244.
93   Lucas, p. 254.

he describes as two thick rounds of home-made bread with a generous amount of treacle.[94]

In 1896, comfortably-off retired newspaper editor William Livesey was a Unionist, while his nephew, a Mr Lee, the owner of a Wakefield worsted mill, of a similar social class, was a Radical. Livesey chose different newspapers to bond with his friend Hewitson and his nephew across political divides. When Livesey arrived at Hewitson's Conservative *Wakefield Herald* office 'he carried in his hand the Liverpool Courier (Conservative) and when he went out to his Radical nephew's he put down this paper and took the Leeds Mercury (Radical) in his hand.'[95]

When readers bought their newspapers rather than reading them in a news room, poorer buyers naturally favoured cheaper newspapers. After cover prices fell when Stamp Duty was reduced to a penny in 1836, sales of stamped newspapers rose from thirty-five million in 1835 to forty-eight million in 1837.[96] In Liverpool, James Whitty saw sales of his *Liverpool Journal* rise from 2,700 to 10,000 per week when he reduced the price to 3d in 1846.[97] Conversely, in 1853, when the Inland Revenue forced William Woods Mitchell to double the price of his fortnightly local papers in West Sussex from a penny to 2d, it had a 'catastrophic' effect, reducing sales by ninety per cent in some places.[98] In 1893 the *Preston Guardian* reduced its price to a penny, in search of new, less well-off readers, explaining that 'the time has come when the area of the constituency may be enlarged, and an appeal made for support to those popular forces which are outside the sphere of higher-priced papers.'[99] Manchester wholesale newsagent Abel Heywood told the 1851 Newspaper Stamp Committee that he sold 4,000 copies of the *Weekly Times* and 3,500 copies of the *News of the World* (both 3d) because, for

---

94   J. R. Williams, *The Whitehaven News Centenary 1852–1952: An Outline of 100 Years* (Whitehaven: Whitehaven News, 1952).

95   Diary of Anthony Hewitson, 23 June 1896, Lancashire Archives, DP512/1.

96   Patricia Hollis, *The Pauper Press: A Study in Working-Class Radicalism of the 1830's* (London: Oxford University Press, 1970), pp. 145–46.

97   Evidence of Michael James Whitty, minutes 574–84, 1851 Newspaper Stamp Committee.

98   William Woods Mitchell, *The Newspaper Stamp and Its Anomalies Practically Considered: A Letter Addressed to the Right Hon. the Chancellor of the Exchequer*, [W. E. Gladstone] (Mitchell, 1854), cited in Martin Hewitt, *The Dawn of the Cheap Press in Victorian Britain: The End of the 'Taxes on Knowledge', 1849–1869* (London: Bloomsbury Academic, 2014), p. xi.

99   *Preston Guardian*, 7 January 1893.

working men, he believed, 'it is not a matter of politics with them, but a question of price; they take it because it is cheap.'[100] Edward Salmon made the same point in 1886, in his survey of working-class reading, arguing that manual workers chose London evening newspapers the *Echo* and the *Evening News* for their readability rather than their politics.[101] These papers pioneered a simpler, more lively writing style with shorter sentences, shorter paragraphs and shorter articles, associated with the New Journalism (something the *Preston Guardian* promised when it cut its price to a penny).

The three readers profiled at the beginning of this chapter, a weaver, a vicar and a cotton mill clerk, were all men, highlighting the importance of gender in who read what. Men seemed to prefer newspapers, women magazines. Men were twice as likely as women to read local evening papers, according to the oral history interviewees (Table 6.12 below), possibly because they contained substantial amounts of political news and sport, particularly football and betting news. Mrs H3L of Lancaster (b. 1903), referring to the *Lancashire Daily Post*, saw the evening paper as typically male reading matter: 'my dad had a daily paper like every other man'. Men were also more likely to read Sunday papers, possibly because of sport again and also their day of publication, when working-class women were doing housework or attending church. Instead, women preferred magazines, as seen in the greater numbers of magazines in mixed reading rooms than in men-only rooms. Observational surveys found ladies looking at fashion magazines and articles in a London branch library in 1892, while in newsagents' shops in Harpurhey, Manchester in 1906, James Haslam found that 'numerous penny "fashion" periodicals have an excellent turnover. They are bought by women and girls, by wives and widows, and female employés in factories, city warehouses, offices and shops'.[102] Women also preferred religious reading — in Preston, Barrow and Lancaster, seven oral history interviewees remembered mothers reading religious magazines and papers, but none remembered fathers reading such material.[103]

---

100 Evidence of Abel Heywood, minute 2551, 1851 Newspaper Stamp Committee.
101 Salmon, p. 110.
102 'A Day at the London Free Libraries', p. 305; Haslam, 'What Harpurhey Reads'.
103 Anglican parish magazines were read mainly by women: Jane Platt, *Subscribing to Faith? The Anglican Parish Magazine 1859–1929* (Basingstoke: Palgrave Macmillan, 2015), p. 135, https://doi.org/10.1057/9781137362445

Table 6.12. Reading preference by gender at the turn of the twentieth century in Preston, Lancaster and Barrow-in-Furness.[104]

Reading preference	Men	Women
Local evening	22	9
Local weekly	3	3
Local other	1	1
Regional news miscellany	5	2
Regional daily	4	2
Regional Sunday	6	1
London Sunday	11	3
Other Sunday	2	1
London daily	12	5
London magazine	5	3
Women's magazine	0	2
Religious magazine/newspaper	0	7
Total	**71**	**39**

Conclusions

Everyone read magazines, and just about everyone read the local paper. For most readers, the local weekly newspaper was the most popular type of paper in the second half of the nineteenth century, particularly working-class readers. Individual readers such as John O'Neil, Joseph Barlow Brooks and the parents of the oral history interviewees preferred it, and no other genre required so many multiple copies to meet reader demand in news rooms and public libraries (at the level of individual titles, only the *Times* required more copies than individual local newspapers in one upper-class news room in Liverpool). Local papers topped the sales figures in a Bacup newsagent's shop, in Manchester and Bradford, supporting Baines's national figures. This evidence corroborates other sources for the importance of the provincial press, such as Reuters' decision to contract exclusively with the provincial press through the Press Association, and the Census figures showing a greater number of reporters and printers in the provinces than in London.

---

104 Note: Instances where reader's gender is ambiguous have been omitted. Source: Elizabeth Roberts archive.

Decade by decade, there was more of everything. But within that overall trend other patterns can be discerned: in the 1850s, penny magazines outsold highly taxed newspapers, and London papers outsold provincial papers by more than two to one. But news room evidence suggests that readership of newspapers, especially provincial papers, may have been closer to magazine readership than the sales figures suggest. Abolition of the compulsory newspaper tax in 1855 began the era of the hugely popular cheap provincial newspaper, as seen in the sales figures of the Bacup newsagent in 1860. By 1864, according to Baines's figures, they had comfortably overtaken the sales of London papers. The 1870s was probably the high point of the local press relative to magazines, as both increased in number of titles and total sales and readership; London papers grew, too, but there was no explosion in new titles, and sales increased at a slower pace than in the provinces. In the 1880s and 1890s new popular magazines and magazine-style content, particularly in London papers, began to threaten the dominance of the local newspaper, but it continued to be the most popular type of paper, particularly with working-class readers, into the 1930s.

Working-class people had always read or heard the local newspaper, but before mid-century this must have felt like eavesdropping rather than being part of a conversation. With the exception of the radical press, most newspapers spoke to middle-class readers, and working-class people were discussed in the third person. But increasingly, they moved from being addressed as 'them' to 'you' and even 'us', as traditional papers tried to address their concerns and interests, and new genres such as the weekend news-miscellany and the halfpenny evening paper were created for them. The presence of the halfpenny evening paper in the homes of so many working-class oral history interviewees by the early twentieth century shows the significance of this relatively new genre in bringing the price of a newspaper within reach of most families, thereby turning working-class readers into purchasers, and making the practice of newspaper reading a domestic habit for them too, as was already the case in middle-class homes.

Some of these conclusions could be reached by studying only the implied reader, addressed in the text of the newspaper. But flesh-and-blood historical readers are so much more complex and interesting than ghostly implied ones. Historical readers were promiscuous readers, hearers of texts read aloud, non-contemporaneous readers consulting a second-hand copy or a bound volume, and public readers, sitting or standing in a room where news and comment was being discussed, often by readers with opposing views. Implied readers are found only in the text of a single publication, whilst historical readers can be found reading more than one publication, they can tell us about preferences between titles and genres (particularly the relationship between reading newspapers and magazines), and about preferences for particular types of article or advert within a single publication. Implied readers can tell us about broad preferences according to gender and class, but the historical reader complicates and sophisticates these generalisations. Gender and class demarcated reading communities, interpretive communities, and local public spheres, in the physical communities of each reading place, and in the choice of reading matter. Yet the local paper was read by members of all classes, and by both genders, particularly the local weekly. The only other publications to have such wide appeal were the *Illustrated London News* and *Punch*. Why was the local newspaper so popular? The next chapter suggests that its promotion of local identity is part of the answer.

7. Exploiting a Sense of Place

Local newspapers, like the brewers Bass (Fig. 7.1 overleaf), used local identity or sense of place to sell their product. Beer was central to the local identity of Burton, which at one time brewed a quarter of all beer sold in Britain. Bass also thought that the local press was an important carrier of local identity, and therefore put a copy of the *Burton Daily Mail* (est. 1898) behind their beer, to proclaim its 'Burton-ness'. Similarly, the painter Walter Langley sometimes used particular local newspapers as props in his realist paintings of life in Cornish fishing villages, to proclaim the specificity of his subject. In 'When the boats are away' (Fig. 7.2), the old fisherman is reading aloud from *The Cornishman* (est. 1878), whose front page in 1903 consisted mainly of classified advertisements.

This chapter examines the techniques used to exploit such attachments to place, what Appadurai calls 'the production of locality as a structure of feeling'.[1] More broadly, it describes how the local press was woven into the fabric of cultural life in a provincial town, as a mirror, magnifier and maker of local culture. Although this has been acknowledged by many historians, the processes and techniques employed have not been studied in detail, especially in one location.[2] Newspapers did more than report their localities, they became part of the loop of making and

---

1   Arjun Appadurai, *Modernity At Large: Cultural Dimensions of Globalization* (Minneapolis: University of Minnesota Press, 1996), p. 181.

2   Jeffrey Hill, 'Rite of Spring: Cup Finals and Community in the North of England', in *Sport and Identity in the North of England*, ed. by Jeffrey Hill and Jack Williams (Keele: Keele University Press, 1996), pp. 85–111 (p. 86); William Donaldson, *Popular Literature in Victorian Scotland: Language, Fiction, and the Press* (Aberdeen: Aberdeen University Press, 1986), p. ix; J. Barry, 'The Press and the Politics of Culture in Bristol 1660–1775', in *Culture, Politics, and Society in Britain, 1660–1800*, ed. by Jeremy Black and Jeremy Gregory (Manchester: Manchester University Press, 1991), p. 49.

      https://doi.org/10.11647/OBP.0152.07

Fig. 7.1. The *Burton Daily Mail* is used to express local identity in a Bass advertising card, 1909. Author's copy, CC BY 4.0.

Fig. 7.2. The title of *The Cornishman* adds realism and specificity to Walter Langley's painting 'When the Boats are Away' (1903). Image courtesy of the Art Renewal Center, www.artrenewal.org, all rights reserved.

re-making culture, giving them the status of a local institution — as in the postcard — part of the events and processes they reported, both arena and actor.[3] They selectively promoted or 'framed' certain aspects while ignoring others, and occasionally intervened directly and self-consciously in local culture, initiating events and movements.[4]

It is argued here that local identity guided the selection, interpretation and presentation of much of the content of the local press, including non-local content. First, the concept of local identity is shown to be both complex and dynamic. We have seen that Preston news and advertising, and news from other parts of Lancashire, dominated the content of Preston's newspapers (Fig. 6.7). This chapter analyses the nature of some of that local content and the techniques used by the local press to promote and sustain local identity. Finally, the contested nature of local identity is acknowledged, and the theory that 'othering' is central to identity formation is questioned, in relation to the local press.

The idea that local newspapers *influenced* local identity was the starting point for this research. It is propounded by journalists and accepted by historians. *Manchester Guardian* editor C. P. Scott wrote: 'A newspaper [...] is much more than a business; it is an institution; it reflects and it influences the life of a whole community.'[5] Broadcaster Andrew Marr, a former newspaper journalist, claimed: 'Anyone who has lived without a local paper quickly comes to realise how important they are; a community which has no printed mirror of itself begins to disintegrate.'[6] Historian Jeff Hill is equally eloquent:

> The press is not simply a passive reflector of local life and thought but an active source in the creation of local feeling. And in reading press

---

3   Jostein Gripsrud, *Understanding Media Culture* (London: Arnold, 2002), p. 232, https://doi.org/10.24926/8668.2601

4   Robert M. Entman, 'Framing: Toward Clarification of a Fractured Paradigm', *Journal of Communication*, 43 (1993), 51–58 (p. 52), https://doi.org/10.1111/j.1460-2466.1993.tb01304.x

5   C. P. Scott, 'A Hundred Years', *Manchester Guardian*, 5 May 1921.

6   Andrew Marr, *My Trade: A Short History of British Journalism* (London: Macmillan, 2004), pp. 44–45; see also William Harvey Cox and David R. Morgan, *City Politics and the Press: Journalists and the Governing of Merseyside* (Cambridge: Cambridge University Press, 1973), p. 1; Daniel J. Monti, *The American City: A Social and Cultural History* (Malden, MA: Blackwell, 1999), p. 5; F. K. Gardiner, 'Provincial Morning Newspapers', in *The Kemsley Manual of Journalism* (London: Cassell, 1952), pp. 204–5.

accounts of themselves and their community the people who buy the newspapers become accomplices in the perpetuation of these legends. To paraphrase a famous observation by Clifford Geertz, the local press is one of the principal agencies for "telling ourselves stories about ourselves".[7]

Peter Fritzsche, in his study of Berlin's local press at the beginning of the twentieth century, argues that 'the city as place and the city as text defined each other in mutually constitutive ways.'[8] But by what techniques and processes would a newspaper change the way that readers thought about themselves and their place? And what historical evidence could be adduced to test this idea?

---

7   Hill, p. 86; see also Clifford Geertz, *Available Light: Anthropological Reflections on Philosophical Topics* (Princeton: Princeton University Press, 2000), p. 193, https://doi.org/10.1515/9781400823406; Aled Gruffydd Jones, 'The 19th Century Media and Welsh Identity', in *Nineteenth-Century Media and the Construction of Identities*, ed. by Laurel Brake, Bill Bell, and David Finkelstein (Basingstoke: Palgrave, 2000), pp. 322–23; John Duncan Marshall, 'Review Article: Northern Identities', *Journal of Regional and Local Studies*, 21 (2000), 40–48 (p. 41); Brad Beaven, 'The Provincial Press, Civic Ceremony and the Citizen-Soldier During the Boer War, 1899–1902: A Study of Local Patriotism', *Journal of Imperial and Commonwealth History*, 37 (2009), 207–28 (p. 212), https://doi.org/10.1080/03086530903010350; Michael Bromley and Nick Hayes, 'Campaigner, Watchdog or Municipal Lackey? Reflections on the Inter-War Provincial Press, Local Identity and Civic Welfarism', *Media History*, 8 (2002), 197–212, https://doi.org/10.1080/1368880022000030559

8   Peter Fritzsche, *Reading Berlin 1900* (London: Harvard University Press, 1996), p. 1; David McKitterick, 'Introduction', in *The Cambridge History of the Book in Britain, Volume 6, 1830–1914*, ed. by David McKitterick (Cambridge: Cambridge University Press, 2009), p. 12, https://doi.org/10.1017/chol9780521866248.002; Peter Clark, 'Introduction', in *The Transformation of English Provincial Towns, 1600–1800*, ed. by Peter Clark (London: Hutchinson, 1984), p. 45; David Eastwood, *Government and Community in the English Provinces, 1700–1870* (Basingstoke: Macmillan, 1997), p. 73; Donald Read, *The English Provinces, 1760–1960: A Study in Influence* (London: Edward Arnold, 1964), p. 250; Michael Wolff and Celina Fox, 'Pictures from the Magazines', in *The Victorian City: Images and Reality, Vol. 2*, ed. by H. J. Dyos and Michael Wolff (London: Routledge and Kegan Paul, 1973), p. 559; Margaret Beetham, 'Ben Brierley's Journal', *Manchester Region History Review*, 17 (2006), 73–83 (p. 75).

The Construction of Local Identities

Patrick Joyce argues that class was not the dominant form of identity in Victorian England; instead, people defined themselves by neighbourhood, workplace, town, region, religion and nation.[9] But few historians have followed his lead, so that the obvious hierarchy of geographical identities still corresponds to a hierarchy of their status within academic history, from national and international, through regional and county to local, despite evidence that local identities were the most powerful on a day-to-day basis.[10] Some of the identities in such a notional hierarchy seem to 'nest' neatly inside each other, but the relationships between these nested territories are complex, and in constant flux.[11] Neither are local identities simply scaled-down versions of national identities. Further, local identities can of course co-exist with local versions or building blocks of national identity, as in the German idea of Heimat or Russell's 'national-provincial' structure of feeling;[12] Jones argues that Welsh *local* papers contributed to the strengthening of Welsh *national* identity in the nineteenth century.[13] However, locality has not been problematised in the same way as the concepts of nation and national identity, despite the fact that most of us live our lives at a local level.

Local identity is a vague yet powerful notion.[14] It overlaps and combines ideas such as sense of community, *genius loci* (spirit of place),

---

9   Patrick Joyce, *Visions of the People: Industrial England and the Question of Class, 1848–1914* (Cambridge: Cambridge University Press, 1994); see also John Duncan Marshall, *The Tyranny of the Discrete: A Discussion of the Problems of Local History in England* (Aldershot: Routledge, 1997), pp. 98–101.

10   Marshall, *Tyranny*, p. 105.

11   Dave Russell, *Looking North: Northern England and the National Imagination* (Manchester: Manchester University Press, 2004), p. 274; Neil Evans, 'Regional Dynamics: North Wales, 1750–1914', in *Issues of Regional Identity: In Honour of John Marshall*, ed. by Edward Royle (Manchester: Manchester University Press, 1998), p. 202.

12   Dave Russell, 'The Heaton Review, 1927–1934: Culture, Class and a Sense of Place in Inter-War Yorkshire', *Twentieth Century British History*, 17 (2006), 323–49 (p. 346), https://doi.org/10.1093/tcbh/hwl018; for the same point for early American magazines, see Robb K. Haberman, 'Provincial Nationalism: Civic Rivalry in Postrevolutionary American Magazines', *Early American Studies: An Interdisciplinary Journal*, 10 (2012), 162–93, https://doi.org/10.1353/eam.2012.0001

13   Jones, 'The 19th Century Media and Welsh Identity'.

14   Shmuel Shamai and Zinaida Ilatov, 'Measuring Sense of Place: Methodological Aspects', *Tijdschrift Voor Economische En Sociale Geografie*, 96 (2005), 467–76, https://doi.org/10.1111/j.1467-9663.2005.00479.x

sense of place, civic pride, local patriotism, parochial loyalties, local attachments and local belonging (phrases used in nineteenth-century journalism and in more recent history, geography and sociology).[15] This loose collection of ideas, feelings and habits was important to people in the past, sometimes a matter of life or death. To paraphrase Royle, the local is assumed to exist, and the historian must therefore seek out its meaning and identity, 'unstable, fluctuating and ambiguous though these meanings and identities are [...]'[16] Here, Russell's definition of local identity is adopted: 'an intense identification with a city, town or village where an individual has been born or has long residence or connection.'[17]

Table 7.1 below brings together some likely factors in the creation and development of local identity. It does not pretend to be an exhaustive list, and it would be difficult to decide which ones were necessary or sufficient. Not all the factors are of the same type or of the same importance. For instance, those grouped under the title 'Self-conscious differentiation and expression of local identity' (the 'collective self-conscious', perhaps) can each subsume almost any of the other factors. The purpose of the table is to show how complex local identity is, how layered and interconnected.[18] It also makes clear that local newspapers are only one factor among many. Local identities were being formed and developed long before newspapers were invented.

There is of course disagreement among members of the same community about the unwritten lists of qualities held in common by local people that differentiate them from outsiders, and this is examined in the last section of this chapter. At its simplest, this contestation might be between elite and popular mentalities. Many historians have been suspicious of local, regional and national identities, seeing them as hegemonic attempts to downplay conflicting class interests; this may be true, but there is more to these identities than that. There is also tension between internal and external characterisations of a place, with internal

---

15   Christopher Ali, *Media Localism: The Policies of Place* (Urbana: University of Illinois Press, 2017), p. 46, https://doi.org/10.5406/illinois/9780252040726.001.0001

16   Edward Royle, 'Introduction: Regions and Identities', in *Issues of Regional Identity*, pp. 2, 4.

17   Russell, *Looking North*, p. 246.

18   For a case study of one such mosaic, see Melanie Tebbutt, 'Centres and Peripheries: Reflections on Place Identity and Sense of Belonging in a North Derbyshire Cotton Town', *Manchester Region History Review*, 13 (1999), 3–20.

Table 7.1. Some factors in the formation of local identities.

Physical characteristics	Location Topography Natural resources Distance from other settlements
Relationships	Administrative status Links to regional, national or international economy and cultural institutions Patterns of immigration and emigration Power relationships within the locality
Economic	Local economy and resultant occupations Individual employers, e.g. small, paternalistic Land ownership patterns Patterns of transport networks
Unconscious differentiation/distinctiveness	
	Accent and dialect Food Architecture
Self-conscious differentiation and expression of local identity	
Memory and custom	Myths Rituals and customs Stories of famous local figures
Organised cultural activities	Sports teams and sporting heroes Newspapers and magazines Festivals Choirs and other amateur performing groups Civic institutions Architecture Trade directories Written local histories Locally set fiction and poetry Personification through famous local personalities
Supra-local affiliations, locally visible or locally expressed	
	Family Class 'Race' Political affiliations Religious affiliations

ones generally more positive.[19] Internal representations, in particular those generated or mediated locally by the local press, are the focus of this chapter. Another aspect of local identity formation — inclusion and exclusion, differentiation or 'othering' — is often taken as central to any identity, individual or collective, but little evidence has been found for this idea in Preston's newspapers.[20]

The *process* of creating, sustaining and sometimes destroying local identities happens when some or all of the elements in Table 7.1 (plus others no doubt omitted) combine in a particular contingent sequence over time. The chronological order in which factors come into play is significant — Gilbert describes the importance of the mining unions in creating community structures in the South Wales village of Ynysbwl, in contrast to Hucknall in Nottinghamshire, where the co-operative movement had already filled the role outside the workplace played by the union in Wales. Following Royle, local identity, 'as a historical concept [...] must be made time-specific if it is to have any useful meaning in historical analysis.'[21]

Here complexity theory, and the idea of emergent phenomena, help to describe the sequencing, overlaps, and complex interactions between so many variables. The concept of emergence describes how complex systems and patterns in nature and in society emerge from a multiplicity of relatively simple interactions, for example an eddy in a stream, which is more than the sum of its parts, is a pattern or arrangement rather than a thing in its own right, and yet is real — it can be seen and it affects other things.[22] This approach uses probability to say that some

---

19 David Smith, 'Tonypandy 1910: Definitions of Community', *Past and Present*, 87 (1980), 158–84, https://doi.org/10.1093/past/87.1.158; compare, for example, the two lists of statement from Hull residents and outsiders in D. C. D. Pocock and Raymond Hudson, *Images of the Urban Environment* (London: Macmillan, 1978), p. 111. Equally, unpleasant events of national significance, such as the capture of Rohm and other 'Brownshirt' leaders by Hitler at Tegernsee in the Bavarian Alps, can be forgotten in the places where they happened, whilst remembered elsewhere: Geert Mak, *In Europe: Travels through the Twentieth Century* (London: Vintage, 2008), p. 269.

20 See also Pat Jess and Doreen B. Massey, 'The Conceptualization of Place', in *A Place in the World? Places, Cultures and Globalization*, ed. by Doreen B. Massey and P. M. Jess (Oxford: Oxford University Press/Open University, 1995).

21 David Gilbert, 'Community and Municipalism: Collective Identity in Late-Victorian and Edwardian Mining Towns', *Journal of Historical Geography*, 17 (1991), 257–70 (p. 266), https://doi.org/10.1016/s0305-7488(05)80002-7; Royle, p. 5.

22 Jeffrey Goldstein, 'Emergence as a Construct: History and Issues', *Emergence: Complexity and Organization*, 1 (1999), https://journal.emergentpublications.com/article/vol1-iss1-1-3-ac/

things are very likely to proceed in a certain way at a general level of description, but at a more detailed level of description, a particular case cannot be predicted.[23] The contingency and dynamism of the process is seen when two seemingly similar places (the Victorian new towns of Barrow-in-Furness and Middlesbrough, for example) develop very different local identities, and these identities change over time.

Just as the local press was only one among many cultural institutions capable of developing local identities in similar ways, it was only one among many institutions using the same techniques and ideas of what characterised a locality. The content of a local paper had strong similarities to the contents of a public library or the lecture programme of a literary and philosophical society, for example.[24] Local newspapers recognised the power of local patriotism and traded on it consciously, often explicitly.[25] Some historians have recognised this, but few have examined the phenomenon in detail.[26] Joyce believes that newspaper 'framing' helped to define a place:

> The local press was extraordinarily important in [...] presenting the town as a universe of voluntary and religious associations in all the range of their many local activities. These it reported on as elements in the life of a single entity.[27]

---

23 Stephen Caunce, 'Complexity, Community Structure and Competitive Advantage within the Yorkshire Woollen Industry, c. 1700–1850', *Business History*, 39 (1997), 26–43, https://doi.org/10.1080/00076799700000144

24 When the Victorian Church of England was reorganised geographically, diocesan officials set out to build a sense of loyalty to the new dioceses by publishing calendars and almanacs among other methods. The contents of these publications were remarkably similar to the contents of local and regional papers of the same period: Arthur Burns, *The Diocesan Revival in the Church of England, c. 1800–1870* (Oxford: Oxford University Press, 1999), pp. 111–14.

25 For the difficulty in untangling commercial and other motives, see Simon Potter, 'Webs, Networks, and Systems: Globalization and the Mass Media in the Nineteenth- and Twentieth-Century British Empire', *Journal of British Studies*, 46 (2007), 621–46 (pp. 644–45), https://doi.org/10.1086/515446

26 Dave Russell, 'Culture and the Formation of Northern English Identities from c.1850', in *An Agenda for Regional History*, ed. by Bill Lancaster, Diana Newton, and Natasha Vall (Newcastle upon Tyne: Northumbria University Press, 2007), p. 280. See, however, Marshall, 'Review Article: Northern Identities', p. 41; Jones, pp. 322–23. For the conceptual problems created by leaving local and regional identities undefined, and the reader perspective ignored, see David Berry, 'The South Wales Argus and Cultural Representations of Gwent', *Journalism Studies*, 9 (2008), 105–16.

27 Patrick Joyce, *The Rule of Freedom: Liberalism and the Modern City* (London: Verso, 2003), p. 125; Aled Gruffydd Jones, *Press, Politics and Society: A History of Journalism in Wales* (Cardiff: University of Wales Press, 1993), p. 240.

As a cultural product, the local press is particularly well suited to sustain and amplify local identities.[28] Its very existence helps to put a locality on the map. Its ability to tell and to enshrine familiar local stories, over and over again, is crucial, in common with most of the other cultural products and institutions listed under the heading 'Self-conscious differentiation and expression of local identity' in Table 7.1, above. News reporting ('facts') is one aspect of this storytelling function, which Nord distinguishes from a second function of the local press, 'forum', the explicit encouragement of community-building.[29] As he point out, this does not require unity or even respect, but the local press can enable readers to meet in print and dispute the nature of local reality. There is no evidence that this 'forum' function declined towards the end of the century. While contemporary commentators noticed the growth of avowedly 'objective' reporting, and a recasting of readers from participants to consumers, other traits of that disputed concept, New Journalism, such as greater reader involvement, could still build communities. Children's nature clubs and competitions in which readers voted for favourite local individuals and institutions are two examples. Three other features of the press are significant here: its constant, gradual, repetitive nature, its miscellaneity and its ability to amplify. Scott-James put the first point well in 1913:

> If the Press is powerful it is as an aggregate, as a multitude of writings, each of small importance when taken by itself. It is in its vast bulk, its incessant repetitions, its routine utterance of truth and falsehood, its ubiquity, its permeation of the whole fabric of modern life, that the Press, however blatant, rather conceals than reveals its insidious power of suggestion.[30]

This argument applies equally to the provincial press, 'powerful as an aggregate'. The second point, the miscellaneity of the press, is made by Joyce above, that the local press is powerful through its function as a container, a box with 'local' emblazoned on its side, so that whatever is

---

28   Newspapers are strangely absent from an account of writing and place in Mike Crang, *Cultural Geography* (London: Routledge, 2004), pp. 44–45.

29   David Paul Nord, 'Introduction: Communication and Community', in *Communities of Journalism: A History of American Newspapers and Their Readers* (Urbana: University of Illinois Press, 2001), pp. 1–27.

30   Rolfe Arnold Scott-James, *The Influence of the Press* (London: S. W. Partridge & Co., 1913), p. 27.

put in the box automatically becomes local, or at least locally mediated. The press is able to roll together many of the factors involved in local identity formation, and it seems likely that the more factors that can be combined, the more powerful is the effect (although emergence theory suggests that the process is not one of simple addition or multiplication). The third feature, amplification or publicity, is central to mass media products. Sport can be a particularly powerful expression of local identity, especially when rival teams play the role of 'other', and the growth of professional football during the high point of the Victorian local press was a symbiotic process. Sports reporting amplified the impact.[31] 'Amplification' rightly suggests that the press reflected and reinforced aspects of local identity much more than it originated or determined them.

Newspaper Techniques for Producing Locality

By mid-century, local newspapers not only mediated news from elsewhere for their local audience, they also published news from their own locality. To the mystification of many Victorian metropolitan journalists and some present-day academics, the minutiae of local life mattered to most of the population.

> Nothing interests a man more than the news of his own neighbourhood [...] We shall therefore continue our endeavours to cram our sheet full of facts — facts possessing as much local interest as possible [...] Our chief object is to make this paper a faithful record of everything of public importance that may transpire in the neighbourhood [...][32]

Local newspapers are skilled in emphasising those identity-forming factors that bring people together and give them and their activities a common label. Take for instance a leader in the *Preston Chronicle*, celebrating the opening of the new town hall in 1867, in which the

---

31 N. A. Phelps, 'Professional Football and Local Identity in the "Golden Age": Portsmouth in the Mid-Twentieth Century', *Urban History*, 32 (2005), 459–80, https://doi.org/10.1017/s096392680500324x; Alan Metcalfe, 'Sport and Community: A Case Study of the Mining Villages of East Northumberland, 1800–1914', in *Sport and Identity*, pp. 13–40.

32 'To Our Readers', *Barrow Herald*, 24 October 1863, p. 4; see also Frederic Carrington, 'Country Newspapers and Their Editors', *New Monthly Magazine*, 105 (1855), 142–52 (p. 147).

frequent use of 'we' and related pronouns is designed to create a sense of inclusion (my emphasis):

> What suited *our* grandfathers does not suit *us*. With the increase of *our* population, the extension of *our* streets, and the spread of education among *us*, has come the desire to meet the needs of *our* town by the erection of a municipal palace [...]. In setting *our* hands to such a work, *we* have felt that *we* had duties to discharge, not only towards the present, but towards the future. *We* inhabit a town, which, for situation, is unrivalled among the districts of the cotton manufacture [...].[33]

These first-person plural pronouns were also used in the same way by other newspapers, particularly 'our' and 'us' in a rhetoric of local identity shared by the speaker and addressee (see below).[34]

Publishers and journalists believed that local patriotism made people more likely to buy a local paper. In 1888 the *Preston Guardian* looked forward to the imminent transfer of powers from county magistrates to county boroughs such as Preston because, 'by promoting and concentrating local patriotism to the full, [this change] should not be without many important direct and indirect effects on the interests of the newspaper press.'[35] They also saw the promotion of local identity as part of their job, and could call on a wide vocabulary of techniques. Just by including the name of the town in its title, the *Barrow Herald* (Fig. 7.3) sent out a powerful message — 'this is about you, your town and your life in this place'.[36]

---

33 *Preston Chronicle* (hereafter *PC*), 5 October 1867, p. 4.

34 These geographical uses of first-person plural pronouns in newspaper discourse are not universal. In the twenty-first century, while they still mean British citizens and/or members of the local community when used in British national and regional newspapers, in Italy they generally include 'the writer and the readers as human beings, rather than specifically as Italian citizens': Gabrina Pounds, 'Democratic Participation and Letters to the Editor in Britain and Italy', *Discourse and Society*, 17 (2006), 29–64, https://doi.org/10.1177/0957926506058064; see also Rudolf De Cillia, Martin Reisigl, and Ruth Wodak, 'The Discursive Construction of National Identities', *Discourse and Society*, 10 (1999), 149–74 (pp. 160–64), https://doi. org/10.1177/0957926599010002002

35 *Preston Guardian* (hereafter *PG*), 22 December 1888, p. 4.

36 'Naming is showing, creating, bringing into existence': Pierre Bourdieu, *On Television and Journalism* (London: Pluto Press, 1998), p. 31, cited in A. Paasi, 'Region and Place: Regional Identity in Question', *Progress in Human Geography*, 27 (2003), 475–85 (p. 480), https://doi.org/10.1191/0309132503ph439pr; see also Tim Cresswell, *Place: An Introduction*, 2nd edition (Chichester: Wiley-Blackwell, 2014), p. 15.

Fig. 7.3. *Barrow Herald* masthead, 10 January 1863, including the place name in the title. Image used by permission of Cumbria Archive and Local Studies Centre, Barrow, CC BY NC ND 4.0.

Many local newspapers portrayed their town or wider circulation area in symbols and emblems, such as that seen between the words 'Barrow' and 'Herald' in Figure 7.4 below. The first paper in this rapidly developing new town was eager to establish an identity for what had been marshland and fields a few decades before. The emblem combines modern images of the railway that created the town, foundry chimneys and a ship in the port, surrounding symbols of the ancient Furness abbey. Another Barrow masthead, that of Joseph Richardson's satirical magazine *Vulcan* (Fig. 7.5 below), personifies the town through portraits of his targets, the small group of leading industrialists and aristocrats with whom he had clashed. Such imagery would have been pointless in most towns, Preston included, where power was shared more widely.

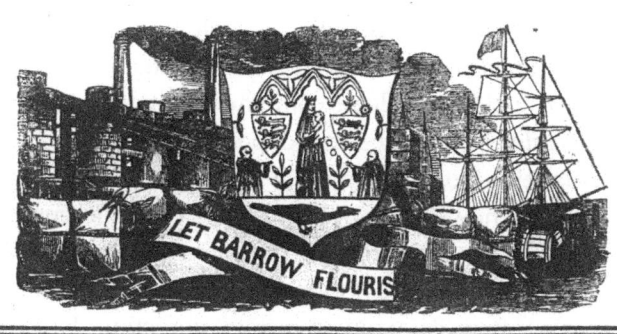

Fig. 7.4. Close-up of *Barrow Herald* masthead, showing local imagery. Image used by permission of Cumbria Archive and Local Studies Centre, Barrow, CC BY NC ND 4.0.

Fig. 7.5. Masthead of the Barrow satirical magazine *Vulcan*, 1874, featuring faces
of the town's governing clique. Image used by permission of Cumbria Archive
and Local Studies Centre, Barrow, CC BY NC ND 4.0.

Equally, in the old, well established town of Preston, where civic
identity was not in doubt, the two leading papers, the *Guardian* and the
Herald, had no masthead images at all (the *Herald* had carried an image
of Britannia in its early years), and those that did tended to choose the
town's coat of arms, as a simple assertion of an identity already well
known — although allied to symbols of political identity. While the
Liberal *Preston Chronicle* gave equal space to the crown and the Magna
Carta either side of the town crest (Fig. 7.6 below), the Tory *Preston Pilot*
omitted any symbols of rights or liberty, and made the crown more
dominant (Fig. 7.7). Both emblems combine national and local imagery.
The *Preston Herald*, like most local papers, mapped territorial space
simply by its labelling of different news columns — with 'local news'
as core and 'district news' as periphery.[37] This extra dimension of place
reduces the miscellaneous nature of the information on a newspaper
page, in a way not available to non-local publications.[38]

Local papers often gave away prints depicting local places or
personalities, such as a handsome engraving of the proposed market
hall 'presented to the purchasers of the *Bolton Chronicle*' in c. 1852,

---

37   See also Jones, 'The 19th Century Media and Welsh Identity', pp. 315, 318–19.

38   This crucial point is missed in Henkin's otherwise profound exploration of one
     city's print culture: David M. Henkin, *City Reading: Written Words and Public Spaces
     in Antebellum New York* (New York: Columbia University Press, 1998), p. 102.

Fig. 7.6. *Preston Chronicle* masthead emblem, 5 April 1862, featuring Magna Carta. Note also use of Lancashire dialect word 'nowt' in advert below date. Image used by permission of E. Michael Atherton, CC BY 4.0.

Fig. 7.7. *Preston Pilot* emblem, 13 September 1851, with a more prominent royal crown and no Magna Carta. Author's copy, CC BY 4.0.

depicting a building obviously designed to increase the town's status.[39] While British local newspapers were not as active as their US

39   Debbie Hodson, 'Civic Identity, Custom and Commerce: Victorian Market Halls in the Manchester Region', *Manchester Region History Review*, 12 (1998), 34–43 (p. 38).

counterparts in promoting lithographed views of towns and cities, they were significant publishers of local images and maps.[40] A town map was given with the *Preston Guardian* in 1865, while views of the town's most elegant buildings were often part of sheet almanacs given away before Christmas, such as the *Preston Chronicle*'s last almanac, for 1894, featuring a photograph of the handsome neo-Gothic Gilbert Scott town hall.[41] Maps and views of Preston had been available long before the town had a newspaper, but in a new town such as Barrow, the press was probably more significant as a disseminator of local images. The *Barrow Herald*, for example, occasionally published lithographed colour maps of Barrow's latest developments, and the *Barrow Times*, linked to the Furness Railway, published a map of the company's network on the front page of every issue for many years.[42]

'All maps are rhetorical. That is, all maps organise information according to systems of priority and thus, in effect, operate as arguments, presenting only partial views, which construct rather than simply describe an object of knowledge [...]'[43] Local papers could use maps and views to convey their particular construction of local reality. In the 1890s the *Preston Guardian* published nostalgic views of the town by local artist Edwin Beattie, at a time of much redevelopment. Besides views and maps, local papers also published portraits of local individuals. In 1893 the *Preston Herald* ran an illustrated series on Preston's temperance pioneers, included portraits of the mayors of each borough in its circulation area on its sheet almanac, and engravings of Lord Salisbury, the town's MPs and Conservative officials with a picture of the new Conservative Working Men's Club as a souvenir of its opening.[44] Sadly, further work on local newspaper iconography is hampered by the fact that few illustrated supplements, almanacs and souvenirs have been preserved.

---

40   John W. Reps, *Views and Viewmakers of Urban America: Lithographs of Towns and Cities in the United States and Canada, Notes on the Artists and Publishers, and a Union Catalog of Their Work, 1825–1925* (Columbia: University of Missouri Press, 1984), pp. 59–60.

41   Almanac given with *PC*, 2 December 1893.

42   Peter J. Lucas, 'The First Furness Newspapers: The History of the Furness Press from 1846 to c.1880' (unpublished M.Litt dissertation, University of Lancaster, 1971), p. 106.

43   Pamela K. Gilbert, *Mapping the Victorian Social Body* (Albany, NY.: State University of New York Press, 2004), p. 16.

44   *Preston Herald* (hereafter *PH*), 14 October 1893, p. 4.

Local newspapers were major publishers of fiction and poetry with local themes. Their wider literary role, which also included original reviews of books and periodicals, has been ignored by literary historians who have mistakenly generalised from the lack of literary content in London newspapers.[45] Around a third of the 4,000 poems published in the 81-year existence of the *Preston Chronicle* alone were written by local or Lancashire writers, from a sample of the first *Chronicle* in each month for 1855 and 1885 (24 issues). Seven of the 12 poems sampled in 1855 were written by local or Lancashire writers, compared with 4 of 17 poems published in the 12 issues sampled in 1885. Although there were no poems with local themes in the 1855 and 1885 *Preston Chronicle* samples, they did appear sporadically, such as 'Stanzas on the Leyland Show, &c' in 1860 and 'Right and Left', a comment on a lock-out, in 1878.[46] Some, such as the long dialect poem 'Traits o' Accrington' published in the *Accrington Gazette* in 1882, addressed local identity head-on.[47] Local newspapers, the main forum for publishing local poets, 'constituted at once a nursery and a shop window for new literary talent'.[48] The majority who failed to progress to publishing in book form served an important 'bardic' function, however, as a 'slightly more articulate neighbour'. They 'remained in a bardic community with their readers, and were able to represent their views'.[49]

Local and localised novels in serial form, short stories and sketches (the last two in both dialect and Standard English) were also staples of

---

45   Laurel Brake, '"The Trepidation of the Spheres": The Serial and the Book in the 19th Century', in *Serials and Their Readers, 1620–1914*, ed. by Robin Myers and Michael Harris (Winchester: Oak Knoll Press, 1993), p. 98.

46   *PH*, 29 September 1860, p. 3; *PC*, 1 June 1878, p. 2.

47   Published in instalments in the *Accrington Gazette*, January and February 1882, quoted in Ronald Y. Digby, J. C. Goddard, and Alice Miller, *An Accrington Miscellany. Prose and Verse by Local Writers* (Burnley: Lancashire County Council Library, Museum and Arts Committee, 1988), pp. 92–96.

48   David Vincent, *Literacy and Popular Culture: England 1750–1914* (Cambridge: Cambridge University Press, 1989), p. 214, https://doi.org/10.1017/cbo9780511560880

49   Brian E. Maidment, 'Class and Cultural Production in the Industrial City: Poetry in Victorian Manchester', in *City, Class and Culture: Studies of Cultural Production and Social Policy in Victorian Manchester*, ed. by Alan J. Kidd and Kenneth Roberts (Manchester: Manchester University Press, 1985), pp. 148–66 (pp. 158–59); Andrew Hobbs and Claire Januszewski, 'How Local Newspapers Came to Dominate Victorian Poetry Publishing', *Victorian Poetry*, 52 (2014), pp. 80–83, https://doi.org/10.1353/vp.2014.0008; Kirstie Blair, 'The Newspaper Press and the Victorian Working Class Poet', in *A History of British Working Class Literature*, ed. by John Goodridge and Bridget Keegan (Cambridge: Cambridge University Press, 2017).

the local press. The ability of fiction to add significance and signification to a place is well expressed by the *Buchan Clown*, a Scottish magazine published in Peterhead: 'Shall Cock Lane have its ghost, Cato St its conspiracy, and shall the Longate of Peterhead sink into oblivion unheeded and unchronicled?'[50] In 1864 the *Preston Chronicle* serialised the historical novel 'The Knoll at Over-Wyresdale' (a rural area twelve miles north of Preston) by 'J. H.' and in 1887 the *Preston Guardian* began the serialisation of 'The Black Dog of Preston'.[51] The author, James Borlase, was not local, but specialised in writing local fiction for newspapers across the Midlands and the North of England.[52] The first episode described him as the author of *The Rose of Rochdale, The Luddites of Leeds, The Lily of Leicester, The White Witch of Worcester, The Nevilles of Nottingham, Leaguered Launceston, '&c.'* The cynical formula behind this alliterative appeal to local patriotism did not necessarily negate the stories' power to endow place with meaning. Attractions of the *Preston Guardian's* expanded Saturday supplement in 1888 included "Locked Out", 'a Lancashire Christmas Tale in the Dialect', by George Hull, 'numerous SHORT STORIES, generally local, and ORIGINAL LANCASHIRE SKETCHES'.[53] Appeals to local, county and regional identities were a selling point.[54] The 'street philosophy' type of sketch, invented in Paris in the 1780s and transferred to London in the 1840s, appeared in the *Preston Chronicle* from the 1860s onwards.[55] In an example from the *Preston Herald* of 1890, an anonymous flaneur described 'Fishergate — most elegant and fashionable of Preston thoroughfares' as part of a series on Preston's main streets:

---

50 *Buchan Clown* 1 August 1838, p. 47, cited in Donaldson, p. 73.

51 The serials began in *PC*, 22 October 1864; in *PG*, 17 December 1887, p. 10.

52 Graham Law, 'Imagined Local Communities: Three Victorian Newspaper Novelists', in *Printing Places: Locations of Book Production & Distribution since 1500*, ed. by John Hinks and Catherine Armstrong (London: British Library, 2005).

53 *PG*, 22 December 1888, p. 4. Hull also wrote the 'The "Guardian" Jubilee Song', sung to the tune of 'The Old Ash Grove', in celebration of the newspaper's 50th anniversary: Jubilee supplement, *PG*, 17 February 1894, p. 16; *LEP*, 29 December 1888.

54 Graham Law, *Serializing Fiction in the Victorian Press* (Basingstoke: Palgrave, 2000), p. 190.

55 Catherine Waters, '"Much of Sala, and but Little of Russia": "A Journey Due North," *Household Words*, and the Birth of a Special Correspondent', *Victorian Periodicals Review*, 42 (2009), 305–23 (p. 310), https://doi.org/10.1353/vpr.0.0090; for an example by Anthony Hewitson, see 'Atticus' [Hewitson], 'Our principal street on the principal day,' *PC*, 25 April 1868.

It was growing dark as I took up my position in a quiet and unpretentious corner [...] standing, so to speak, in the shadows of the Town Hall clock. It was Saturday night [...][56]

There are many more examples, particularly from the Hewitson era *Preston Chronicle*. The local press brought together this local literary material, which previously would have appeared as street literature, pamphlets or not at all.[57]

A local press technique for presenting foreign news demonstrates the extra dimension of place available to these publications, connecting readers more closely to far-away events. As Hess & Waller note, 'local journalism's view extends beyond the parish boundaries to interpret the world through a local lens that makes meaning for audiences'.[58] Individuals who found themselves in foreign lands often asked relatives back home to forward their letters to the local press, such as the young man who joined the Pontifical Zouaves, the volunteer force formed to assist Pope Pius IX in defending the Papal States against the Italian *Risorgimento* in 1868. The letter describes his daily routine, his companions, a 'first-class cricket match', and likens Rome's 'Corse' to Preston's main street, Fishergate.[59] Here, the reader is invited to identify with another Prestonian, and to see foreign places and events through Prestonian eyes, a process of localising the global.[60] Another English volunteer in the same conflict, but on the opposite side, described his journey from Birmingham to Italy, noting that in the Bay of Biscay 'the water was as smooth as Soho Lake or Kerby's Pool', two well-known Birmingham boating lakes.[61] John

---

56 *PH*, 8 October 1890, p. 7.

57 *An Accrington Miscellany* was first published in 1970 'to witness to [Accrington's] life and culture' at a moment of civic crisis, the imminent abolition of Accrington Municipal Borough Council. Commissioned by the Libraries and Art Gallery Committee, its material comes chiefly from Accrington's local press, thereby acknowledging these publications, in the words of Jones, as 'an essential component of a community's identity, its remembrancer': foreword and acknowledgements, Digby et al; Jones, *Press, Politics and Society*, p. 8.

58 Kristy Hess and Lisa Waller, *Local Journalism in a Digital World: Theory and Practice in the Digital Age* (London: Palgrave, 2017), p. 110.

59 *PC*, 4 April 1868, p. 2; see also 'The War — Letter from a Prestonian in Belgium', *PC*, 24 September 1870, p. 5.

60 See also 'Letters from Prestonians in America', *PC*, 11 September 1875, p. 2. This local press technique was a significant genre of war reporting during the First World War: Mike Finn, 'The Realities of War', *History Today*, 52 (2002), 26–31.

61 R. L., 'The English excursion to South Italy', *Birmingham Daily Post*, 19 October 1860.

Macklin Eyre from Newcastle emphasised his local identity by dropping a dialect word, 'canny', into his 'Letter from Capua', during the battle of Volturnus, comparing the terrain to a Newcastle beauty spot:

> I will give you a slight sketch — plain and impartial — of my career since leaving canny Newcastle [...] Caserta [...] is a place of no small order, being surrounded by the Volturno, excepting the south side, where there is a flat plain, something like our Leazes.[62]

A journalist used the same technique when describing a suburb of Istanbul to Sheffield readers, during the 1877 Constantinople peace conference:

> Many of the people of Pera speak of life [...] in Stamboul proper [...] as Attercliffe is viewed by the sons of certain good men who made their fortunes in that busy if not beautiful neighbourhood [...] throughout a large portion of its extent the "Grand Rue" of Pera is about one-third the width of High-street, Sheffield, and almost as rugged under foot as the slopes of the Mam Tor [a hill in the Peak District near Sheffield].[63]

Advertisements for local businesses and events unwittingly made each district's newspapers distinctive, reflecting the local economy and local concerns, 'part of the process whereby newspapers were cemented in to the life of their communities.'[64] This function gave local papers a competitive edge over London papers.[65] This local distinctiveness made some places more profitable for advertising than others, for example Milne and Jones believe that the heavy extractive industries of the North East and Wales had little need to advertise in the local press.[66] Such statements are difficult to test without advertising revenue figures for the period, although proxy figures are available for some earlier years, using government returns of advertising duty collected from each newspaper. Table 7.2 below, using figures for 1838 (information for later years has

---

62   John Macklin Eyre, 'Letter from Capua', *Newcastle Courant*, 23 November 1860.

63   'Sketches from Stamboul', by 'One of Our Staff', *Sheffield Daily Telegraph*, 23 January 1877, p. 2.

64   Lucy Brown, *Victorian News and Newspapers* (Oxford: Clarendon Press, 1985), p. 20.

65   Scott-James, p. 121.

66   Maurice Milne, 'Survival of the Fittest? Sunderland Newspapers in the Nineteenth Century', in *The Victorian Periodical Press: Samplings and Soundings*, ed. by Joanne Shattock and Michael Wolff (Leicester: Leicester University Press, 1982), pp. 193–223 (p. 195); Maurice Milne, *The Newspapers of Northumberland and Durham: A Study of Their Progress during the 'Golden Age' of the Provincial Press* (Newcastle upon Tyne: Graham, 1971), p. 133; Jones, *Press, Politics and Society*, p. 69.

not been traced) gives qualified support to the views of Milne and Jones, with Merthyr Tydfil in the South Wales coalfield producing the least advertising duty, but Newcastle upon Tyne, a port serving a coal, iron and shipbuilding area, producing the most. Port cities probably produced more advertising because of their associated commerce and the needs of middle-class merchants. However Preston, with its commercial and administrative functions, produced a similar amount of duty to Bolton, which lacked such functions and had fewer markets. The relationship between local economies, newspapers and their advertising is clearly complex.[67]

Table 7.2: Advertising duty per head of population, 1838.[68]

	Population (1841)	No. of newspapers (1838)	Total advertisement duty (£ s d, 1838)			Duty per head of population (pence, 1838)
Newcastle	69,430	5	1,915	8	0	6.6
Liverpool	282,656	12	5,807	2	6	4.9
Manchester	240,367	6	3,561	14	9	3.6
Sunderland	52,818	3	425	6	6	1.9
Preston	50,332	3	365	2	0	1.7
Swansea	32,649	2	222	6	0	1.6
Bolton	50,163	2	316	1	0	1.5
Merthyr Tydfil	42,917	3	137	0	0	0.8

Some individual advertisements were used more explicitly to capitalise on local patriotism, such as that for Preston butcher Richard

---

67 The 1838 returns also show that Chartist newspapers had significant amounts of advertising, challenging the view of Curran and others that they operated outside the commercial market: James Curran, 'The Industrialization of the Press', in *Power Without Responsibility: The Press and Broadcasting in Britain*, ed. by James Curran and Jean Seaton (London: Routledge, 1991), pp. 32–48 (p. 39).

68 1839 (548) Return of Number of Stamps issued to Newspapers and Amount of Advertisement Duty, 1836–38; Enumeration abstract, 1841 Census, p. 465.

Myerscough and his North of England Steam Pork Factory, making a play on the letters 'PP' in Preston's coat of arms. Headed 'PP — Proud Preston — Prize Pigs. Prime Pork', it begins:

> In hist'ry we're told
> Proud Preston of old
> Was famous for Tories and Whigs;
> Time changes; we see,
> At present PP
> Is noted for Pork and for Pigs.[69]

The 'hist'ry' of 'Proud Preston' was another popular local press genre, perhaps because, by its nature, local history writing demands 'expression of a definable identity', as Vickery notes of this genre in book form. Indeed awareness of continuity, or memory, is central to the classical philosophical understanding of personal identity.[70] Volumes of local history were popular, and 'a staple of modest family libraries', but history was probably more widely read in newspaper form, because of the newspaper's frequent appearance and wide readership.[71] One writer saw the work of the weekly newspaper publisher as, first, to provide local news, but second, to give 'attention to local history and antiquities'.[72] As Janowitz notes of the mid-twentieth-century local press in Chicago, the linking of local history and local identity goes beyond overtly addressing local historical topics, 'through a style of writing which proudly refers to the age of individuals or to the number of years an organisation has been in local existence. Even routine announcements try to emphasise the stability and persistence of organisations and institutions [...]'[73]

---

69 *Catholic News*, 4 January 1890, p. 8; see also Alison Toplis, 'Ready-Made Clothing Advertisements in Two Provincial Newspapers, 1800–1850', *International Journal of Regional and Local Studies*, 5 (2009), 85–103 (p. 99), https://doi.org/10.1179/jrl.2009.5.1.85; for local identity in advertising poetry, see Kirstie Blair, 'Advertising Poetry, the Working-Class Poet and the Victorian Newspaper Press', *Journal of Victorian Culture*, 23 (2018), 103–18.

70 Brian Garrett, 'Personal Identity', in *Routledge Encyclopedia of Philosophy* (Taylor & Francis), https://doi.org/10.4324/9780415249126-V024-1

71 Amanda Vickery, 'Town Histories and Victorian Plaudits: Some Examples from Preston', *Urban History Yearbook*, 15 (1988), 58–64 (pp. 58, 63), https://doi.org/10.1017/s0963926800013924; see also Pocock and Hudson, p. 82.

72 Alexander Paterson, 'Provincial Newspapers', in *Progress of British Newspapers in the Nineteenth Century* (London: Simpkin, Marshall, Hamilton, Kent & Co., 1901), pp. 79–80.

73 M. Janowitz, *The Community Press in an Urban Setting* (Glencoe: Free Press, 1952), p. 71.

There was a boom in local history in the local press from the 1870s onwards. Biographies of local figures such as the *Preston Herald*'s series on temperance pioneers in 1893 and obituaries attempted to personify Preston's history.[74] Almanacs such as that given by the *Preston Herald* in December 1893 (Fig. 7.8), intended to hang on walls for the following year, listed, for each day of the year, the deaths of local worthies, dates of lock-outs and riots, the opening of the town hall, notorious local murders and the purchase of the town's first steam fire engine, among anniversaries of national and international events. Local history in Preston showed 'no hint of pastoral regret or nostalgia'. Instead it was written to praise the present, with an understanding that 'identity is always, and always has been, in process of formation', hence the recurring mockery of Garstang as a 'finished town' that neither progressed nor changed.[75]

Many genres and formats of historical writing are found in local newspapers, including biography, memoir/reminiscences, chronology (sometimes as separate articles, sometimes in almanacs), historical background to news stories, extracts of historical documents, topography, archaeology (finds during demolition and construction, for example), architecture, folklore, legends, customs and superstitions. Typical formats are 'notes and queries' columns, dedicated history columns and series, reports or summaries of lectures and talks, touristic guides, dialect writing, drawings, maps, photographs and diagrams, poetry and fiction.

Newspapers explicitly linked history to local identity. A poem in memory of local historian T. T. Wilkinson of Burnley, a frequent contributor to local papers, praises him for connecting ordinary local places to ancient legends and famous events, adding glamour to familiar, much-loved landmarks:

> For he that is dead set my heart aflame,
>   While as yet with my schoolmates surrounded,
>
> With the legends that lurked in each dear old name
>   And the myths on the hills that abounded.

---

74 For more on obituaries, see Bridget Fowler, 'Collective Memory and Forgetting: Components for a Study of Obituaries', *Theory, Culture & Society*, 22 (2005), 53–72, https://doi.org/10.1177/0263276405059414

75 Vickery, pp. 59–60; Doreen B. Massey, 'Places and Their Pasts', *History Workshop Journal*, 39 (1995), 182–92 (p. 186), https://doi.org/10.1093/hwj/39.1.182; leader column, *PH*, 15 September 1860, p. 4; see also *PC*, 9 October 1853, p. 4, 7 June 1879, p. 6. There was similar mockery of Ulverston's lack of development in the Barrow press.

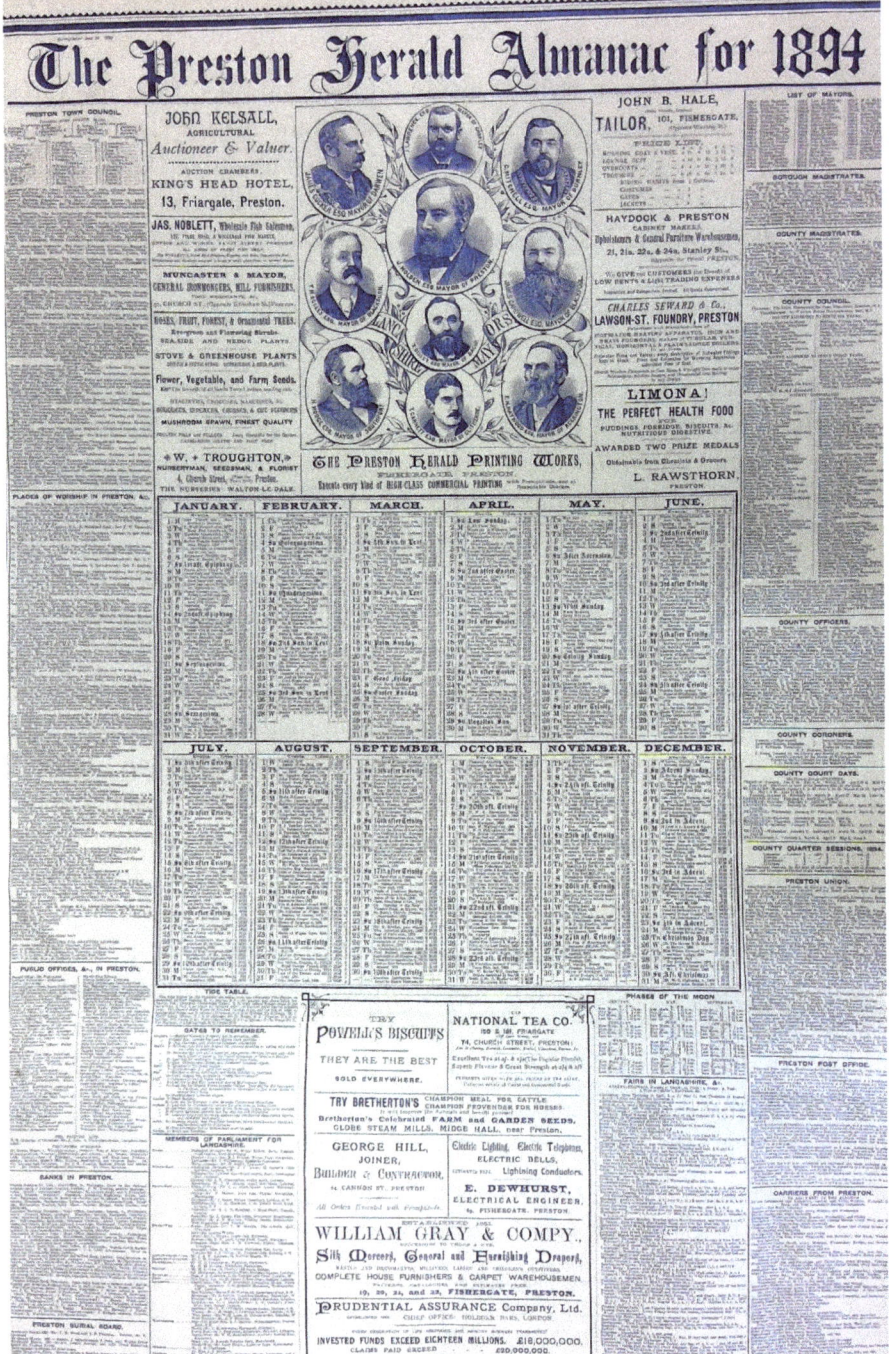

Fig. 7.8. *Preston Herald* sheet almanac for 1894, measuring 87cm x 55cm, including a chronology of local historical events (centre). Author's copy, CC BY 4.0.

> He called forth the heroes of story and song
> > Great Thor, greater Woden and Balder,
>
> And linked them for aye to the homesteads along
> > The banks of the Brun and the Calder.[76]

The introduction to a new local history column, 'Burnleyana, Notes new and old on Burnley and its neighbourhood', in the *Burnley Advertiser* of 1880 reveals the connection between memory and local identity:

> our first wish will be to afford pleasure and recreation to Burnley men and women to whom all that appertains to the smoky busy place is very dear for the sake of hallowed memories.[77]

Newspaper editors were aware of this deep connection to place among many of their readers. Alfred Gregory, editor of the *Tiverton Gazette* for more than fifty years, recalled how one reader once said of Tiverton, 'I love every stone in the place.'[78] Some editors shared this love; most of them exploited it. Local history writing traded on the power of local identities, but in a circular way it also helped to create shared public memory and the continuity that is central to local identities. It had the power to make ordinary places sacred, to confer meaning on locations far from the centres of cultural power.

Boosterism, more a tone of voice than a type of content, was a happy duty for most local publications. Souvenir histories of provincial newspapers stress how their fortunes were tied to those of the area they served, and how the papers helped to promote and develop those areas.[79] Local paper boosterism addressed a wider audience than the locality, as when the *Barrow Times* countered criticism of Barrow in the Liverpool press in 1871, or when the *Barrow Herald* compared local steel production favourably with that of Belgium in 1878. 'Three days later the *Herald* reported that the story had created a stir among the Belgians,

---

76   'The Burnley Antiquary', *Burnley Advertiser*, 17 January 1880.

77   *Burnley Advertiser*, 17 January 1880.

78   Alfred Thomas Gregory, *Recollections of a Country Editor* (Tiverton Gazette, 1932), p. 15.

79   Anon., *A Century of Progress 1844–1944, Southport Visiter* (Southport: Southport Visiter, 1944), p. 1; *Rendezvous with the Past: One Hundred Years' History of North Staffordshire and the Surrounding Area, as Reflected in the Columns of the Sentinel, Which Was Founded on January 7th, 1854* (Stoke-on-Trent: Staffordshire Sentinel Newspapers, 1954), p. 8. Both these newspapers claimed to be instrumental in achieving the incorporation of their towns.

"as we have received orders for papers containing the paragraph, besides instructions to forward the *Herald* regularly".'[80] Boosterism was particularly prevalent in a new town such as Barrow, especially in the pages of the *Barrow Herald* (motto: 'Let Barrow flourish') and the *Barrow Times*, associated with the town's leading industrialists.[81] In 1871 the *Barrow Times* published a 2,000-word article on a 'near perfect' new steam corn mill, and when James Ramsden, the town's most powerful figure, was honoured in 1872, the same paper dedicated four pages to the unveiling of his statue, including a 7,000-word history of the town.[82]

While the *Barrow Times* could be dismissed as the mouthpiece of the town's ruling clique, the rival *Barrow Herald*, not part of the interconnected companies that had built Barrow, was equally patriotic. The frequency of words such as 'progress', 'rapid', 'unique' and 'increasing' in leader articles in the *Barrow Times*, *Barrow Herald* and *Vulcan* in the early 1870s gives a flavour of the promotional nature of the writing. However, the much lower level of boosterism in the more Radical *Barrow Pilot* shows that it was not an inevitable aspect of new-town Victorian newspapers, and even in the *Barrow Times* this discourse declined during the depression of the late 1870s, although the paper still presented an encouraging picture.

In the papers of Preston, a town with a more stable economic position, boosterism was more muted, particularly in the last decades of the century. However, it can be seen in the 'Opening Address' of the *Preston Herald* in 1855: 'Natives of the town ourselves, we have at heart the good of our neighbours, and shall always be ready to render zealous support to every measure that promises improvement to our locality.'[83] An 1860 *Preston Guardian* leader extolled 'the extraordinary progress and present prosperity of the town [...] No other nearer than Glasgow, can expect to attain the dimensions and influence of a large city, as Preston is certain of doing.' Similarly, in 1867 a *Preston Chronicle*

---

80   This account of local paper boosterism in Barrow is taken from Lucas, 'First Furness Newspapers', pp. 99, 105, 113, 119.

81   Lucas, 'First Furness Newspapers', pp. 100–1, 109. Likewise, the *Barrow Advertiser & District Reporter*'s motto was 'Prosperity to Barrow'. For the more extreme version of boosterism seen in frontier America, see David Fridtjof Halaas, *Boom Town Newspapers: Journalism on the Rocky Mountain Mining Frontier, 1859–1881* (Albuquerque: University of New Mexico Press, 1981).

82   Lucas, 'First Furness Newspapers', pp. 100–1.

83   *PH*, 7 July 1855.

leader described Preston as 'a town, which is historically famous, as well as commercially important [...]'[84] Impressionistic comparisons of some civic high and low points in Preston during the period were made, to examine whether the town's identity was discussed more explicitly at these times. This exercise revealed that high points such as the opening of a new town hall and park in 1867, and Preston North End Football Club winning the 'double' in 1888 did produce more characterisations of the town, but low points such as a strike and lock-out in 1878, and the near collapse of Preston North End in 1893 were not linked to local identity, showing the selectiveness of Preston's press.

However, more systematic analysis of explicit characterisations of Preston in the *Preston Herald* found a propensity to criticise the town almost as much as to praise it, as in an 1890 leader arguing that 'Preston enjoys advantages that Oldham does not and cannot command, but the town has been out-distanced in the race through lack of modern mills, and machinery brought up to date'.[85] Yet the editorial voice was more likely to boost Preston than were readers and the local individuals whose comments were reported. Explicit representations of the town were noted in seventy-nine issues of the *Preston Herald* between 1860 and 1900, and grouped into categories. The representations were differentiated by their source, whether from readers' letters, reported speech or the editorial voice of the paper (Table 7.3 below). In its leader columns and other forms of direct editorial address, the *Herald* showed a slight preference for the positive, with twenty-five positive comments about Preston and eighteen negative ones — a close ratio of four to three in favour of the positive. However, in reported speech, negative outweighed positive by two to one, and in readers' letters even more so, by four to one. Typical examples are a municipal election speech by J. Whittle, the Progressive candidate, referring to Preston's high infant mortality rate, claiming that 'There were at least a thousand people every year murdered in Preston [...] The death-rate of Preston was simply appalling', or a letter from 'Ventilator', saying that 'the town appears to be in a disreputable condition so far as regards sanitary matters [...]'[86] Boosterism was only one viewpoint among many in the contest for local identity, and many people claimed the right to criticise their town as an expression of local identity.

---

84 *PH*, 1 September 1860; *PG*, 22 September 1860; *PC*, 5 October 1867.
85 *PH*, 3 September 1890.
86 *PH*, 17 October 1900, 23 October 1880.

Table 7.3. Representations of Preston in the *Preston Herald*, 1860–1900.

Type of representation	Positive or negative	Source of representation		
		Readers' letters	Reported speech	Editorial voice
High death rates	-	2	13	3
Needs improving	-	10	2	2
Backward in comparison to other towns	-	2	4	7
Dirty town	-	11	0	1
Town in decline	-	0	5	2
Corrupt politics	-	1	1	0
Uncultured	-	2	2	3
Immoral town	-	1	4	0
Stronghold of Toryism	+	2	6	7
Patriotic town	+	1	3	0
Garrison town		1	1	0
Pro-Stanley		1	1	0
Progressive	+		1	1
Anti-Stanley town		0	1	0
Radical past		0	1	0
Sporting prowess	+	1	0	7
Cultured/educated	+		1	4
Musical		1		
Pleasant, attractive town	+	2	2	3
Large and growing town	+	1	1	3
Market town/ agricultural centre		0	1	3
Generous, compassionate	+		2	
Catholic town		1	0	3
Birthplace of teetotalism		0	2	1
Total positive		7	16	25
Total negative		29	31	18

Sometimes the local press moved beyond its publishing role in its interventions in local culture, initiating social, charitable and educational activities. The most visible, constant way in which local papers claimed a place in local culture beyond their pages was their physical presence as prominent businesses, usually on the main square or commercial street of the town. This visibility was heightened when publishers commissioned purpose-built premises, as the Toulmins did for the *Preston Guardian* in 1872, making their offices 'unique in Preston — or for that matter in the whole of the northern and eastern divisions of the county', as the paper proudly stated in a two-column celebration. The 'great carved and marbled halls of newspaper offices in the largest cities mimicked the libraries and town halls being raised at the same time.'[87] The status of newspapers as local institutions was confirmed by their inclusion in trade directories alongside banks, theatres and gas companies. Newspapers also brought readers together, through initiatives such as the *Preston Guardian* Animals' Friend Society, or the charity entertainment at Preston's Public Hall in 1895, featuring 150 young performers, organised by the *Lancashire Catholic* magazine.[88] Local papers often set up, or acted as collecting points for, local charitable appeals such as the smallpox relief fund organised by the *Lancashire Evening Post* in 1888.[89] The *Preston Guardian* claimed that its campaign against steaming in weaving sheds led to the 1889 Cotton Cloth Factories Act, and that its programme of agricultural instruction and related farmers' associations had

> enormous consequences [...] affecting the whole country. The movement started from Preston, and *The Guardian* was the initiating force [...] it is only two years since that a farmer declared in the [...] Public Hall that he would not sell for £200 the knowledge gained by the instruction thus inaugurated.[90]

---

87 'The New Offices of "The Guardian"', *PG*, 14 December 1872, p. 6; Marr, p. 27; the history of the newspaper building has yet to be written, but the *Hereford Times* may boast one of the earliest purpose-built provincial offices, from 1838: *Hereford Times* 150th anniversary special, 2 July 1982.

88 *Lancashire Catholic*, December 1895, p. 260. Much higher levels of reader participation were found in regional weekly miscellany papers such as the Scottish *People's Journal* and the *Newcastle Weekly Chronicle*: Frederick S. Milton, 'Newspaper Rivalry in Newcastle upon Tyne, 1876–1919: `Dicky Birds' and `Golden Circles'', *Northern History*, 46 (2009), 277–92 (p. 286); Donaldson, *passim*.

89 *PG*, 30 June 1888, p. 2.

90 *PG*, 30 June 1888; *PG* jubilee supplement, 17 February 1894, p. 4; Alan Fowler, *Lancashire Cotton Operatives and Work, 1900–1950: A Social History of Lancashire Cotton Operatives in the Twentieth Century* (Aldershot: Ashgate, 2003). The tradition of the provincial press as watchdog is an old one, the *Leeds Mercury* exposing an agent provocateur, Oliver the Spy, in 1817.

Competitions, introduced in the 1880s, encouraged readers to respond to local (and other) publications, and to see their writing, ideas, names and addresses in print. Virtually the only local content in the *Preston Monthly Circular* (1895–1915) was a prize competition, launched in 1896, in which readers had to guess what other readers had voted for, in a series of popularity contests including the ten most popular men in Preston, the twelve finest buildings, most popular clergymen, finest streets, most popular doctors, '12 most attractive pictures in the Art Gallery of the Harris free library' and the twelve finest hotels in Preston. Local newspapers went beyond merely reflecting local culture, to shape it, and to mobilise readers.

'Us' and 'Them' and Contested Identities

'Othering', or the definition of self through differentiation from an other, is seen by many modern writers as central to identity.[91] This technique may fit nineteenth-century Western views of the Orient, for example, but it is less common in nineteenth-century local papers than one might expect, even in football coverage. The idea of 'us' can do its work without its binary opposite, 'them', if 'we' are confident and unthreatened in 'our' identity, as in the ancient, established town of Preston.[92] By contrast, in Wales, where nation status had to be asserted self-consciously, the newspapers differentiated the Welsh from the English 'other', and in the new town of Barrow-in-Furness, local papers differentiated Barrow from its sleepy neighbour Ulverston, its new-town rival Middlesbrough, and from other ports and iron and steel areas.[93]

But in Preston, for the most part, othering was absent. Only occasionally did Preston newspapers define the town in opposition to an 'other'.[94] This could be London ('We ought to have nothing in

---

91 'All "identities" require an other': R. D. Laing, *Self and Others* (London: Tavistock Publications, 1969), p. 82; Colley's argument that British identity was formed in opposition to Catholic, aristocratic, decadent France has been influential on this point: Linda Colley, *Britons: Forging the Nation, 1707–1837* (New Haven: Yale Nota Bene, 2005); Edward W. Said, *Orientalism* (London: Penguin, 2003).

92 Stephen Caunce, 'Northern English Industrial Towns: Rivals or Partners?', *Urban History*, 30 (2003), 338–58 (p. 339), https://doi.org/10.1017/s0963926804001397

93 Jones, 'Welsh Identity', p. 315; Lucas, p. 104.

94 'The denigration of others' places provides a way to assert the viability and incipient power of one's own': David Harvey, *Justice, Nature and the Geography of Difference* (Cambridge, MA: Wiley-Blackwell, 1997), p. 322.

Preston approaching in loathsomeness the purlieus of Drury Lane and Baldwin's Gardens and the New Cut') or a generalised south ('Southern agricultural societies might be described as medieval in character [...] in Lancashire and the North we smile at such evidences of rural eccentricity').[95] More often, however the 'other' was the next town. The Victorians kept a close eye on what rival towns were doing, whether it was building a grander library than them, or ensuring more of their children survived to adulthood, and 'very few wanted their own town to be publicly denounced as worse than their neighbours'.[96] A leader column from the *Chronicle* during a strike and lock-out in 1878 categorises Blackburn's cotton workers very clearly as 'them':

> [...] the operative classes of Preston are much more peaceably disposed than those of Blackburn. There is a rough, turbulent, vehemence — a defiant, quarrelsome bull-neckedness about the Blackburnian body [...] this, luckily, is not the spirit of Preston operatives — they are more docile, enduring, and order-loving [...][97]

But this was the exception rather than the rule in Preston's papers.[98] 'Othering' was less common than the other techniques of exploiting local patriotism. Only when there was a threatening level of competition for resources or status (as in the Lancashire-wide strike above), did the town's newspapers define Preston against the other. Even then, 'othering' was not inevitable; there was no scapegoating when Preston North End nearly collapsed in 1893 (see next chapter). A subtler way of defining Preston's identity than invoking the 'other' was through editing out undesirable aspects of the town, a different process of inclusion and exclusion. Internal conflict, however, was a different matter, at least at the start of the period.

---

95 Leader column, *PH*, 9 October 1880, p. 2; leader column, *PG*, 1 September 1860, p. 4. For more on northern self-definitions against the south, see Russell, *Looking North: Northern England and the National Imagination*, p. 250; Richard Holt, 'Heroes of the North: Sport and the Shaping of Regional Identity', in *Sport and Identity in the North of England*, ed. by Jeffrey Hill and Jack Williams (Keele: Keele University Press, 1996), p. 160; Hill, pp. 102–4.

96 Hodson, p. 37; Caunce believes that such rivalry had a positive effect: Caunce, 'Northern English Industrial Towns', p. 350.

97 *PC*, 18 May 1878, p. 4.

98 In mid-twentieth-century Chicago, by contrast, 'controversies which are most popular are those of the local community against the outside urban metropolis; there are few internal dissenters': Janowitz, p. 77.

Community does not necessarily imply harmony.[99] The quiet confidence of Preston's identity did not preclude internal conflicts over the nature of that identity, although the amount of conflict declined after mid-century (see Table 7.4 below).[100] Explicit conflict (defined as two opposing viewpoints in the same article) was identified in all sampled issues of the *Preston Herald* (all those published during September and October every ten years from 1860 to 1900). In the *Herald*, explicit conflict appeared predominantly in readers' letters (thirty-one of forty-nine instances of conflict over Preston identity, see Table 7.5 below), but also in reports of public meetings and the deliberations of councillors and Poor Law Guardians, and occasionally in leader columns. Conflicting characterisations of the town included Preston's relationship to the Stanley family (powerful, politically active landowners), the tension between tradition and modernity, whether the town centre should be industrial or exclusively retail and residential, Preston as a Conservative or a Radical town, a Protestant town or a more diverse, tolerant place, and a progressive town with high local taxation or a retrenching, business-led place. Some of these conflicts concerned power and inequalities, but some did not. Less explicit but more frequent differences in how the town was characterised would also be apparent to those who read more than one local paper. As we saw in Chapter 2, the many reading rooms and news rooms provided plenty of opportunity for such comparisons.

Table 7.4. Conflict in the *Preston Herald*, 1860–1900.

	1860	1870	1880	1890	1900
Articles displaying conflict	29	51	66	23	23
Articles displaying conflict over Preston identity	12	9	14	8	7
No. of columns of type published weekly	48	84	128	132	148

99 Hess and Waller, p. 8.
100 See also Bromley and Hayes, p. 204.

Table 7.5: Where conflicts about Preston appeared, *Preston Herald*, 1860–1900.

Type of item	No. of items featuring explicit conflict
Letters to the editor	31
Report of public meeting	6
Leader columns	5
Other news report	4
Report of public body	3

There was constant conflict between rival newspapers. Irish disestablishment and a long general election campaign in 1868 produced much vituperation, particularly between the *Herald* and the two Liberal papers, the *Chronicle* and the *Guardian*. At less turbulent times, each paper would present their political viewpoint as the norm, by weaving together local and political identities and retelling old stories that characterised Preston either as Tory or Radical. In October 1893 former Conservative Prime Minister Lord Salisbury visited Preston, to open new purpose-built premises for the Conservative Working Men's Club. The *Herald* published a special supplement including 'a finely executed engraving' of the new club, with portraits of Lord Salisbury and leading local Conservatives. Extra copies were printed due to the 'unprecedented sale' of the paper, and Lord Salisbury's admiration of Preston's Conservative history drew a 'jealous' response from a Blackburn Tory paper. The *Herald* retorted with a brief history lesson on Conservative organisation in the town, and added a lament for the 'sport of the old-fashioned sort' in the days when the Stanley family led Preston's social and political life.[101] In fact the Stanleys who had sponsored racing and cock-fighting in Preston at the start of the century had actually been Whigs, but the Tory *Herald* assimilated them into a 'fantasy' place representation (to use David Harvey's term) of Preston as a loyally Tory town, fond of traditional pleasures now defended by Conservatives against Liberal killjoys.[102]

---

101 *PH*, 21 and 28 October 1893. For politics and local identity, see Alex Windscheffel, *Popular Conservatism in Imperial London 1868–1906* (London: Royal Historical Society, 2007); V. C. Barbary, 'Reinterpreting "Factory Politics" in Bury, Lancashire, 1868–1880', *Historical Journal*, 51 (2008), 115–44.

102 Harvey, p. 321.

When the three-fold increase in the amount of material published weekly by the *Preston Herald* is taken into account, the fourth column of Table 7.4 above suggests that the proportion of conflict, in this paper at least, greatly reduced during the period. But each newspaper was different: in Furness, the editor of the *Ulverston Advertiser* believed that 'local dissensions are, in all cases, greatly to be deprecated' while his opposite number on the *Ulverston Mirror* relished conflict as part of his anti-authority stance.[103] One might expect even less conflict in a situation of local monopoly, as became the norm in the twentieth century, and further research on this point would be helpful.

For Preston's papers, the most significant 'other' was the enemy within, showing the fractured nature of local identity, or rather identities. As sociolinguistic studies would predict, the pronouns 'they', 'their' and 'them' were used to distinguish in-groups from outsiders, 'us' from 'them" in the endless conflict over Preston's true identity (Table 7.6 below).[104] These third-person plural pronouns denoted the political, moral and religious opponents — overwhelmingly local — of each paper. Such differentiation in order to create 'an ingroup identity', may be central to all mass media language.[105] For Preston's two Liberal, Nonconformist papers, the *Chronicle* and the *Guardian*, the 'others' were Preston's parsons, Churchmen, Orangemen and Tory politicians. Table 7.6 shows the five most common uses of these pronouns in leader columns before and after Anthony Hewitson bought the *Preston Chronicle*, in his opinionated 'Atticus' columns, and in the leader columns of the rival *Preston Guardian*. Third-person plural pronouns were used more in Atticus columns than in the leader columns (18.1 occurrences per 1000 words for Atticus columns, 12.1–13.7 per 1000 words in leader columns). In Hewitson's 'Atticus' columns, his leaders and those of the rival *Preston Guardian*, 'they', 'their' and 'them' have a negative meaning, occasionally neutral. 'Atticus' uses them heavily in his descriptions of Poor Law Guardians and parsons, less so for

---

103 *Ulverston Advertiser*, 31 January 1861, cited in Peter J. Lucas, 'J. A. Bernard's Challenge: Journalists on Journalism in a Victorian Country Town', *Transactions of the Cumberland and Westmorland Antiquarian and Archaeological Society* 7 (2007), 193–213 (p. 196).

104 Katie Wales, *Personal Pronouns in Present-Day English* (Cambridge: Cambridge University Press, 1996), p. 8.

105 Allan Bell, 'Language Style as Audience Design', *Language in Society*, 13 (1984), 145–204 (p. 192), https://doi.org/10.1017/S004740450001037X

Table 7.6: Use of 'they'/'their'/'them' (five most frequent meanings, %), in leading articles about Preston and in 'Atticus' columns.

Hewitson-era *Preston Chronicle*, April 1868	%
Preston Tory MPs	17
Revivalists	11
Orangemen of Preston	9
Magistrates	6
Parsons	6
'Atticus' columns, April 1868	
Parsons	25
Preston Poor Law Guardians	24
Preston councillors	15
Tradesmen	6
Reporters	5
Pre-Hewitson *Preston Chronicle*, Sept–Nov 1867	
The Romans	26
Prestonians	18
Preston corporation	8
Ribble Co & shareholders	8
Commissioners	7
Preston Guardian, April 1868	
Churchmen of Preston	32
Parsons	10
Irish Church	10
Preston Tory MPs	8
Tory rump of Preston council	8

councillors, and very little in his sketch of Fishergate, which is peopled by 'us' — shopkeepers (Hewitson among them), shoppers, workers and market-goers. Describing some of the Guardians, he writes that 'they prate and preach, and rant to poor people' and of some young clergymen he says: 'They have graduated at some fifty-fifth collegiate establishment'. But the tradition that leading articles are against rather than for something does not explain why 'them' is used negatively more in Hewitson's opinion columns than his leaders, nor why there is little antagonism nor 'othering' in pre-Hewitson *Chronicle* leaders.[106] In these articles, the ancient Romans and modern Prestonians are 'them', but a positive 'them'. The writer has chosen subjects he can praise rather than condemn, and is more conciliatory and less opinionated, even on controversial topics such as the debate over whether to improve Preston's port at ratepayers' expense. This suggests that the technique of 'othering' was, in part, the editor's personal choice.

Conclusions

Local identity is highly complex, constructed as it is from many different elements, layered and interconnected in different ways in each place. While local newspapers were only one among many factors involved in the development and promotion of local identity, they were involved in an explicit project of promoting and exploiting local patriotism. This may explain why local newspapers are used so heavily by historians in studies of local identity; when the rhetoric is taken at face value, the dangers are obvious. This chapter has built on the insights of Hill, Jones and Joyce to offer a detailed analysis of some techniques used by nineteenth-century local newspapers. Many of the techniques are so banal that they are rarely noticed, such as including the name of the town in the paper's title. Others are more sophisticated, such as the 'rhetorical web'[107] woven by careful use of 'we', 'our' and 'us', for example. Newspapers also published visual images of the locality, labelled news items in a way that divided the world's events into local, district, general or foreign news; published local and localised fiction and poetry, advertisements and history. The newspaper as a cultural form is well suited to the promotion of place identities, thanks to its iterative, repetitive nature, its ability to roll together many disparate elements of local identity, thereby increasing their power, and its ability to present highly constructed, artificial notions as normal and implicit, seen in its division of the world into 'us' and 'them'. Defining local identity through differentiating from an external 'other' was present, but weakly expressed and not central to the Preston papers' methods; the local press focused on 'us' far more than 'them'. Othering may have

---

106 Simon Goldsworthy, 'English Nonconformity and the Pioneering of the Modern Newspaper Campaign', *Journalism Studies*, 7 (2006), 387–402 (p. 393), https://doi.org/10.1080/14616700600680690

107 Jones, 'Welsh Identity', p. 316.

been important in places with less established, or more embattled, identities, such as Barrow or Wales. In such places, the role of the local press in conjuring up Benedict Anderson's imagined communities may have been more significant, too, than in more confident, established places such as Preston, where the official signs of geographical status were more visible and therefore less imagination was required.

The local press was a mirror and a magnifier of local events, but it also helped to shape local culture, becoming an institution in its own right, with its premises at the heart of the provincial town, collecting together the miscellaneous advertising previously published in other formats, and sponsoring sporting, musical and charitable endeavours. Provincial culture had managed without the press in previous ages, but it is hard to imagine late Victorian society functioning without the infrastructure it provided.[108] Lee was unduly pessimistic when he claimed that, by the early twentieth century, 'the press had become a business, not only first, but increasingly a business almost entirely, and a political, civil and social institution hardly at all.'[109] Lee also underplayed the cultural function of the local press. The next chapter focuses in detail on one part of local culture, the use of dialect, and on how local papers used it to include and exclude, whilst combining their commercial and cultural roles.

---

108 Modern recognition of the power of these techniques at national level can be seen in initiatives such as USAID's 'Civil Society and Independent Media' initiatives, and the BBC's charter, recently amended to include the purpose of 'sustaining citizenship and civil society': U. S. Agency for International Development, 'Supporting Vibrant Civil Society & Independent Media', https://www.usaid.gov/what-we-do/democracy-human-rights-and-governance/supporting-vibrant-civil-society-independent-media; 'BBC — Public Purposes: Citizenship and Civil Society —Inside the BBC', http://www.bbc.co.uk/corporate2/insidethebbc/whoweare/publicpurposes/citizenship.html

109 Alan J. Lee, *The Origins of the Popular Press in England: 1855–1914* (London: Croom Helm, 1976), p. 232.

8. Class, Dialect and the Local Press: How 'They' Joined 'Us'

Moses Cocker, the vice-chairman of Blackburn Board of Guardians, delivered himself in the barbarious [sic] dialect of the district, which was rendered literally by Mr Brooks, the then editor and reporter for the *Blackburn Mercury*[1] [...] Mr Lumley [a Poor Law inspector] came down from Somerset House when Moses was upholding the law at the Board of Guardians.[2] When Mr Lumley entered the Board-room he was sainted by Moses holding up and shaking his giant hand and saying to him, "Pousy jackanapes, if I hev ever to set thi limbs o'll mek um crack." To Mr Lumley this threat was just so much Latin. An applicant for relief next presented herself, when Moses said, "Tha coms fro Tockholes, o'll gether thee some brass — thart a daysent lass, and so is thi mother." These words were addressed to Isabel Holden, a "lass" that was 76 years of age, and the "lass" alluded to as her mother was 93 [...] To listen to Moses Cocker giving evidence, amounted to the pursuit of knowledge under great difficulties, for every sentence had to be transposed into English by the advocate employed, who had to turn interpreter [...] One day Moses met Mr Brooks and asked him if there was anything he could "tice" him with. His family felt very keenly that he (Mr B) made him into a public laughing stock by not writing his speeches "gradely." He would give him anything to be thick with him. Mr Brooks replied that it was the

---

1   I have found no trace of a Mr Brooks connected to the *Blackburn Mercury* (1843–46); the paper's last editor was Robert Wilson Smiles, brother of the author Samuel Smiles, who went on to work for the Lancashire Public Schools Association and became chief librarian of Manchester Free Library in 1858: 'Demise of the Blackburn Mercury', *Blackburn Standard*, 29 July 1846, 7 October 1846.

2   William Golden Lumley, a barrister, was Assistant Secretary to the Poor Law Commission from c. 1841 to 1847: Correspondence between Lumley and Charles Mott, The National Archives ref: MH 12/6040-43. I am grateful to Peter Park for this reference.

         https://doi.org/10.11647/OBP.0152.08

province of the press to show up the shortcomings of public men, and he then turned on his heel.[3]

This passage from an anonymous memoir, serialised in the *Preston Chronicle*, describes an editorial decision taken in the 1840s, to render the speech of a Blackburn public figure, Moses Holden, as Lancashire dialect. In later years, local and regional dialects became an established provincial newspaper technique for profiting from local patriotism and playing down class differences. But before then, dialect was used more divisively, as in the passage above, to emphasise social and moral difference. The deployment of dialect, as with other techniques for promoting and profiting from local identities, was self-conscious, considered and highly constructed.

This chapter shows how local papers in Lancashire went from using dialect largely as a class marker, to embracing its potential to hide class differences and emphasise the common ground of local identity. This was part of newspapers' adaptation to an expanding working-class readership. These readers had previously been positioned as eavesdroppers on middle-class newspaper conversations, but in the last decades of the nineteenth century, they moved from reading and listening, to purchasing and therefore influencing local newspapers and their content. Place trumped class in the changing discourse of local newspapers, as a theoretically neutral technique — dialect — was used to include rather than exclude. This was part of complex changes in the relationship between spoken and written language, and the crossover between literary and journalistic techniques. In all of this, the differentiated local markets of the provincial press, and their position at the heart of distinctive local cultures, gave them a commercial advantage over London newspapers.

Moses Cocker, the subject of the reminiscence that opens this chapter, was a tenant farmer (a middle-class occupation) who practised the ancient art of bone-setting (continued today by chiropractors and osteopaths), on the fringes of orthodox medicine, and seen as a craft rather than a profession. He was the vice-chairman of a local government body responsible for Poor Law administration, but he did not receive the respect usually accorded to men of his position and class. Other Poor Law

---

3   'Recollections of Blackburn and its Neighbourhood', 'by an old East Lancashire man', *Preston Chronicle* (hereafter *PC*), 22 December 1877.

Guardians treated him differently, addressing him as 'Moses' rather than 'Mr Cocker'.[4] He was a local character, generous with ratepayers' money when demanding food and drink for himself at the workhouse, but also generous with his own money and time. He was happy to accept hospitality from tradesmen bidding for workhouse contracts, and resisted attempts by liberal Guardians to admit the press to meetings of the Guardians. All of this may have led the radical *Blackburn Mercury* (and its Tory rival, the *Blackburn Standard*) to render Cocker's dialect literally in their reports. This was an established journalistic technique, of embarrassing a speaker by refusing to perform the usual editorial tidying-up of speech ready for print. In 1870 a writer in the *Printers' Register* recalled how

> we once heard a very ungrammatical councilman gravely bring it before the town council as a grievance that a certain reporter had, with malice aforethought, put into the newspaper a verbatim report of one of his speeches.[5]

It was not unusual for nineteenth-century middle-class Lancashire professionals to speak in dialect; what is noteworthy here is that it was 'rendered literally' by the newspaper, suggesting that the orthography was a matter of editorial choice, and that it was usual for newspapers to 'translate' the dialect of middle-class speakers into the higher-status variety of Standard English.[6] This editorial policy irked Mr Cocker and his family, making him a 'public laughing stock', not because he spoke in dialect, but because this oral form was maintained in print, usually a marker of the speaker's working-class status. The editorial policy was adopted to highlight Mr Cocker's 'shortcomings' as a Poor Law Guardian. However the speech of other Guardians associated with the same corrupt practices was not rendered in dialect. Perhaps Moses Cocker was monolingual, unable to use any kind of English other than Lancashire dialect, whereas men of his position were expected to have the cultural capital that went with bilingualism or, in the terminology of linguistics, style-shifting.[7] 'Use of dialect was designed to produce a

---

4   *Blackburn Standard*, 15 April 1846.

5   'Reporters and reporting', February 7, 1870, p. 27.

6   James Vernon, *Politics and the People: A Study in English Political Culture, c. 1815–1867* (Cambridge: Cambridge University Press, 1993), p. 147.

7   Style-shifting, or code-switching, is when 'speakers routinely draw on different varieties of English [...] to communicative effect': Joan Swann, 'Style Shifting, Code Switching', in *English: History, Diversity and Change*, ed. by David Graddol, Dick Leith, and Joan Swann (London: Routledge, 1996), pp. 301–37 (p. 301).

comic effect and also create distance between the object of humour and the reader (who possessed, by implied contrast, a command of flawless, standard English).'[8]

Mr Cocker's monolingualism contrasts with the ability of the advocate in court, who was able to 'transpose into English' the evidence given in dialect by Mr Cocker, in cases of personal injury. There are two further clues to the strategy adopted by the newspaper: first, the incomprehension of the London Poor Law official at Mr Cocker's dialect greeting, illustrating how 'language is an instrument of both communication and excommunication', a method of inclusion and exclusion, in this case a marker of status;[9] second, the graphic, vivid, robustly affectionate register of much Lancashire dialect, exemplified in the promise of Mr Cocker, a local functionary of the central state, to 'gether thee some brass'. From a literary perspective, it is clear why journalists seized on such snatches of dialect, because of their communicative and emotional power. Reporters used dialect speech as a literary technique, in the same ways as novelists such as Elizabeth Gaskell, and aimed for similar effects.

A Typology of Dialect in Lancashire Newspapers

This discussion of Lancashire dialect follows the definitions used by Dave Russell, taken from current mainstream thinking in linguistics:

> "Dialect" is defined here simply as a regional variant of a language that also has a standardised and thus more prestigious form [...] dialects are not debased or incorrect versions of "Standard English" but valid linguistic systems derived from Old English, Norse and Norman roots and possessing their own distinctive accent, vocabulary and grammar. Standard English is itself a dialect but one which, through association with the nation's geographical and social power bases, has come to dominate, first of all in print from the late fifteenth century, and increasingly in spoken form from the late eighteenth.[10]

---

8   Christine Pawley, *Reading on the Middle Border: The Culture of Print in Late-Nineteenth-Century Osage, Iowa* (Amherst, MA: University of Massachusetts Press, 2001), p. 175.

9   P. J. Waller, 'Democracy and Dialect, Speech and Class', in *Politics and Social Change in Britain: Essays Presented to A. F. Thompson*, ed. by P. J. Waller (Brighton: Harvester Press, 1987), pp. 1–33 (p. 2).

10   Dave Russell, *Looking North: Northern England and the National Imagination* (Manchester: Manchester University Press, 2004), pp. 111–12.

Accent is only part of dialect, and it is possible to deliver the syntax and vocabulary of Standard English with a pronounced accent, as did Friedrich Engels and three-times Prime Minister Lord Derby, for example.[11]

The use of dialect has been examined systematically in those Lancashire newspapers digitised in the *British Newspaper Archive* database.[12] Dialect passages were identified by searching for three common words, 'skrike' (to shriek or scream), 'anenst' (opposite or against) and 'gradely' (meaning good, proper, right); this elicited 277 articles containing at least 1 of these words between 1830 and 1899. Each article was examined, and the use of dialect grouped and classified. The growth over time in the number and physical size of newspapers included in the BNA, and this database's patchy coverage, was controlled for by dividing instances of dialect by the number of pages digitised in each decade. A rough estimate of the number of pages was gained by searching for a common word, 'Mr', which appeared approximately 4.25 times per page.

The layering of newspapers as texts is revealed in the processes leading to the appearance of dialect in print. The writing of dialect prose or fiction, for publication, was less mediated than most forms (although of course it emerged from a tradition and set of genres already familiar to local readers and writers). However, when a witness gave evidence in court, using dialect, and this was reported verbatim, there were two stages, the speaking and the writing. It was also fairly common to see a three-stage process, when an individual spoke in dialect, perhaps at the scene of a crime; these words were then described in court by a witness, also in dialect, before again

---

11 A. N. Wilson, *The Victorians* (London: Arrow, 2003), p. 114; Augustine Birrell, 'Sir Robert Peel', *The Collected Essays & Addresses of the Rt. Hon. Augustine Birrell, 1880–1920* (London: J. M. Dent & Sons, 1922), p. 331, http://archive.org/details/collectedessaysa01birr

12 www.britishnewspaperarchive.co.uk. The search was limited to material added to the database before 16 January 2018. The twenty-three Lancashire titles available between 1830–99 comprised the *Blackburn Standard, Blackburn Times, Bolton Chronicle, Bolton Evening News, Burnley Advertiser, Burnley Gazette, Burnley Express, Bury Times, Lancashire Evening Post (Preston), Lancaster Gazette, Leigh Chronicle, Liverpool Mercury, Liverpool Mail, Liverpool Daily Post, Manchester Courier, Manchester Times, Preston Chronicle, Preston Herald, Rochdale Observer, Todmorden Advertiser, Todmorden News, Warrington Guardian* and *Wigan Observer*. Every instance of 'skrike/skriking' and 'anenst' was included, but the more common word 'gradely' was only searched for in the fifth year of each decade, to make the exercise more manageable. For a spreadsheet of the full results, see supplementary online material.

being reported verbatim by a newspaper reporter. As we will see, considerations of class came into play more in the second and third instances than in the first.

Analysis of the 277 instances of Lancashire dialect reveals 3 main types: first, dialect in reported speech; second, dialect words and phrases used alongside Standard English in writing such as letters and travelogues written for publication and the editorial voice of the newspaper; and third, the established genre of dialect writing, encompassing poetry, prose and non-fiction. This typology can be subdivided into 8 distinct usages, a wider range of dialect genres than previously acknowledged (see Table 8.1 below).

Table 8.1. A typology of Lancashire dialect usage in local newspapers, 1830–99.

1.	Reported speech
1a	Reported speech, court case defendant or witness
1b	Reported speech in news/feature article
1c	Reported speech in reader's letter
1d	Reported speech in non-dialect fiction or poetry
2.	Writer's own words
3.	Dialect literature
3a	Dialect poetry/dialect in poetry
3b	Dialect fiction/dialect in fiction
3c	Dialect non-fiction

In the first genre of dialect in the local press, reported speech, the original speaker has no control over the literal, cultural and social meanings of their speech once it has been noted by a reporter and published in a newspaper. Dialect used in this way had a low status, and was associated with working-class speakers and 'country bumpkins', regardless of the fact that it was also spoken by people of all classes, in both urban and rural areas.

The most common use of dialect in reported speech was in court reports, or 'Police Intelligence,' as the columns of Police Court cases were headed. The word 'skrike' often appeared in evidence in court, for obvious reasons:

He married my sister, and on Sunday last, I heard her skriking out, un I went in un I knocked im deawn [...][13]

He was so smothered that he could neither see nor speak, and "skriked out murder".[14]

Less often, the more positive word 'gradely' also appeared in court reports, as when a wife was reported by a witness as having encouraged her husband to hit a schoolmaster, urging her spouse to 'give it him gradely [...]'[15] In another case, Thomas Kershaw, 'charged with being drunk and riotous, in extenuation pleaded that he was not "gradely" drunk.'[16] As with Moses Cocker's colourful turn of phrase, the decision to include the dialect word may have been taken to enliven a court report; but it was also a decision to emphasise the class of the speaker. For other people in the same courtroom, a different decision was made, to translate their dialect into Standard English.

Dialect in reported speech was sometimes used to demarcate another distinction, that between the town and the less sophisticated countryside. In 1835 'a simple looking countryman' told a Liverpool court: 'I skriked out "Murder", but that lass there told me if I did not hold my din she would cut my bloody throat'.[17] In 1845, under the heading 'Fiddling, otherwise diddling a country bumpkin', the court report rendered all the evidence of the complainant — a rural fiddle-player cheated out of two violins — in dialect, interspersed with '(loud laughter)', '(renewed laughter)' and '(roars of laughter)'.[18] The heading invites the reader to join in the merriment by laughing at simple country folk. Dialect speech was often used for comic effect in court reporting, as with many working-class characters in Dickens, giving a clear invitation for the reader to look down on the speaker.[19]

---

13   *Manchester Times*, 8 June 1833, p. 3
14   *Bolton Chronicle*, 25 February 1843, p. 2.
15   *Bolton Chronicle*, 16 August 1845.
16   *Rochdale Observer*, 9 December 1865.
17   *Liverpool Mercury*, 2 October 1835, p. 6.
18   *Bolton Chronicle*, 13 December 1845.
19   For example, the Cockney characters of Sam Weller in *The Pickwick Papers* or Sarah Gamp in *Martin Chuzzlewit*. 'English writers have seldom felt able to take the risk of depicting a hero or heroine as a dialect speaker [...] Of course, if the intention was to portray a character as ignorant and comical, the use of dialect would serve very well': William Robert O'Donnell and Loreto Todd, *Variety in Contemporary English* (London: Routledge, 1992), p. 133.

When dialect in speech was reported outside court, the social range of the speakers was wider, as were the social meanings of dialect use. In the passage below, headed 'AN ORATOR OF THE WORKING CLASS,' a report of a public meeting in Bury in 1841, published in the *Preston Chronicle* and reprinted from the *Bolton Free Press*, features the 'extraordinary speech of an Anti-Corn Law Tim Bobbin'.

> [...] Henry Rostron, a working man, from Radcliffe-bridge, came forward to address the meeting. His speech, which was full of wit and humour, set the whole assembly laughing like to split their sides. "Ye mun kno," said he, "yesthurday wur th' day for choosin' kunstables i' eawr place, un th' rate-payurs han chosn me ogen. Neaw, wen aw went ofore th' paason o' Ratcliffe, who's no gud will to th' Repeelers, he sed as he oped to see me at th' church ofthur nur aw ad bin latly. Aw towd im awd mey noan sitch promisus o' that swort, but awd goo a deeol aufthur if he'd preytch i' favur ov' a gud ballyful o' beef for th' workin' mon. (Cheers and laughter.) Thoose ut ud pinch th' ballies o' th' poor wud n't do mitch gud to their sowls. (Renewed laughter.) Th' clergy tell'n me ut aw mun hev o kreawn o' glory wen awm deeod, iv awl behaive gradely; boh aw oalus say ut awd loik to ha summut to be gooin on wi meon whioile. (Roars of laughter and cheers.) [...] Aw wur tellin yo abeawt choosin t'kunstables yesthurday. Well, afthur it war o'er, we'd o rare gud dinnr. Thir wur plenty o' beef, un plenty o' summat ut they koed church puddin. (Laughter.) Yo mey leawf, but its o foine thing is that church puddin; un, moor nur that, its mey opinion, un aw towd th' paason, if teyd o sitch a dinnur us that, wi church puddin, it ud kill o' th' Chartists i' th' kunthry. (Great cheering and laughter.) [...]'[20]

In contrast to the court reports, there is clear admiration for the wit and style of the speaker, and the reference to the revered eighteenth-century dialect writer 'Tim Bobbin' (pen-name of John Collier, 1708–86) enhances the speaker's status. This report is a complex text: a skilled dialect speaker, reported by a skilled dialect writer; the Anti-Corn Law line of the speech is in tune with the *Bolton Free Press* but goes against the editorial policy of the *Preston Chronicle* which reprinted it; the speaker is working-class, but is not stigmatised for this (perhaps because his respectability was guaranteed by his position as constable, and his rejection of Chartism); the inclusive, cross-class register of Lancashire dialect is here turned into a class weapon, or more precisely,

---

20   *PC*, 8 May 1841.

as a weapon of the virtuous poor against the idle and immoral rich.[21] As a rhetorical device, spoken or written, dialect was well suited to mocking pomposity and challenging social status. However, as Vernon notes, the dialect speech of middle-class speakers was more likely to be transcribed into 'Queen's English', apart from the heckles of the working-class crowd. Vernon sees this as a sign of the closer association between Standard English and power, and the growing power of print over oral media.[22]

Occasionally, upper- and middle-class speakers from outside Lancashire would use dialect to say, 'I'm the same as you' to a working-class Lancashire audience, like US President John F. Kennedy telling a Berlin crowd, 'Ich bin ein Berliner'. In 1885, Lord Harris, an Eton-educated baron, told the annual soiree of the Oldham Conservative Working Men's League that 'he knew that the Lancashire "gate" [crowd] was always of the "gradely" character, and that it would give him a fair hearing. (Laughter and applause.)'[23] A year before, a newly arrived clergyman used dialect in the same way, to play down class differences and pay homage to local patriotism. Rev Mr Gordon, vicar of Goosnargh, speaking at the 1884 anniversary celebrations of a friendly society, said that

> [he] had not been long in Lancashire, and had not got their lingo off, but he fancied they were something like "jannock." (Laughter.) He could only say in conclusion that he had been enjoying himself "gradely." (Loud laughter and applause.)[24]

Bourdieu's phrase 'strategy of condescension' seems appropriate here.[25] Why did the audience laugh? Was the incomer's use of their language merely a pleasant surprise? Or was it mocking laughter, at a blatant attempt to patronise them? Russell believes that such 'unifying narratives' of regional identity, expressed here through the middle-class outsider's use of the language of his working-class audience, were used 'consciously or otherwise, to maintain social advantage.' Such 'modes of northernness'

---

21 Patrick Joyce, *Visions of the People: Industrial England and the Question of Class, 1848–1914* (Cambridge: Cambridge University Press, 1994), pp. 245, 249.

22 Vernon, p. 147.

23 'Conservatism at Oldham: Lord Harris on the land question', *Manchester Courier*, 28 September, 1885.

24 *PC*, June 14, 1884.

25 John Brookshire Thompson, 'Editor's Introduction', in Pierre Bourdieu, *Language and Symbolic Power*, ed. by John Brookshire Thompson (Cambridge: Polity, 1991), p. 19.

were used 'by the northern middle and upper classes in their attempts to manage the field of class relationships.'[26]

However, it appears that dialect was part of the native tongue, to varying degrees, of many middle-class people, and was occasionally used in formal situations, for effect.[27] A report of an 1865 meeting of the Bedford Local Board, Leigh, Lancashire, records how discussion turned to paying for new sewers:

> Mr Birchall: I wonder if you would allow it if you [had a financial interest in the affected properties]. — Mr Horrocks: He would "skrike" hard enough. (Laughter.) — Mr Birchall: There is not a man in this Boardroom that would "skrike" harder.[28]

The speaker, John Horrocks, could be classified as lower middle class — a farmer's son, a baker and provision dealer, a 'staunch Conservative and Churchman' who had been a special constable during the time of local Chartist riots, and had kept his truncheon as a souvenir. His obituary claimed that 'he was highly respected in the town'.[29] The laughter suggests that dialect was not usually spoken in public, formal settings such as a local government meeting, by respectable people such as Horrocks. There is also an overtone of mockery, suggesting the word may have associations with schooldays, childhood or play, which would diminish the person associated with the word. A famous example from the 1980s was British Prime Minister Margaret Thatcher's mocking taunt that political opponent Denis Healey was 'frit' (frightened).[30] In 1893, another lower-middle-class figure, a court clerk, insisted that a man prosecuting two women for stealing £20 from him should use the correct dialect term. Samuel Fielden, a draper, told the court that one of the women started screaming when he accused her of theft:

> The Clerk: What kind of screaming was it? Was it crying or skriking out?
> Prosecutor: Skriking out. The Clerk: Why don't you use the correct term?

26　Russell, p. 278.

27　Katie Wales, *Northern English: A Cultural and Social History* (Cambridge: Cambridge University Press, 2006), p. 128, https://doi.org/10.1017/cbo9780511487071

28　*Leigh Chronicle*, 11 March 1865.

29　*Leigh Chronicle* 30 October 1896, p. 8.

30　Fiona McPherson, 'The Iron Lady: Margaret Thatcher's Linguistic Legacy', *OxfordWords Blog*, 2013, https://blog.oxforddictionaries.com/2013/04/10/margaretthatcher/

Sympathetic middle-class characters adopting dialect are sometimes found in nineteenth-century fiction, such as Hiram Yorke in Charlotte Brontë's *Shirley* (1849) and Margaret Hale in Elizabeth Gaskell's *North and South* (1854–55). Towards the end of the century, Stephen Caunce believes that in Northern England, 'the middle class muted their speech [...] increasingly not fully part of their local culture yet not able to live out their class ideal in a satisfactory way. Northernness was thus becoming [...] a *spoiled* version of a generally accepted unitary national ideal.'[31]

Further evidence comes from the contrasting treatment of Preston town councillors in news reports of council meetings and the light-hearted sketches of *Preston Chronicle* reporter and subsequent editor, Anthony Hewitson. While the middle-class professionals and tradesmen who sat on the council spoke Standard English in the news reports, in Hewitson's 1868 sketch, 'Preston Roundabout', on 'Our Town Council and its Members', the same people, in the same meetings, are portrayed as speaking in dialect. Hewitson, writing under his pen-name Atticus, describes the reporters struggling with the councillors' 'bad grammar', and suggests that

> it is probable that one of [the councillors] at least, if asked on the way whether he has been at the meeting, will sapiently reply "I were"; and if he has said anything at it he will, on the following Saturday, quiz the newspaper report, examine his utterance, and genially whisper to himself the old tale of expressiveness, "Them's my sentiments."[32]

Hewitson's irreverence was part of his pioneering adoption of New Journalism techniques in Preston, but he was careful to avoid naming the perpetrators of 'bad grammar', thereby reducing the damage to any individual's middle-class status. Of course, many readers would have heard the councillors speak, and would know full well that they used dialect.

The next usage of dialect, as reported speech in readers' letters, appeared occasionally towards the end of the period surveyed. Here, dialect was used in the same way as in light-hearted news articles,

---

31   Stephen Caunce, 'British, English or What? A Northern English Perspective on Britishness as a New Millennium Starts', Unpublished Conference Paper Delivered at "Relocating Britain" Conference, University of Central Lancashire', 2000, n. p.

32   *PC*, 4 April 1868.

to add vivacity and verisimilitude, and the dialect speaker quoted was almost always working-class. The journalistic technique of using quotes to reveal individuals' emotions was used, as in the letter below, reprinted in the *Preston Chronicle* from the London monthly *The Quiver*, describing the pleasure of textile workers in a village near Blackburn at the sight of a waggon full of raw cotton, at the end of the Cotton Famine in 1864:

> Round this ungainly lurry a crowd of hundreds was gathered. Men laid their hands on the huge, and to us unsightly, parcels with a loving touch, and as though greeting an unlooked-for friend who had long been given up for lost. Others gave the bags a hearty slap, and added, "Hey, owd chaps, but I'm fain to see yo agen."[33]

In other instances, the dialect speaker was implicitly commended by the correspondent for making a sound, commonsense point, the dialect once again emphasising down-to-earth practicality.

The fourth setting for reported dialect speech, in non-dialect fiction or poetry, has already been discussed briefly, with reference to middle-class characters in Charlotte Brontë and Elizabeth Gaskell (Mrs Gaskell's husband published two lectures on the history of Lancashire dialect).[34] This was a breach of novelistic practice, which had previously decreed that 'narrators and other middle-class characters used only "good" or "standard" English'.[35] This usage more commonly tended to denote working-class, uneducated or rural characters, but not always unsympathetically.

These speakers, whose words were reported by someone else, had far less control over how their words were used (often against them) than writers, who interspersed dialect words or phrases with Standard English. This usage also tended to appeal to the common-sense associations of dialect, as in a letter from W. Streight in 1872, using a local hero's exclusion from a civic function to make a dig at the poor creditworthiness of some Preston dignitaries:

> [...] Well, all I have to say is this, that if he cannot get invited to the Mayor's garden party he can do this, at all events, namely, keep agate

---

33   *PC*, 3 September 1864.

34   William Gaskell, *Two Lectures on the Lancashire Dialect* (London, 1854).

35   Patricia Ingham, 'Introduction', in *North and South*, by Elizabeth Gaskell, ed. by Patricia Ingham (London: Penguin, 1995).

paying his debts, and that is more than some of the heavy swells can do who were present.[36]

Another letter, supporting Russia against Turkey in 1877, uses the inclusive undertones of the word 'gradely' to add emotional power to the writer's argument:

> [...] "Do unto others as thou wouldst have others do unto thee" was never intended to guide our dealings with such people as the Mahommedans. Not a bit of it. They are not "gradely" people you know [...][37]

As with other techniques for promoting and profiting from local identities, dialect appeared in local newspaper advertisements. A Liverpool bakery selling a foreign delicacy, 'Yorkshire parkin', used Yorkshire dialect to establish the authenticity of its cake. The advert included a testimonial 'signed by a Live Yorkshireman [...] given *verbatim et literatim*' confirming that the parkin was the genuine article.[38] Throughout 1865 Ralph Holden, a Burnley tailor, used dialect in doggerel advertising his goods on the front page of the *Burnley Advertiser*, while the tea sold by Preston's Consumer Tea Company in 1875 was advertised as 'gradely', of course.[39] In 1895 a small ad in a Blackburn paper offered 'gradely lodgings for two gradely lads' (Fig. 8.1).

L ODGINGS.— Gradely Lodgings for two gradely lads :
bath and piano.— Apply " Express and Standard "
Office, Blackburn.

Fig. 8.1. Dialect word in classified advertisement, *Blackburn Weekly Standard & Express*, 12 October 1895, p. 4. Author's transcription, CC BY 4.0.

In later years this interspersing of Standard English and dialect was also used occasionally by the editorial voice of local newspapers, for its commonsense associations and to establish the publication as local. The *Burnley Express* columnist 'Sportsman', commenting on the new committee of Burnley Football Club, wrote in 1895: 'I hope the management will act in unity, and, as the old saying goes, "shape gradely."'[40]

---

36 *PC*, 24 August 1872.
37 *PC*, 10 February 1877.
38 *Liverpool Daily Post*, 15 June 1855, p. 1.
39 *Preston Herald*, 23 January 1875.
40 *Burnley Express*, 6 April 1895, p. 6.

The most prestigious use of dialect went beyond journalistic writing to claim the status of literature, whether poetry, fiction or non-fiction. When used in literary genres, or as part of a bilingual written vocabulary clearly showing the writer's mastery of Standard English, the status of dialect was almost equal to Standard English.[41] The standing of dialect literature can be seen in the *Papers of the Manchester Literary Club* for 1893, in which a highly complimentary paper on Edwin Waugh's dialect poetry is sandwiched between papers on Shelley's lyrics and *Macbeth*. Here, status or social class was not an issue.[42]

Most local newspapers carried some dialect writing, making them central players in this literary market, alongside other middle-class patrons of the genre. This was part of their broader role as a major publishing platform for poetry and many other genres.[43] Newspaper editors and journalists were involved in local literary cultures, nurturing, publishing and critiquing the poetry and prose of local writers, when they were not writing it themselves. F. B. Peacock of the *Manchester Examiner & Times* was the first to publish Lancashire's most famous dialect poem, 'Come Whoam to thi childer an' me', by Edwin Waugh; John Harland, a reporter and partner in the *Manchester Guardian*, published articles on dialect poetry in 1839 and wrote extensively on Lancashire's culture, later compiling *The Ballads and Songs of Lancashire* and *Lancashire Lyrics*. In Blackburn, William Abram of the *Blackburn Times* was a great enabler of that town's working-class literary culture, much of it written in dialect.[44]

Lancashire and Yorkshire produced more dialect literature than any other part of England, published in broadsides and ballad form,

---

41   Martha Vicinus, *The Industrial Muse: A Study of Nineteenth Century British Working-Class Literature* (London: Croom Helm, 1974); Brian Hollingworth, *Songs of the People: Lancashire Dialect Poetry of the Industrial Revolution* (Manchester: Manchester University Press, 1977); Joyce, chap. 6; Paul Salveson, 'Region, Class, Culture: Lancashire Dialect Literature, 1746–1935' (unpublished PhD dissertation, University of Salford, 1993); Russell, chap. 4.

42   Table of contents, *Papers of the Manchester Literary Club*, vol 19, 1893, in Sutton, Charles W, and William Credland, eds. *Manchester Literary Club: Index to Publications, Catalogue of the Library and List of Members 1862–1903* (Manchester: Sherratt & Hughes, 1903), http://archive.org/details/indexpapers00mancuoft, p. 15.

43   Andrew Hobbs and Claire Januszewski, 'How Local Newspapers Came to Dominate Victorian Poetry Publishing', *Victorian Poetry*, 52 (2014), p. 83, https://doi.org/10.1353/vp.2014.0008

44   Thanks to Professor Brian Hollingworth for these points.

pamphlets, newspapers, books and almanacs, and read, or performed, in public and at home.[45] Below is an example of dialect poetry published by the *Preston Chronicle*, reprinted from the *Manchester Guardian*, and signed '"J. D.", Preston.' The poem was published during the Cotton Famine, when many Lancashire mills closed due to a trade glut and the disruption of the American Civil War. The crisis was seen at the time as a cross-class disaster for Lancashire, although mismanagement by mill owners played a large part in it.

A'ARE FACTORY'S GOOIN' TO BEGIN.

We'est manidge, owd lass, to poo throo,
    If we'll nobbut howd eawt a bit lunger;
Tho' it hez bin' a terrable doo,
    We'an hed wi' starvation un hunger.

Baw gum! when aw luk i' thi face,
    Un see thi so haggert un thin,
Mi hart welly brasts, aw confess,
    Un th' wayter will rise to mi e'en.

[...][46]

It is typical of the dialect literature published in local newspapers, in its domestic focus, its sentimentality and its stoic acceptance of the status quo. Salveson believes that writers selected their more non-political pieces for submission to local papers.[47] There is a similar lack of political questioning, alongside a belief in the shared interests of capital and

---

45   Graham Shorrocks, 'Non-Standard Dialect Literature and Popular Culture', in *Speech Past and Present: Studies in English Dialectology in Memory of Ossi Ihalainen*, ed. by Juhani Klemola, Merja Kyto, and Matt Rissanen (Frankfurt am Main: P. Lang, 1996), pp. 390–91.

46   *PC*, April 16, 1864.

We must manage, old girl, to pull through,
If we can hold out a bit longer
Though it's been a terrible do
We've had with starvation and hunger.

By gum! When I look in your face
And see you so haggard and thin,
My heart well nigh bursts, I confess
And the water will rise to my eyes.

47   Salveson, p. 133.

labour, in the poor-quality piece of prose below, from 1878, at the end of a pay dispute in which workers had been locked out of most Preston mills.

EAUR FOLKS WUR LOCKED OUT, BUT THEY'N GETTEN TO THEIR WARK AGAIN.

(By a Weaver's Wife.)

[...]

Whatever should we ha' done but for those good, kind ladies an' gentlemen, who so nobly come forrad wi' a helpin' hond — awm not th' only one who says "God bless 'em, and may they never know what it is to want what they connot get till they go to their reward i' heaven." Awst taich my childher to pray for 'em aw th' days o' their lives [...] Thoose waistrils 'at went about riotin' wanted eaur Josh to jine 'em, but he said he'd rather clem fust. He towd 'em plainly they wur nowt but a pack o' foos to goo about desthroyin' what wur like their own property — it wur like chopping their own legs off, so as they couldn't walk. They said if th' mesthers wouldn't oppen th' mills they'd brun 'em down. Eaur Josh towd 'em 'at him, an' a few moor, meant to keep a sherp watch on their facthry an' it shouldn't be set on fire beaut somebody knowin'.[48]

It is quite possible that the author of the piece above was indeed 'a Weaver's Wife', but it is equally possible that it was written by a reporter or other member of the *Chronicle* staff, as it chimes with the paper's editorial attitude to the dispute. In this passage, the employers' point of view has been put clearly, but clothed in the accent and dialect conventionally assigned to workers. It uses local patriotism to appeal for consensus. Dialect writing was often harnessed in this way, appealing to cross-class interests by exploiting its down-to-earth, common-sense register.[49] Peter Lucas has shown that much dialect writing in the newspapers of Furness, in the far north of Lancashire, was produced by employees of the publications, in one case, three individuals sharing a pseudonym.[50] But some dialect literature appears to come from readers.

---

48   *PC*, 29 June 1878.
49   Salveson, PhD, summary [n.p.].
50   Peter J. Lucas, 'The First Furness Newspapers: The History of the Furness Press from 1846 to c.1880' (unpublished M.Litt, University of Lancaster, 1971), p. 16; Peter J. Lucas, 'The Dialect Boom in Victorian Furness', *Transactions of the Cumberland & Westmorland Antiquarian & Archaeological Society*, 5 (2005), 199–216 (p. 205).

Certain papers published in south and east Lancashire, the heartland of Lancashire dialect, solicited readers' contributions to the genre. In Blackburn, the rival Radical *Times* and Conservative *Standard* both supported the town's thriving working-class literary culture.[51] In the 1870s the *Standard* had a reader competition (as did the *Burnley Advertiser*), while the *Blackburn Times* often published half a page of dialect literature per issue, featuring the town's roster of poets plus Lancashire's most famous nineteenth-century dialect writer, Edwin Waugh.[52] Waugh's most famous poem, 'Come Whoam to thi childer an' me', was the subject of a reader's prize essay in the *Blackburn Standard* of 1895; the paper also ran a weekly competition for the 'best anecdote or short Lancashire sketch' in the same year.[53]

Dialect was less often used as a mocking marker of class in newspapers where there were vibrant working-class literary cultures, such as Blackburn or Burnley. Table 8.2 below provides a rough comparison of how dialect was used in two different towns (each represented by two newspapers in the BNA database). Blackburn, with its exceptional literary culture, treated dialect mainly as a literary form, allowing working-class writers to speak for themselves. In contrast, in the Preston papers, working-class users of dialect were more likely to be objects of derision than subjects with agency.

Table 8.2. Usage of Lancashire dialect in Blackburn and Preston, 1840s–90s.

	Blackburn	Preston
Dialect literature	31	10
Reported speech (excluding fiction):	12	25
In news/feature articles	4	14
In court reports	8	10
Writer's own words	2	1

---

51   George Hull, *The Poets and Poetry of Blackburn* (Blackburn: G. & J. Toulmin, 1902).

52   For example, 'Tales i' the Nook by Edwin Waugh: It's Noan o Mine!', 16 November 1878.

53   *Blackburn Standard*, 24 August, 10 August 1895.

Change Over Time

The use of dialect in local papers also changed over time, with a move away from using it as a class marker, towards using it in cross-class ways. Table 8.3 below confirms a boom in dialect literature from the 1840s onwards, with fiction first, followed by poetry and non-fiction (typically comic correspondence on local and national issues) later.[54] The use of dialect in the reported speech of defendants and witnesses peaked in the 1840s and declined steeply thereafter. Donaldson believes that Isaac Pitman's breakthrough in rendering the *sound* of language rather than its spelling in his shorthand inspired dialect writers to experiment with orthography from the late 1830s onwards.[55] The use of reported dialect speech in other news reports and feature articles peaked in the 1850s and '60s, and it is tempting to see the influence of Gaskell, Charlotte and Emily Brontë and other novelists in the greater use of this literary trope. Journalists were likely to pick up literary trends before most of their readers, which could explain the later use of reported dialect speech in readers' letters, in the 1870s, after the use of the device had become established first in fiction and poetry, and then in newspaper reporting.[56] This could also explain the peak in the 1870s of the use of dialect by letter-writers and journalists using the editorial voice, showing a peak of confidence in local dialect.

Many literary tropes were shared by journalistic and more 'literary' writing, which is less surprising when we consider that journalists, like novelists, were in the business of telling stories. As Dallas Liddle and Matthew Rubery have demonstrated, a focus on content (for example Lancashire dialect, or particular news stories), rather than forms of publication (books or newspapers) can help us see how techniques and attitudes were passed between and within genres such as literature and journalism which are anachronistically viewed as

---

54 Hollingworth, *Songs of the People*, p. 2. Hollingworth dates the boom to 1856–70.

55 William Donaldson, *Popular Literature in Victorian Scotland: Language, Fiction, and the Press* (Aberdeen: Aberdeen University Press, 1986), pp. 53–54.

56 In Manchester many journalists worked through the Manchester Literary Club to compile a *Glossary of Lancashire Dialect*: Margaret Beetham, 'Healthy Reading', in *City, Class and Culture: Studies of Social Policy and Cultural Production in Victorian Manchester*, ed. by Alan J. Kidd and Kenneth W Roberts (Manchester: Manchester University Press, 1985), pp. 173–74.

Table 8.3: Usage of dialect in selected Lancashire newspapers, 1830s–'90s (instances per 100,000 pages).

	1830-1839	1840-1849	1850-1859	1860-1869	1870-1879	1880-1889	1890-1899
Reported speech, court case defendant or witness	20	123	42	41	26	9	4
Reported speech in news/ feature article	0	36	81	67	19	47	33
Reported speech in reader's letter	0	0	0	0	81	0	0
Reported speech in non-dialect fiction or poetry	0	0	0	31	32	53	55
Writer's own words	0	2	22	1	65	16	25
Dialect poetry or song	0	0	0	80	65	19	33
Dialect fiction	64	72	24	30	20	35	25
Dialect non-fiction	64	39	20	1	32	0	84

separate spheres.[57] The case of dialect reminds us that an interplay was also taking place between print and oral culture, further challenging simplistic ideas of print replacing oral traditions.[58]

The increasingly cross-class use of dialect can be seen more clearly in Fig. 8.2 below. Working-class witnesses and defendants were marked out for their use of dialect in court cases less and less, while dialect literature,

---

57   Dallas Liddle, *The Dynamics of Genre: Journalism and the Practice of Literature in Mid-Victorian Britain* (Charlottesville: University of Virginia Press, 2009); Matthew Rubery, *The Novelty of Newspapers: Victorian Fiction After the Invention of the News* (Oxford: Oxford University Press, 2009).

58   For a discussion of these themes exemplified in another publishing genre, the local magazine, see Margaret Beetham, 'Ben Brierley's Journal', *Manchester Region History Review*, 17 (2006), 73–83, particularly pp. 81–82.

written by members of all classes, increased in popularity. Most dialect writing in newspapers was anonymous, and it has not been possible to ascertain most authors' identities and hence their class. However, Joyce, Lucas, Russell and Salveson suggest that many nineteenth-century writers of dialect prose and poetry were middle-class, with Russell's analysis of Yorkshire dialect writers up to 1945 finding that the class distribution was about even.[59] Some were not even native speakers, but had the technical facility to convincingly reproduce dialect speech, aided by the growing volume of glossaries and other dialect literature; these writers included M. R. Lahee, an Irish woman celebrated as one of Rochdale's finest dialect poets;[60] the Middlesbrough-born journalist Joseph Richardson and the Nottingham-born surgeon-turned-vicar Dr Barber, who both published literature in the dialect of Lancashire 'north of the sands'.[61] Frederic W. Moorman, Devon-born Professor of English Language at the University of Leeds at the turn of the twentieth century, wrote and edited Yorkshire dialect poetry and prose.[62]

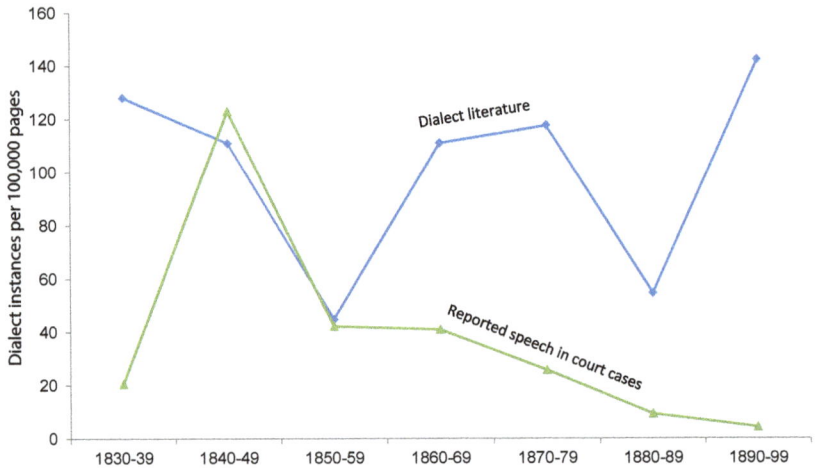

Fig. 8.2. Dialect literature and dialect in court reporting, 1830–99, selected Lancashire newspapers, per 100,000 pages. Author's graph, CC BY 4.0.

59   Salveson, p. 4; Joyce, p. 258; Lucas, 'Dialect Boom', p. 205; Russell, pp. 120–21.

60   Taryn Hakala, 'M. R. Lahee and the Lancashire Lads: Gender and Class in Victorian Lancashire Dialect Writing', *Philological Quarterly*, 92 (2013), 271–88.

61   Lucas, M.Litt, p. 16; Lucas, 'Dialect Boom', p. 205.

62   William Marshall, 'An Eisteddfod for Yorkshire? Professor Moorman and the Uses of Dialect', *Yorkshire Archaeological Journal*, 83 (2011), 199–217, https://doi.org/10.117 9/008442711X13033963454633

There appear to be two separate processes at work: the rise in popularity of dialect literature from the late 1850s to the early 1870s, and a greater sensitivity to the growing numbers of working-class local newspaper readers. The peak of reported dialect speech in the 1840s could be related to the renewed popularity of dialect literature, and its subsequent decline could be caused by the growing editorial realisation that the paper's new working-class readers might be offended by the supercilious way in which their class was portrayed through the comic use of dialect quotes. By the time of the second Reform Act (1867), newspapers were beginning to claim a working-class readership.[63] As Gareth Stedman Jones has noted, 'Changes in the use of language can often indicate important turning points in social history'.[64] It may also be that, as the literature boom raised the status of dialect, so its usefulness as a class marker declined.

As dialect increased in legitimacy as a written form, it became one literary device among many, to be used in a growing range of contexts. For example, *Cross Fleury's Journal*, a Preston monthly magazine, comfortably mixed Standard English, French, Latin and Lancashire dialect in a report of an 1897 royal jubilee celebration, while the *Preston Argus*, a weekly paper, introduced itself to readers thus:

> As this is our first appearance under the new name, we take off our hat and give you kindly greeting, if only for the purpose of proving to you that we have "larn't manners."[65]

The dialect may have been in inverted commas, but it was now found in sections of these publications where previously only Standard English had appeared.

While there may have been renewed respect for written dialect, at least in some quarters, dialect speech was probably in decline. The debate among teachers around the 1862 Revised Code for teaching in schools showed that many valued dialect speech, and respected the language spoken by children at home.[66] But after the 1870 Education

---

63 Lucy Brown, *Victorian News and Newspapers* (Oxford: Clarendon Press, 1985), pp. 73–74.

64 Gareth Stedman Jones, *Outcast London: A Study in the Relationship between Classes in Victorian Society* (Penguin Books, 1984), preface, p. v.

65 'Sparks from the Anvil', *Cross Fleury's Journal*, July 1897, 10; *Preston Argus*, 17 September 1897, p. 1.

66 Brian Hollingworth, 'Education and the Vernacular', in *Dialect and Education: Some European Perspectives*, ed. by Jenny Cheshire (Multilingual Matters, 1989), pp. 293–302.

Act, and compulsory education from 1880, there was a push for standardised English, and policies were introduced into Lancashire schools to 'eradicate' dialect speech.[67] In 1890 the debate was revived in Rochdale, when the local inspector of schools called for dialect writer 'Tim Bobbin' to be studied alongside Shakespeare (in an equally dry manner); the *Rochdale Observer* opposed the inspector and declared in an editorial that 'dialect is dying through schooling and the newspapers'.[68]

Readers seemed to like the use of dialect in local newspapers, judging from their many responses to competitions encouraging them to send contributions. Dialect writing (like many other genres published in the local press, week by week) was often republished in book form, by the same newspaper publishers. For example, *Giles's Trip to London: A Farm Labourer's First Peep at the World*, by James Spilling, first appeared in the *Eastern Daily Press* and *Ipswich and Colchester Times*. Reprinted in book form by the *Eastern Daily Press*, it had gone through 58 editions (239,000 copies) by 1903. For the most part, we can only guess at readers' responses. As Maidment and Hollingworth have noted of dialect poetry, it evoked a sense of belonging and community, of inclusion.[69] Conversely, it may have excluded those who did not read, speak or understand the particular dialect. Translation was sometimes necessary, if dialect was part of a sensational court case that received national coverage, as in a widely reported murderer's confession which included the word 'skrike'. In Lancashire newspapers the word was given without explanation, but in other parts of the country the translation '(scream)' was added.[70]

Conclusions

Dialect in print, far from being a sub-genre of low-quality comic or sentimental folk literature, or a simple marker of working-class

---

67 Brian Hollingworth, 'Dialect in Schools —an Historical Note', *Durham and Newcastle Research Review*, 39 (1977), 15–20 (p. 16).

68 *Rochdale Observer*, 22 March 1890, cited in Hollingworth, 'Dialect in Schools', p. 19. The newspaper's view is consistent with James Vernon's argument that the local press harmed local oral cultures: Vernon, p. 147.

69 Brian Hollingworth, 'From Voice to Print: Lancashire Dialect Verse, 1800–70', *Philological Quarterly*, 92 (2013), 289–308 (p. 297).

70 *PC*, 29 November 1890.

status — a sociolect — had a variety of uses in local newspapers, revealing the linguistic and literary sophistication of these texts. The very fact of who was represented as using it sent a simple message of social distinction; more subtly, it could be used as a rhetorical device to strengthen supposedly 'commonsense' arguments, and more subtly still, the untranslatable nuances of dialect words and phrases could add depth to any piece of writing. In these ways, publishers and writers in areas with a lively dialect tradition had literary advantages over less linguistically diverse areas, being able to call on an extra set of meanings.[71] Comparisons with other 'bilingual' publishing situations, such as English-language newspapers in Wales, would be instructive.

However, some dialect speakers may have felt excluded. The orthography used to render dialect in print was one of the subtle ways in which certain readers could be excluded because of their educational level. Dialect in print was harder to read than Standard English, perhaps particularly for dialect speakers, who naturally read Standard English in a Lancashire accent, and so may have been confused by many of the phonetic spellings. A reader who does not speak in Received Pronunciation receives a clear message, 'this text was not written for you'.[72]

Power relations are central to any understanding of language, and the 'value-laden' nature of dialect shows this clearly.[73] Working-class writers increasingly had the power to represent themselves in print, in local newspapers, to be subjects rather than objects. The changing uses of dialect in local papers reveal editors deciding who is represented as 'them', who as 'us'. Increasingly, working-class readers went from the former category to the latter. Some papers in some towns made more efforts in this regard than others.

Dialect in print highlights two competing discourses, of place (region or locality) and class. Local newspapers' use of dialect to

---

71   Hollingworth, 'From Voice to Print', p. 294.

72   In the same way, twenty-first-century London newspapers' attempts to render the northern accent phonetically (for example, spelling a well-known swear-word as 'fook') automatically exclude readers with that accent. Oral historians in Scotland found that transcripts of interviews which were written phonetically were almost incomprehensible to the interviewees: Stephen Caunce, *Oral History and the Local Historian* (London: Longman, 1994); Graham Shorrocks, 'A Phonemic and Phonetic Key to the Orthography of the Lancashire Dialect Writer, Teddy Ashton', *Journal of the Lancashire Dialect Society*, 27 (1978), 45–59 (p. 59); Wales, p. 138.

73   Nikolas Coupland, *Dialect in Use: Sociolinguistic Variation in Cardiff English* (Cardiff: University of Wales Press, 1988), p. 95.

capitalise on their readers' sense of place was inclusive, in the main, with surprisingly little reference to an 'other', perhaps because of their very localised markets. But they also used dialect as a strategy of exclusion, by class rather than geography, particularly at the start of the period under discussion, when readers were mainly middle-class. In contrast, working-class listeners to such a paper being read aloud may have felt like eavesdroppers, being talked about rather than included in the conversation. The use of dialect in reported speech emphasised class differences, while dialect literature played them down. Newspapers colluded in the fiction that middle-class people did not speak in dialect in formal settings, by putting Standard English words into their mouths — even though this was no more than a convention, and most of their readers knew it was a fiction. Moses Cocker was penalised by the *Blackburn Mercury* not because he was monolingual, but because he was not respectable. The phonetic rendering of his dialect was a punishment, an example of policing the borders of social distinction by the press. However, the middle-class institution of the local paper occasionally allowed glimpses of working-class dialect speakers using this language variety to mock and defy other institutions of authority, a sign of the complexity of dialect, and of local newspapers, which were not monolithic, mono-glossal bourgeois institutions, but poly-glossal, multi-authored texts. Over time, as more working-class newspaper readers became newspaper purchasers, dialect was used less to exclude, and more to include. The use of dialect in reported speech declined; conversely, the use of dialect in a wider range of literary contexts grew, as it became more established as a legitimate writerly device. New working-class readers influenced the language of newspapers, which were eager to cater to their tastes and sensibilities. The cross-class nature of much dialect literature made it a safe selling point to these new readers, who were thus welcomed into an expanded 'imagined community' of other readers for mainly commercial reasons.[74]

Local newspapers' use of dialect reveals the dynamic and contested nature of local identities. In a newspaper, 'what is arrayed before the

---

74   James Curran, 'The Press as an Agency of Social Control', in *Newspaper History from the Seventeenth Century to the Present Day*, ed. by David George Boyce, James Curran, and Pauline Wingate (London: Constable, 1978), pp. 51–75 (p. 71); Russell, p. 127; Benedict Anderson, *Imagined Communities: Reflections on the Origin and Spread of Nationalism* (London: Verso, 2006).

reader is not pure information but a portrayal of the contending forces in the world.'[75] These contending forces were present in the multiple local identities fought over within and between each publication, class identities amongst them. There was more than one imagined community. Many historians have noted a lessening of conflict in the pages of late nineteenth century local newspapers (see Table 8.4). Murphy believes that the 'ideology of impartiality' was a result of newspapers' move from the political arena into the marketplace: 'the new commercial papers of the late nineteenth century identified themselves with a sort of parish-pump patriotism, a supra-factional, local, public interest [...]'[76] Factors beyond the press may also have been involved in the reduction of class and religious conflict, such as a calmer political atmosphere after the Second and Third Reform Acts, higher real wages and shorter working hours, and more tolerance of Catholics. However, the evidence from this study of dialect suggests another commercial reason, an attempt to welcome new working-class readers into a classless conception of the locality. They downplayed conflict and 'encouraged positive identification with the local community, its local traditions and its middle-class leadership.'[77] This was certainly true when Preston's football club nearly collapsed in 1893, the subject of the next chapter.

---

75 James Carey, *Communication as Culture: Essays on Media and Society* (London: Routledge, 1989), p. 20, https://doi.org/10.4324/9780203928912

76 David Murphy, *The Silent Watchdog: The Press in Local Politics* (London: Constable, 1976), p. 28.

77 Curran, p. 71.

9. Win-win: The Local Press and Association Football

Football made the local evening newspaper, and the local evening newspaper made football. From the 1880s onwards, the huge popularity of organised professional association football fed, and fed off, the local press. Both were part of national structures, both relied on local patriotism for their success. It was a win-win situation. Sports coverage was a significant part of the changes in British journalism that coalesced in the 1880s as the 'New Journalism', bringing in new readers and purchasers, particularly among the working classes. The coverage of professional football in Preston's newspapers represented a conscious broadening of appeal, in the same way that most Lancashire newspapers had changed their use of dialect in an attempt to attract working-class readers (Chapter 8). The symbiotic relationship between football and the local press, and the techniques used by the press to incorporate the game into its conventions of local patriotism, are illustrated by coverage of a high point and a low point in the fortunes of Preston North End Football Club. In 1889 PNE reached the pinnacle of their career, becoming champions of the new Football League in its first season without losing a match, and winning the FA Cup without conceding a goal. But four years later, in the summer of 1893, the club nearly collapsed under heavy debts, was suspended by the sport's governing body, the Football Association, and only just scraped together enough money to relaunch as a limited company.

Sports history has produced some perceptive writing on the nature of local — and regional — identities. It seems that sport, and football in

    https://doi.org/10.11647/OBP.0152.09

particular, is the quintessential creator and sustainer of local identity. Like the local press, it has the capacity to incorporate almost any other aspect of local identity, thereby combining and magnifying elements into a more powerful whole — but with the added ingredient of emotional involvement.[1] Jeff Hill's classic study of the ritual of the Cup Final demonstrates powerfully the number of elements at play, magnified and mythologised by the local press, which 'often stepped into the realm of myth-making. By offering comment and opinion on the events, or simply by selecting certain aspects for attention, newspaper editors and reporters played upon notions of identity which drew on and at the same time reinforced a sense of local distinctiveness.'[2] As this chapter demonstrates, Preston newspapers, like many others, incorporated into their sports coverage many of the techniques discussed previously, such as local history, boosterism and 'othering', in an appeal to local patriotism.

Working-class interest in football developed in Lancashire before many other parts of the country, with association football (as distinct from rugby football) reaching Preston from East Lancashire, where it had been popular since the late 1870s.[3] Preston North End (PNE), originally a cricket club, switched from rugby to the 'dribbling game' fully in 1882.[4] They quickly adapted to the new code, and began to import Scottish players and the Scottish passing style of play. While other clubs were still concocting ad hoc teams for each fixture, PNE concentrated on building a stable, consistent team, better able to play in an 'organised scientific style'. From August 1885 to April 1886 the club had an undefeated run, although success in the Lancashire and FA cup competitions eluded them. By 1886 the club had 'assumed the prerogative of using the ancient town crest', thereby claiming to represent the whole of Preston.[5] In 1888 they reached the finals of

---

1   For a superb account from an earlier period of local identity and sport (in this case cricket), see Mary Russell Mitford, 'A Country Cricket-Match', in *The Works of Mary Russell Mitford, Prose and Verse* (Philadelphia: Crissy & Markley, 1846), pp. 41–45.

2   Jeffrey Hill, 'Rite of Spring: Cup Finals and Community in the North of England', in *Sport and Identity in the North of England*, ed. by Jeffrey Hill and Jack Williams (Keele: Keele University Press, 1996), pp. 85–111 (pp. 102, passim).

3   Dave Russell, *Looking North: Northern England and the National Imagination* (Manchester: Manchester University Press, 2004), pp. 13, 19.

4   David Hunt, *The History of Preston North End Football Club: The Power, the Politics and the People* (Preston: PNE Publications, 2000), p. 44.

5   Hunt, p. 54.

the FA Cup and the Lancashire Cup, but refused to compete for the latter trophy against Accrington, in Blackburn, because of the hostility of Blackburn supporters (demonstrating the fierce inter-town rivalries expressed through football).[6]

Football and the Local Press

The rise of association football assisted, and was assisted by, the rise of the local press. Contemporary reading surveys found that many men, particularly among the working classes, read sporting papers and halfpenny local evening papers, featuring a great deal of sport (see Chapter 6). These publications developed around the same time as professional football, and Mason is one of many sports historians to have identified an 'important symbiotic relationship between the expansion of the game, both amateur and professional, and both the growth of a specialised press and the spread of football coverage in the general newspapers.'[7] The local and regional sporting press grew enormously in the last two decades of the nineteenth century, with evening papers (and some weeklies) adding special late football editions to their Saturday papers, including the *Blackburn Times* (1883), owned by the Toulmins, publishers of the *Preston Guardian* and *Lancashire Evening Post*.[8] These football and sports specials, such as Sheffield's *Green 'Un* (Fig. 9.1 below) were 'arguably the most important consumer product produced for supporters'.[9] Mason claims that 'sports coverage in local papers helped shape local identities and boost partisanship.'[10] This is certainly what the local press set out to do, but whether they were successful is harder to prove.

---

6   Hunt, pp. 17, 42, 76.

7   Anthony Mason, *Association Football and English Society, 1863–1915* (Brighton: Harvester Press, 1980), p. 187; Thomas Preston, 'The Origins and Development of Association Football in the Liverpool District, c.1879 until c.1915' (unpublished PhD dissertation, University of Central Lancashire, 2007), pp. 309, 311.

8   Mason, p. 193; Bob Clarke, *From Grub Street to Fleet Street: An Illustrated History of the English Newspaper to 1899* (Aldershot: Ashgate, 2004), p. 129.

9   Alexander Jackson, 'Reading the *Green 'Un*: The Saturday Football and Sports Special as a Consumer Product and Historical Source', 2007, unpublished manuscript, p. 12.

10 Tony Mason, 'All the Winners and the Half-Times', *The Sports Historian*, 13 (1993), 3–13 (p. 12), https://doi.org/10.1080/17460269309446373

Fig. 9.1. A speedy results service was as important as local patriotism for newspaper readers, as seen in this illustrated column header in the *Football and Sports Special of the Yorkshire Telegraph and Star*, known colloquially as *The Green 'Un* because of the distinctive colour of its newsprint, 31 October 1908 (British Library NEWS979). © The British Library Board, all rights reserved.

Local evening papers, and Saturday sports specials in particular, had two distinct selling points: first, their local flavour, and, second, the speed with which they delivered results, reports and comment (Fig. 9.1), on football but also on non-local sports, notably horse racing. Lee claims that 'London evening papers sold a quarter to a third more copies during the racing season'.[11] Evidence that the local and localised content was a large part of the appeal of sports news comes, paradoxically, from the 'national' press, in which sports reporting was the most localised content. The *Daily Mail*, for example, utilised the ability to publish variant regional editions, thanks to its publishing operation in Manchester, in which sports content was the most differentiated type of content. Content analysis of two Monday editions of the *Mail* in 1900, after the launch of its Northern edition, and in 1908, found that the sports news accounted for fifty-five of the eighty-seven column inches that were different in the two sampled issues, and the same First Division football matches were reported

---

11   Alan J. Lee, *The Origins of the Popular Press in England: 1855–1914* (London: Croom Helm, 1976), p. 127.

differently in each edition, with reports in the northern edition written from the perspective of northern fans, and those in the London edition written from the perspective of southern fans.[12] The local and regional nature of interest in professional football was well understood and catered for.

Sports coverage grew rapidly in Preston's papers in the last two decades of the century, but there was fierce competition and careful differentiation between titles within the same stable. A comparison of the main Preston papers shows that sports coverage was minimal in 1880, with the one weekly and two bi-weekly papers devoting between one and three columns to it per week, the bi-weekly *Herald* and *Guardian* giving slightly more space than the weekly *Chronicle* (Table 9.1 below). James Catton, an apprentice reporter on the *Herald* at the time, later wrote of PNE captain Harry Cartmel, 'how desperately he used to try and secure the support of the local press, which just tolerated football in an off-hand kind of way at that date.'[13] By 1890, sport (mainly football) was now a significant part of the contents of the *Herald*, with more than fourteen columns per week devoted to it, or 11.1 per cent of its total space, while twenty-five columns of sport in the new *Lancashire Evening Post* accounted for more than twenty per cent of its space. Sometimes there was even more, as in the Saturday 2 September 1893 *Evening Post*, in which sport accounted for more than two-thirds of editorial content. The *Herald*'s focus was narrower, concentrating more on Preston and Lancashire sport, while the *Evening Post* featured more regional and national sport. Generally, football coverage was more focused on Preston than was cycling or cricket coverage. By 1890 the *Guardian* had

---

12 Both editions of Monday 5 February 1900 carried results from Divisions 1 and 2, but where the northern edition had results from the Lancashire League, the Lancashire Combination, the Lancashire Alliance and other Manchester and Lancashire leagues, the southern edition had instead results from the Southern League, the Midland League and the Kent League. For 5 February and 3 December 1900, there was an average of sixty-four column inches of sports coverage from north of Watford in the northern edition, compared with an average of twenty-three inches in the southern edition. Quantitative analysis of the 1908 editions does not capture the differences as well: the same FA Cup matches were given equal space in each edition in February 1908, but were written from northern or southern perspectives.

13 J. A. H. Catton, *The Rise of the Leaguers: A History of the Clubs Comprising the First Division of the Football League : Reprinted from the Sporting Chronicle* (Manchester: Sporting Chronicle, 1897), p. 95, cited in Steve Tate, 'The Professionalisation of Sports Journalism, c.1850 to 1939, with Particular Reference to the Career of James Catton' (unpublished PhD dissertation, University of Central Lancashire, 2007), p. 219.

decreased its coverage, probably to avoid competition with its sister evening paper, while the ailing *Chronicle*, now in new hands, had only slightly more sport than under Hewitson's ownership. By 1900 the *Evening Post* was clearly dominant in its sports coverage, devoting a third of its space to it, more than seventeen columns. The *Herald* had ceded to this dominance, reducing sport from around fourteen to about four columns per week, or less than three per cent of its space.

Table 9.1. Sports coverage, selected Preston newspapers, 1880–1900 (number of columns published per week).[14]

	1880	1890	1900
Preston sport			
Lancashire Evening Post		3.4	5
Preston Chronicle	0.8	0.6	
Preston Guardian	0.3	0.3	0
Preston Herald	0.7	4.6	1.5
Lancashire sport			
Lancashire Evening Post		8.8	25.5
Preston Chronicle	0.2	0.6	
Preston Guardian	1.6	0.3	0
Preston Herald	1	5.5	0.3
Total sport			
Lancashire Evening Post		25.1	57.3
Preston Chronicle	1	1.5	
Preston Guardian	2.9	0.8	0.3
Preston Herald	1.7	14.7	4.3

In 1888 the four-page *Evening Post* concentrated most of its football coverage in its two Saturday late editions, the 7pm 'football edition' and the 8pm 'extra special edition'.[15] All Saturday editions carried previews of the day's matches around Lancashire. Another column, 'We Hear and See', comprised snippets of news, gossip and comment, plus excerpts from other papers, metropolitan and provincial, about Lancashire

---

14   'Total sport' includes sport from outside Lancashire and international fixtures.

15   Multiple editions were viewed on microfilm at the *Lancashire Evening Post* (LEP) office, Preston.

clubs and football in general. The two late editions also carried match reports of league and cup matches and the final scores of other matches, professional and amateur. Monday's late editions featured a round-up of significant Lancashire games and how they affected the league and cup standings, plus commentary and descriptions of the main matches. While the evening paper could report Saturday's matches within hours of the final whistle, with additional comment two days later, the bi-weekly *Herald* had to wait until the following Wednesday. Both papers professed to circulate in and report on the whole of North Lancashire, home to some of the most successful clubs of the era, but both gave precedence to Preston North End, in order of priority and amount of editorial space; this suggests that Preston was the core of their sales area. However, the *Herald* often hedged its bets when reporting a Preston game against another North Lancashire side, for example in the 24 October 1888 issue, when Preston played Accrington in the League. One paragraph of notes and analysis of the game from Preston's perspective is followed by a paragraph beginning, 'The Accrington view of the game was as follows […]'[16] This technique is still used in the northern and southern editions of twenty-first-century national newspapers, but one version replaces the other, rather than sitting together in the same edition, as in the *Herald*. Did this accentuate local patriotism, whilst allowing each team's fans to learn how others saw their club — or was it merely confusing? The *Preston Guardian* Wednesday edition carried three or four columns of sports news in 1888, but most of this material was identical to that published in its sister paper, the *Evening Post*, and so has been excluded from this account.

In contrast, the *Preston Chronicle* covered cricket, bowls and rifle volunteer shooting matches, but under Hewitson's editorship, no football. His diary explains why. He saw his first football match in 1884: 'I don't care for the game and I believe it would not by any means be so very popular as it is if it were not for the betting & gambling mixed up with it.'[17] When a North End player broke a leg a month later, Hewitson commented, 'I wish lots would do same. I'm disgusted with it & the gambling associated with it.'[18] What annoyed him most were

---

16   See also *Preston Herald* (hereafter *PH*), 19 December 1888, 16 January and 20 February 1889.

17   Diary of Anthony Hewitson, Lancashire Archives DP512 (Hewitson Diaries hereafter), 15 November 1884.

18   Hewitson Diaries, 13 December 1884.

the large crowds outside rival newspaper offices in Fishergate during matches, gathered to read, hear and discuss telegraphed reports of the games. At the start of the 1886 season the only mention of football in the *Chronicle* was a paragraph in the 'Local Chit-Chat' column calling on the Watch Committee or police authorities to 'stop the insane crowding of Fishergate, especially on Saturday evenings, by persons waiting for football returns' as it affected trade.[19] The *Chronicle* was the only paper to publish letters critical of football, such as one headed 'Is footballing a game, or what?' from 'Old Prestonian' in 1887.'[20] Hewitson's diary entry for 5 March 1887 reads:

> Preston North End footballers beaten to day by West Bromwichers at Nottingham. A big, idle, godless, hands-in-breeches-pockets, smirking, spitting crowd in Fishergate waited a considerable time for the result [...] Could like to see a hose pipe opened or turned full on them.

Besides snobbery and a personal dislike of the game, no doubt there was envy at the popularity of football coverage in the *Herald* and the *Evening Post*. In contrast, one of the purchasers of the *Chronicle* when Hewitson sold up in 1890 was Francis Coupe, who went on to become one of twelve directors when PNE became a limited company in 1893.[21] Strangely, Coupe's name disappeared from the imprint of the paper in the same week that he was elected to the committee overseeing the conversion of the football club into a company. The influence of the *Chronicle*'s new owners was apparent from their first issue, when football coverage increased from nothing to almost two columns.[22] By 1893, the *Chronicle* typically published a single column of sports news, either cricket or football depending on the season, comprising very brief match reports, league tables and a county round-up. Hewitson's decision to ignore football shows the influence of an individual publisher, and the business costs of missing a significant journalistic trend.

The crowds outside newspaper offices were a symbol of the mutual benefits derived by football clubs and local papers. A description of

---

19 *Preston Chronicle* (hereafter *PC*), 22 September 1886, p. 5.

20 *PC*, 26 March 1887. This letter received an appreciative response from another reader the following week.

21 Hunt, pp. 92–93. I am grateful to Dr Steve Tate for information on Coupe; see also Tate, pp. 125–26.

22 *PC*, 6 September 1890.

the crowd during an FA Cup tie at Aston Villa in 1888 shows how the supporters shared the limelight with the players in football reportage, how newspapers revelled in their new role, and how hard it is to imagine professional football becoming so successful without the infrastructure provided by the local press.

> By half-past two there would be at least a couple of hundred people in front of the office of the *Lancashire Evening Post,* and half an hour later there was a [...] busy bustling crowd which reminded one of the exciting days of electoral conflict. The excitement became intense, and groups of people were discussing the probabilities with great animation [...] By four o'clock the gathering had assumed very large proportions, the crowd extending almost to the Town Hall in one direction and to Guild Hall street in the other. The notes on the progress of the game, periodically posted, were read with the most absorbing interest [...] round after round of cheering went up at the splendid win. The news was speedily carried to all parts of the district [...] The final result was first announced from the door of the *Evening Post* Offices, by Mr John Toulmin [...] Coloured lights were ignited on the balcony of the Conservative Club, in Church-street, and fireworks were discharged in other parts of the town.[23]

While pubs, sports outfitters and tobacconists also posted telegraphic football news, many supporters preferred to stand outside a newspaper office. The reference to Preston's lively electoral history gives a flavour of the heightened atmosphere, and the fact that a proprietor of the paper gave the final score shows the importance attached to this duty. However, the carrying of the news 'to all parts of the district', the Conservative working men's club lights and the fireworks, show that football fever was more than a press-inspired fad.

That said, the local press was 'absolutely indispensable' to the organisation and popularity of the game, especially the local amateur game.[24] The 'Brief Results' column of the *Evening Post* in 1888, for example, listed the scores of some fifty amateur Preston teams, from information supplied by 'secretaries of clubs desirous of making the exploits of their organisations known'.[25] Newspapers met the demand for facts and figures through their 'Notices to Correspondents' sections and 'offered prizes, management, commitment, even judges and

---

23   *LEP,* 7 January 1888, p. 3.
24   Preston PhD, pp. 302–3, 306–7.
25   *LEP,* 20 October 1888; *PH,* 10 September 1890, p. 2.

referees. Newspapers helped to form those sporting sub-cultures that grew up around particular sports and particular competitions.'[26]

In football as in other spheres, Preston's most potent 'other' was Blackburn. 'There are signs that the Blackburn crowd is slowly learning to appreciate really good football', the *Preston Herald* condescended in 1889.[27] In 1893, when Blackburn defeated Preston at Deepdale, 'The enemy came over from Blackburn, and literally took possession of the Proud town on Saturday. Fishergate was captured, and Prestonians were generally walked over [...]'[28] A gentler 'othering' is seen in the mockery of a traumatised Wolverhampton Wanderers fan at the end of the Cup Final, whose Midlands accent is rendered phonetically, as he protests at the sight of the cup denied to his team: 'Toike it away! Toike it away! Ow yes, send it to Preston!'[29] We can see the many techniques for producing locality in the coverage of two contrasting seasons in the early career of Preston North End FC.

Winning the Double, 1888–89

The underlying tone of this season's coverage was that Preston were the best team in the country and deserved to win the League and the Cup. Preston played well, and it was hard to find an article about the team that neglected to praise their current or past performance, so that no other section of each newspaper published the name of the town so frequently, or so positively.[30] In the *Herald*, localised pseudonymous bylines added to the effect, including 'Red Rose' (the emblem of Lancashire) and 'North Ender' in 1890, and a column, 'Notes by "Prestonian"' by 1893. If the team lost a friendly match (which did not affect their standings in the League or Cup), or played poorly, the papers always offered a defence: a defeat in Glasgow was excused by a tiring journey, and

---

26   Mason, 'All the Winners', p. 3; Mason suggests that this tradition was created by the pioneering sporting paper *Bell's Life in London*, which promoted and sponsored sport, and whose editors often acted as stakeholders in wagers: Tony Mason, 'Sporting News, 1860–1914', in *The Press in English Society from the Seventeenth to Nineteenth Centuries*, ed. by Michael Harris and Alan J. Lee (London: Associated University Presses, 1986), p. 172.

27   *PH*, 16 January 1889.

28   *PH*, 1 November 1893.

29   *LEP*, 1 April 1889.

30   Russell, *Looking North: Northern England and the National Imagination*, p. 241.

after a lacklustre performance at Christmas, 'no one can justly blame a team who can win three League matches in what may be called a week, besides travelling the best part of two nights'.[31] Statistics were used to show that a weak game was merely an aberration, as when North End drew with Blackburn Rovers in January 1889 and the *Herald* reminded readers that 'the Prestonians are [...] the winner of the thirteen out of the last sixteen matches played between the clubs', above a table listing all Preston-Blackburn results since February 1884.[32] Repetition, which came naturally to serial publications, was also apparent in the league tables published every week, always with Preston at the head. The serial nature of League and Cup football can only have added power to sport's ability to promote local identities.[33]

Although North End had been playing association football for less than a decade, the press, the club and its supporters already had a strong sense of history. At the start of the season, in September 1888, many fans and commentators believed that the club, widely accepted as England's top team, had already seen its best years. Reporting carried a 'golden-age' undertone, which gradually disappeared as the team won match after match. But the historical perspective remained. In January the *Herald* reminded readers of North End's 'brilliant record' and both papers seized on a collection of match statistics given at the club's annual general meeting in early February, including forty-four consecutive wins in the previous season, the *Post* proclaiming that 'no other club in the annals of football has ever come near achieving such a magnificent performance.'[34] The *Post* repeated the figures in its Saturday edition for good measure.[35] Statistics were used in the same way in both papers' preview coverage of the semi-finals and final, while Preston's record of no appeals for the replay of any match they had lost, was invoked in coverage of West Bromwich's appeal after a pitch invasion during the semi-final.[36]

'Association football thrived on the pitting of one local identity against another local identity in a national framework,' according to

---

31   *LEP*, 15 September 1888; *PH*, 2 January 1889.

32   *PH*, 16 January 1889.

33   John Bale, 'The Place of "Place" in Cultural Studies of Sports', *Progress in Human Geography*, 12 (1988), 507–24 (p. 514).

34   *PH*, 2 January 1889; *LEP*, 5 February 1889; *PH*, 6 February 1889.

35   *LEP*, 9 February 1889.

36   *PH*, 27 March 1889.

Jeffrey Hill.[37] This suited the local press perfectly, which was structured, as we have seen, as a national network of local 'nodes'. Alexander Jackson has highlighted how local sports commentators ensured 'that the local was linked to regional and national competitions and topics', never more so than when this national network of writers entered into debates with each other, reproducing and responding to press comment from elsewhere. Simultaneously, this technique promoted local and national identities.[38] Praise from outsiders carried extra prestige, and amplified local achievements already known to supporters, as when the *Herald* quoted a 'Scotch paper' at the end of the season as saying that 'Preston's play was simply perfection'.[39] Criticism in other papers was often answered point by point.[40] In February, when North End became the first champions of the new Football League, completing all their fixtures without defeat, the *Herald* and *LEP* both devoted half a column to press extracts praising PNE, from the *Birmingham Daily Gazette*, *Birmingham Daily Times* and *Birmingham Daily Post*, the Wolverhampton *Evening Express & Star*, the national football paper *Athletic News* and London's *Daily News*.[41] The *LEP*'s subsequent remarks on this laudatory 'criticism' reveal the circuit of press comment, pub conversation and official club discussion in which local newspapers created, supported and magnified a local footballing public sphere, and connected it to a national one:[42]

> this criticism was taken into a certain bar-parlour on Tuesday last, and read aloud; [...] subsequently a great authority who lately complained about the croakings of a section of the local press held this up as a sample of how he wished the team to be treated; [...] if this is the kind of matter the North End want reeling off every week, the general opinion is they desire to have their powers and abilities over-estimated.[43]

37 Jeffrey Hill, 'Anecdotal Evidence: Sport, the Newspaper Press and History', in *Deconstructing Sport History: A Postmodern Analysis*, ed. by Murray G. Phillips (Albany: State University of New York Press, 2006), pp. 117–29 (p. 122).

38 Jackson, 'Reading the Green 'Un', p. 5; Alexander Jackson, 'Football Coverage In The Papers Of The *Sheffield Telegraph*, c.1890–1915', *International Journal of Regional and Local Studies*, 5 (2009), 63–84 (pp. 80, 63), https://doi.org/10.1179/jrl.2009.5.1.63

39 *PH*, 5 September 1888.

40 *PH*, 16 January 1889.

41 *PH*, 13 February 1889.

42 Martin Johnes, *Soccer and Society: South Wales, 1900–39* (Cardiff: University of Wales Press, 2002), p. 10.

43 *LEP*, 16 February 1889.

One aspect of local identity formation was problematic for North End, and for the local papers that supported the team: the fact that few of the players were local (only three out of eleven in the 1888/89 season).[44] A Birmingham club, Mitchell's St George's, the *LEP* noted, were proud that all the team were born within six miles of the brewery that sponsored them, and a comment on Wolverhampton Wanderers — 'they all hail from one town, I believe' — by FA president Major Marindin, in his Cup Final speech, was probably a dig at Preston's imported team.[45] However, North End's pragmatic approach to the business of football was applauded by the *Evening Post*, who commented that 'nobody desires to see more Scotchmen introduced and yet the local talent is not of a sufficiently high order.'[46] Winning came first. Nonetheless, the Preston newspapers made the best of what they had, with the *Herald* emphasising the local origins of the three Preston-born players, such as left full-back Robert Holmes, 'a Preston lad, born and bred'. In the same Cup Final preview supplement, the *Herald* stressed the local links of the club's committee, led by William Sudell, the chairman, whose ancestors included a seventeenth-century Guild Mayor, the very epitome of Preston-ness.[47] After the final, the *Evening Post* described 'the best football team in the world' as 'Proud Prestonians', bestowing honorary citizenship on the predominantly Scottish players.[48]

Wider identities beyond the local were also emphasised in the coverage. The *LEP*'s preview of the semi-final games appealed to Lancastrian identity, noting how well the county's teams had done in the cup in recent years.[49] In the same paper's preview of the final a headline, 'Lancashire champions', introduced an article explaining that North End 'seek to regain for Lancashire the possession of the "blue riband" of the Association code.' A potted history of the competition told how 'the North has advanced by leaps and bounds while the Metropolitan district has remained to all intents and purposes stationary[...]'[50] Earlier

---

44   This was not unusual: Dave Russell, *Football and the English: A Social History of Association Football in England, 1863–1995* (Preston: Carnegie, 1997), p. 65.
45   *LEP*, 2 March 1889, 1 April 1889.
46   *LEP*, 17 November 1888.
47   *PH*, 30 March 1889.
48   *LEP*, 3 April 1889.
49   *LEP*, 16 March 1889.
50   *LEP*, 30 March 1889. At other times, Lancashire dialect was used, as in 'those who were not present may lay the flattering unction to their soul that, to use a Lancashire term, "they missed nowt"': 'Notes by Prestonian,' *PH*, 6 September 1893, p. 6.

in the season, regional identity was combined with class consciousness in a comment on North End's victory over the leading amateur side, ex-public schoolboys the Corinthians. North-south rivalry, overlain with the class-inflected conflict between amateurism and professionalism, and pride in the fact that football was then largely a game of the North and the Midlands, is encapsulated in a remark about the Corinthians tour, said to have made a £1000 profit. 'Of this, about £400 has been paid to "Pa" Jackson and his boys; and information as to how they have disposed of it would be gladly received by Northerners.'[51] The implicit reference to North End's previous victories in the battles over payment of players would be apparent to many readers.[52]

The local press techniques for creating attractive, profitable coverage of local football teams outlined above are all adaptations of established methods. But the most distinctive aspect of football coverage — the treatment of football consumers as subjects of reportage in their own right — has few antecedents, unless we look to reporting of rowdy local elections in the era before the secret ballot. This motif may have been established in the early years of association football, when the size of crowds for this new sport was newsworthy;[53] it may have been an acknowledgement that, in a commercial business, the number of paying customers was crucial; perhaps, where few players were native, the local nature of the supporters could be fixed on;[54] perhaps the sayings and doings of the fans were so colourful that they deserved coverage;[55] or it

---

51   *LEP*, 12 January 1889. For more north-south rivalry concerning the Corinthians, see *LEP*, 2 February 1889; Jackson, 'Football coverage', p. 64. 'In the South there is not the enthusiasm shown in the sport as in other parts, and the lethargic Southern amateur will wait for the cool breezes of October before he ventures on his exertions': *LEP*, 26 August 1893. For more on sport and northern identity, see Jeff Hill and Jack Williams, 'Introduction', in *Sport and Identity in the North of England*, ed. by Jeffrey Hill and Jack Williams (Keele: Keele University Press, 1996), pp. 1–12; in the same book, Richard Holt, 'Heroes of the North: Sport and the Shaping of Regional Identity', pp. 137–64 and Tony Mason, 'Football, Sport of the North?', pp. 41–52.

52   Hunt, pp. 17, 59.

53   Stacy Lorenz believes that high numbers of supporters were evidence that the host city 'had successfully demonstrated its energy and vitality': Stacy L. Lorenz, '"In the Field of Sport at Home and Abroad": Sports Coverage in Canadian Daily Newspapers, 1850–1914', *Sport History Review*, 34 (2003), 133–67 (p. 149), cited in Preston, p. 289, https://doi.org/10.1123/shr.34.2.133

54   Bale, p. 516.

55   The Preston papers occasionally contrasted the behaviour of football and cricket crowds, without making judgments (*PH*, 20 March 1889); cricket spectators were not incorporated into the reportage in the same way, perhaps because cricket was a participatory rather than a spectator sport.

may have been a controlled way of allowing predominantly working-class men access to the columns of a middle-class medium, a public sphere by proxy.[56] Northern crowds in this period had a reputation for partisanship, and it would be interesting to compare the treatment of southern football supporters by their local papers with that of northern papers such as Preston's.[57]

Whatever the reason, the crowd was written into professional football reportage at every opportunity. Large crowds ('gates') were a source of pride, as when Preston's attendance of 6,000 was second only to Everton's 10,000, or linked to almost any evaluation of North End's performance, good or bad — 'not only the team, but every Prestonian who takes an interest in the club, will be justly proud' or 'the spectators were evidently tired of the exhibition being made by [Preston], and repeatedly shouted at them to "play up" […]'[58] Quips were reported, such as one about the recent departure of star defender Nick Ross to Everton: 'the question was asked, "Where has North End's defence gone to?" and the reply came readily, "Everton".'[59] The manner in which supporters celebrated was described, for example after Preston completed their last League fixture, before their Cup run:

> the pride of their supporters has been raised considerably by their newly gained honour, and last Saturday night it required a considerable number of refreshers to quench the enthusiasm of some of the players and their admirers […] there is yet hope for them bringing that "blessed pot" to the banks of the Ribble.[60]

The crowd was also part of the match reports and analyses, for example in a report of an away match against Blackburn:

---

56 Russell, *Looking North*, p. 56. For the view that the late nineteenth-century press saw itself as 'representative', see Mark Hampton, *Visions of the Press in Britain, 1850–1950* (Urbana: University of Illinois Press, 2004).

57 Alexander Jackson, 'The Chelsea Chronicle, 1905 to 1913', *Soccer & Society*, 11 (2010), 506–21 (pp. 515–19), https://doi.org/10.1080/14660970.2010.497341; the Sheffield publication *Football and Cricket World* exemplified this northern attitude. 'We do not believe in the wishy-washy talk about no partisanship being felt. We want to see Sheffield football triumphant': *Football and Cricket World*, 9 September 1895, cited in Jackson, 'Football Coverage', p. 69.

58 *LEP*, 15 September 1888, 11 February 1889; *PH*, 12 December 1888.

59 *LEP*, 13 October 1888. The *Liverpool Echo* 'Saturday Night Football Edition' included imagined dialogues between fans: Preston, p. 287.

60 *LEP*, 12 January 1889.

when play started it was quickly evident that there was a strong contingent of Prestonians present, for there was a huge cheer when Graham neatly grassed Jack Southworth [...] The failure of Thomson to lead through was received with a groan. A loud cheer at the end of 23 minutes announced that Thomson had scored for the visitors.[61]

All of the other techniques described above could be given extra local value when voiced and amplified by supporters, such as the appeal to North End's proud history when a victory over West Bromwich Albion 'brought back to the memories of thousands the grand battle fought by the North End when making their name, and after the match the exploits of the men in their famous games were recounted with gusto.'[62]

Fan culture was supported and reported in other ways. The *Evening Post* published a 180-word review of the PNE fixture card in October 1888, noting that 'Mr J Miller, lithographer, Preston, has surpassed all his previous efforts on behalf of the club. The style is less pretentious than in past years, but is much neater and more artistic.'[63] Adverts next to or within the sports columns promoted 'football houses', pubs devoted to the game, including the Lamb, on Church Street, run by North End goalkeeper Jim Trainer, whose name appeared prominently in the advert.

The reporting of northern teams playing in London FA Cup Finals followed a formula in the early twentieth century, according to Hill: the spectators' journey to London, enjoyment of the match in the stadium and at home, and the welcoming home of the team.[64] In 1889 the *Preston Herald* and the *Lancashire Evening Post* followed only part of this formula, with heavy preview coverage, barely a mention of travelling fans, fairly 'straight' reporting of the match itself, but detailed coverage of the victorious homecoming. The *Herald*'s four-and-a-half columns of match-day preview coverage was twice the length of the *Post*'s, perhaps because it was unable to publish a match report that evening.[65] But both were similar in content: an engraving of the FA Cup, a history of northern club appearances in the competition, a history of PNE, recent statistics, including favourable comparisons with opponents Wolves, and

---

61 *LEP*, 12 January 1889.

62 *LEP*, 20 October 1888.

63 *LEP*, 13 October 1888, p. 4.

64 Hill, 'Rite of Spring', p. 94.

65 *PH*, 30 March 1889. Without access to all editions of the *Herald*, it is impossible to know for sure that no post-match edition appeared.

biographies of players (and of club officials, both with portraits, in the *Herald*). The *Post's* preview merged into its reporting of the day itself, with a piece headed 'Reception of the News at Preston' describing the crowd outside its office on Fishergate.[66] A week later the *Post* had a short item on the experiences of supporters in London, of Lancastrians bumping into 'brother Northerners' and out-cheering the 'Cockneys' at the Oval.[67]

The team's return to Preston followed the ritual already established for these occasions. Beneath a headline, 'Return of the North End team. Brilliant ovation from twenty-seven thousand people', the *Herald* reported that the Public Hall 'was packed as it has never been packed before by an audience representative of all classes of the community', emphasising the unifying nature of the occasion. The platform party included the town's great and good, with councillors and aldermen, doctors, solicitors and businessmen. A message was read from the mayor (absent through illness), linking the success of the 'Invincibles' to the prestige of the town and to imperial themes: 'Outdoor sports have been important factors in forming and maintaining the manly robust, invincible character of the British race, and it is most gratifying to know that one's town can take the foremost place in them.' In the absence of the town's MPs and other political leaders (away in London, steering a Bill through Parliament), solicitor T. M. Shuttleworth, Esq, took the chair. He declared the occasion 'unique in the history of the good old town — (hear, hear)' and admitted that he

> was not an habitué of the football field, but he was one of those who had followed with keen interest every move of the celebrated North Enders — (hear, hear and cheers) — and nobody rejoiced more than he did on Saturday, when he elbowed his way through the crowd to look at the window of the *Herald*-office, and saw to his delight the result […] He asked them to give the North End team a right royal Lancashire welcome, for they were the finest football team in the world.[68]

As with any speeches on such an occasion, the oratory aimed to crystallise and celebrate North End's achievement, and link it to civic and wider

---

66 *PH, LEP*, 30 March 1889.

67 *LEP*, 6 April 1889.

68 *PH*, 3 April 1889, p. 5. Even at this early date, the occasion was less a 'spontaneous celebration of club' and more a 'semi-official glorification of town', challenging Hill's chronology: Hill, 'Rite of Spring', p. 100.

themes.[69] The next speaker, Alderman Walmsley, described himself as 'one of the spectators of the matches at Deepdale'. The following speaker also linked North End's qualities to imperial triumphs, and evoked inter-town rivalry when he 'ventured to express a hope that the club would be able to outrival even the achievements of the Blackburn Rovers in the Cup competition' (Blackburn had won it three times). The coverage of the *Evening Post* and even the usually disdainful *Chronicle* was similar to the *Herald*'s, with the *Post* measuring the crowds favourably against Preston's highest benchmark, the audience for the huge textile trades procession of the Guild civic festival.[70] The press reported these speeches and resolutions, confirming the audience's experience and informing those not present. By committing the occasion to print, the papers lent it status and permanence.

All this must have come as a surprise to readers of the *Chronicle*. Hewitson's paper had studiously ignored North End's greatest season, not even giving final scores, nor mentioning their League champion status, until the Saturday following the cup final. Then, a news report, headed 'The Champion Exponents of Association Football' grudgingly admitted that, 'In the eyes of the Press, local and otherwise, they constitute the finest Association all-round football team that has ever graced the Oval.' The *Chronicle* followed the same model of reportage as the other papers for the homecoming, describing the same events in the same way (indeed the account may have been taken from the other papers). While Hill's general point is accepted, that the local press used such occasions to create and sustain myths, it is hard to imagine any other way of describing the home-coming.[71] Even the cynical *Chronicle* had no other vocabulary, in its news reporting at least.

Hewitson's commentary was a different matter. On the same page as the news report, in his 'Local Chit-Chat' column, he found

> the massing of so many thousands of Preston people in the streets, &c [...] to see eleven vanquishers in the domain of ball-kicking [...] quite inexplicable, and absurd on account of its excess [...] The town has a right to feel proud of its football champions; but the town need not go silly [...]

---

69 Mike Huggins, 'Oop for t' Coop: Sporting Identity in Britain', *History Today*, 55 (2005), 55–61.

70 *PH*, *LEP*, 3 April 1889; *PC*, 6 April 1889, p. 5.

71 Hill, 'Rite of Spring', p. 102.

North End Close to Collapse, 1893

The coverage was very different when crisis hit the club four years later. By 1893, Preston had won the league again, been runners-up three times and reached the FA Cup semi-finals once. Between late July and early September of that year, an alarming story unfolded, of debt, FA suspension, a plan to save the club by converting it into a limited company, the suspense of a slow take-up of shares, and — finally — resolution, after the bare minimum of shares had been sold, debts were paid and the club reinstated by the FA. The *Herald*, *Evening Post* and *Chronicle* (the latter now under new ownership, and featuring more sport, particularly football) all reported the story in a similar way, demonstrating how the presence of a successful football club was seen as essential both for the prestige of the town and for the commercial well-being of its press.[72]

Optimism was the dominant tone throughout, beginning with stories in the *Herald* and the *Chronicle* in advance of the much-delayed annual general meeting in late July, when the club's financial problems were exposed.[73] Optimism continued throughout the summer, whether it was warranted or not.[74] The boosterism took on almost desperate tones in mid-August, after Preston's suspension from the FA (for an unpaid debt to Everton FC), but 'the new committee [...] may be relied upon to set matters right,' predicted the *Chronicle*. Against all the evidence, it added that 'the shares in the new company [...] are being quickly taken up, and there is every promise of a prosperous future for North End', a formula repeated the following week almost word for word.[75] As time ran out for the share issue in late August, day after day the *Post* reported that, whilst yesterday's sales had been disappointing, today's were picking up.[76] The *Chronicle*'s confidence was confirmed by support from the spirit world. A séance at the Public Hall included a question to

---

72 Hill, 'Anecdotal Evidence', p. 121; Bale, p. 516.

73 *PC*, 15 July 1893; *PH*, 19 July 1893.

74 *PH*, 22 July 1893; *LEP*, 11 August 1893. Surprisingly, none of the papers set an example by publicly buying shares themselves, although the Toulmins later 'became large shareholders in the club': Hunt, p. 12; the owners of the *Eastern Daily Press* bought twenty-five shares in Norwich City FC in the early twentieth century: Tony Clarke, *Pilgrims of the Press: A History of Eastern Counties Newspapers Group 1850–2000* (Norwich: Eastern Counties Newspapers, 2000), p. 22.

75 *PC*, 12 August 1893.

76 *LEP*, 22, 23, 24 August 1893.

the medium 'as to whether North End would head the League during the coming season. The lady had no hesitation about her answer. It was a decided affirmative [...].' The medium's husband, Professor Baldwin, confirmed this evidence by offering to make 'a reasonable wager'.[77]

The corollary of such optimism was a willingness to play down the bad news. The *Post* was the most even-handed, for example reporting the AGM without comment but nonetheless describing irregularities in the accounts, the disquiet of some members, and the defensiveness of the chairman, William Sudell, who had run the club successfully for more than a decade as a benevolent dictator. The *Herald* gave a fuller account, diluting the bad news slightly, while the *Chronicle* (now co-owned by a future club director) omitted those parts reflecting poorly on Sudell. When Preston were suspended by the FA, the *Post* devoted only four lines to it, the *Herald* and *Chronicle* two. The language was generally defensive. The *Post* claimed there were 'no grounds for alarm' over whether the players would sign with Preston again for the coming season, and 'no fear' that one player, Cowan, wanted to leave; words and phrases such as 'satisfaction', 'satisfactory' and 'no fear of difficulty' jarred with the grim news they accompanied.[78]

Readers were exhorted to unite behind the new regime and to buy shares. 'Whatever little difference there may have been should now be forgotten,' the *Chronicle* pleaded. 'All well wishers of the winter pastime will best consult the interests of the club by forwarding their deposits at once', the *Post* urged.[79] These exhortations were made chiefly on two grounds: an appeal to civic pride, and to the club's proud history and reputation. Unlike four years previously, football was now considered a fit subject for a leading article in the *Post*, which urged members to unite in promoting 'the interests of the great club, the fortunes of which, in a way, may raise or lower the reputation of the town.' The *Herald* urged 'the lovers of football in Preston [to] combine together in support of the winter sport and those who so well maintain the credit of the town in its practice'.[80] There were many appeals in the name of North End's distinguished history, such as the *Post*'s reminder that 'in the past, as everyone knows,

77   *PC*, 29 July 1893.
78   *LEP*, 10, 12 August 1893.
79   *PC*, 5 August 1893; *LEP*, 22 August 1893.
80   *LEP*, 21 July 1893; *PH*, 23 August 1893.

the team has been in the front rank of Association elevens, and with the support of the townspeople it will retain its old and proud position'.[81] The arguments put forward, and the vocabulary employed, were almost identical in all three papers, suggesting that reporters were receiving the same briefings from the club, perhaps simultaneously, or that there was only one way for the local press to report the story, within the conventions of late nineteenth-century local journalism.

When the crisis ended, days before the start of the new season, it became apparent that another side to the story had been suppressed. As it became clear that enough shares had been sold to pay the club's debts, the papers began to refer to earlier widespread fears among fans, now past, that the club might collapse. The papers had closed ranks, underplaying the depth of the crisis and adopting a boosting role, which left no room for the untidy, uncertain and fickle voices of the fans. Unlike the coverage at North End's high point in 1888–89, the fans were noticeably absent from the reporting of the 1893 crisis. Only in mid-September did the *Herald* acknowledge 'the, more or less, twaddle talked by some individuals during the heated period when the new company was being floated'.[82] The slow take-up of shares suggests that many North End fans did not share the papers' confidence in the viability of the club nor the ability of its managers.

Conclusions

Close reading and comparison of rival publications has revealed how Preston's main newspapers reacted to another cultural movement, professional football. The symbiotic relationship of the local press and professional football benefited both parties, and the press took full advantage of the regional and local nature of the new phenomenon, adapting established techniques and adopting new ones to capitalise on local identity in its coverage. Whilst rivalry was intrinsic to football coverage, there was surprisingly little 'othering' of rival teams, beyond the bounds of sportsmanlike fair play. The emphasis was on 'us' rather than 'them'.[83] Sports coverage, particularly of football,

---

81 *PC*, 22 July 1893; *LEP*, 19 August 1893.
82 *PH*, 13 September 1893.
83 In Mary Mitford's words, 'to be authorised to say *we*': Mitford, p. 43.

enabled newspapers to package together many other elements of local identity into one topic, making local patriotism more intense and emotional. Football reporting provides a particularly good example of local newspaper boosterism — although there is little evidence that this boosting had any direct impact — and was well suited to combining identities at local, county, regional and national level. The habit of quoting and debating comment on local teams from other newspapers around the country strengthened and made use of the national network that was the local press.

Preston's papers, regardless of their political stance, followed the same template when reporting the new phenomenon of professional football. It is hard to imagine how else they could have reported PNE's triumphal homecoming after winning the FA Cup, an event that drew a quarter of the town's population onto its main street. The exception was Hewitson's *Chronicle*, perhaps confirming that by the late 1880s, he was out of step with contemporary journalism, despite his stylistic innovations in the 1860s and 1870s. The Preston press's football coverage was usually more passive than Hill suggests, creating myths through selective repetition and through reporting, such as that around the FA Cup in 1889, in which the speech-makers at the Public Hall rather than the newspapers did the work of connecting North End's victory to civic identity. But when PNE was nearly destroyed by a financial crisis in 1893, the Preston papers offered more active, partial constructions of reality, playing down bad news, wishing good news into existence and adopting a tone of exhortation, urging readers to buy shares and save the ailing club, for the sake of the town. The only other time such direct appeals to the reader were seen was during election campaigns. This is a case study of how the local press applied established techniques to the new phenomenon of organised, professional association football, to the mutual benefit of the press and the football club. The next chapter argues that such selection and framing of stories did have an impact on some readers.

10. How Readers Used the Local Paper

In 1890, Guildford Workhouse housed

> one inmate who has a local paper sent him, but (wicked man!) he keeps it to himself, reads it all through, and keeps it under his bed. He calls it his only remaining comfort. The matron thinks it should be lent round and then used for waste paper. He says *NO!*[1]

What is comforting about a local newspaper? Perhaps it was full of familiar names and familiar places, and enabled this man to imagine that once again he was part of a community. Although, if indeed it made him part of an imagined community, with a shared local identity, he nevertheless insisted on using the paper privately ('wicked man!'). The local paper also enabled individual pleasures to be shared communally. In Fig. 10.1, members of the mythical Slocum Football Club shout 'We're in!' as they read about themselves in the Sheffield sporting newspaper, the *Green 'Un*. They are triumphant that their achievements on the pitch have been validated before the entire imagined community of *Green 'Un* readers. Not only had the new team played its match, this public event had now been validated, elevated, by being recorded in the local paper.

But the local paper was more than a record; as David Paul Nord writes, it offered not only facts, but also a forum, the facilities for a local public sphere, where citizens could debate public matters.[2] In the same

---

1   Report of Guildford Workhouse, 'The Association of Helpers: Service for July', *Review of Reviews*, July 1890, p. 14.

2   David Paul Nord, 'Introduction: Communication and Community', in *Communities of Journalism: A History of American Newspapers and Their Readers* (Urbana: University of Illinois Press, 2001), pp. 1–27 (p. 4).

   https://doi.org/10.11647/OBP.0152.10

way that only a local publication could sustain the workhouse inmate's local identity, only the local paper had the space, and the market demand, to host discussions of local issues. The content was local, as in the continued debates of the 1870s and 1880s over whether to spend ratepayers' money on improving Preston's port on the River Ribble; but the form of the debate was also a unique product of its place. Readers wove the Ribble into similes to strengthen the rhetoric of their letters to the editor, or resorted to Lancashire dialect in an appeal to the local patriotism of other readers.

Fig. 10.1. '"We're in! [A 'Green Un' is bought by special subscription] A banquet follows.' Cartoon from *Football and Sports Special* [The 'Green 'Un'], Sheffield, 21 September 1907, British Library NEWS979. © The British Library Board, all rights reserved.

Earlier chapters have established that the local press was popular. This chapter explains why — by examining how readers used it, publicly to circulate the information necessary for Victorian society to function, and privately to sustain local identities. Many of the uses were unique to these types of publication. The local newspaper was still merely raw material when it came off the press. Readers completed the manufacturing process, as they brought local newspapers to life through the many uses to which they put them.[3]

We are all familiar with the idea that reading books changes lives, but Jonathan Rose gives only one example of a newspaper having the same impact, in his survey of autodidactic reading habits. The future Labour Party leader J. R. Clynes recalled how 'some of the articles I read from the local Oldham papers of the time must have been pretty poor stuff I suppose, but they went to my head like wine [...]'[4] The rarity of newspaper epiphanies points to an important contrast with book-reading, due to newspapers' serial nature: newspaper reading tends to be a continuous process, while reading a book in volume form is experienced more as a discrete event.

The local press was an important part of public and private life in this period. However, the scarcity of evidence for how readers used the local press might raise doubts about its significance. It is hard to argue from an absence, but this study, following Lucy Brown, has demonstrated that the local press was like furniture, or a roof over one's head, part of the basic infrastructure of life. The lack of historical evidence for the appreciation of chairs or roofs does not mean that they were not significant in people's lives. The provincial press was 'embedded in the social fabric of [readers'] everyday lives', integrated through networks, 'habits (more or less unreflective routines) and interests (more conscious or rationalised calculations)'. Local papers mediated 'between the system-world and the life-world'.[5] Preston newspaper reporter and editor Anthony Hewitson could not have done his job without reading scores of local papers from near and far every week, yet his diary mentions only high-status books he read for relaxation on Sundays. Like the *Burton Daily Mail* in the background of Fig. 8.1, the local press formed the background to many aspects of readers' lives. The quantitative evidence of Chapter 6 — numbers of titles, copies sold, and copies taken in reading rooms — demonstrated that local papers were a significant part of each

---

3   Similar ideas can be found in Elihu Katz and Paul F. Lazarsfeld, *Personal Influence; the Part Played by People in the Flow of Mass Communications* (Glencoe: Free Press, 1955); Heikki Heikkilä, Risto Kunelius, and Laura Ahva, 'From Credibility to Relevance: Towards a Sociology of Journalism's "Added Value"', *Journalism Practice*, 4 (2010), 274–84 (p. 279), https://doi.org/10.1080/17512781003640547

4   Jonathan Rose, *The Intellectual Life of the British Working Classes* (London: Yale University Press, 2001), p. 26.

5   Heikkilä, Kunelius, and Ahva, pp. 274, 278, 275.

place's reading world. Most individual readers did not think that reading the local paper was important or unusual enough to be worth recording, but evidence does exist, in oral history material, autobiographies, diaries and company histories. One of the most important types of evidence for readers' uses of the local press comes from correspondence columns within the papers themselves, although these can be problematic.

Readers' Letters as Evidence

Historically, newspapers developed from manuscript and printed newsletters, so that letters from readers to the editor could be seen as the vestigial core of the newspaper as a form.[6] These origins are more visible in certain types of overtly reader-led periodical such as *Notes and Queries*, consisting entirely of questions posed and answered by readers; or the *English Mechanic*, also mostly written by its readers.[7] Even in the second half of the nineteenth century, local newspaper genres that we might expect to be produced by professional journalists were submitted as correspondence: a letter from Leicester political activist William Biggs to the *Leicestershire Mercury* in 1850 appeared as a leading article, as did some of the young W. T. Stead's letters to the *Northern Echo* in 1870.[8]

On the one hand, a lively correspondence column was considered essential to a newspaper; on the other, publishers, journalists and readers understood that some letters were not genuine.[9] They might be the Victorian equivalent of online 'sockpuppeting', written by a journalist to stimulate genuine correspondence;[10] or for rhetorical effect where an opinion would gain more support if it was seen to come from the public rather than the press, as when Edward Baines began the campaign for a

---

6   Charles John Sommerville, *The News Revolution in England: Cultural Dynamics of Daily Information* (Oxford: Oxford University Press, 1996), p. 6.

7   James Mussell, *Science, Time and Space in the Late Nineteenth-Century Periodical Press: Movable Types* (Aldershot: Ashgate, 2007), p. 29, https://doi.org/10.4324/9781315243658

8   Derek Fraser, 'The Press in Leicester c. 1790–1850', *Transactions of the Leicestershire Archaeological and Historical Society*, 42 (1967), 53–75 (p. 67); Tony Nicholson, 'The Provincial Stead', in *W. T. Stead: Newspaper Revolutionary*, ed. by Roger Luckhurst and others (London: British Library, 2012), pp. 7–21.

9   'How to improve a country business; or, hints to a young beginner', *London, Provincial, and Colonial Press News*, 16 January 1871, p. 10.

10   *Press News*, 16 January 1871, p. 10.

literary and philosophical society in Leeds with a pseudonymous letter in the newspaper he owned and edited, the *Leeds Mercury*, in 1818.[11] But evidence from journalists, readers and commentators suggests that most letters were genuinely from readers, with only a minority written by journalists or other local 'insiders', and passed off as readers' efforts. The difficulty is knowing which ones. Even made-up letters need to tap into something genuine to be convincing, but nonetheless it is unsafe to put much weight on any individual letter. Using letters in aggregate, quantitatively, can overcome this problem, although the number of letters rose and fell, depending on the news agenda and the amount of space available (itself partly dictated by the week's news — war news often squeezed out correspondence, for example). But taken together, readers' letters point in the same direction as evidence from outside the newspaper such as readers' diaries, correspondence, oral history interviews and lists of periodicals provided by free libraries.

We may accept that most letters were genuinely from readers, but who *were* those readers who wrote, who used a local newspaper in a public way, leaving historical traces? They probably had more in common with the publishers and journalists than with the readership as a whole, so we should be careful not to generalise too much from their evidence. Letter-writers were representative of what Stanley Fish called 'interpretive communities' from which each local paper sprang, rather than the wider readership, yet their output was read avidly by less active readers. At mid-century only public figures signed letters with their real name; everyone else used pseudonyms. This practice declined rapidly, from fifty-nine per cent of letters signed pseudonymously in 1860 to only ten per cent in 1900, in the *Preston Herald* at least (mirroring a similar trend from anonymous to signed periodical articles). However, both pseudonyms and genuine signatures tell the same story, of the local newspaper correspondence column as an overwhelmingly male, bourgeois public sphere. Indeed it is quite possible that the lifting of the cloak of anonymity reduced the opportunities for women and working-class letter-writers, who had previously been judged on the merits of their letters rather than their class or gender.

---

11 *Leeds Mercury*, 26 September 1818, cited in John B. Hood, 'The Origin and Development of the Newsroom and Reading Room from 1650 to Date, with Some Consideration of Their Role in the Social History of the Period' (unpublished FLA dissertation, Library Association, 1978), p. 163.

In nineteenth-century Preston, readers used the local paper correspondence column in many different ways, as an interactive reference source, as a noticeboard, a stimulus to action, a visitors' book, a substitute for the duel in defending reputations, as a permanent record, and most of all, as a debating forum, an essential tool in the creation of a public sphere in the late nineteenth century. They may have been a minority, but their contributions were one of the most popular parts of the paper. One self-deprecating letter-writer claimed 'that proud prerogative of the Englishman [...] to thrust his grievances into the columns of newspapers', and grievance was indeed the default register, typically complaints about local government, or public nuisances.[12] Others sought fellow feeling and community (imagined and real), such as John Hagan, incensed at the injustice of poor tenants having to pay their own rates: 'Last Saturday morning, as soon as I could get a *Preston Guardian* to buy I did so. I thought to find your columns devoted to letters of correspondence filled up with indignation [...]'[13] But some had a lower opinion of readers' letters, with one writer dismissing 'those foolish persons who wish to see their names in print, by writing long letters to the papers'. This was a short letter, of course.[14]

The popularity of readers' correspondence was due in large part to its local focus. It concerned matters close to the hearts of most readers, with local topics accounting for the majority of letters in the *Preston Herald* in all but one of the sampled years.[15] The only exception in the Preston papers was 1870, when the Franco-Prussian War dominated the correspondence columns. Local identity was a common topic in readers'

---

12 Letter complaining about uncomfortable trains, from Lumbaginiensis, *Preston Guardian* (hereafter *PG*), 12 October 1872, p. 6; Ian Jackson, *The Provincial Press and the Community* (Manchester: Manchester University Press, 1971), p. 153; Gabrina Pounds, 'Democratic Participation and Letters to the Editor in Britain and Italy', *Discourse and Society*, 17 (2006), 29–64 (p. 55), https://doi.org/10.1177/0957926506058064. For quantitative analysis, see Andrew Hobbs, 'Reading the Local Paper: Social and Cultural Functions of the Local Press in Preston, Lancashire, 1855–1900' (unpublished PhD dissertation, University of Central Lancashire, 2010), Tables A30-31, appendices.

13 Letter from John Hagan, *PG*, 28 September 1867.

14 Letter, 'Mr Harper and the Orangemen of Preston', from TB, *Preston Chronicle* (hereafter *PC*), 25 April 1868, p. 6.

15 Hobbs, p. 219. This British preference continues into the twenty-first century, when readers' letters are still more likely to be about 'specific and localised topics' such as the quality of Bury black puddings, whereas Italian letters, by contrast, 'tend to deal with issues of more general interest such as the meaning of life': Pounds, p. 53.

letters, explicitly and implicitly.[16] Correspondents debated the state of the town, compared it to other places, looked back on its history and tried to characterise it. Writers occasionally used local metaphors, for example arguing that one could 'as well try to stop the flow of the Ribble as to stop the advance of public opinion' or that 'a Protestant might as well attempt to fly up to the pinnacle of the Town Hall spire as attempt to get work at [a hypothetical Catholic-owned] mill [...]'[17]

Read all About Us:
The Appeal of Local News and Views

The local press was successful because it fulfilled the desires of readers to read about themselves, and about others who lived their lives in the same place as them. In 1890, a Staffordshire letter-writer described how 'one opens one's *Leek Times* on a Friday night, to see what one's neighbours are doing [...]'[18] In one home in Barrow, the *North Western Evening Mail* was taken every night 'to see who was dead and born'. A Lancaster interviewee, referring to the early twentieth century, stated the rarely-spoken obvious when he said: 'the only literature that ever came into the house was the *Lancashire Daily Post* which we used to read for the local news.'[19] In 1820, the preface to a bound volume of the *Lonsdale Magazine, or Provincial Repository for the Year 1820* declared:

> we build our hopes of obtaining the support and patronage of our neighbours (and we solicit no higher honour) upon this simple excellence, that ours is a PROVINCIAL work. The subjects are consequently within the sphere of the reader's acquaintance — the allusions are familiar to

---

16   Hobbs, Tables A30 and A31, appendices; Table 42, p. 219.

17   Untitled letter, from 'W. W.', *PG*, 11 April 1868; Letter, 'Messrs "Atticus" and Tate,' from 'A Conservative From Conviction', *Preston Herald* (hereafter *PH*), 12 September 1868, p. 6.

18   Letter to *Leek Times*, quoted in letter, 'Controversy', from John Hobson Matthews, Cardiff, *Antidote*, 4 November 1890.

19   Mrs C2B (b. 1887), 'Social and family life in Preston, 1890–1940', transcripts of recorded interviews, Elizabeth Roberts archive, Lancaster University Library (hereafter *ER*; the letters P, B or L at the end of the interviewee's identifier denotes whether the interviewee was from Preston, Barrow or Lancaster). The transcripts are being digitised, with some available at www.regional-heritage-centre.org; Mr M1L (b. 1910), *ER*. 'Community news' was the most popular type of content in mid-twentieth-century Chicago local papers: Morris Janowitz, *The Community Press in an Urban Setting* (Glencoe: Free Press, 1952), p. 133.

his mind — the contributors are his neighbours — and the scene is his home. These are properties, and valuable ones, which no other Magazine can boast of.[20]

This reason for reading local newspapers, not available to metropolitan or national publications, has been underplayed in press history and the history of reading, in which betting news and romantic fiction have been highlighted as more significant motivations for new working-class readers to develop and maintain their literacy skills.[21] For example, the compiler of an anonymous 1890s scrapbook of cuttings from the *Newcastle Weekly Chronicle* appears to have treasured the localness of this weekly news miscellany; most of the scrapbook is filled with images of beauty spots near Newcastle, and columns of 'local anecdotes', full of amusing stories about local characters.[22]

The ability of local media to report on people and places known to its audience has continued. In the mid-twentieth century, readers of small weekly community papers in Chicago evinced the same desire to know and be known through the local press, seeing these papers as an extension of their own social networks. One Chicago interviewee liked the paper because there were 'so many people you see in it that you know', while another said: 'I like to read about the people I know.'[23] Janowitz describes this pleasure at seeing one's community captured in print as the democratisation of prestige.[24] In late twentieth-century Lancaster and twenty-first-century Australia, people read in order to take part in their local community, with the local paper a key text, and this seems equally true for nineteenth-century Preston.[25]

It was one thing to read about people you knew in the local paper, but to read about oneself was even better.[26] There are numerous

---

20   *Lonsdale Magazine*, 1820, LA12/NOR, Lancashire Archives.

21   David Vincent, *Literacy and Popular Culture: England 1750–1914* (Cambridge: Cambridge University Press, 1989), p. 190, https://doi.org/10.1017/cbo9780511560880

22   Scrapbook in author's collection.

23   Morris Janowitz, 'The Imagery of the Urban Press', *Public Opinion Quarterly*, 15 (1951), 519–31 (pp. 522, 529).

24   Janowitz, 'Imagery', p. 527.

25   David Barton and Mary Hamilton, *Local Literacies: Reading and Writing in One Community* (London: Routledge, 1998), p. 153; Kristy Hess and Lisa Waller, *Local Journalism in a Digital World* (Palgrave, 2017), p. 94, https://doi.org/10.1057/978-1-137-50478-4

26   Sommerville argues that the *Athenian Mercury* and *London Spy*, followed by Steele's journals, saw 'the commercial possibilities in periodicals as a way of reading about oneself' in the early eighteenth century: Sommerville, p. 148.

examples, from this period and others, of readers' pride in becoming part of the text they revered. W. E. Adams, a compositor who went on to edit the *Newcastle Weekly Chronicle*, had his first letter published in the *Cheltenham Free Press* in 1851, defending the right of asylum of Polish and Hungarian fighters against Russia: 'The printing of that letter produced an exaltation that no similar honour has ever produced since,' he wrote at the end of a successful career.[27] Most of the 300 or so wedding guests listed (with details of the presents they gave) in a 2-column report of the marriage of Arthur Mossop and Mary Catt in Lindfield, Sussex in 1892 probably bought a copy of the *Sussex Agricultural Express* to read what they already knew, that they had been there.[28] Fred Ching sold the *Dursley Gazette* on Dursley station on Saturday mornings in 1918, where the 'workmen who played for the local football teams [...] would come rushing up to buy a *Gazette*, to see their names and the teams listed for the weekend matches.'[29] Likewise, a company history of the *Eastern Football News* (the '*Pink 'Un*', established 1913) remarks: 'Isn't it strange how the Norwich City match reports are always most eagerly devoured by people who were actually at the game?'[30] These representations of local people and local places, the recording of names and deeds, did more than confirm that they existed or had happened, they made them glow with significance. Once again, Carey's insight applies: for such readers, 'nothing new is learned but [...] a particular view of the world is portrayed and confirmed'.[31] The local paper enabled a worldview in which any reader, even a child, was granted cultural citizenship, as part of a cultural democracy.

Frederick Milton believes that hundreds of thousands of children were motivated by the desire to have their lives affirmed by the prestige of local print, when they joined the national network of wildlife protection clubs set up by local newspapers in the late nineteenth and

---

27 William Edwin Adams, *Memoirs of a Social Atom* (London: Hutchinson, 1903), pp. 271–72.

28 *Sussex Agricultural Express*, 21 October 1892, p. 8.

29 Anne Hayes, *Family in Print: Bailey Newspaper Group Ltd, a History* (Dursley: Bailey Newspaper Group, 1996), p. 21.

30 Tony Clarke, *Pilgrims of the Press: A History of Eastern Counties Newspapers Group 1850–2000* (Norwich: Eastern Counties Newspapers, 2000), p. 31.

31 James Carey, *Communication as Culture: Essays on Media and Society* (London: Routledge, 1989), p. 20, https://doi.org/10.4324/9780203928912

early twentieth centuries. 'The overriding impression from this mass of correspondence is the sheer pleasure they took in simply seeing their names in print in a newspaper that was likely to be read by their parents, relatives, neighbours and, possibly, their peers.' 'It is my greatest desire to see my name in print,' Annie Trousdale wrote to the *Northern Weekly Gazette* in 1911.[32] A similar club in Preston, the *Preston Guardian* Animals' Friend Society, had a membership of more than 8,000 children, each of whom had the pleasure of seeing their name included in the lists of new members published every week.

Adult readers also believed that the local paper conferred status on its subjects. One reader of the *York Herald*, on seeing his verses published in 1827, wrote: 'I cannot describe the sensation I felt. It was the pride of a conqueror. That, I thought, is celebrity.'[33] John Rushton, a coalminer from Walkden near Bolton, gave a paper at a mutual improvement class in 1868, on gas in coal mines, and 'had preserved — and quoted in full — the short report which the *Farnworth Weekly Observer* published of that meeting.'[34] The memoirs of many nineteenth-century journalists describe the same pride at first seeing their name in the local paper.[35] Entering competitions was another way to get into print — with the chance of a prize, too, and this channel of reader involvement was as popular in the local press as in metropolitan publications. Children entered a competition to select extracts for reading in the *Preston Herald* in 1890, while women competed in a prize draw for ladies' gloves in the same paper in 1900. Readers responded enthusiastically to competitions promoting local identity in the *Preston Monthly Circular* in 1896, in which they nominated their favourite local people, places or objects, and they sent their photographic work to the *Empire Journal* in 1897. Even the Vicar of Wrightington, who favoured London papers over the local

---

32   Frederick Milton, 'Uncle Toby's Legacy: Children's Columns in the Provincial Newspaper Press, 1873–1914', *International Journal of Regional and Local Studies*, 5.1 (2009), 104–20 (pp. 112–14).

33   *Yorkshire Herald*, 7 September 1920, cited in N. Arnold, 'The Press in Social Context: A Study of York and Hull, 1815–1855' (unpublished PhD dissertation, University of York, 1987), p. 126.

34   Unpublished autobiography of John Rushton of Walkden, coalminer, 1833-c.1914, written 1908, in John J. Bagley, *Lancashire Diarists: Three Centuries of Lancashire Lives* (London: Phillimore, 1975), p. 178.

35   'Journalistic Autobiographies. I. Sir John Leng, MP, DL, Etc.', *Bookman*, February 1901, p. 157.

press, was eager to see the reports of his parish and its events in local and regional papers, and for his Preston friend to read them too. 'Please look in your *Manchester Courier* beginning with yesterday's under the heading of local Gleanings — Lancashire and Cheshire — for something about Heskin School', he wrote in 1877.[36]

Private scrapbooks often included cuttings from the local press, suggesting that readers prized reports of themselves and their families, further testament to the status conferred by publicity in the local paper. The scrapbook of J. J. Myres, a Preston solicitor and alderman, includes his electoral addresses and reports of his and his family's activities and achievements, all from the local press.[37] The scrapbook pictured in Figure 4.7 was used to save cuttings from Northampton and Norfolk newspapers from the 1860s to the 1890s, about the achievements, lives and deaths of members of the inter-related Jeffery, Hawes and Ratcliffe families, including school prizes, amateur dramatic performances and obituaries.[38] Here was evidence of involvement in local life, sanctioned and recorded by local newspapers, and preserved by readers because of its importance to them. The status of the local press meant that the promise of appearing in print was sometimes used as an incentive, as when 'a lady' was encouraged to attend a meeting in defence of the Irish Church in 1868, with the promise that 'arrangements had been made for the accommodation of ladies [...] all of whose names it had been arranged to publish in a certain Church paper [probably the *Preston Herald*], whose reporter was sure to be in attendance.'[39]

This is a supercharged version of Benedict Anderson's 'imagined community', the idea that the very act of privately reading a newspaper encourages each reader to imagine the thousands of others who are performing the same act or 'ceremony' — thereby connecting them, in

---

36 Anne R. Bradford, *Drawn by Friendship: The Art and Wit of the Revd. John Thomas Wilson* (New Barnet: Anne R. Bradford, 1997), 22 September 1877; see also 10 January 1879.

37 J. J. Myres's scrap book relating to Preston, 1857–1892, Community History Library, Harris Library, Preston, LE02. See also Scrapbook of Douglas C Logan, 1901–1916, Highland Council Archives, Lochaber, GB3218/L/D1, which includes reports of shooting matches in which he was successful, his activities as a committee member of local sporting and social bodies, and a letter published in the local paper.

38 Scrapbook, author's collection.

39 'How to enlist the sympathy of the ladies', letter from 'One in the Secret', PG, 19 September 1868.

their imagination, to other readers.[40] 'I should say nearly every home took the [*Lancashire Evening*] *Post*', one interviewee said of Preston in the early decades of the twentieth century.[41] Whether they did or not, this reader imagined that they did. But when local newspaper readers saw their own names in print, two further dimensions were added to the reading experience: both the readers and the place of reading were known and loved by each reader.

The Public Sphere and Other Uses of the Local Press

In the second half of the nineteenth century, long after Habermas and other scholars believe that the public sphere had been corrupted by commercialisation, reasoned argument was thriving in the correspondence columns of the local press in England (although there may have been a splintering into smaller local public spheres at the end of the century).[42] This was one of the most significant ways in which readers used their local newspapers — to discuss matters of local, national and international import, but particularly the local. The provincial press provided a forum for debate and for the art of controversy, an art often practised by skilled and self-aware rhetoricians. These debates could move back and forth between the page, the platform and the street, revealing the integration of oral and print cultures. Readers sometimes created national networks through their local correspondence.

Readers used correspondence columns to talk to each other, rather than to the paper or its editor. This can be seen when readers' letters are analysed according to their orientation — whether they were responding to leader columns, news articles, or other readers' letters

---

40   Benedict Anderson, *Imagined Communities: Reflections on the Origin and Spread of Nationalism* (London: Verso, 2006), pp. 35–36.

41   Mr G1P (b.1907), *ER*.

42   Jurgen Habermas, *The Structural Transformation of the Public Sphere: An Inquiry into a Category of Bourgeois Society* (Oxford: Polity, 1992), pp. 168–69; Mark Hampton, *Visions of the Press in Britain, 1850–1950* (Urbana: University of Illinois Press, 2004), pp. 30, 130.

(Table 10.1 below).[43] It is rare to find a letter beginning 'Thanks for your leader [...]' so that 'letters from readers' would be a more accurate description than 'letters to the editor'.[44] Readers were much more likely to make announcements, complain, take issue with the reported comments of a public figure, or to respond to other readers, for example arguing over rival conceptions of local identity, as in the political dialect letters in Chapter 8.[45] Some proactive letters (setting their own agenda, rather than responding to someone else's) stood alone, generating no response, while others initiated long-running debates. (The proactive category is probably overstated, as it includes responses to public meetings, sermons, placards and rumours, and no doubt responses to news articles and leaders to which allusions have been missed.)

Table 10.1. Orientation of readers' letters, *Preston Herald* 1860–1900.[46]

Proactive (setting own agenda)	112
Response to news report, same publication	84
Response to letter, same publication	73
Response to news report, other publication	15
Response to letter, other publication	7
Response to leader column	6
Response to advert	1
Total	**298**

Editorial concerns, reflected in leader columns or the proportion of Preston news, were not reflected in readers' letters, suggesting that readers

---

43　See also Hobbs PhD, Table A34, appendices. Similar categories are used in Sarah Pedersen, 'Within Their Sphere?: Women's Correspondence to Aberdeen Daily Newspapers, 1900–1918' (unpublished PhD dissertation, Robert Gordon University, 2004) and David Paul Nord, 'Reading the Newspaper: Strategies and Politics of Reader Response, Chicago, 1912–1917', in *Communities of Journalism: A History of American Newspapers and Their Readers* (Urbana: University of Illinois Press, 2001), pp. 246–77.

44　For a rare exception, see 'The Next Election and the Liberals of Preston', Correspondence, *PC*, 16 May 1868, p. 6; Ross Connelly, '"Letters from Readers" a More Appropriate Heading', *Grassroots Editor*, 47 (2006), 14.

45　Nick Hayes, 'The Construction and Form of Modern Cities: Exploring Identities and Community', *Urban History*, 29 (2002), 413–23 (p. 416), https://doi.org/10.1017/s0963926802003061; Nord, 'Introduction: Communication and Community', p. 13.

46　Based on all letters published in September and October of five sample years (1860, 1870, 1880, 1890, 1900).

brought their own frames of reference to the newspaper, rather than any mechanistic following of the newspaper's worldview. Lack of response to leader columns also calls into question their use by historians as an index of public opinion (although there were other types of response to the editorial view, as will become apparent).[47] As we saw in Chapter 7, readers were more negative than public figures quoted in news reports, and much more negative than editorial comment in the newspapers themselves (see Table 7.3). This only partly explains the mismatch between the point of view of readers and the publications they read — they also preferred to engage more with other readers, or follow their own agendas. Similarly, the proportion of readers' letters about Preston in the *Preston Herald* bore little relation to the proportion of Preston news in the paper, as Fig. 10.2 shows.

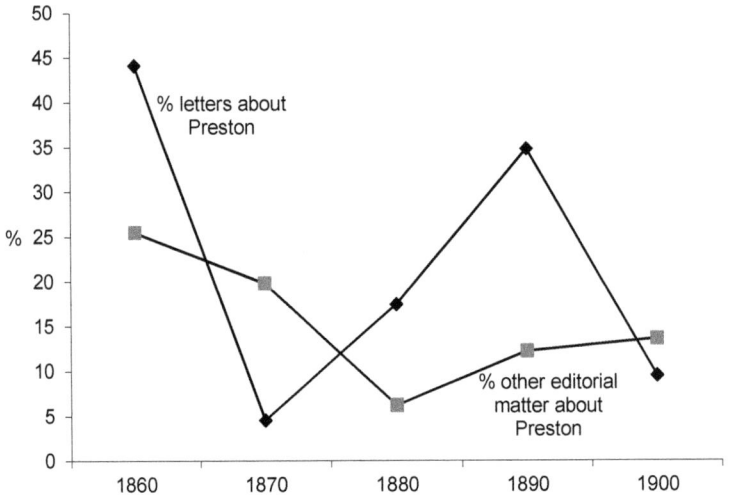

Fig. 10.2. Letters about Preston and proportion of Preston content, *Preston Herald* 1860–1900. Author's graph, CC BY 4.0.

The anonymity of the letters helped to achieve one of the conditions of a public sphere, or deliberative democracy, that participants meet as equals (although badly written letters were less likely to be published,

---

47   See, for example, the otherwise excellent Donald Read, *Press and People, 1790–1850: Opinion in Three English Cities* (London: Edward Arnold, 1961), p. 73.

because of the extra editing time required, if for no other reason).[48] Pseudonymous correspondence was like a masked ball, at which readers did not know who they were dancing with — although they knew who the host was, and therefore the sort of guest who might attend. As Barker argues, pseudonyms were used 'to suggest that an individual was speaking not for him or herself, but as the representative of a wider social group, or even of the public as a whole.'[49]

Controversy and the art of rhetoric were central to this public sphere, as they were to the nineteenth-century press as a whole.[50] The *Preston Herald* boasted that it 'advocates the principles of the Constitution in a vigorous and argumentative manner'.[51] Rather than something to be avoided, disputation was pursued and embraced, and was seen as a high-minded exercise in establishing and defending the truth, involving courage and skilful technique, akin to a martial art. It was important to know one's enemy, and to use the right methods. Catholic letter-writers who had defeated the Anglican controversialist Richard Littledale were commended to other Catholics for using

> the simple tactic of going straight at him, like a fox-terrier at a rat, utterly neglecting all the side issues which he raised up, and forcing him to keep to the point first raised, until he either owned himself in the wrong, or took refuge in sullen silence [...][52]

---

48 Karin Wahl-Jorgensen, 'The Construction of the Public in Letters to the Editor: Deliberative Democracy and the Idiom of Insanity', *Journalism*, 3 (2002), 183–204 (p. 71), https://doi.org/10.1177/146488490200300203; Karin Wahl-Jorgensen, 'Letters to the Editor in Local and Regional Newspapers', in *Local Journalism and Local Media*, ed. by Bob Franklin (London: Routledge, 2006), pp. 221–31 (p. 223). In 1820 an eighteen-year-old Manchester machine maker John Bagguley invited the editor of the *Manchester Observer* to 'select the Wheat and burn the Chaff', in a note accompanying his letter for publication: Robert Poole, 'The *Manchester Observer*: Biography of a Radical Newspaper', *Bulletin of the John Rylands Library*, forthcoming (2019), p. 8.

49 Hannah Barker, 'England, 1760–1815', in *Press, Politics and the Public Sphere in Europe and North America, 1760–1820*, ed. by Hannah Barker and Simon Burrows (Cambridge: Cambridge University Press, 2002), pp. 93–112 (p. 94). Paradoxically, the same value — the public sphere — is expressed in exactly opposite terms in modern US newspapers, many of which now refuse anonymous letters, even if the writer supplies their name and address as bona fides: 'the newspaper is a public forum. If one enters a public forum they need to be public about who they are': Connelly, p. 7, https://doi.org/10.1017/s0018246x07006607

50 For the tradition of controversy in religious publishing, see Josef L. Altholz, *The Religious Press in Britain, 1760–1900* (London: Greenwood, 1989), pp. 16, 18, 141.

51 Advertisement, Mitchell's *Newspaper Press Directory*, 1871.

52 *Antidote*, 1 February 1890, p. 14.

This analysis was published in a Preston publication that claimed a small national circulation in the early 1890s, and was devoted to equipping and encouraging Roman Catholics to use the public sphere of the correspondence column — chiefly in the provincial press — to defend and promote their faith. It provides further evidence of the importance of the provincial newspaper letters column as a public sphere. The publication in question, the *Antidote*, began as a column in the *Catholic News*, a weekly paper published from Preston for a regional readership; the column was also issued separately as an independent inquarto (roughly A4-size) publication from 1890 to 1892, and operated as a Victorian Catholic 'rapid rebuttal' service, similar to those established by Bill Clinton's Democratic party and Tony Blair's New Labour in the late twentieth century.[53] Every week it carried this appeal on its front page:

> It would be doing a great service to the cause of Catholic Truth if our friends up and down through the country would send us — immediately they come across it — any slander upon the Catholic religion published either in the Press or from the platform. A prompt refutation will be given in these columns, and the evil can be met by circulating THE ANTIDOTE freely on the spot where the slander arose.[54]

This publication sustained a 'counterpublic', to use Nancy Fraser's phrase, a community who used print to resist dominant narratives, in this case anti-Catholicism.[55]

The cultural capital of rhetorical skills and supporting facts was needed to take part in the public sphere of the correspondence column, according to a book reviewer in the *Antidote*:

---

53   Thomas Quinn, *Modernising the Labour Party: Organisational Change since 1983* (Springer, 2004), p. 167, https://doi.org/10.1057/9780230504912

54   An antidote to poison was a common metaphor in cultural debates about the press, and was chosen as the title of publications opposed to Chartism, Tractarianism and the Mormon church among others: Aled Gruffydd Jones, *Powers of the Press: Newspapers, Power and the Public in Nineteenth-Century England* (Aldershot: Scolar Press, 1996), p. 99; *The Waterloo Directory of English Newspapers and Periodicals, 1800–1900*, ed. by John S. North (North Waterloo Academic Press), http://www.victorianperiodicals.com

55   Nancy Fraser, 'Rethinking the Public Sphere: A Contribution to the Critique of Actually Existing Democracy', in *Habermas and the Public Sphere*, ed. by Craig J. Calhoun (Cambridge, MA.: MIT Press, 1997), pp. 109–42, https://doi.org/10.2307/466240, cited in Ellen Gruber Garvey, *Writing with Scissors: American Scrapbooks from the Civil War to the Harlem Renaissance* (Oxford: Oxford University Press, 2012), ch. 4, 'Alternative histories in African American scrapbooks', https://doi.org/10.1093/acprof:oso/9780195390346.001.0001

anyone who can write correct English and condense his ideas, armed with this little book, need not fear to do battle in the public Press with any of the champions of Church Defence. There is not one whose sophistries, shallowness and unhistorical fables cannot be refuted [...] by the treasures of <u>facts</u> crowded together in these pages, and wisely woven together in a letter to a newspaper.[56]

Controversy was also pleasurable, as evinced by one letter-writer who was attempting to initiate a debate about the financial problems of local co-operative societies:

I think a good newspaper discussion might help them. I did get two on in one paper some time ago, but I cannot draw them out now. I have just had a discussion in a Chorley paper with two co-operative persons [...] I intend to keep the subject sore and open.[57]

The Manchester poet Edwin Waugh records in his diary that, after a pub discussion on the existence of God, 'Wm Mallalieu, an intelligent and hearty man about forty-five years of age, owner of the Jacky Lane Brown Woollen Mill, challenged me to a correspondence on the subject. I accepted it, and agreed to write first.'[58] This was probably published in a Manchester paper.

A letter from 'Fakradeen', a pseudonym taken from Disraeli's novel *Tancred*, reveals sporting pleasure, an appreciation of rhetoric and promiscuous reading habits ranging between rival local titles:

I have ascertained that my good friend "Saxon" has, in another quarter, undertaken to demolish the Rev. J. Taylor on the very points that "Deplorer" defends him. I intend, therefore, to let "Deplorer" off this week, as I intend next week to throw all my strength and energy in an endeavour to help W. Singleton to smash "Deplorer's" twin-brother "Explainer," if that gentleman "shifts" himself into the *Chronicle* again on Saturday [...] meantime, I would advise "Deplorer" to read "Saxon's" ebullition, against the Turkish part of the Rev. J. Taylor's sermon. As a matter of reasoning, it is a species of small thunder. It is really.'[59]

---

56 Anonymous review of *Continuity or Collapse?* by Canon McCave DD, and Rev J. D. Breen BA, OSB, edited by R. J. B. Mackinlay OSB, *Antidote*, 19 August 1890, p. 224.

57 'Co-operation', letter from 'Live and Let Live', Correspondence, *PC*, 24 August 1889.

58 Edwin Waugh, *The Diary of Edwin Waugh: Life in Victorian Manchester and Rochdale 1847–1851*, ed. by Brian Hollingworth (Lancaster: Carnegie, 2008), Sunday 8 October 1848.

59 'A few words from Fakradeen in reply to "Deplorer"', Correspondence, *PC*, 29 October 1870.

As with any well-matched contest, there was mutual respect between combatants, and an 'agreed behavioural code to which even bickering groups within communities can subscribe', as in a tribute to a Southport paper from the Dean of Liverpool, who recalled 'good scrapping with the *Visiter* and that in itself is one of the best compliments I know [...]'[60] Editors also subscribed to this view, with a journalism handbook from 1894 advising that

> wordy strife may provide a means of escape for bitterness, malice, and uncharitableness [...] enabling [...] a visible and immediate growth of the spirit of toleration and of sweet reasonableness.[61]

Controversies between public figures were treated respectfully, as when a Catholic and a Protestant clergyman took part in an eleven-month debate on Papal jurisdiction in the *Manchester Courier* in 1889–90 and 'the editor, with much courtesy, placed a column at the disposal of each of the disputants, and carefully shut out all intervention of others than themselves.'[62] Debates at such length were not uncommon. These exchanges were sometimes considered valuable enough to be re-published as pamphlets.[63] Not everyone admired such disputes, however. A Barrow clergyman wrote that, 'of all religious controversies, so called, those carried on [in] a newspaper are the least profitable.'[64]

Active readers who wrote regularly to the Preston papers formed a small community, with regular signatures continuing to appear over the years, such as 'Saxon', 'Fakradeen' and some writers who gave their names, such as E. Foster and Albert Simpson. No doubt other readers tired of their constant appearances in the correspondence columns, but there is evidence from the twenty-first century that many readers grow fond of such characters, and that they are missed when they go.[65]

---

60 Hayes, p. 416.

61 John Beveridge Mackie, *Modern Journalism, a Handbook of Instruction and Counsel for the Young Journalist* (London: Crosby, Lockwood and Son, 1894), p. 76.

62 'The last of a long controversy', *Antidote*, 23 September 1890, p. 265.

63 For example, this pamphlet advertised in the *Antidote*, 16 December 1890, p. 36: "All roads lead to Rome," an account of a recent controversy in the *Lakes Herald* [...] To be had of Father Sellon, Ambleside (Westmoreland), price 2½d, post free.'

64 Letter from T. D. Anderson, *Barrow Herald*, 29 October 1870.

65 Jackson, pp. 169–71. The prolific British newspaper letter-writer Keith Flett is a case in point.

The public sphere created by readers' letters, and other newspaper content, provoked oral debate, too. We saw in Chapter 2 that newspaper-reading was associated with discussion, in pubs and in news rooms. Edward Ambler told the Preston Liberal candidate George Melly that Ambler's anonymous letters promoting Melly's cause were being talked about.[66] Letters sometimes went beyond 'wordy strife' and broke out of the rule-bound safety of rational discussion. In 1860 a letter published in the *Blackburn Times*, criticising the Darwen shoemakers' union, led to the picketing of a cobbler's shop after he was heard to agree with the letter, and the same letter was then the subject of a public meeting.[67] Violent opposition to the stance of a local paper can be interpreted as readers defining their identities in opposition to the views of particular publications, as when a Church and King mob let off a cannon near the offices of the *Preston Review* in 1793, and Chartists fired a pistol at the *Preston Pilot* offices in the 1840s.[68] (These were, of course, also attempts to intimidate and silence those papers.) In 1893 striking dockers in Hull burnt copies of two local evening papers (whilst a band played the 'Dead March' from *Saul*), as a sign of their displeasure at the reporting of their dispute.[69] Crowds who burnt piles of newspapers and editors' effigies, and individuals who physically assaulted editors such as Hewitson, obviously cared about what the local press wrote.[70] In 1844 the *Hull Advertiser* claimed that one old Holderness farmer was so attached to the paper that he shed tears when it declared itself against the Corn Laws.[71] Readers and non-readers alike cared deeply about what was written in the local press. These violently non-textual reactions to editorial opinion suggest that the correspondence columns under-represented the wider readership's response to leading articles.

We saw in Chapter 4 that the provincial press functioned as a national system and as a national network, thanks largely to the efforts of publishers and journalists. However, readers were also involved

---

66   Letter from E. Ambler to George Melly, 21 April 1864, George Melly Collection, Liverpool Archives, 920 MEL 13 Vol. IX, 1996.

67   *PG*, 1 September 1860, p. 7.

68   Edward Baines Jr, *The Life of Edward Baines, Late M. P. for the Borough of Leeds, by His Son* (Leeds: Reid Newsome, 1851), p. 20.; 'Death of Mr T. W. Clarke', *PG*, 15 August 1863, p. 5.

69   *Lancashire Evening Post*, 14 April 1893, p. 3.

70   Frederick Large, *A Swindon Retrospect, 1855–1930* (Wakefield: S. R. Publishers, 1970), p. 73.

71   *Hull Advertiser*, 12 April 1844, cited in Arnold, p. 126.

in knitting publications into national networks, by using one paper
to reply to a letter or editorial comment in a rival paper (particularly
at the start of the period). They also did this on a national and even
international scale. Their responses to the content of one paper, when
published in another, wove the publications and their readers into a
larger public sphere. At the local level, for example, 'An Old Political
Pioneer' wrote a letter to the *Preston Chronicle*, encouraging Catholics to
vote Liberal in the November 1868 general election. A rhetorical question
in his letter was quoted out of context by a Conservative councillor at a
public meeting and then printed on placards posted around the town.
The original correspondent then replied to his Tory opponents, from
the safety of the Liberal *Chronicle*'s correspondence column.[72] The same
process of dialogue and controversy across a number of publications
also linked distant papers, as when 'Latris' wrote a letter from Preston
to the *South Bucks Standard*, nearly 200 miles away:

> A friendly controversy has been going on between the editor of the
> *Wycombe Leaflet* and myself, writing in the CATHOLIC NEWS, a Preston
> paper, and I understand that it has been followed with interest by several
> of your readers. May I ask the favour of insertion of this short letter, in
> reply to what appears in the current number of the *Leaflet*?[73]

This letter was then republished in the *Catholic News* and the *Antidote*,
thus connecting four publications hundreds of miles apart through one
correspondence. Such long-distance exchanges were not unusual, and
if drawn on a map, they show how these active reader-correspondents
created a national network of local papers, by circulating, recirculating
and responding to texts from these publications. 'Such correspondence
provides the clearest indication that the reading of newspapers was a
creative process that could add to or alter intended meanings and in
turn produce a vast amount of new, unsolicited writing.'[74] This public
sphere encompassed other forms of print, including pamphlets,
placards, books and magazines, and also the platform and the pulpit. In
1870 'Fakradeen', a regular correspondent to the *Preston Herald*, wrote
a letter mocking the 'mad teetotal preachers in the Orchard on Sunday

---

72 Correspondence, *PC*, 3 and 17 October 1868.
73 *Antidote*, 25 November 1890, p. 335. In 1868 a *Preston Chronicle* reader wrote to
    comment on an article in the *Belfast Times*: Correspondence, *PC*, 12 September 1868.
74 Aled Gruffydd Jones, *Press, Politics and Society: A History of Journalism in Wales*
    (Cardiff: University of Wales Press, 1993), p. 198.

night' (Chadwick's Orchard was a public meeting place in the centre of Preston). The following week 'Fakradeen' returned to the Orchard and saw one of the preachers

> with the *Herald* in his hand, and I tell you, Mr Editor, he did give your paper a character and no mistake, simply because you had allowed a poor simple correspondent like me to have my say on a few matters [...][75]

These active readers had a clear understanding of the networked nature of the press. In 1851 a Preston Catholic bookseller described how 'newspaper transcribed from newspaper' to publish slanders against the Catholic church.[76] In 1891 *The Antidote* asked readers 'to have an eye on [Anglican] parish magazines' after one had repeated the supposed Catholic 'curse' from *Tristram Shandy*: 'This paragraph will probably be repeated right and left, and be spread through hundreds of towns and villages in England.'[77] In 1890 *The Antidote* warned readers about a false reference to Aquinas first used by Charles Hastings Collette, the 'no-Popery lecturer', in a controversy in the *Midlands Counties Express* in 1867–68. Such detailed reference to correspondence from more than twenty years earlier suggests some kind of cuttings archive, perhaps an indexed scrapbook or the use of a press cuttings agency.[78] Active reader-correspondents were numerous enough to have publications such as the *Antidote* dedicated to them; likewise, 'the editors of Temperance periodicals despised the passive reader: they wanted readers who would [...] scrutinise hostile papers for heresies requiring exposure [...]'[79] Such readers may have been cranks, but they were legion.

---

75 Correspondence, *PH*, 10 September 1870, p. 6; see also 'A few words from Fakradeen in reply to "Deplorer"', Correspondence, *PC*, 29 October 1870.

76 Speech of Evan Buller reported in 'Catholic Defence Association, meeting in Preston', *PC*, 18 October 1851; a similar organisation, the Preston Society for the Defence of Catholic Principles through the Medium of the Press, had been formed in 1823: Tom Smith, 'Preston Catholics before Emancipation', *North West Catholic History*, 26 (1999), 33–61.

77 *Antidote*, 24 February 1891, p. 53; much of the content of Anglican parish magazines was indeed syndicated: Jane Platt, *Subscribing to Faith? The Anglican Parish Magazine 1859–1929* (Basingstoke: Palgrave Macmillan, 2015), https://doi.org/10.1057/9781137362445

78 For example, Walker's *"Century" Scrap & Newscuttings Book (patented) No.2*, c.1901, 'for authors, clergymen, students, lawyers, and all literary men. specially prepared for those who desire to conveniently keep their cuttings relating to one subject within two boards for ready reference.' For the use of a cuttings service by an active provincial newspaper reader, see Pedersen, p. 51.

79 Brian Harrison, '"A World of Which We Had No Conception." Liberalism and the English Temperance Press: 1830–1872', *Victorian Studies*, 13 (1969), 125–58 (p. 130).

The local press was particularly important to these readers in allowing them to express and defend their religious, moral and political identities and views. Of the eighty-six publications dealt with in the first volume of the Catholic rapid response journal the *Antidote*, the most common type was the local press, with thirty-one mentions.[80] Local papers, particularly Conservative ones, were routinely anti-Catholic, but no more than other types of publication.[81] The next most common category, London non-denominational papers and reviews, received twenty mentions. When the local press was cited, it was the correspondence columns that provoked response, while for London papers and Anglican publications, it was the editorial content, typically articles or answers to correspondents. This shows the importance of the provincial letters column to this public sphere (albeit a far-from-inclusive public sphere). Local papers may have been at the heart of such public debate because it was easier to have one's views published there (a strength, not a weakness), but also because the local press was more pervasive.

However, this reasoned argument no longer took place in a unified public sphere in Preston's press at the end of the century. Instead, there was a growing divergence between papers in the topics addressed in letters. Earlier in the period, in September and October 1860, 72 per cent of letters in the Liberal *Preston Guardian* and the Conservative *Preston Herald* were on the same topics (62 out of a total of 86). But by the last decade of the century, this common ground had reduced from 72 per cent to 29 per cent (58 out of 198 letters), in a comparison of letters published in the *Herald* and the Liberal *Lancashire Evening Post* for the same months of 1890 and 1900. The same story is told in a decline in the number of readers' letters responding to either news or correspondence in other papers. In September and October 1860, the *Preston Herald* published 9 responses to material in other papers, and in 1868, the *Preston Chronicle* and *Preston Guardian* each published 10 letters in response to other papers. But by 1900, the *Herald* published only 1 such letter in the same 2 months, and the *Evening Post* only 3. At the end of the period, there were 2 distinct readerships, members of politically differing interpretive communities, who probably bought a copy of their favourite paper, rather than reading it in a news room alongside rival titles.

---

80   Hobbs PhD, Table A35, appendices.
81   Denis G. Paz, *Popular Anti-Catholicism in Mid-Victorian England* (Stanford: Stanford University Press, 1992), pp. 1–2.

Other Uses

The local press was woven into the expanding public life of towns such as Preston in many other ways besides the public sphere, lubricating local life with information. The local press served as a noticeboard on which information could be posted, for example to attract support for new initiatives such as a free library, public readings or the campaign against steaming in weaving sheds.[82] This sharing of information led to action, as with some of the complaints made in readers' letters. In Preston, a reader thanked the tram company for following his suggestions for a more efficient service, and in Barrow, the council's surveyor returned a 'fine, fat goose' sent by a builder after the gift was revealed in a reader's letter.[83] Sometimes this noticeboard function was exploited by visitors to the area, such as the letter from 'A Fortunate Visitor at Poulton-le-Fylde' keen to record his favourable impressions of the town, using the newspaper like a visitors' book.[84]

Readers in business needed the local press, alongside regional and metropolitan publications, for commercial information, and, logistically, publications from elsewhere were unable to compete in offering such detailed and up-to-date information as could be found in the 'market editions' of the Preston papers, which listed that day's prices at Preston's markets within hours of the farmers' carts trundling into town.[85] In Kent, William Hickson told the 1851 Newspaper Stamp Committee that only the local press could provide some types of commercial information: 'I am sometimes a buyer of stock, and I want to know what the price of heifers and horses is, and what the price of corn is especially, not at Mark-lane [in London] as the "Times" gives it, but at Maidstone Market.'[86] The members of Preston's Exchange and News Room ordered

---

82 Letter from J. A. Ferguson, Secretary of Preston Temperance Society, *PG*, 13 October 1860.

83 *PG*, 6 December 1890, p. 4; Peter J. Lucas, 'The First Furness Newspapers: The History of the Furness Press from 1846 to c.1880' (unpublished M.Litt, University of Lancaster, 1971), pp. 72, 82.

84 *PH*, 2 October 1880.

85 Stephen Caunce, 'Market Reports', in *Dictionary of Nineteenth Century Journalism*, ed. by Laurel Brake and Marysa Demoor, C19: The Nineteenth Century Index, Online Edition (London: ProQuest).

86 House of Commons, 'Report from the Select Committee on Newspaper Stamps; Together with the Proceedings of the Committee, Minutes of Evidence, Appendix, and Index 1851 (558) XVII. 1', para. 3201.

later editions of the three Preston papers and the *Manchester Guardian*, presumably for these purposes, as well as receiving market prices and other information from across the country by telegraph.[87]

Earlier, in the mid-1830s, the *Manchester Guardian* increased its sale when it focused on local news, according to an unpublished analysis by Alfred Wadsworth, editor of the paper between 1944 and 1956.[88] Wadsworth compared weekly sales figures with content, to analyse what attracted new readers to the paper, and identified a pattern of 'intensely *local* interests. The *Guardian* was still very much a local Manchester paper and clearly its readers liked it that way. The paper's reporting of local events seems to have had a direct relation to its circulation'.[89] Readers seemed to like national politics with local impact, such as the Manchester Improvement Bill, news affecting local businesses, such as the Budget, local railway ventures, and local bankruptcies, and court reports and meetings of local government bodies. 'Local government was a topic of great interest, sales always increasing when the *Guardian* contained a report of an important meeting of the Police Commissioners [...]'[90] In Shrewsbury in the 1860s, Henry Lucy claimed that readers preferred leader columns about 'the new sewage system and the proposed Market Hall' rather than the American Civil War, 'and when they found these matters discussed in the columns of the *Observer* [...] they rushed to buy the paper. Its sale went up in inspiriting fashion [...].'[91]

The local press was used for political manoeuvring, as seen in the letters from the Liberal 'wire-puller' Edward Ambler in support of Parliamentary candidate George Melly.[92] Reputations, personal and civic, were defended publicly, such as the letter claiming that Preston, rather than Garstang or Lancaster, had the oldest charter in Lancashire; or the plea from the curate of Leyland to his accuser over allegations of rabble-rousing at an election meeting:

87　Preston Exchange and Newsroom minutes, 4 January 1869, 3 December 1872, Lancashire Archives, CBP 53/4.

88　Alfred Wadsworth, typescript, *Manchester Guardian* archive, John Rylands Library, Manchester, 324/5A.

89　Wadsworth typescript, 324/5A, p. 4.

90　Wadsworth typescript, 324/5A, p. 3.

91　Henry W. Lucy, *Sixty Years in the Wilderness: Some Passages by the Way* (London: Smith, Elder, 1909), p. 46.

92　H. A. Taylor, 'Politics in Famine Stricken Preston: An Examination of Liberal Party Management, 1861–65', *Transactions of the Historic Society of Lancashire & Cheshire*, 107 (1956), 121–39.

I respectfully request you, as a gentleman, to give to another gentleman all the satisfaction in your power by making me an apology for the serious charges contained in your letter published in the *Preston Guardian* and *Preston Chronicle* of Saturday last.[93]

The role of the local press, in aggregate, as a major publisher of a wide range of literary genres enabled it to offer opportunities of self-expression to many readers (see Chapters 4 and 5). Amateur poets, novelists, historians, naturalists, archaeologists, travel writers, literary critics and journalists all contributed significant amounts of material that rivalled if not outweighed the output of book publishers. These readers who wrote formed interpretive communities around each newspaper and their large numbers cast further doubt on any decline of a public sphere in the nineteenth century.

Less active readers sometimes relied on the local press to put into words thoughts and feelings that they could not express themselves. Rev W. D. Thompson, vicar of St Saviour's in Preston, quoted from Hewitson's *Preston Chronicle* series 'Our Churches And Chapels' (later republished in book form) when recounting the history of his church's schoolroom.[94] In Lancashire's northern Furness peninsula, an editor's catchphrase became part of the local vocabulary. J. A. Bernard, editor of the *Ulverston Mirror*, often ended his leaders in condemnation of the police with the phrase, 'Who rules in Furness?' When a police superintendent was told to move out of a private train carriage at Furness Abbey station, an onlooker mocked him by shouting,"Who rules in Furness?' 'and a host of voices, in concert, rejoined, "Who rules in Furness Abbey?"'[95] Here, the words of the journalist were taken off the page by the mocking passengers and used against their target, demonstrating these readers' support of the paper's editorial stance.

---

93 'Garstang Historical Oratory', letter from 'A Preston Freeman', *PC*, 7 June 1879; 'The great Jacques question', letter from Rev Kinton Jacques, *PG*, 19 September 1868.

94 'Tea-party at St Saviour's: Inaugural opening of the new schools', *PC*, 10 September 1870, p. 6.

95 *Ulverston Mirror*, 4 August 1860, cited in Peter J. Lucas, 'J. A. Bernard's Challenge: Journalists on Journalism in a Victorian Country Town', *Transactions of the Cumberland and Westmorland Antiquarian and Archaeological Society* 7 (2007), 193–213 (p. 206).

Local Identity

The local press moved from background to foreground at times of crisis for local identity, as seen in the twentieth-century examples of local government reorganisation that threatened the status of Accrington and Herefordshire.[96] Individuals also turned to the local press when the geographical aspects of their personal identities were threatened, particularly by exile from their birthplace. The contrasting reading matter available in Preston and Barrow Free Libraries is a good example of how the local press was used to sustain expatriate local identities. The more settled population of Preston required only four weekly papers from other parts of the country at any one time, while the 'shifting and fluctuating' population of Barrow, a smaller town full of migrants, required sixteen such publications.[97] The papers in Barrow free library were from other parts of Furness and Lancashire, from Cumberland, Westmorland, the Isle of Man and Cheshire, matching the places of birth revealed in the Census. The only surprise is the lack of any papers from Staffordshire, a significant source of immigration to Barrow, although the publications auctioned at Barrow Working Men's Club and Institute in 1870 included one from Wolverhampton, among a similar geographical spread of titles.[98] A generation later, around the turn of the century, the parents of Barrow oral history

---

96 For Accrington, see Chapter 7, p. 281, n. 57. When the county identity of Herefordshire was threatened by its planned merger with Worcestershire in the early 1970s, the county paper, the *Hereford Times,* was the obvious forum in which to protest. Correspondence grew to 'record proportions' and sales of the paper increased: C. R. Goulding, 'Defeat in the battle for Herefordshire,' *Hereford Times* 150th anniversary special, 2 July 1982.

97 Barrow Free Library annual reports, Cumbria Archive and Local Studies Centre, Barrow. As well as looking back to their places of origin, Barrow Library's readers also looked forward to opportunities elsewhere, as seen in the higher number of specialist migration titles; John Duncan Marshall, *Furness and the Industrial Revolution: An Economic History of Furness, 1711–1900, and the Town of Barrow, 1757–1897* (Beckermet: Moon, 1981), p. 310.

98 See also Marie-Louise Legg, *Newspapers and Nationalism: The Irish Provincial Press, 1850–1892* (Dublin: Four Courts Press, 1999), p. 69. 'Barrow Working Men's Club and Institute', *Barrow Herald,* 8 October 1870, p. 3. In 1871 40.7 per cent of Barrow's population had come from Staffordshire, Westmorland, Ireland, Cumberland, Yorkshire, Worcestershire and Scotland, in that order. During the 1880s, an estimated 12 per cent of the town's population, 5,700 people, migrated elsewhere: Marshall, p. 355; T. H. Bainbridge, 'Barrow in Furness: A Population Study', *Economic Geography,* 15 (1939), 379–83 (pp. 380–81).

interviewees preferred local newspapers, from their places of origin and from Barrow, to London papers. The local press was mentioned in similar numbers as in Preston, and more than in Lancaster, but there were also more non-local papers, especially from Scotland, where many interviewees' parents were born. Often the same family took a Barrow paper and a paper from their home town — of the nine families who took provincial papers from elsewhere (including Manchester mornings and Sundays), six also took a Barrow paper. These six families felt no need to choose between their previous home and their present one, perhaps like those cricket fans whose parents were born in Pakistan, who see no contradiction between being British and supporting Pakistan.

Expatriates who travelled further afield likewise used local papers to keep informed of events back home, and to sustain their local identities.[99] Thomas Parkinson, who emigrated from Preston to the United States in 1851, regularly received Preston papers from his mother and sister, and almost a century later, Southport clergyman Rev N. C. Oatridge described the response of local soldiers to receiving copies of the *Southport Visiter* overseas: 'their letters of appreciation show what it means to them. The provincial paper [...] provides an indispensable link for those away from home [...].'[100] Nearer home, 'Bert', reading his paper by the fire with his Woodbine at the ready (Chapter 3), probably read the Blackpool *Evening Gazette* because he was a Blackpool expatriate exiled to Preston. Similarly, a Lancaster oral history interviewee's parents, both from Penrith, received the Penrith paper every week in Lancaster, 50 miles from their birthplace.[101] The most eloquent evidence for the use of the local paper to nourish local identities is found in John O'Neil's diaries. O'Neil, born in Carlisle but

---

99 Bill Bell, 'Bound for Australia: Shipboard Reading in the Nineteenth Century', in *Journeys through the Market: Travel, Travellers, and the Book Trade*, ed. by Robin Myers and Michael Harris (Folkestone: Oak Knoll Press, 1999); Andrew Crisell and Guy Starkey, 'News on Local Radio', in *Local Journalism and Local Media: Making the Local News*, ed. by Bob Franklin (London: Routledge, 2006), p. 23, https://doi.org/10.4324/9780203969205

100 Thomas A. Parkinson, 'A Preston Emigrant to America 1851, His Diary & Letters from England' (1983), typescript, Marian Roberts Collection, University of Central Lancashire; Anon., *A Century of Progress 1844–1944, Southport Visiter* (Southport: Southport Visiter, 1944), p. 29.

101 Mrs W2L (b.1910), ER.

settled in Clitheroe, 100 miles away, summarised in his diary what he learnt from the paper each week, but rarely recorded his feelings. Yet when he occasionally received a paper from his home town, his writing became more emotional:

> I got the *Carlisle Journal* today which was sent me and I was very glad to get it, it is the first news I have had from Carlisle this many a month and it is very full of news it being the assize week. I read it all through advertisements and all I was so keen of it.
>
> I got a newspaper from Carlisle [...] I read the local news and advertisements which makes me think I am at home again.[102]

Similarly, James Lonsdale, a Blackburn man who had emigrated to South Africa, wrote to a hometown paper in 1889, describing 'the pleasure with which I receive my Standard & Express each week in this far-off land. It seems to take me once again amongst old friends [...] But there is another pleasure, and that is the really good poetry and prose in our dear old dialect [...].'[103]

The Uniqueness of the Local Press

Readers took from the local press things they could not find elsewhere, which explains why the mid-nineteenth-century prophecies of doom for the provincial press did not come to pass. Nowhere else could people read so much and so often about people and places they knew or knew of, about other Prestonians' activities and opinions, thereby connecting them with their neighbours or former neighbours, family and friends. Nowhere else were they as likely to gain the prestige of print themselves, with a positive mention, set in the permanence of type. The local press offered active readers a platform for self-expression and for action. None of this could be supplied in such quantity, or so powerfully, by non-local publications. While all newspapers were prestigious, the limited space and subject matter of the high-status London press could not provide the opportunities, spread across the nation, that the local press exploited, for

---

102 John O'Neil, *The Journals of a Lancashire Weaver: 1856–60, 1860–64, 1872–75*, ed. by Mary Brigg (Chester: Record Society of Lancashire and Cheshire, 1982), Wednesday 13 August 1856, 2 March 1857. See also 14 August 1859.

103 Letter, *Blackburn Standard & Weekly Express*, 22 June 1889, p. 6.

distributing and democratising the prestige of seeing oneself and one's place in print. The hundreds of names printed in each edition, of people at public meetings, members of committees, subscribers to charitable causes, defendants and witnesses, public officials, people at funerals, pub cricketers and church football teams, all provided fifteen minutes of local fame, a century before Warhol's prediction. The *Dudley Weekly Times* eloquently expressed the unique role of the local paper in 1856:

> In the economy of nature we have not only great and stupendous objects, but also, those which are minute and apparently of little importance [...] As in nature, so in the world of letters — so with the public press. It is not only important that great national events should be chronicled and commented upon, but also those which are of a local character and of a more limited interest, and this can only be done by the local press.[104]

It could be argued that the popularity of the regional and local press lay not in its localness but in its faster, more up-to-date news service. For Preston readers, Manchester and Liverpool papers had several hours' advantage over London papers; and in the twenty-four hours before publication of any Preston paper, a local title had the same advantage over the big-city Lancashire dailies. For the most important stories, they published special editions within minutes of receiving telegraphed news. However, speed was not the main attraction. In Nord's words, 'how readers read the newspaper suggests what the newspaper is', and in Preston as elsewhere, the local newspaper was valuable to readers in two ways: for its local content, and its ability to validate and elevate readers' lives in a particular place.[105] No other print product performed these functions as effectively.

Conclusions

The active readers discussed in this chapter responded as journalists hoped, in many instances, such as supporting the editorial stance, defending the paper against attacks, basking in the status of print and deferring to the editor's bottomless knowledge. But they also maintained an independent attitude, often setting their own agenda when writing to

---

104 *Dudley Weekly Times* supplement, 20 December 1856.
105 Nord, 'Reading the Newspaper', p. 247.

the paper, and rarely responding to the hallowed leader column. They constructed their own networks of readers, through correspondence with other papers. Readers' uses of the paper were influenced by but not *determined* by the content of local papers, nor by the conscious decisions and intentions of publishers and journalists.[106]

We have seen how readers used the local press as public persons — to build and sustain political, social, commercial and cultural infrastructures and to take part in a local public sphere of reasoned discussion. In the same way today, use of local news media in the United States is associated with a sense of place and active citizenship.[107] The importance of the provincial press to the public sphere is shown by its dominance (particularly its readers' letters) among the publications which the *Antidote* responded to in the early 1890s. Such reader-to-reader relationships are not a given — twenty-first-century research has found it lacking in Italian newspapers, for example.[108] However, it is important not to overstate the role of the local press in fostering deliberative democracy. The papers more often followed local initiatives than led them, as with the Preston shop assistants' half-day holiday in 1890. The success of the initiative was due mainly to canvassing of shopkeepers, rather than publicity in the newspapers. This chapter has also shown how readers used local newspapers as private persons, for relaxation and leisure, and to feel part of a community.

Readers liked local news of local personalities and places; they saw the local press as a welcoming platform on which to perform dialect writing; they valued fiction, poetry and historical writing about the locality; and they believed that a mention in the paper raised the status of local people and places. When newspapers organised social and cultural events and competitions on a local theme, readers and their families took part enthusiastically. Readers relied on the local press as the infrastructure for local professional and amateur sport, particularly football. They used the local press to argue about local identity. All

---

106 Michel de Certeau, *The Practice of Everyday Life* (Berkeley: University of California Press, 1988), pp. xiii, xvi–xvii.

107 Michael Barthel and others, 'Civic Engagement Strongly Tied to Local News Habits', *Pew Research Center's Journalism Project*, 2016, http://www.journalism.org/2016/11/03/civic-engagement-strongly-tied-to-local-news-habits/

108 'The writer's interaction with the readers is markedly stronger in Britain than in Italy [...] references and direct address to the readers are much more common in Britain': Pounds, p. 49.

these are positive responses — no doubt the majority response was more passive, as with readers' responses to leader columns; only one type of negative response has been found, that of readers' resistance to the boosterism of local newspapers. In Chapter 7 we saw that the local press in the new town of Barrow tried harder to evoke and exploit a rapidly developing local identity, but the only reader evidence traced so far suggests that many readers looked to the press 'back home' for sustenance of their local identities.

Readers used the local paper to propose, sustain and contest local identities by taking generic journalistic methods and focusing them on their own locality; they enjoyed the prestige that print gave to local people and places, and the permanence bestowed on fleeting events by their being recorded in the local paper. They also brought their interpretations of other aspects of local identity, such as dialect and local history, to the newspaper. Usually these uses of the paper were implicit, but crises of local identity — public and private — made the value of this cultural product more explicit. When distance from home threatened the local identity of the reader, or when the continuity of a place was disrupted, as in local government reorganisation, people turned to the local press. Many of the local newspaper's functions could not be fulfilled by publications from elsewhere.

Conclusions

Karl Marx's 1855 predictions of a 'revolution in the provincial press', 'emancipation from London' and 'decentralisation of journalism' largely came to pass, for the next eighty years at least. The second half of the nineteenth century was the golden age of the provincial press. More copies of provincial newspapers were sold and read between the early 1860s and 1900 than any other type of newspaper. In most news rooms and reading rooms, no other type of publication required so many multiple copies to meet reader demand as the local paper, and it was this print genre that was most often recalled from the childhood homes of oral history interviewees. While local papers had to compete with other newspaper genres for popularity among upper-middle-class readers, they were pre-eminent for readers lower down the social scale. None of this is apparent if we conduct impressionistic studies using low-circulation London newspapers, read by small but powerful minorities.

Local papers were the most popular type of newspaper for two reasons: they appealed to local identities and their networked national structure was the fastest news delivery system available. Local newspaper publishers and journalists consciously set out to promote local identity, seeing this as part of their cultural role, whilst also aware of the commercial benefits. Content exploiting local patriotism could not practically be provided by London papers. An extra vocabulary of place was available to the local press, literally so in the case of Lancashire dialect, whose untranslatable nuances could add depth to any piece of writing. Football reportage, with its focus on local supporters, gave readers the opportunity to read about themselves. Unlike the *Daily Mail,*

     https://doi.org/10.11647/OBP.0152.11

for example, the local press could provide local football information and infrastructure, for both the amateur and the professional game. Local papers were exclusive providers of other local — or locally relevant — content, such as market prices, Parliamentary speeches by local MPs, or prize winners at agricultural shows. Furthermore, non-local news could reach readers more quickly if it was telegraphed to hundreds of local newspaper offices throughout the nation and then printed in newspaper form and distributed across small areas. The alternative, of telegraphing the same news to London newspaper offices and printing and transporting newspapers hundreds of miles by rail, was much slower.

These competitive advantages have been confirmed by evidence from the readers themselves. They often used local papers for purposes that publications from elsewhere could not fulfil, and incorporated them into local politics, social movements, commerce and culture, and used them as local public spheres. They also used them more personally, for leisure and as extensions of their social networks. Local papers were better able to fulfil these functions because there were more of them, providing more opportunities, across the nation, for Janowitz's 'democratisation of prestige', the mundane glamour of appearing in print under the gaze of one's neighbours. But there was more than a logistical, quantitative difference between readers' uses of the local press and of publications from elsewhere — there was also a qualitative difference, enabling readers to write in their own dialect, to discuss local issues, and to feel connected to the people and places given status in the local paper. However, as regards local identity, the local press played only a small part in the formation and development of sense of place. Even at the height of the local newspaper's powers, it was only one among many factors 'producing locality'. Local identity was more significant to the newspaper than the newspaper was to local identity.

The forty-five years covered by this book encompass a fast-changing, dynamic period in periodical print culture and reading behaviour. In Preston as elsewhere, more titles were published, more copies were sold, and established publications grew in their physical dimensions and in the number of their pages and editions. New genres appeared, such as the provincial evening newspaper. The local press diversified, with more periodicals and specialist publications serving particular religious denominations, leisure interests and occupational groups. Local papers adapted their content to a larger, more socially diverse readership, with shorter articles, shorter paragraphs and more variety in their non-news articles. Newspapers' address shifted from middle-class to classless, as new working-class readers influenced journalists' language; the boundaries of 'us' were expanded to include readers previously represented as 'them', expressing more consensus and less conflict. Rising literacy and cheaper newspapers encouraged more reading, more public places in which to read and an exponential increase in shops from which to buy papers.

News was at the heart of the most dynamic changes in the reading world of a provincial town like Preston. The rise of the news room, and the even greater rise of the newsagent, eclipsed any other changes in the circumstances of reading. The comparative significance of newspapers in the public life of a town is illustrated by the contrast with the far fewer institutions dedicated to the reading of fiction, such as circulating libraries. Facilities to read and discuss the news were thought attractive enough to be offered as benefits for members of clubs and societies, and to be used as bait to lure men into churches and political parties, pubs and temperance halls. As the pace of publication quickened and news rooms, newsagents and a purpose-built newspaper office appeared in the town, newspaper-reading began to change the appearance and routines of Preston — and most of the newspapers being read were provincial ones, particularly those published in Preston.

While news was widely available at the beginning of the period, it was often heard rather than read, or read from a newspaper owned by somebody else, in a public place. As time went on, more hearers became readers, and more readers became purchasers. News rooms became integrated in the activities of political parties, clubs and societies, and, with the opening of Preston's free library, became available to all if they so desired. Meanwhile, reading the newspaper at home became more common at the end of the period, first for lower-middle-class readers and then for working-class readers, with a consequent decline in the use of middle-class news rooms (and a decline in the second-hand value of papers and periodicals). Yet, at the end of the period, when newspaper-reading was becoming part of the domestic routine of even working-class readers, reading a newspaper in a public news room was still a normal activity, and one that often involved discussion.

Consequently, there may indeed have been a decline in one type of bourgeois public sphere, that of the middle-class news room. However, other public spheres such as Co-op reading rooms and political clubs flourished, where a variety of reading material encouraged promiscuous reading and where discussion was the norm. The decline in 'non-aligned' news rooms unattached to specific creeds is consistent with evidence from readers' letters, which suggests that newspaper readers ranged more freely across political and religious lines at the start of the period than at the end. The local public sphere splintered. Certainly by the turn of the century, if not long before, most readers used the press to confirm what they already believed, rather than to engage in genuine debate. However, the growth of political clubs with reading facilities in Preston and the opening of the public library suggest that motives of education, and of political persuasion, continued in the era of the commercial press. It may be that some historians have overestimated the political and self-improving motives of readers of the early nineteenth-century political press, who may have been as keen on the crime news as the political interpretation of it. Conversely, they may have underestimated the political use of the later capitalist press.[1] Perhaps its commercial nature was less the end of the bourgeois public sphere, and more the rejuvenation of a boisterous, democratic working-class public sphere.[2]

Many of the dominant paradigms in press history and the history of reading are peculiarly unsuited to the study of the local press. A focus on centralised modes of cultural production misses a nationally networked phenomenon such as the local press, and dismisses local phenomena as unimportant. The anachronistic and confused concept of the 'national' newspaper would not have been familiar to the

---

1   Aled Gruffydd Jones, 'Constructing the Readership in 19th-Century Wales', in *Serials and Their Readers, 1620–1914*, ed. Robin Myers and Michael Harris (Winchester/New Castle, DE: St Paul's Bibliographies/Oak Knoll Press, 1993), p. 160; James Curran, 'The Industrialization of the Press', in *Power without Responsibility: The Press and Broadcasting in Britain*, ed. James Curran and Jean Seaton (London: Routledge, 1991), 32–48.

2   David M. Henkin, *City Reading: Written Words and Public Spaces in Antebellum New York* (New York: Columbia University Press, 1998), pp. 12–13.

creators and readers of nineteenth-century newspapers, and it has hindered press scholarship; further, by concentrating on the London daily, a print genre that was part of high politics, diplomacy and elite culture, we have ignored the more popular genre of the local weekly, which was relatively insignificant in these areas of human endeavour. Scholarship on 'significant' literary figures has taken little account of their writings in the local press, since the low status of local newspapers at the time often led famous writers and intellectuals to hide or downplay such work.

A number of misconceptions about the metropolitan and provincial press have been challenged in this book. First, that provincial newspapers were parochial during this period.[3] Content analysis shows that national and international news, and non-news items, almost matched local news in most of Preston's papers. The idea that metropolitan newspapers were national papers in this period has been dealt with in Chapter 1; in fact, London papers circulated mainly in south-east England, and to local elites elsewhere, and contained little news of British events outside the south-east. The idea that newspapers contain only news is demonstrably false, as shown by the examination of content related to local identity in Chapters 7–9, including sport, poetry, serialised fiction, history, geography, biography, book reviews, maps, portraits and other illustrations. As Laurel Brake, Margaret Beetham and others have demonstrated, newspapers cannot be dismissed as shallow, transparent, 'sub-literary' texts. In fact, newspapers are as complex as novels, made by many authors, using many genres, for a variety of motives, most of them concealed or unconscious. Many of the authors of each issue never met nor agreed with each other, and readers' responses were routinely incorporated into the text.[4] The example of Hewitson has shown that provincial editors and newspaper proprietors were far from anonymous. The nameless metropolitan editor was the exception rather than the rule in Victorian journalism. Another misconception, that profit replaced politics as the primary motive for newspaper publishing in the late nineteenth century, has

---

3   Anon., 'On the Parish', *All The Year Round*, 29 December (1860), 273–76.
4   Laurel Brake, 'The Old Journalism and the New: Forms of Cultural Production in London in the 1880s', in *Papers for the Millions: The New Journalism in Britain, 1850s to 1914*, ed. by Joel H. Wiener (London: Greenwood, 1988), p. 1; Margaret Beetham, 'Ben Brierley's Journal', *Manchester Region History Review*, 17 (2006), 73–83 (p. 76).

found no support in the case study of Preston, or elsewhere in provincial journalism.[5] A complex mix of motives continued to motivate the launch, purchase and continuation of newspapers, and many papers were founded chiefly for political reasons into the twentieth century.

Turning to misconceptions about newspaper readership, the bound file copies kept in news rooms, and the demand for second-hand copies, complicate ideas about the ephemeral nature of newspapers. There is some truth in the idea that readers' political views can be inferred from a paper's political stance, but users of news rooms and reading rooms read promiscuously, and technically superior papers or those with specialist content, such as farming news, were read even by those who disagreed with the papers' politics. Historical readers were much more complex than implied readers. Finally, Chalaby's assertion that 'the popular classes and the elites' have never read the same papers is contradicted by the presence of the *Times* even in working class news rooms; further, a divide between a 'quality' press and a 'popular' press is harder to sustain when examining local weekly and evening papers.[6]

The argument presented here — that readers preferred the local press because, among other reasons, they liked to read about themselves, people they knew, and the places they loved — is, of course, open to challenge. Even when one accepts that the local paper was the most widely read type of newspaper in the second half of the nineteenth century, the significance of this phenomenon can still be questioned. People may have read the local press, but perhaps it had little impact on them, on their society, and on the nation. This can be addressed in two ways: first, the local press may have been a small part of most people's lives, but the reader evidence suggests that other newspapers and periodicals had even less significance for them. Second, we have

---

5   In contrast, Rachel Matthews believes that 'the provincial newspaper is, and always has been, a commercial venture to its core': Rachel Matthews, *The History of the Provincial Press in England* (New York: Bloomsbury Academic, 2017), p. 4, https://doi.org/10.5040/9781501324680. But two Preston examples contradict this commercial focus: the Anti-Corn Law League subsidised the launch of the town's main nineteenth-century newspaper, the *Preston Guardian*, while its rival, the *Preston Herald*, was subsidised by the Conservatives from 1860 into the twentieth century. And from the Conservative local papers edited by Alaric Watts in the 1820s to the Carnegie-Storey syndicate of Radical evening and weekly papers in the 1880s, a political mission was an important aspect of the nineteenth-century local press.

6   Jean Chalaby, *The Invention of Journalism* (Basingstoke: Macmillan, 1998), p. 179.

seen that, for some readers at least, the local paper was integrated into their daily routines, their sense of self (as an exiled native of Carlisle, for example) or their way of doing business. At a community level, this study does not claim that the local press was indispensable in local society, but that the information circulated by local newspapers became increasingly important as the Victorian state and associative culture developed. They were not essential, but local Victorian society would have been very different without them. Rightly or wrongly, people believed that the presence of a local paper gave status to a town, enhanced local democracy, elevated the public events it reported and held leaders and criminals alike to account. Objections to the study of the local press on the grounds that it was nationally insignificant are based on misunderstandings of the national nature of the local press, of how national culture was produced and reproduced at local level, and of the English nation itself, as no more than a small group of powerful individuals living within fifty miles of Westminster.

It could be argued that a faster news service and lower price were the main attractions of the halfpenny local paper, and no doubt these were important. International news, particularly of wars, increased newspaper sales significantly. However, journalists and readers alike saw local content as valuable, and the circulations of local (but not regional) papers continued to rise until the 1950s, despite London newspapers and radio being able to deliver non-local news more speedily and cheaply.

Can this examination of reading Preston's local press be generalised to other places? This is a weakness of any case study, and if local distinctiveness is as important as I believe it is, then this objection applies even more. The distinctive (yet far from unique) character of Preston must be taken into account when extrapolating the findings of this research, but only two aspects would make the local press unusually popular here: the tradition of wider political participation, and lower literacy rates (the oral history material demonstrated a link between poor literacy and a preference for the local paper). Even after these phenomena had disappeared, the traditions established by them could have persisted. However, only two minor differences were detected between Preston and a comparator town, Barrow. As an old, established town, the boosterism of Preston's newspapers was more muted than in the striving new town of Barrow (except when reporting the 1893 Preston North End crisis). Further, as a *de facto* county town and market centre, Preston's press may have had less need to appeal to working-class readers until the late 1880s, unlike that of Barrow, where there were not enough middle-class readers to go round.[7] However, secondary literature from elsewhere suggests that Preston was broadly similar to other places in its print culture and reading behaviour. Only further studies will test this point, and the eventual aim must be to synthesise the scholarship on the London and the provincial press. Only when such work has been done can we begin to approach a truly national history of print culture, rather than the distortedly London-focused account we have at present.

This book helps to explain many seemingly anomalous aspects of nineteenth-century press history. The greater popularity of the local press is unfathomable without a recognition of the importance of place to the majority of the population. The lack of a truly national press in the nineteenth century, and the difficulties with the notion of a national press, explain the seemingly odd strategies of newspaper publishers, such as partly printed sheets, the daily 'newspaper' issued by the Central Press and printed on one side of the paper only to aid speedy typesetting, the group of Catholic local papers with syndicated content published by Charles Diamond, or the ability of a syndication agency in the northern industrial town of Bolton to commission *Tess of the D'Urbervilles* from Thomas Hardy. Equally, the lack of a national press, and the high value placed on local news, explains the methods of popular London papers in the twentieth century as they developed national news-gathering, distribution and sales operations. These methods included the opening of 'secondary' centres of 'national' newspaper production in Manchester and Glasgow and the resort to regional and occasionally local editions, paradoxically achieving national status by becoming more local. Sense of place, combined with the effective national system created by the provincial press, also explains the attitude of provincial readers such as J. B. Priestley's father in Bradford, a teacher who never read a London newspaper,

---

7   There were 828 middle-class Barrow residents in 1911, in a population of 63,770: Caroline Joy, 'War and Unemployment in an Industrial Community: Barrow-in-Furness 1914–1926' (unpublished PhD dissertation, University of Central Lancashire, 2004), p. 31.

finding all he needed in the Bradford morning paper. These provincial morning dailies were to suffer the most when the London dailies began to become genuinely national in the twentieth century, because they contained the least local content of any provincial genre.

This study has implications for the disciplines of media history, the histories of reading and publishing, and perhaps even for present-day provincial journalism. It demonstrates that an acknowledgement of the importance of place to media audiences can cast new light on audience behaviour. It suggests that some theories of the nineteenth-century newspaper are applicable only to London publications, representing a minority of the field. Chalaby's chronology of pre-repeal political 'publicists' being replaced by post-repeal commercial 'journalists' is too simplistic, especially as the same individuals were often involved.[8] The provincial press, like the London press, adapted to the new market conditions post-1855, but current knowledge of the diverse nature of this adaptation is too limited to say anything beyond the fact that it did not fit the London pattern suggested by Chalaby.[9] The same is true for recent formulations of New Journalism as the death of the Liberal educational press ideal.[10] The tradition of direct political control of newspapers continued longer in the provinces than in the capital, and the greater provincial diversity of newspaper genres, allied with innovations in style and content around the country, meant that recognisably New Journalistic approaches could go hand-in-hand with 'old-fashioned' didactic style and content. Equally, a slight decline in readers' correspondence and in the level of conflict displayed in the Preston press does not in itself constitute evidence for a decline in the public sphere.[11]

---

8   This was also true of Manchester wholesale newsagent and publisher Abel Heywood. For an analysis of his career which offers a convincing narrative of the development of the nineteenth-century newspaper press, see Brian E. Maidment, 'The Manchester Common Reader — Abel Heywood's "Evidence" and the Early Victorian Reading Public', in *Printing and the Book in Manchester, 1700–1850*, ed. by Eddie Cass and Morris Garratt, *Transactions of the Lancashire and Cheshire Antiquarian Society* 97 (Manchester: Lancashire and Cheshire Antiquarian Society, 2001), pp. 99–120.

9   Jean Chalaby, *Invention*.

10 Mark Hampton, *Visions of the Press in Britain, 1850–1950* (Urbana: University of Illinois Press, 2004).

11 Jurgen Habermas, *The Structural Transformation of the Public Sphere: An Inquiry into a Category of Bourgeois Society* (Oxford: Polity, 1992).

For the 'history of the book' and its sub-discipline, the history of reading, the name 'book history' becomes positively misleading when attempting to encompass the nineteenth century, in which newspapers — particularly provincial newspapers — were far more widely read than books. Subsuming newspapers and periodicals under nineteenth-century 'book history' is rather like subsuming aviation history under stage-coach history. Sources and methods more suited to the history of bound volumes of text produced by individual authors, pre-eminently the novel, need to adapt to capture the distinctive nature of newspaper publishing (decentralised, produced by multiple authors, most of them anonymous) and newspaper reading. The focus on books has understandably led to a concentration on London as a publishing centre, with the unfortunate consequence that place, and sense of place, has once again been downplayed. For the publishing histories of specific genres such as fiction, poetry and history, more material was published in aggregate in local weekly newspapers than in books or magazines. For reading, as Secord has demonstrated, 'each experience of reading becomes more generally revealing the more locally it can be situated.'[12] When book history starts from readers rather than books it is better equipped to recover the print culture of past ages, as opposed to the texts we retrospectively value.[13]

I now realise that I experienced Victorian local journalism myself, when I started work as a reporter in 1984, because later, when I began to study it, so much was already familiar to me: the daily routines as a reporter; the rolled-up exchange newspapers from around the country, connecting my paper to a national network; the newspaper's organisational structure, job roles and job titles; the district offices (feeling autonomous but marginal, small centres, yet subjugated to a larger centre); the jargon; the Press Association news arriving in the 'wire room'; the contributions from village correspondents; the slightly racy freelances who dropped in; the

12   James A. Secord, *Victorian Sensation: The Extraordinary Publication, Reception, and Secret Authorship of Vestiges of the Natural History of Creation* (Chicago, IL: University of Chicago Press, 2003), p. 338.

13   Paraphrasing Robert J. Mayhew, 'Review of William St Clair, *The Reading Nation in the Romantic Period*', *Journal of Historical Geography*, 31 (2005), 199, https://doi.org/10.1016/j.jhg.2005.01.016; cited in William St. Clair, 'Following up *The Reading Nation*', in *The Cambridge History of the Book in Britain, Volume 6, 1830–1914*, ed. by David McKitterick (Cambridge: Cambridge University Press, 2009), pp. 704–35 (709), https://doi.org/10.1017/CHOL9780521866248.022

moonlighting for 'the nationals' in Manchester; and the news values that dictated what was a story, what was not, and which one might be sold to a London news desk for some extra cash.

Our attitude to the readers — they were tiresome but were always politely entertained — was also Victorian. I met, and later read about their Victorian forerunners, the ones who queued for the early edition of the evening paper outside the office on the main shopping street; the ones who, like me, believed there was something magical about seeing your name in the paper; those who wrote letters in green ink; those who drank with us on a Friday afternoon; those who, I later realised, politely used me for their various agendas, sometimes to fight battles, sometimes to right wrongs. I experienced the changing worth of the paper throughout the day, its original significance symbolised by the flurry of calls from readers as soon as the paper came out and the delivery vans had sped off to the four corners of the circulation area, down to the stack of unread papers on the greengrocer's counter at day's end, used to wrap my cauliflower.[14]

In the Victorian building where I worked, I was aware of the demarcations, the differing cultures and atmospheres of each department: my news room; the 'stone' where the 'comps' (compositors) assembled the pages; the print room where the men wore inky overalls; and the uninteresting advertising offices, whose occupants believed that it was *they* who provided what the readers actually wanted. Later, I put my ignorance of the business side of journalism into practice, running a small local magazine. It soon went bust in a very Victorian way (under-capitalised and incompetently managed, by me), but not before I learnt that we had created a community among our readers, expressing and reflecting their feelings about the place where they lived. After that I worked on a broadsheet 'national' in London, where I was shocked at the ignorance of some journalists about their own country; they felt that, because they lived at the centre, there was no need to know the periphery.

Those London journalists reminded me of a university friend who was determined never to return to his small provincial town; instead, he made his way to the centres of power. The last time I saw him we argued;

---

14   For more on discarded texts as grocery wrappings, see Leah Price, *How to Do Things with Books in Victorian Britain* (Princeton, NJ: Princeton University Press, 2012), pp. 231–34, https://doi.org/10.23943/princeton/9780691114170.001.0001

he thought lives lived in the provinces were worth less than those at the metropolitan centre. But for me, like most Victorian reporters moving from place to place (or present-day football fans who follow their lower league club around the country), every place mattered, had meaning, was sacred to those who lived there. The local press made money out of those feelings, with the help of the advertising-led Victorian business model. That business model is now broken, and perhaps if British local newspapers had left the Victorian era sooner, they would have been better equipped to enter the twenty-first century. I have no answers from history, beyond the banal: it doesn't have to be this way, some things change, some things stay the same. The internet has changed the economics of local journalism, but what has not changed is the desire for local lives to be celebrated, validated and recorded, as they were in Victorian local newspapers.

Bibliography

Archival material

British Library

Catholic News 1889 Microform. MFM.M30054 [1889]

Cross Fleury's Journal P.P.6080.ka

Empire Journal PP.6080.K

The Journalist and Newspaper Proprietor LOU.LON 247

Newspaper Press Directory (Mitchell) P.P.2495.gab

The London, Provincial and Colonial Press News NEWS11930 NPL

Preston Evening News NEWS16131 NPL

The Printers' Register LOU.LON 5

Cumbria Archive and Local Studies Centre, Barrow

Barrow Working Men's Club Reading Committee minute book 1881–91, BDSO 85

Barrow Library annual reports BA/L

Harris Library, Community History Library, Preston

Preston Evening Express, Local LA11

Preston Illustrated Times LA11 PRESTON ILLUSTRATED TIMES/PRE

Preston Magazine & Christian Miscellany LJ2 PRESTON/PRE

The Wasp LA12/WAS

Annual report of the committee of the free public library and museum of the borough of Preston, LT T251 PRE

Anthony Hewitson, miscellaneous items Local LG3 HEWITSON, Anthony/ ANT

Lancashire Archives

Anon, *The Lancaster Guardian. History of the Paper, And Reminiscences by "Old Hands", Published in Connection with Its Diamond Jubilee* (Lancaster: E & J Milner, 1897), Local LA11 LANCASTER GUARDIAN

Diaries of Anthony Hewitson DP512

Longworth's Preston Advertiser LA12/LON

Lonsdale Magazine, 1820, LA12/NOR

Minutes of Preston Exchange & News Room committee, CBP 53/4

Oakey's Commercial and Trade Directory of Preston (Preston: Henry Oakey, 1853)

Winckley Club minute book, DDX 1895/1

Lancashire Post, Preston

Lancashire Evening Post/Daily Post multiple editions, microfilm

Lancaster University Library

'Social and family life in Preston, 1890–1940', transcripts of recorded interviews, Elizabeth Roberts archive, Special Collections 8MW (R)

Liverpool Archives

George Melly Collection, 920 MEL 13

Northern Photographic Exhibition, Walker Art Gallery, Liverpool 1907, programme 708.6 PHO (print), https://archive.org/details/ northernphotogra00walk (online)

University of Manchester Library

Manchester Guardian Archives

Talbot Library, Liverpool Hope University

Lancashire Catholic

Antidote

The National Archives

Poor Law Commission, Correspondence between William Golden Lumley and Charles Mott, MH 12/6040-43

University of Central Lancashire, special collections

Marian Roberts Collection

Illustrated London News

Institution for the Diffusion of Knowledge, annual reports, Livesey Collection

Databases and websites

Web addresses are only given if individual subscriptions are available; others are available only through institutions such as universities or research libraries.

19th Century British Library Newspapers (includes *Preston Chronicle*)

British Newspaper Archive, *https://www.britishnewspaperarchive.co.uk/* (includes *Preston Herald*)

British Periodicals (ProQuest)

Dickens Journals Online, http://www.djo.org.uk/

Dictionary of Nineteenth Century Journalism, online edition, C19: The Nineteenth Century Index (ProQuest)

The Economist Historical Archive 1843–2013

Historic Hansard, https://api.parliament.uk/historic-hansard/

Parliamentary Papers 1800–2000 (ProQuest)

Fourth annual report of the registrar-general, 1840–41 [year ending June 30, 1841] (1842)

Twenty-third annual report of the registrar-general, 1860 (1862)

1872 [C.667] Registrar General of Births, Deaths and Marriages in England Thirty-third Annual Report (Summary of Marriages, Births and Deaths registered, 1861–70)

1882 [C.3208] Registrar General of Births, Deaths and Marriages in England Forty-third Annual Report

1854–55 (83) Return of Number of Stamps issued at One Penny to Newspapers in United Kingdom, 1854 [House of Commons Parliamentary Papers Online].

Census reports:

1851 (1852–53) C.1691 (parts 1 & 2)

1861 (1863) C.3221

1871 (1873) C.872

1881 (1883) C.3722

1891 (1893–94) C.7058

1901 (1904) Cd. 2174

1851 (558) XVII. 1House of Commons, 'Report from the Select Committee on Newspaper Stamps; Together with the Proceedings of the Committee, Minutes of Evidence, Appendix, and Index'

1887 (C. 5158), Royal Commission Appointed to Inquire into the Working of the Elementary Education Acts in England and Wales, Third Report, Evidence

Reading Experience Database www.open.ac.uk/Arts/RED

Times Historical Archive

Waterloo Directory of English Newspapers and Periodicals, 1800–1900 (North Waterloo Academic Press) www.victorianperiodicals.com/series3/

Print and individual online sources

A Conservative Journalist, 'The Establishment of Newspapers', *National Review*, 5 (1885), 818–28.

Abram, William Alexander, *Blackburn Characters of a Past Generation* (Blackburn: Toulmin, 1894).

Adams, William Edwin, *Memoirs of a Social Atom* (London: Hutchinson, 1903), https://archive.org/details/memoirsasociala00adamgoog

Aldridge, Meryl, *Understanding the Local Media* (Maidenhead: Open University Press, 2007).

Ali, Christopher, *Media Localism: The Policies of Place* (Urbana, IL: University of Illinois Press, 2017), https://doi.org/10.5406/illinois/9780252040726.001.0001

Allan, Stuart, 'News and the Public Sphere: Towards a History of Objectivity and Impartiality', in *A Journalism Reader*, ed. by Michael Bromley and Tom O'Malley (London: Routledge, 1997), pp. 296–329.

Allen, Joan, and Owen R. Ashton, *Papers for the People: A Study of the Chartist Press* (London: Merlin Press, 2005).

Allen, Joan, 'Diamond, Charles', in *Dictionary of Nineteenth Century Journalism*, ed. by Laurel Brake and Marysa Demoor, C19: The Nineteenth Century Index, online (ProQuest).

Altholz, Josef L., *The Religious Press in Britain, 1760–1900* (London: Greenwood, 1989).

Altick, Richard, *The English Common Reader: A Social History of the Mass Reading Public, 1800–1900* (Chicago, IL: University of Chicago Press, 1963).

Anderson, Benedict, *Imagined Communities: Reflections on the Origin and Spread of Nationalism* (London: Verso, 2006).

Andrew, Alison, 'The Working Class and Education in Preston 1830–1870: A Study of Social Relations' (unpublished PhD dissertation, University of Leicester, 1987).

Andrews, Alexander, *The History of British Journalism: From the Foundation of the Newspaper Press in England to the Repeal of the Stamp Act in 1855, with Sketches of Press Celebrities* (London: Richard Bentley, 1859), http://books.google.co.uk/books?id=_dFZAAAAMAAJ

Appadurai, Arjun, *Modernity At Large: Cultural Dimensions of Globalization* (Minneapolis, MN: University of Minnesota Press, 1996).

Arnold, N., 'The Press in Social Context: A Study of York and Hull, 1815–1855' (unpublished MPhil dissertation, University of York, 1987).

Ashton, Owen R., *W. E. Adams: Chartist, Radical and Journalist (1832–1906) : 'An Honour to the Fourth Estate'* (Whitley Bay: Bewick Press, 1991).

Aspden, Hartley, *Fifty Years a Journalist. Reflections and Recollections of an Old Clitheronian* (Clitheroe: Advertiser & Times, 1930).

Aspinall, Arthur, 'The Circulation of Newspapers in the Early Nineteenth Century', *The Review of English Studies*, 22 (1946), 29–43.

Aspinall, Arthur, *Politics and the Press, c.1780–1850* (Brighton: Harvester Press, 1973).

Asquith, Ivon, 'The Structure, Ownership and Control of the Press, 1780–1855', in *Newspaper History from the Seventeenth Century to the Present Day*, ed. by David George Boyce, James Curran, and Pauline Wingate (London: Constable, 1978), pp. 98–116.

Atteridge, A. Hilliard, 'Catholic Periodical Literature', *Catholic Encyclopedia*, Vol. 11 (New York: Robert Appleton, 1911), http://www.newadvent.org/cathen/11673a.htm

Ayerst, David, *Guardian: Biography of a Newspaper* (London: Collins, 1971).

[Bagehot, Walter], 'The Position of the Metropolitan Press', *The Economist*, 14 May 1870, pp. 595–96.

Baggs, Christopher M., 'The Libraries of the Co-Operative Movement: A Forgotten Episode', *Journal of Librarianship and Information Science*, 23 (1991), 87–96.

Bagley, John J., *Lancashire Diarists: Three Centuries of Lancashire Lives* (London: Phillimore, 1975).

Bainbridge, T. H., 'Barrow in Furness: A Population Study', *Economic Geography*, 15 (1939), 379–83.

Baines, Edward, jnr, *The Life of Edward Baines, Late M. P. for the Borough of Leeds, by His Son* (Leeds: Reid Newsome, 1851).

Baines, Edward, *Extension of the Franchise: Speech of Edward Baines on Moving the Second Reading of the Borough Franchise Bill, in the House of Commons, on the 11th May, 1864* (London, 1864), https://play.google.com/store/books/details/Extension_of_the_Franchise_Speech_on_moving_the_se?id=Ln3Aspp9ovwC&hl=en_SG

Bale, John, 'The Place of "Place" in Cultural Studies of Sports', *Progress in Human Geography*, 12 (1988), 507–24.

Barbary, V. C., 'Reinterpreting "Factory Politics" in Bury, Lancashire, 1868–1880', *Historical Journal*, 51 (2008), 115–44, https://doi.org/10.1017/s0018246x07006607

Barker, Hannah, 'England, 1760–1815', in *Press, Politics and the Public Sphere in Europe and North America, 1760–1820*, ed. by Hannah Barker and Simon Burrows (Cambridge: Cambridge University Press, 2002), pp. 93–112, https://doi.org/10.1017/cbo9780511496660.005

Barry, J, 'The Press and the Politics of Culture in Bristol 1660–1775', in *Culture, Politics, and Society in Britain, 1660–1800,* ed. by Jeremy Black and Jeremy Gregory (Manchester: Manchester University Press, 1991), pp. 49–81.

Barthel, Michael, Jesse Holcomb, Jessica Mahone, and Amy Mitchell, 'Civic Engagement Strongly Tied to Local News Habits', *Pew Research Center's Journalism Project,* 2016, http://www.journalism.org/2016/11/03/civic-engagement-strongly-tied-to-local-news-habits/

Barton, David, 'Exploring the Historical Basis of Contemporary Literacy', *The Quarterly Newsletter of the Laboratory of Comparative Human Cognition,* 10 (1988), 70–76.

Barton, David, and Mary Hamilton, *Local Literacies: Reading and Writing in One Community* (London: Routledge, 1998).

Barton, Roger Neil, 'New Media: The Birth of Telegraphic News in Britain 1847–1868', *Media History,* 16 (2010), 379–406, https://doi.org/10.1080/13688804.20 10.507475

Basu, Jitendra Nath, *Romance of Indian Journalism* (Calcutta: Calcutta University, 1979).

Bates, Denise, *Historical Research Using British Newspapers* (Barnsley: Pen & Sword, 2016).

Bauman, Zygmunt, *Liquid Modernity* (Cambridge: Polity Press, 2000).

Bayard, Pierre, *How to Talk About Books You Haven't Read* (Granta Books, 2008).

'BBC — Public Purposes: Citizenship and Civil Society— Inside the BBC', http://www.bbc.co.uk/corporate2/insidethebbc/whoweare/publicpurposes/citizenship.html

Beaven, Brad, 'The Provincial Press, Civic Ceremony and the Citizen-Soldier During the Boer War, 1899–1902: A Study of Local Patriotism', *Journal of Imperial and Commonwealth History,* 37 (2009), 207–28, https://doi.org/10.1080/03086530903010350

Beetham, Margaret, 'Ben Brierley's Journal', *Manchester Region History Review,* 17 (2006), 73–83.

—, 'Healthy Reading', in *City, Class and Culture: Studies of Social Policy and Cultural Production in Victorian Manchester,* ed. by Alan J. Kidd and Kenneth W. Roberts (Manchester: Manchester University Press, 1985).

—, '"Oh! I Do like to Be beside the Seaside!": Lancashire Seaside Publications', *Victorian Periodicals Review,* 42 (2009), 24–36, https://doi.org/10.1353/vpr.0.0060

—, 'Open and Closed: The Periodical as a Publishing Genre', *Victorian Periodicals Review,* 22 (1989), 96–100.

—, 'Time: Periodicals and the Time of the Now', *Victorian Periodicals Review,* 48 (2015), 323–42, https://doi.org/10.1353/vpr.2015.0041

Bell, Allan, 'Language Style as Audience Design', *Language in Society*, 13 (1984), 145–204, https://doi.org/10.1017/s004740450001037x

Bell, Bill, 'Bound for Australia: Shipboard Reading in the Nineteenth Century', in *Journeys through the Market: Travel, Travellers, and the Book Trade*, ed. by Robin Myers and Michael Harris (Folkestone: Oak Knoll Press, 1999), pp. 119–40.

Bell, Florence Eveleen Eleanore Olliffe, *At the Works: A Study of a Manufacturing Town* (Middlesbrough: University of Teesside, 1907/1997).

Berridge, Virginia, 'Popular Sunday Newspapers and Mid-Victorian Society', in *Newspaper History from the Seventeenth Century to the Present Day*, ed. by David George Boyce, James Curran, and Pauline Wingate (London: Constable, 1978), pp. 247–64.

Berry, David, 'The South Wales Argus and Cultural Representations of Gwent', *Journalism Studies*, 9 (2008), 105–16, https://doi.org/10.1080/14616700701768170

Birrell, Augustine, 'Sir Robert Peel', in *The Collected Essays & Addresses of the Rt. Hon. Augustine Birrell, 1880–1920* (London: J. M. Dent & Sons, 1922), pp. 326–48, http://archive.org/details/collectedessaysa01birr

Blair, Kirstie, 'Advertising Poetry, the Working-Class Poet and the Victorian Newspaper Press', *Journal of Victorian Culture*, 23 (2018), 103–18, https://doi.org/10.1093/jvc/vcx003

—, 'The Newspaper Press and the Victorian Working Class Poet', in *A History of British Working Class Literature*, ed. by John Goodridge and Bridget Keegan (Cambridge: Cambridge University Press, 2017), pp. 264–80, https://doi.org/10.1017/9781108105392.018

Bourdieu, Pierre, *On Television and Journalism* (London: Pluto Press, 1998).

Bourne, H. R. Fox, *English Newspapers: Chapters in the History of Journalism, Vol. II* (London: Routledge/Thoemmes Press, 1887), https://archive.org/details/englishnewspaper02bouriala

Bradford, Anne R., *Drawn by Friendship: The Art and Wit of the Revd. John Thomas Wilson* (New Barnet: Anne R. Bradford, 1997).

Brake, Laurel, 'The Longevity of "Ephemera"', *Media History*, 18 (2012), 7–20, https://doi.org/10.1080/13688804.2011.632192

—, 'Magazine Day', in *Dictionary of Nineteenth-Century Journalism in Great Britain and Ireland*, ed. by Laurel Brake and Marysa Demoor (Ghent; London: Academia Press; British Library, 2009).

—, 'Markets, Genres, Iterations', in *Routledge Handbook to Nineteenth-Century British Periodicals and Newspapers*, ed. by Andrew King, Alexis Easley, and John Morton (Abingdon: Routledge, 2016), pp. 237–48.

—, 'Nineteenth-Century Newspaper Press Directories: The National Gallery of the British Press', *Victorian Periodicals Review*, 48 (2016), 569–90, https://doi.org/10.1353/vpr.2015.0055

—, 'The Old Journalism and the New: Forms of Cultural Production in London in the 1880s', in *Papers for the Millions: The New Journalism in Britain, 1850s to 1914*, ed. by Joel H. Wiener (London: Greenwood, 1988).

—, '"The Trepidation of the Spheres": The Serial and the Book in the 19th Century', in *Serials and Their Readers, 1620–1914*, ed. by Robin Myers and Michael Harris (Winchester: Oak Knoll Press, 1993).

—, 'Writing, Cultural Production, and the Periodical Press in the Nineteenth Century', in *Writing and Victorianism*, ed. by J.B. Bullen (London: Longman, 1997), pp. 54–72.

Brake, Laurel, and Marysa Demoor, eds., *Dictionary of Nineteenth Century Journalism*, C19: The Nineteenth Century Index, Online edition (ProQuest).

Brake, Laurel, and Mark W. Turner, 'Rebranding the News of the World: 1856–90', in *The News of the World and the British Press, 1843–2011*, ed. by Laurel Brake, Chandrika Kaul, and Mark W. Turner (Basingstoke: Palgrave Macmillan, 2015), pp. 27–42, https://doi.org/10.1057/9781137392053_3

Bramwell, William, *Reminiscences of a Public Librarian, a Retrospective View* (Preston: Ambler, 1916).

Brett, Peter, 'Early Nineteenth-Century Reform Newspapers in the Provinces: The Newcastle Chronicle and Bristol Mercury', in *Studies in Newspaper and Periodical History: 1995 Annual*, ed. by Tom O'Malley and Michael Harris (London: Greenwood, 1997), pp. 49–67, https://doi.org/10.1080/13688809509357917

'The British Newspaper: The Penny Theory and Its Solution', *Dublin University Magazine*, 61 (1863), 359–76, https://babel.hathitrust.org/cgi/pt?id=njp.32101064302472;view=1up;seq=361

Bromley, Michael, and Nick Hayes, 'Campaigner, Watchdog or Municipal Lackey? Reflections on the Inter-War Provincial Press, Local Identity and Civic Welfarism', *Media History*, 8 (2002), 197–212, https://doi.org/10.1080/1368880022000030559

Brooks, Joseph Barlow, *Lancashire Bred: An Autobiography* (Oxford: Church Army Press, 1951).

Brown, James Duff, and W. C. Berwick Sayers, *Manual of Library Economy*, 3rd edn (Grafton & Co., 1920), http://gutenberg.polytechnic.edu.na/4/9/8/9/49895/49895-h/49895-h.htm

Brown, Lucy, *Victorian News and Newspapers* (Oxford: Clarendon Press, 1985).

Buckley, Colin, 'The Search for "a Really Smart Sheet": The Conservative Evening Newspaper Project in Edwardian Manchester', *Manchester Region History Review*, 1 (1987), 21–28, http://web.archive.org/web/20061209065627/http://www.mcrh.mmu.ac.uk/pubs/pdf/mrhr_01i_buckley.pdf

Burns, Arthur, *The Diocesan Revival in the Church of England, c. 1800–1870* (Oxford: Oxford University Press, 1999).

Burt, Arnold G., 'Newsroom Arrangement', *Library World*, 1902, 256–64.

Bussey, Harry Findlater, *Sixty Years of Journalism: Anecdotes and Reminiscences* (Bristol: J. W. Arrowsmith, 1906).

Carey, James, *Communication as Culture: Essays on Media and Society* (London: Routledge, 1989), https://doi.org/10.4324/9780203928912

—, 'A Cultural Approach to Communication', in *Communication as Culture: Essays on Media and Society* (London: Routledge, 1989), pp. 13–36.

Carrington, Frederic, 'Country Newspapers and Their Editors', *New Monthly Magazine*, 105: 418 (1855), 142–52, https://babel.hathitrust.org/cgi/pt?id=umn .31951t00079615n;view=1up;seq=152

Catton, J. A. H., *The Rise of the Leaguers: A History of the Clubs Comprising the First Division of the Football League: Reprinted from the Sporting Chronicle* (Manchester: Sporting Chronicle, 1897).

Caunce, Stephen, 'British, English or What? A Northern English Perspective on Britishness as a New Millennium Starts', Unpublished Conference Paper Delivered at "Relocating Britain" Conference, University of Central Lancashire, 2000.

—, 'Complexity, Community Structure and Competitive Advantage within the Yorkshire Woollen Industry, c. 1700–1850', *Business History*, 39 (1997), 26–43, https://doi.org/10.1080/00076799700000144

—, 'Market Reports', in *Dictionary of Nineteenth Century Journalism*, ed. by Laurel Brake and Marysa Demoor, C19: The Nineteenth Century Index, Online Edition (London: ProQuest).

—, 'Northern English Industrial Towns: Rivals or Partners?', *Urban History*, 30 (2003), 338–58, https://doi.org/10.1017/s0963926804001397

—, *Oral History and the Local Historian* (London: Longman, 1994).

Cavallo, Guglielmo, and Roger Chartier, 'Introduction', in *A History of Reading in the West*, ed. by Guglielmo Cavallo and Roger Chartier (Amherst, MA: University of Massachusetts Press, 1999), pp. 1–36.

Census of Great Britain, 1851: Religious Worship in England and Wales Abridged from the Official Report (London: Routledge, 1854), https://archive.org/details/ censusgreatbrit00manngoog

A Century of Progress 1844–1944, Southport Visiter (Southport: Southport Visiter, 1944).

Certeau, Michel de, *The Practice of Everyday Life* (Berkeley, CA: University of California Press, 1988).

'A Chapter On Provincial Journalism', *Tait's Edinburgh Magazine*, July 1850, 424–27, https://babel.hathitrust.org/cgi/pt?id=nyp.33433081663357

Chalaby, Jean, *The Invention of Journalism* (Basingstoke: Macmillan, 1998).

Clark, Peter, 'Introduction', in *The Transformation of English Provincial Towns, 1600–1800*, ed. by Peter Clark (London: Hutchinson, 1984), pp. 13–61.

Clarke, Bob, *From Grub Street to Fleet Street: An Illustrated History of the English Newspaper to 1899* (Aldershot: Ashgate, 2004).

Clarke, Tony, *Pilgrims of the Press: A History of Eastern Counties Newspapers Group 1850–2000* (Norwich: Eastern Counties Newspapers, 2000).

Clay, Walter Lowe, *The Prison Chaplain: A Memoir of the Rev. John Clay, B. D., with Selections from His Reports and Correspondence, and a Sketch of Prison Discipline in England* (Cambridge: Macmillan, 1861).

Colclough, Stephen, *Consuming Texts: Readers and Reading Communities, 1695–1870* (Basingstoke: Palgrave Macmillan, 2007), https://doi.org/10.1057/9780230590540

—, '"A Larger Outlay than Any Return": The Library of W. H. Smith & Son, 1860–1873', *Publishing History*, 54 (2003), 67–93.

—, 'Procuring Books and Consuming Texts: The Reading Experience of a Sheffield Apprentice, 1798', *Book History*, 3 (2000), 21–44, https://doi.org/10.1353/bh.2000.0004

Colley, Linda, *Britons: Forging the Nation, 1707–1837* (New Haven, CT: Yale Nota Bene, 2005).

Collins, Mortimer, 'Country Newspapers', *Temple Bar*, 10 (December 1863), pp. 128–41, https://babel.hathitrust.org/cgi/pt?id=coo.31924057354296;view=1up;seq=132

[Collins, Wilkie], 'The Unknown Public', *Household Words*, 18 (1858), 217–22, http://www.djo.org.uk/household-words/volume-xviii/page-217.html

Connelly, Ross, '"Letters from Readers" a More Appropriate Heading', *Grassroots Editor*, 47 (2006), 14, http://bloximages.chicago2.vip.townnews.com/iswne.org/content/tncms/assets/v3/editorial/4/39/4392babd-cbbc-5bd9-a2ca-3d8f030a9081/4ec18d6577b7d.pdf.pdf

Convey, John, *The Harris Free Public Library and Museum, Preston 1893–1993* (Preston: Lancashire County Books, 1993).

'Country Books of the Quarter', *Countryman*, April 1928, p. 90.

'Country News', *Household Words*, 2 July 1853, pp. 426–30, http://www.djo.org.uk/household-words/volume-vii/page-426.html

Coupland, Nikolas, *Dialect in Use: Sociolinguistic Variation in Cardiff English* (Cardiff: University of Wales Press, 1988).

Cox, Howard, and Simon Mowatt, *Revolutions from Grub Street: A History of Magazine Publishing in Britain* (Oxford: Oxford University Press, 2014).

Crang, Mike, *Cultural Geography* (London: Routledge, 2004), https://doi.org/10.1093/acprof:oso/9780199601639.001.0001

Credland, William Robert, *The Manchester Public Free Libraries; a History and Description, and Guide to Their Contents and Use* (Manchester: Public Free Libraries Committee, 1899), http://archive.org/details/manchesterpublic00mancrich

Cresswell, Tim, *Place: An Introduction*, 2nd edition (Chichester: Wiley-Blackwell, 2014).

Crisell, Andrew, and Guy Starkey, 'News on Local Radio', in *Local Journalism and Local Media: Making the Local News*, ed. by Bob Franklin (London: Routledge, 2006), pp. 16–26, https://doi.org/10.4324/9780203969205

Cross, Gary, *A Quest for Time: The Reduction of Work in Britain and France, 1840–1940* (Berkeley, CA: University of California Press, 1992).

Curran, James, 'The Press as an Agency of Social Control', in *Newspaper History from the Seventeenth Century to the Present Day*, ed. by David George Boyce, James Curran, and Pauline Wingate (London: Constable, 1978), pp. 51–75.

—, 'The Industrialization of the Press', in *Power without Responsibility: The Press and Broadcasting in Britain*, ed. by James Curran and Jean Seaton (London: Routledge, 1991), pp. 32–48.

—, 'Media and the Making of British Society, c.1700–2000', *Media History*, 8 (2002), 135–54, https://doi.org/10.1080/1368880022000047137

Darnton, Robert, 'First Steps Towards a History of Reading', in *The Kiss of Lamourette: Reflections in Cultural History*, ed. by Robert Darnton (London: Faber & Faber, 1990), pp. 154–87.

Dawson, John, *Practical Journalism, How to Enter Thereon and Succeed. A Manual for Beginners and Amateurs* (London: Upton Gill, 1885).

'A Day at the London Free Libraries', *All the Year Round*, 7 (1892), 305–9.

De Cillia, Rudolf, Martin Reisigl, and Ruth Wodak, 'The Discursive Construction of National Identities', *Discourse and Society*, 10 (1999), 149–74, https://doi.org/10.1177/0957926599010002002

Delafield, Catherine, *Serialization and the Novel in Mid-Victorian Magazines* (Routledge, 2016), https://doi.org/10.4324/9781315608440

Denvir, John, *The Life Story of an Old Rebel* (Shannon: Irish University Press, 1972).

[Dicey, Edward], 'Provincial Journalism', *Saint Pauls Magazine* 3 (December 1868), 61–73, https://babel.hathitrust.org/cgi/pt?id=mdp.39015004102474;view=1up;seq=73

Dickens, Charles, *Our Mutual Friend* (London: Chapman and Hall, 1865).

—, *Hard Times*, ed. by Fred Kaplan (Norton, 2016).

Digby, Ronald Y., J. C. Goddard, and Alice Miller, *An Accrington Miscellany. Prose and Verse by Local Writers* (Burnley: Lancashire County Council Library, Museum and Arts Committee, 1988).

Disraeli, Benjamin, *Benjamin Disraeli Letters 1848–51*, ed. by J. B. Conacher and M. G. Wiebe (Toronto: University of Toronto Press, 1982), V, https://utorontopress.com/ca/benjamin-disraeli-letters-20

Dixon, Diana, 'New Town, New Newspapers: The Development of the Newspaper Press in Nineteenth-Century Middlesbrough', in *The Moving Market*: *Continuity and Change in the Book Trade*, ed. by Peter C. G. Isaac and Barrie McKay (New Castle, DE: Oak Knoll Press, 2001), pp. 107–16.

—, 'Navigating the Maze: Sources for Press Historians', *Media History*, 9 (2003), 79–90, https://doi.org/10.1080/1368880032000060005

Donaldson, William, *Popular Literature in Victorian Scotland*: *Language, Fiction, and the Press* (Aberdeen: Aberdeen University Press, 1986).

Dooley, Brendan Maurice, 'Introduction', in *The Politics of Information in Early Modern Europe*, ed. by Brendan Maurice Dooley and Sabrina A. Baron (London: Routledge, 2011), pp. 1–16, https://doi.org/10.4324/9780203991855

Douglas, Susan J., 'Does Textual Analysis Tell Us Anything about Past Audiences?', in *Explorations in Communication and History*, ed. by Barbie Zelizer (London: Routledge, 2008), pp. 66–76, https://doi.org/10.4324/9780203888605

Duffy, Patrick, *The Skilled Compositor, 1850–1914*: *An Aristocrat Among Working Men* (Aldershot: Ashgate, 2000).

Dutton, H. I., and John Edward King, *'Ten per Cent and No Surrender'* : *The Preston Strike, 1853–1854* (Cambridge: Cambridge University Press, 1981).

Eastwood, David, *Government and Community in the English Provinces, 1700–1870* (Basingstoke: Macmillan, 1997).

Easley, Alexis, Andrew King, and John Morton, eds., *Researching the Nineteenth-Century Periodical Press*: *Case Studies* (London: Routledge, 2017), https://doi.org/10.4324/9781315605616

Eliot, Simon, *Some Patterns and Trends in British Publishing, 1800–1919* (London: Bibliographical Society, 1994).

Eliot, T. S., 'American Literature and the American Language', in *To Criticize the Critic and Other Writings* (Lincoln, NE: University of Nebraska Press, 1965), pp. 43–60.

Ellegard, Alvar, 'The Readership of the Periodical Press in Mid-Victorian Britain II. Directory', *Victorian Periodicals Newsletter*, 13 (1971), 3–22.

Ellegard, Henrik Alvar, 'The Readership of the Periodical Press in Mid-Victorian Britain', *Göteborgs Universitets Arsskrift*, 63 (1957).

Elliott, Robert, 'On Working Men's Reading Rooms, as Established since 1848 at Carlisle', *Transactions of the National Association for the Promotion of Social Science*, 1861, 676–79, https://archive.org/stream/transactionsnat25britgoog#page/n746/search/On+Working+Men%E2%80%99s+Reading+Rooms%2C+as+Established+since+1848+at+Carlisle

Engel, Matthew, 'Local Papers: An Obituary', *British Journalism Review*, 20 (2009), 55–58, https://doi.org/10.1177/0956474809106672

Entman, Robert M., 'Framing: Toward Clarification of a Fractured Paradigm', *Journal of Communication*, 43 (1993), 51–58, https://doi.org/10.1111/j.1460-2466.1993.tb01304.x

Erickson, Lee, 'The Market', in *A Companion to Victorian Poetry*, ed. by Richard Cronin, Alison Chapman, and Antony H. Harrison (Malden, MA.: Blackwell, 2002), pp. 345–60, http://dx.doi.org/10.1002/9780470693537

—, *The Economy of Literary Form: English Literature and the Industrialization of Publishing, 1800–1850* (London: Johns Hopkins University Press, 1996).

Esbester, Mike, 'Nineteenth-Century Timetables and the History of Reading', *Book History*, 12 (2009), 156–85, https://doi.org/10.1353/bh.0.0018

Evans, Neil, 'Regional Dynamics: North Wales, 1750–1914', in *Issues of Regional Identity: In Honour of John Marshall*, ed. by Edward Royle (Manchester: Manchester University Press, 1998), pp. 201–25.

Ferdinand, C. Y., *Benjamin Collins and the Provincial Newspaper Trade in the Eighteenth Century* (Oxford: Clarendon Press, 1997).

Finn, Mike, 'The Realities of War', *History Today*, 52 (2002), 26–31.

Fish, Stanley Eugene, 'Interpreting the Variorum', *Critical Inquiry*, 2 (1976), 465–85, https://doi.org/10.1086/447852

Fowler, Alan, *Lancashire Cotton Operatives and Work, 1900–1950: A Social History of Lancashire Cotton Operatives in the Twentieth Century* (Aldershot: Ashgate, 2003).

Fowler, Bridget, 'Collective Memory and Forgetting: Components for a Study of Obituaries', *Theory, Culture & Society*, 22 (2005), 53–72, https://doi.org/10.1177/0263276405059414

Fraser, Derek, 'The Press in Leicester c. 1790–1850', *Transactions of the Leicestershire Archaeological and Historical Society*, 42 (1967), 53–75

—, 'The Editor as Activist: Editors and Urban Politics in Early Victorian England', in *Innovators and Preachers: The Role of the Editor in Victorian England*, ed. by Joel H. Wiener (Westport, Conn: Greenwood Press, 1985), pp. 121–42.

Fraser, Nancy, 'Rethinking the Public Sphere: A Contribution to the Critique of Actually Existing Democracy', in *Habermas and the Public Sphere*, ed. by Craig J. Calhoun (Cambridge, MA: MIT Press, 1997), pp. 109–42, https://doi.org/10.2307/466240

Fritzsche, Peter, *Reading Berlin 1900* (London: Harvard University Press, 1996).

Fyfe, Paul, *By Accident or Design: Writing the Victorian Metropolis* (Oxford, New York: Oxford University Press, 2015), https://doi.org/10.1093/acprof:oso/9780198732334.001.0001

Gardiner, F. K., 'Provincial Morning Newspapers', in *The Kemsley Manual of Journalism* (London: Cassell, 1952), pp. 204–08.

Gardner, FitzRoy, 'The Tory Press and the Tory Party, I. —a Complaint', *National Review*, 21 (1893), pp. 357–74.

Gardner, Victoria E. M., 'The Communications Broker and the Public Sphere: John Ware and the Cumberland Pacquet', *Cultural and Social History*, 10 (2013), 533–57, https://doi.org/10.2752/147800413X13727009732164

—, *The Business of News in England, 1760–1820* (Basingstoke: Palgrave, 2016), https://doi.org/10.1057/9781137336392

Garrett, Brian, 'Personal Identity', in *Routledge Encyclopedia of Philosophy* (Taylor & Francis), https://doi.org/10.4324/9780415249126-V024-1

Garvey, Ellen Gruber, *Writing with Scissors: American Scrapbooks from the Civil War to the Harlem Renaissance* (Oxford: Oxford University Press, 2012), https://doi.org/10.1093/acprof:oso/9780195390346.001.0001

Gaskell, William, *Two Lectures on the Lancashire Dialect* (London, 1854).

Geertz, Clifford, *Available Light: Anthropological Reflections on Philosophical Topics* (Princeton, NJ: Princeton University Press, 2000), https://doi.org/10.1515/9781400823406

'Gentlemen of the Press. IV. The Reporter', *St. James's Magazine*, February 1882, 173–79.

George, Lisa M., and Joel Waldfogel, 'The New York Times and the Market for Local Newspapers', *American Economic Review*, 96 (2006), 435–47, https://doi.org/10.1257/000282806776157551

'Getting Through the Morning Newspaper', *The Journalist and Newspaper Proprietor*, 20 October 1900, p. 329.

Gilbert, David, 'Community and Municipalism: Collective Identity in Late-Victorian and Edwardian Mining Towns', *Journal of Historical Geography*, 17 (1991), 257–70, https://doi.org/10.1016/s0305-7488(05)80002-7

Gilbert, Pamela K., *Mapping the Victorian Social Body* (Albany, NY: State University of New York Press, 2004).

Gillow, Joseph, and Anthony Hewitson, eds., *The Tyldesley Diary: Personal Records of Thomas Tyldesley (Grandson of Sir Thomas Tyldesley, the Royalist) during the Years 1712-13-14* (Preston: A. Hewitson, 1873), https://archive.org/details/tyldesleydiaryp00attigoog

Goffman, Erving, *Frame Analysis: An Essay on the Organization of Experience* (Cambridge, MA: Harvard University Press, 1974).

Goldgel-Carballo, Víctor, '"High-Speed Enlightenment"', *Media History*, 18 (2012), 129–41, https://doi.org/10.1080/13688804.2012.663865

Goldstein, Jeffrey, 'Emergence as a Construct: History and Issues', *Emergence: Complexity and Organization*, 1 (1999), https://journal.emergentpublications.com/article/vol1-iss1-1-3-ac/

Goldsworthy, Simon, 'English Nonconformity and the Pioneering of the Modern Newspaper Campaign', *Journalism Studies*, 7 (2006), 387–402, https://doi.org/10.1080/14616700600680690

[Goodair, John] 'A Preston Manufacturer', *Strikes Prevented* (Manchester: Whittaker, 1854), http://books.google.co.uk/books?vid=BL:A0018944155

Goodwyn, Helena, 'A "New" Journalist: The Americanization of W. T. Stead', *Journal of Victorian Culture*, 23 (2018), 405–20, https://doi.org/10.1093/jvcult/vcy038

Graff, Harvey J., and W. B. Hodgson, 'Exaggerated Estimates of Reading and Writing as Means of Education (1867), by W. B. Hodgson', *History of Education Quarterly*, 26 (1986), 377–93, https://doi.org/10.2307/368244

Grant, James, *The Newspaper Press: Its Origin, Progress and Present Position, Vol.3. The Metropolitan Weekly and Provincial Press* (London: Routledge, 1872), http://www.archive.org/details/newspaperpressit03granuoft

Gregory, Alfred Thomas, *Recollections of a Country Editor* (Tiverton Gazette, 1932).

Griest, Guinevere L., *Mudie's Circulating Library and the Victorian Novel* (Newton Abbot: David and Charles, 1970).

Gripsrud, Jostein, *Understanding Media Culture* (London: Arnold, 2002), https://doi.org/10.24926/8668.2601

Gunn, Simon, *The Public Culture of the Victorian Middle Class: Ritual and Authority in the English Industrial City, 1840–1914* (Manchester: Manchester University Press, 2000).

Haas, Sabine, 'Victorian Poetry Anthologies: Their Role and Success in the Nineteenth Century Book Market', *Publishing History*, 17 (1985), 51–64.

Haberman, Robb K., 'Provincial Nationalism: Civic Rivalry in Postrevolutionary American Magazines', *Early American Studies: An Interdisciplinary Journal*, 10 (2012), 162–93, https://doi.org/10.1353/eam.2012.0001

Habermas, Jurgen, *The Structural Transformation of the Public Sphere: An Inquiry into a Category of Bourgeois Society* (Oxford: Polity, 1992).

Hakala, Taryn, 'M. R. Lahee and the Lancashire Lads: Gender and Class in Victorian Lancashire Dialect Writing', *Philological Quarterly*, 92 (2013), 271–88.

Halaas, David Fridtjof, *Boom Town Newspapers: Journalism on the Rocky Mountain Mining Frontier, 1859–1881* (Albuquerque, NM: University of New Mexico Press, 1981).

Hall, Stuart, 'Encoding/Decoding', in *Media and Cultural Studies*: *Keyworks*, ed. by Meenakshi Gigi Durham and Douglas Kellner (Malden: Blackwell, 2006), pp. 163–73.

Hammond, Mary, 'Wayward Orphans and Lonesome Places: The Regional Reception of Elizabeth Gaskell's Mary Barton and North and South', *Victorian Studies*, 60 (2018), 390–411, https://muse.jhu.edu/article/703351

Hampton, Mark, 'Journalists and the "Professional Ideal" in Britain: The Institute of Journalists, 1884–1907', *Historical Research*, 72 (1999), 183–201, https://doi.org/10.1111/1468-2281.00080

—, 'Newspapers in Victorian Britain', *History Compass*, 2 (2004), 1–8, https://doi.org/10.1111/j.1478-0542.2004.00101.x

—, *Visions of the Press in Britain, 1850–1950* (Urbana, IL: University of Illinois Press, 2004).

Hardwick, Charles, *History of the Borough of Preston and Its Environs, in the County of Lancaster* (Preston: Worthington, 1857), https://archive.org/details/historyofborough00harduoft

Harrison, Brian, '"A World of Which We Had No Conception." Liberalism and the English Temperance Press: 1830–1872', *Victorian Studies*, 13 (1969), 125–58.

Harvey, David, *Justice, Nature and the Geography of Difference* (Cambridge, MA: Wiley-Blackwell, 1997).

Haslam, James, *The Press and the People*: *An Estimate of Reading in Working-Class Districts, Reprinted from the 'Manchester City News'* (Manchester, 1906).

—, 'What Harpurhey Reads', *Manchester City News*, July 7 (1906).

Hatton, Joseph, *Journalistic London*: *Being a Series of Sketches of Famous Pens and Papers of the Day* (London: Routledge/Thoemmes, 1882), https://archive.org/details/journalisticlond00hatt

Hayes, Anne, *Family in Print*: *Bailey Newspaper Group Ltd, a History* (Dursley: Bailey Newspaper Group, 1996).

Hayes, Nick, 'The Construction and Form of Modern Cities: Exploring Identities and Community', *Urban History*, 29 (2002), 413–23, https://doi.org/10.1017/s0963926802003061

Hegel, Georg Wilhelm Friedrich, *Hegel's Political Writings*, ed. by Z. A. Pelczynski and T. M. Knox (Oxford: Clarendon Press, 1964).

Heikkilä, Heikki, Risto Kunelius, and Laura Ahva, 'From Credibility to Relevance: Towards a Sociology of Journalism's "Added Value"', *Journalism Practice*, 4 (2010), 274–84, https://doi.org/10.1080/17512781003640547

Henkin, David M, *City Reading*: *Written Words and Public Spaces in Antebellum New York* (New York: Columbia University Press, 1998).

Hesketh, Phoebe, *What Can the Matter Be?* (Penzance: United Writers, 1985).

Hess, Kristy, and Lisa Waller, *Local Journalism in a Digital World* (London: Palgrave, 2017).

Hewitson, Anthony, *Hewitson's Guild Guide and Visitors' Handbook: An up-to-Date History of Preston, Its Guild, Public Buildings, Principal Objects of Interest* (Preston: Hewitson, 1902).

—, *History of Preston* (Wakefield: SR Publishers [first published 1883], 1969).

Hewitt, Martin, 'Confronting the Modern City: The Manchester Free Public Library, 1850–80', *Urban History*, 27 (2000), 62–88, https://doi.org/10.1017/s0963926800000146

—, *The Dawn of the Cheap Press in Victorian Britain: The End of the 'Taxes on Knowledge', 1849–1869* (London: Bloomsbury Academic, 2014).

Heyd, Uriel, *Reading Newspapers: Press and Public in Eighteenth-Century Britain and America* (Oxford: Voltaire Foundation, 2012).

Heywood, Abel, 'Newspapers and Periodicals: Their Circulation in Manchester, II', *Manchester Literary Club Papers II*, 1876, 39–58.

Hill, Jeffrey, 'Rite of Spring: Cup Finals and Community in the North of England', in *Sport and Identity in the North of England*, ed. by Jeffrey Hill and Jack Williams (Keele: Keele University Press, 1996), pp. 85–111.

Hill, Jeff, and Jack Williams, 'Introduction', in *Sport and Identity in the North of England*, ed. by Jeffrey Hill and Jack Williams (Keele: Keele University Press, 1996), pp. 1–12.

Hill, Jeffrey, 'Anecdotal Evidence: Sport, the Newspaper Press and History', in *Deconstructing Sport History: A Postmodern Analysis*, ed. by Murray G Phillips (Albany, NY: State University of New York Press, 2006), pp. 117–29.

Hinks, John, Catherine Armstrong, and Matthew Day, eds., *Periodicals and Publishers: The Newspaper and Journal Trade, 1750–1914* (New Castle, DE: Oak Knoll Press, 2009).

Hobbs, Andrew, 'Carnegie-Storey Syndicate', in *Dictionary of Nineteenth Century Journalism*, C19: The Nineteenth Century Index, online (ProQuest).

—, 'The Deleterious Dominance of *The Times* in Nineteenth-Century Scholarship', *Journal of Victorian Culture*, 18 (2013), 472–97, https://doi.org/10.1080/13555502.2013.854519

—, 'History as Journalistic Discourse in 19th-Century British Local Newspapers', *Academia.Edu*, 2016, https://www.academia.edu/27138940/History_as_journalistic_discourse_in_19_th_century_British_local_newspapers

—, 'Partly Printed Sheets', in *Dictionary of Nineteenth Century Journalism*, C19: The Nineteenth Century Index, online (ProQuest).

—, 'Preston Guardian', in *Dictionary of Nineteenth Century Journalism*, C19: The Nineteenth Century Index, online (ProQuest).

—, 'Preston's Nineteenth-Century Newspaper Wars', *Bulletin of Local and Family History*, 5 (2012), 41–47, https://www.academia.edu/37304449/Prestons_19_th_-century_newspaper_wars

—, 'The Provincial Nature of the London Letter', in *The Edinburgh History of the British and Irish Press, Vol. 2: Expansion and Evolution, 1800–1900*, ed. by David Finkelstein (Edinburgh: Edinburgh University Press, 2019).

—, 'Provincial Periodicals', in *The Routledge Handbook to Nineteenth-Century British Periodicals and Newspapers*, ed. by Andrew King, Alexis Easley, and John Morton (London: Routledge, 2016), pp. 221–33, https://doi.org/10.4324/9781315613345

—, 'Reading the Local Paper: Social and Cultural Functions of the Local Press in Preston, Lancashire, 1855–1900' (unpublished PhD dissertation, University of Central Lancashire, 2010), http://clok.uclan.ac.uk/1866/

—, 'When the Provincial Press Was the National Press (c.1836-c.1900)', *International Journal of Regional and Local Studies*, 5 (2009), 16–43, https://doi.org/10.1179/jrl.2009.5.1.16

—, 'William Saunders and the Industrial Supply of News in the Late Nineteenth Century', in *The Edinburgh History of the British and Irish Press, 2: Expansion and Evolution, 1800–19000*, ed. by David Finkelstein (Edinburgh: Edinburgh University Press, 2019).

Hobbs, Andrew, and Claire Januszewski, 'How Local Newspapers Came to Dominate Victorian Poetry Publishing', *Victorian Poetry*, 52 (2014), 65–87, https://doi.org/10.1353/vp.2014.0008

Hodson, Debbie, 'Civic Identity, Custom and Commerce: Victorian Market Halls in the Manchester Region', *Manchester Region History Review*, 12 (1998), 34–43, http://web.archive.org/web/20061209065627/http://www.mcrh.mmu.ac.uk/pubs/pdf/mrhr_12_hodson.pdf

Hole, James, *An Essay on the History and Management of Literary, Scientific, & Mechanics' Institutions* (London: Longman/Society of Arts, 1853), http://archive.org/details/essayonhistoryma00holeuoft

Hollingworth, Brian, 'Dialect in Schools — an Historical Note', *Durham and Newcastle Research Review*, 39 (1977), 15–20.

—, 'Education and the Vernacular', in *Dialect and Education: Some European Perspectives*, ed. by Jenny Cheshire (Multilingual Matters, 1989), pp. 293–302.

—, 'From Voice to Print: Lancashire Dialect Verse, 1800–70', *Philological Quarterly*, 92 (2013), 289–308.

—, *Songs of the People: Lancashire Dialect Poetry of the Industrial Revolution* (Manchester: Manchester University Press, 1977).

Hollis, Patricia, *The Pauper Press: A Study in Working-Class Radicalism of the 1830's* (London: Oxford University Press, 1970).

—, *Ladies Elect: Women in English Local Government 1865–1914* (Oxford: Clarendon Press, 1987).

Holt, Richard, 'Heroes of the North: Sport and the Shaping of Regional Identity', in *Sport and Identity in the North of England*, ed. by Jeffrey Hill and Jack Williams (Keele: Keele University Press, 1996), pp. 137–64.

Hood, John B, 'The Origin and Development of the Newsroom and Reading Room from 1650 to Date, with Some Consideration of Their Role in the Social History of the Period' (unpublished FLA dissertation, Library Association, 1978).

Hopkin, Deian, 'The Left-Wing Press and the New Journalism', in *Papers for the Millions: The New Journalism in Britain, 1850s to 1914*, ed. by Joel H. Wiener, (London: Greenwood, 1988), pp. 225–41.

Houston, Natalie M, 'Newspaper Poems: Material Texts in the Public Sphere', *Victorian Studies*, 50 (2008), 233–42, https://doi.org/10.2979/vic.2008.50.2.233

Huggins, Mike, 'Oop for t' Coop: Sporting Identity in Britain', *History Today*, 55 (2005), 55–61.

Hughes, Linda K., and Michael Lund, *The Victorian Serial* (Charlottesville, VA: University of Virginia Press, 1991).

Hughes, Linda K, 'On New Monthly Magazines, 1859–60', in *BRANCH: Britain, Representation and Nineteenth-Century History*, ed. by Dino Franco Felluga, Romanticism and Victorianism on the Net, http://www.branchcollective. org/?ps_articles=on-new-monthly-magazines-1859-60

Hull, George, *The Poets and Poetry of Blackburn* (Blackburn: G & J Toulmin, 1902), http://gerald-massey.org.uk/hull/b_blackburn_poets.htm

Hunt, David, *A History of Preston* (Preston: Carnegie/Preston Borough Council, 1992).

—, *The History of Preston North End Football Club: The Power, the Politics and the People* (Preston: PNE Publications, 2000).

Hunt, Frederick Knight, *The Fourth Estate: Contributions Towards a History of Newspapers, and of the Liberty of the Press* (London: Bogue, 1850), http://archive.org/details/fourthestatecon03huntgoog

Ingham, Patricia, 'Introduction', in Elizabeth Gaskell, *North and South* (London: Penguin, 1995).

Jackson, Alexander, 'Football Coverage in the Papers of the Sheffield Telegraph, c.1890–1915', *International Journal of Regional and Local Studies*, 5 (2009), 63–84, https://doi.org/10.1179/jrl.2009.5.1.63

—, 'Reading the Green 'Un: The Saturday Football and Sports Special as a Consumer Product and Historical Source', unpublished manuscript, 2007.

—, 'The Chelsea Chronicle, 1905 to 1913', *Soccer & Society*, 11 (2010), 506–21, https://doi.org/10.1080/14660970.2010.497341

Jackson, Andrew J. H., 'Provincial Newspapers and the Development of Local Communities: The Creation of a Seaside Resort Newspaper for Ilfracombe, Devon, 1860–1', *Family & Community History*, 13 (2010), 101–13, https://doi.org/10.1179/146311810X12851639314110

Jackson, Ian, *The Provincial Press and the Community* (Manchester: Manchester University Press, 1971).

Janowitz, Morris, 'The Imagery of the Urban Press', *Public Opinion Quarterly*, 15 (1951), 519–31.

—, *The Community Press in an Urban Setting* (Glencoe: Free Press, 1952).

Jefferies, Richard, 'The Future of Country Society', *The New Quarterly Magazine*, 1877, 379–409, https://babel.hathitrust.org/cgi/pt?id=uc1.a0007881212;view=1up;seq=387

Jess, Pat, and Doreen B Massey, 'The Conceptualization of Place', in *A Place in the World? Places, Cultures and Globalization*, ed. by Doreen B Massey and Pat M. Jess (Oxford: Oxford University Press/Open University, 1995), pp. 45–85.

Johnes, Martin, *Soccer and Society: South Wales, 1900–39* (Cardiff: University of Wales Press, 2002).

Jones, Aled Gruffydd, 'The 19th Century Media and Welsh Identity', in *Nineteenth-Century Media and the Construction of Identities*, ed. by Laurel Brake, Bill Bell, and David Finkelstein (Basingstoke: Palgrave, 2000), pp. 310–25.

—, 'Constructing the Readership in 19th-Century Wales', in *Serials and Their Readers, 1620–1914*, ed. by Robin Myers and Michael Harris (Winchester/New Castle, DE: St Paul's Bibliographies/Oak Knoll Press, 1993), pp. 145–62.

—, *Powers of the Press: Newspapers, Power and the Public in Nineteenth-Century England* (Aldershot: Scolar Press, 1996).

—, *Press, Politics and Society: A History of Journalism in Wales* (Cardiff: University of Wales Press, 1993).

Jones, Gareth Stedman, *Outcast London: A Study in the Relationship between Classes in Victorian Society* (Penguin Books, 1984).

Jones, T. Artemus, 'Our Network of News: The Press Association and Reuter', *Windsor Magazine*, July 1896, pp. 517–24.

'Journalistic Autobiographies. I. Sir John Leng, MP, DL, Etc.', *Bookman*, February 1901, p. 157.

Joy, Caroline, 'War and Unemployment in an Industrial Community: Barrow-in-Furness 1914–1926' (unpublished PhD dissertation, University of Central Lancashire, 2004).

Joyce, Patrick, *The Rule of Freedom*: *Liberalism and the Modern City* (London: Verso, 2003).

—, *Visions of the People*: *Industrial England and the Question of Class, 1848–1914* (Cambridge: Cambridge University Press, 1994).

Kaestle, Carl F., 'Studying the History of Literacy', in *Literacy in the United States* : *Readers and Reading since 1880*, ed. by Carl F. Kaestle, Helen Damon-Moore, Lawrence C Stedman, Katherine Tinsley, and William Vance Trollinger (New Haven, CT: Yale University Press, 1991), pp. 1–32.

Katz, Elihu, and Paul F. Lazarsfeld, *Personal Influence; the Part Played by People in the Flow of Mass Communications* (Glencoe, IL: Free Press, 1955).

Keith-Lucas, Brian, *The English Local Government Franchise*: *A Short History* (Oxford: Blackwell, 1952).

Kenneally, Ian, *From the Earth, A Cry*: *The Story of John Boyle O'Reilly* (Collins Press, 2011).

Kent, Christopher, 'The Editor and the Law', in *Innovators and Preachers*: *The Role of the Editor in Victorian England*, ed. by Joel H. Wiener (Westport, CT: Greenwood Press, 1985), pp. 99–119.

Kidd, Alan J., 'Between Antiquary and Academic: Local History in the Nineteenth Century', *Local Historian*, 26 (1996), 3–14.

—, '"Local History" and the Culture of the Middle Classes in North-West England, C1840–1900', *Transactions of the Historic Society of Lancashire and Cheshire*, 147 (1998), 115–38, https://www.hslc.org.uk/wp-content/uploads/2017/05/147-6-Kidd.pdf

Kilgour, Frederick G., *The Evolution of the Book* (Oxford: Oxford University Press, 1998).

King, Andrew, *The London Journal, 1845–1883* : *Periodicals, Production, and Gender* (Aldershot: Ashgate, 2004), https://doi.org/10.4324/9781315238555

King, Andrew, Alexis Easley, and John Morton, eds., *The Routledge Handbook to Nineteenth-Century British Periodicals and Newspapers* (London: Routledge, 2016), https://doi.org/10.4324/9781315613345

Kingsley, Charles, *Alton Locke*: *Tailor and Poet* (London: Cassell, 1969).

Koss, Stephen, *The Rise and Fall of the Political Press in Britain, Vol.1, The Nineteenth Century* (London: Hamish Hamilton, 1981).

Kristeva, Julia, 'Women's Time', in *The Kristeva Reader*, ed. by Toril Moi (Oxford: Wiley-Blackwell, 1991), pp. 187–213.

Laing, R. D., *Self and Others* (London: Tavistock Publications, 1969).

Large, Frederick, *A Swindon Retrospect, 1855–1930* (Wakefield: S. R. Publishers, 1970).

Larkin, Felix M., '"Green Shoots" of the New Journalism in the Freeman's Journal, 1877–1890', in *Ireland and the New Journalism*, ed. by Karen Steele and Michael de Nie (New York: Palgrave Macmillan, 2014), pp. 35–55, https://doi.org/10.1057/9781137428714_32014

Law, Graham, 'Imagined Local Communities: Three Victorian Newspaper Novelists', in *Printing Places: Locations of Book Production & Distribution since 1500*, ed. by John Hinks and Catherine Armstrong (London: British Library, 2005), pp. 185–204.

—, *Serializing Fiction in the Victorian Press* (Basingstoke: Palgrave, 2000) https://doi.org/10.1057/9780230286740

—, 'Weekly News Miscellany', in *Dictionary of Nineteenth Century Journalism*, ed. by Laurel Brake and Marysa Demoor, C19: The Nineteenth Century Index, online (ProQuest).

Lawrence, Jon, 'Class and Gender in the Making of Urban Toryism, 1880–1914', *English Historical Review*, 108 (1993), 629–52 https://doi.org/10.1093/ehr/cviii.428.629

Lee, Alan J., *The Origins of the Popular Press in England: 1855–1914* (London: Croom Helm, 1976).

—, 'The Structure, Ownership and Control of the Press, 1855–1914', in *Newspaper History from the Seventeenth Century to the Present Day*, ed. by David George Boyce, James Curran, and Pauline Wingate (London: Constable, 1978), pp. 117–29.

Legg, Marie-Louise, *Newspapers and Nationalism: The Irish Provincial Press, 1850–1892* (Dublin: Four Courts Press, 1999).

Leigh, John Garrett, 'What Do the Masses Read?', *Economic Review*, 4 (1904), 166–77.

Levitt, Ian, ed., *Joseph Livesey of Preston: Business, Temperance and Moral Reform* (Preston: University of Central Lancashire, 1996).

Lewis, Brian, *The Middlemost and the Milltowns: Bourgeois Culture and Politics in Early Industrial England* (Stanford: Stanford University Press, 2002).

Liddle, Dallas, *The Dynamics of Genre: Journalism and the Practice of Literature in Mid-Victorian Britain* (Charlottesville, VA: University of Virginia Press, 2009).

—, 'The News Machine: Textual Form and Information Function in the London Times, 1785–1885', *Book History*, 19 (2017), 132–68, https://doi.org/10.1353/bh.2016.0003

Lippard, Lucy R., *The Lure of the Local: Senses of Place in a Multicentered Society* (New York: The New Press, 1998).

Little, Bryan, 'Two Chronicles in a Fight to the Death'. *Bath Evening Chronicle*. 1 June 1977, Centenary supplement marking 100 years of daily publication.

Lopatin, Nancy P, 'Refining the Limits of Political Reporting: The Provincial Press, Political Unions, and The Great Reform Act', *Victorian Periodicals Newsletter*, 31 (1998), 337–55.

Lorenz, Stacy L, '"In the Field of Sport at Home and Abroad": Sports Coverage in Canadian Daily Newspapers, 1850–1914', *Sport History Review*, 34 (2003), 133–67 https://doi.org/10.1123/shr.34.2.133

Lowe, J. C., 'The Tory Triumph of 1868 in Blackburn and in Lancashire', *The Historical Journal*, 16 (1973), 733–48 https://doi.org/10.1017/s0018246x00003927

Lucas, Peter J., 'The Dialect Boom in Victorian Furness', *Transactions of the Cumberland & Westmorland Antiquarian & Archaeological Society, Series 3*, 5 (2005), 199–216.

—, 'The First Furness Newspapers: The History of the Furness Press from 1846 to c.1880' (unpublished M.Litt dissertation, University of Lancaster, 1971).

—, 'J. A. Bernard's Challenge: Journalists on Journalism in a Victorian Country Town', *Transactions of the Cumberland and Westmorland Antiquarian and Archaeological Society, Series 3*, 7 (2007), 193–213.

—, 'The Regional Roots of Feminism: A Victorian Woman Newspaper Owner', *Transactions of the Cumberland & Westmorland Antiquarian & Archaeological Society, Series 3*, 2 (2002), 277–300.

Lucy, Henry W, *Sixty Years in the Wilderness: Some Passages by the Way* (London: Smith, Elder, 1909), https://archive.org/details/sixtyyearsinwild00lucyiala

Mackeson, Charles, 'Curiosities of the Census. V.', *The Leisure Hour*, 1874, 390–92, https://babel.hathitrust.org/cgi/pt?id=mdp.39015068401085;view=1up;seq=410

Mackie, John Beveridge, *Modern Journalism, a Handbook of Instruction and Counsel for the Young Journalist* (London: Crosby, Lockwood and Son, 1894).

Maidment, Brian E, 'Almanac', in *Dictionary of Nineteenth Century Journalism*, ed. by Laurel Brake and Marysa Demoor, C19: The Nineteenth Century Index, online (London: ProQuest).

—, 'Beyond Usefulness and Ephemerality: The Discursive Almanac 1828–1860', in *British Literature and Print Culture*, ed. by Sandro Jung (Cambridge: D. S. Brewer, 2013), pp. 158–94.

—, 'Class and Cultural Production in the Industrial City: Poetry in Victorian Manchester', in *City, Class and Culture: Studies of Cultural Production and Social Policy in Victorian Manchester*, ed. by Alan J. Kidd and Kenneth Roberts (Manchester: Manchester University Press, 1985), pp. 148–66.

—, ed., 'The Literary Culture of Nineteenth-Century Manchester', *Special Issue of Manchester Region History Review*, 17 (2006).

—, 'The Manchester Common Reader — Abel Heywood's "Evidence" and the Early Victorian Reading Public', in *Printing and the Book in Manchester, 1700–*

1850, ed. by Eddie Cass and Morris Garratt, *Transactions of the Lancashire and Cheshire Antiquarian Society* 97 (Manchester: Lancashire and Cheshire Antiquarian Society, 2001), pp. 99–120.

Mak, Geert, *In Europe: Travels through the Twentieth Century* (London: Vintage, 2008).

Marr, Andrew, *My Trade: A Short History of British Journalism* (London: Macmillan, 2004).

Marshall, John Duncan, *Furness and the Industrial Revolution: An Economic History of Furness, 1711–1900, and the Town of Barrow, 1757–1897* (Beckermet: Moon, 1981).

—, 'Review Article: Northern Identities', *Journal of Regional and Local Studies*, 21 (2000), 40–48.

—, *The Tyranny of the Discrete: A Discussion of the Problems of Local History in England* (Aldershot: Routledge, 1997).

Marshall, William, 'An Eisteddfod for Yorkshire? Professor Moorman and the Uses of Dialect', *Yorkshire Archaeological Journal*, 83 (2011), 199–217, https://doi.org/10.1179/008442711X13033963454633

Marx, Karl, 'The English Middle Classes [1 August 1854]', in *Dispatches for the New York Tribune: Selected Journalism of Karl Marx*, ed. by James Ledbetter (London: Penguin Classics, 2007), pp. 142–45.

—, 'Prince Albert's Toast. — The Stamp Duty on Newspapers', *Neue Oder-Zeitung*, 21 June 1855, MarxEngels.public-archive.net, http://marxengels.public-archive.net/en/ME0913en.html

Mason, Anthony, 'All the Winners and the Half-Times', *The Sports Historian*, 13 (1993), 3–13 https://doi.org/10.1080/17460269309446373

—, *Association Football and English Society, 1863–1915* (Brighton: Harvester Press, 1980).

—, 'Football, Sport of the North?', in *Sport and Identity in the North of England*, ed. by Jeffrey Hill and Jack Williams (Keele: Keele University Press, 1996), pp. 41–52.

—, 'Sporting News, 1860–1914', in *The Press in English Society from the Seventeenth to Nineteenth Centuries*, ed. by Michael Harris and Alan J. Lee (London: Associated University Presses, 1986), pp. 168–86.

Massey, Doreen B, 'Places and Their Pasts', *History Workshop Journal*, 39 (1995), 182–92 https://doi.org/10.1093/hwj/39.1.182

Matthew, H. C. G., 'Gladstone, Rhetoric and Politics', in *Gladstone*, ed. by Peter John Jagger (London: Hambledon, 1998), pp. 213–34.

Matthews, Rachel, *The History of the Provincial Press in England* (New York: Bloomsbury Academic, 2017) https://doi.org/10.5040/9781501324680

Mayhew, Robert.J., 'Review of William St Clair, The Reading Nation in the Romantic Period', *Journal of Historical Geography*, 31 (2005), 199 https://doi.org/10.1016/j.jhg.2005.01.016

McKitterick, David, 'Introduction', in *The Cambridge History of the Book in Britain, Volume 6, 1830–1914*, ed. by David McKitterick (Cambridge: Cambridge University Press, 2009), pp. 1–74 https://doi.org/10.1017/chol9780521866248.002

McAllister, Annemarie, 'Temperance Periodicals', in *The Routledge Handbook to Nineteenth-Century British Periodicals and Newspapers*, ed. by Andrew King, Alexis Easley, and John Morton (London: Routledge, 2016), pp. 342–54.

McPherson, Fiona, 'The Iron Lady: Margaret Thatcher's Linguistic Legacy', *OxfordWords Blog*, 2013, https://blog.oxforddictionaries.com/2013/04/10/margaretthatcher/

Merrett, Stephen, and Fred Gray, *Owner Occupation in Britain* (London: Routledge & Kegan Paul, 1982).

Metcalfe, Alan, 'Sport and Community: A Case Study of the Mining Villages of East Northumberland, 1800–1914', in *Sport and Identity in the North of England*, ed. by Jeffrey Hill and Jack Williams (Keele: Keele University Press, 1996), pp. 13–40.

Milne, Maurice, *The Newspapers of Northumberland and Durham: A Study of Their Progress during the 'Golden Age' of the Provincial Press* (Newcastle upon Tyne: Graham, 1971).

—, 'Periodical Publishing in the Provinces: The Mitchell Family of Newcastle-Upon-Tyne', *Victorian Periodicals Newsletter*, 10 (1977), 174–82.

—, 'Survival of the Fittest? Sunderland Newspapers in the Nineteenth Century', in *The Victorian Periodical Press: Samplings and Soundings*, ed. by Joanne Shattock and Michael Wolff (Leicester: Leicester University Press, 1982), pp. 193–223.

Milton, Frederick S., 'Newspaper Rivalry in Newcastle upon Tyne, 1876–1919: `Dicky Birds' and `Golden Circles''', *Northern History*, 46 (2009), 277–92.

—, 'Uncle Toby's Legacy: Children's Columns in the Provincial Newspaper Press, 1873–1914', *International Journal of Regional and Local Studies*, 5 (2009), 104–20.

Mitchell, William Woods, *The Newspaper Stamp and Its Anomalies Practically Considered: A Letter Addressed to the Right Hon. the Chancellor of the Exchequer, [W. E. Gladstone]* (Mitchell, 1854).

Mitford, Mary Russell, 'A Country Cricket-Match', in *The Works of Mary Russell Mitford, Prose and Verse* (Philadelphia, PA: Crissy & Markley, 1846), pp. 41–45, https://archive.org/details/worksmaryrussel01mitfgoog

'The Modern Newspaper', *British Quarterly Review*, 110 (1872), 348–80, https://babel.hathitrust.org/cgi/pt?id=inu.30000080764453;view=1up;seq=356

Monti, Daniel J., *The American City*: *A Social and Cultural History* (Malden, Mass: Blackwell, 1999).

Moretti, Franco, 'Conjectures on World Literature', *New Left Review*, 1 (2000), 54–68, https://newleftreview.org/II/1/franco-moretti-conjectures-on-world-literature

[Morley, Henry], 'The Labourer's Reading Room', *Household Words*, 3 (1851), 581–85, http://www.djo.org.uk/household-words/volume-iii/page-581.html

Mott, Frank Luther, *A History of American Magazines, Vol. 3: 1865–85* (Cambridge, MA: Harvard University Press, 1938).

Mullins, J. D., *Free Libraries and Newsrooms*: *Their Formation and Management.*, 3rd edn (London, 1879), http://hdl.handle.net/2027/mdp.39015033882336

Murphy, David, *The Silent Watchdog*: *The Press in Local Politics* (London: Constable, 1976).

Mussell, James, '"Characters of Blood and Flame": Stead and the Tabloid Campaign', in *W. T. Stead, Newspaper Revolutionary*, ed. by Laurel Brake, Ed King, Roger Luckhurst, and James Mussell (London: British Library, 2012), pp. 22–36.

—, 'Repetition: Or, "In Our Last"', *Victorian Periodicals Review*, 48 (2015), 343–58, https://doi.org/10.1353/vpr.2015.0043

—, *Science, Time and Space in the Late Nineteenth-Century Periodical Press*: *Movable Types* (Aldershot: Ashgate, 2007) https://doi.org/10.4324/9781315243658

Mynott, Malcolm T, *The Postal History of Preston, Garstang and the Fylde of Lancashire from the Civil War to 1902* (Preston: Preston & District Philatelic Society, 1987).

'New York Literary Correspondence', *Ladies' Repository* 18, August 1858, p. 505, https://babel.hathitrust.org/cgi/pt?id=nyp.33433104825652

Nicholson, Bob, 'Looming Large: America and the Late-Victorian Press, 1865–1902' (unpublished PhD dissertation, Manchester University, 2012).

Nicholson, John, 'Popular Imperialism and the Provincial Press: Manchester Evening and Weekly Papers, 1895–1902', *Victorian Periodicals Review*, 13 (1980), 85–96.

Nicholson, Tony, 'The Provincial Stead', in *W. T. Stead*: *Newspaper Revolutionary*, ed. by Roger Luckhurst, Laurel Brake, James Mussell, and Ed King (London: British Library, 2012), pp. 7–21.

Nisbet, J. F., 'The World, the Flesh and the Devil', *The Idler*, November 1896, p. 548.

Nodal, John H, 'Newspapers and Periodicals: Their Circulation in Manchester, I', *Manchester Literary Club Papers II*, 1876, 33–38.

Nord, David Paul, *Communities of Journalism: A History of American Newspapers and Their Readers* (Urbana: University of Illinois Press, 2001).

—, 'Introduction: Communication and Community', in *Communities of Journalism: A History of American Newspapers and Their Readers* (Urbana, IL: University of Illinois Press, 2001), pp. 1–27.

—, 'Reading the Newspaper: Strategies and Politics of Reader Response, Chicago, 1912–1917', in *Communities of Journalism: A History of American Newspapers and Their Readers* (Urbana, IL: University of Illinois Press, 2001), pp. 246–77.

'Nothing Like Example', *All the Year Round*, 19 (1868), 583–87, http://www.djo. org.uk/all-the-year-round/volume-xix/page-583.html

Nulty, Geoffrey, *Guardian Country 1853–1978: Being the Story of the First 125 Years of Cheshire County Newspapers Limited* (Warrington: Cheshire County Newspapers Ltd, 1978).

Ogborn, Miles, and Charles W. J. Withers, 'Introduction: Book Geography, Book History', in *Geographies of the Book* (Farnham: Ashgate, 2010), pp. 1–26 https://doi.org/10.4324/9781315584454

'On the Parish', *All The Year Round*, December 29 (1860), 273–76, http://www.djo. org.uk/all-the-year-round/volume-iv/page-273.html

O'Donnell, William Robert, and Loreto Todd, *Variety in Contemporary English* (London: Routledge, 1992).

John O'Neil, *The Journals of a Lancashire Weaver: 1856–60, 1860–64, 1872–75*, ed. by Mary Brigg (Chester: Record Society of Lancashire and Cheshire, 1982).

Paasi, A, 'Region and Place: Regional Identity in Question', *Progress in Human Geography*, 27 (2003), 475–85 https://doi.org/10.1191/0309132503ph439pr

Palmegiano, Eugenia M, *Perceptions of the Press in Nineteenth-Century British Periodicals: A Bibliography* (London: Anthem, 2012) https://doi.org/10.7135/upo9781843317562

Paterson, Alexander, 'Provincial Newspapers', in *Progress of British Newspapers in the Nineteenth Century* (London: Simpkin, Marshall, Hamilton, Kent & Co., 1901).

Pawley, Christine, *Reading on the Middle Border: The Culture of Print in Late-Nineteenth-Century Osage, Iowa* (Amherst, MA: University of Massachusetts Press, 2001).

—, 'Retrieving Readers: Library Experiences', *Library Quarterly*, 76 (2006), 379–87 https://doi.org/10.1086/511761

Paz, Denis G., *Popular Anti-Catholicism in Mid-Victorian England* (Stanford: Stanford University Press, 1992).

Pebody, Charles, *English Journalism, and the Men Who Have Made It* (London: Cassell, Petter, Galpin & Co., 1882), https://archive.org/details/englishjournali00pebogoog

Pedersen, Sarah, 'Within Their Sphere?: Women's Correspondence to Aberdeen Daily Newspapers, 1900–1918' (unpublished PhD dissertation, Robert Gordon University, 2004), https://openair.rgu.ac.uk/handle/10059/628

Phegley, Jennifer, 'Family Magazines', in *The Routledge Handbook to Nineteenth-Century British Periodicals and Newspapers*, ed. by Andrew King, Alexis Easley, and John Morton (Abingdon: Routledge, 2016), pp. 276–92.

Phelps, N. A., 'Professional Football and Local Identity in the "Golden Age": Portsmouth in the Mid-Twentieth Century', *Urban History*, 32 (2005), 459–80 https://doi.org/10.1017/s096392680500324x

Phillips, Paul T., *The Sectarian Spirit: Sectarianism, Society, and Politics in Victorian Cotton Towns* (Toronto: University of Toronto Press, 1982).

Pilkington, William, *The Makers of Wesleyan Methodism in Preston, and the Relation of Methodism to the Temperance and Teetotal Movements* (Preston: W. Pilkington, 1890), http://www.archive.org/stream/themakersofwesl00pilkuoft/themakersofwesl00pilkuoft_djvu.txt

Platt, Jane, *Subscribing to Faith? The Anglican Parish Magazine 1859–1929* (Basingstoke: Palgrave Macmillan, 2015) https://doi.org/10.1057/9781137362445

Pocock, D. C. D., and Raymond Hudson, *Images of the Urban Environment* (London: Macmillan, 1978).

Pollard, William, *A Hand Book and Guide to Preston* (Preston: H Oakey, 1882)

Poole, Robert, 'The *Manchester Observer*: Biography of a Radical Newspaper', *Bulletin of the John Rylands Library*, 2019.

—, *Popular Leisure and the Music Hall in Nineteenth-Century Bolton* (Lancaster: Centre for North-West Regional Studies, University of Lancaster, 1982).

Potter, Simon, 'Webs, Networks, and Systems: Globalization and the Mass Media in the Nineteenth- and Twentieth-Century British Empire', *Journal of British Studies*, 46 (2007), 621–46 https://doi.org/10.1086/515446

Pounds, Gabrina, 'Democratic Participation and Letters to the Editor in Britain and Italy', *Discourse and Society*, 17 (2006), 29–64 https://doi.org/10.1177/0957926506058064

Powell, Michael, and Terry Wyke, 'Manchester Men and Manchester Magazines: Publishing. Periodicals in the Provinces in the Nineteenth Century', in *Periodicals and Publishers: The Newspaper and Journal Trade 1740–1914*, ed. by John Hinks, Catherine Armstrong, and Matthew Day (London: British Library and Oak Knoll Press, 2009), pp. 161–84.

Preston, Thomas, 'The Origins and Development of Association Football in the Liverpool District, c.1879 until c.1915' (unpublished PhD dissertation, University of Central Lancashire, 2007), http://clok.uclan.ac.uk/9733/

Price, Leah, *How to Do Things with Books in Victorian Britain* (Princeton, NJ: Princeton University Press, 2012) https://doi.org/10.23943/princeton/9780691114170.001.0001

Priestley, J. B., 'An Outpost', in *The Book of Fleet Street*, ed. by T.Michael Pope (London: Cassell, 1930), pp. 174–82.

Procter, Richard Wright, *Literary Reminiscences and Gleanings* (Manchester: Thomas Dinham, 1860), https://archive.org/stream/literaryreminis00procgoog#page/n5/mode/2up

'Provincial Journalistic Enterprise', *Printers' Register*, 7 March 1870, p. 49.

Qureshi, Sadiah, *Peoples on Parade*: *Exhibitions, Empire, and Anthropology in Nineteenth-Century Britain* (Chicago, IL: University of Chicago Press, 2011) https://doi.org/10.7208/chicago/9780226700984.001.0001

Quinn, Thomas, *Modernising the Labour Party*: *Organisational Change since 1983* (Springer, 2004) https://doi.org/10.1057/9780230504912

Read, Donald, *The English Provinces, 1760–1960*: *A Study in Influence* (London: Edward Arnold, 1964).

—, 'John Harland, Father of Provincial Reporting', *Manchester Review*, 8 (1958), 205–12.

—, *Press and People, 1790–1850*: *Opinion in Three English Cities* (London: Edward Arnold, 1961).

Reade, Alfred Arthur, *Literary Success:Being a Guide to Practical Journalism.*, 2d ed. (London, 1885), http://hdl.handle.net/2027/uiug.30112056958892

Reid, Arnot, 'How a Provincial Paper Is Managed', *The Nineteenth Century*, 20 (1886), 391–402.

Reid, Stuart Johnson, *Memoirs of Sir Wemyss Reid, 1842–1885* (London: Cassell, 1905).

Rendezvous with the Past: *One Hundred Years' History of North Staffordshire and the Surrounding Area, as Reflected in the Columns of the Sentinel, Which Was Founded on January 7th, 1854* (Stoke-on-Trent: Staffordshire Sentinel Newspapers, 1954).

Reps, John W., *Views and Viewmakers of Urban America*: *Lithographs of Towns and Cities in the United States and Canada, Notes on the Artists and Publishers, and a Union Catalog of Their Work, 1825–1925* (Columbia, MO: University of Missouri Press, 1984).

Rhode, Dyke, 'Round the London Press, XI. Turveydrop and Weller in Type', *New Century Review*, January 1899, 61.

Roberts, Elizabeth, *A Woman's Place*: *An Oral History of Working-Class Women 1890–1940* (Oxford: Blackwell, 1985).

Roberts, F. David, 'Still More Early Victorian Newspaper Editors', *Victorian Periodicals Newsletter*, 18 (1972), 12–26.

Roberts, Matthew, 'Constructing a Tory World-View: Popular Politics and the Conservative Press in Late-Victorian Leeds', *Historical Research*, 79 (2006), 115–43 https://doi.org/10.1111/j.1468-2281.2006.00367.x

Roberts, Robert, *The Classic Slum*: *Salford Life in the First Quarter of the Century* (Harmondsworth: Penguin, 1973).

Robinson, Deborah, and Andrew Hobbs, 'How the Audience Saved UK Broadcast Journalism', in *The Future of Quality News Journalism*: *A Cross-Continental Analysis*, ed. by Peter J. Anderson, George Ogola, and Michael Williams (New York: Routledge, 2014), pp. 162–83 https://doi.org/10.4324/9780203382707

Robinson, Lionel, *Boston's Newspapers* (Boston: Richard Kay Publications, for the History of Boston Project, 1974).

Rose, Jonathan, *The Intellectual Life of the British Working Classes* (London: Yale University Press, 2001).

Rothenbuhler, Eric W., Lawrence J. Mullen, Richard DeLaurell, and Choon Ryul Ryu, 'Communication, Community Attachment, and Involvement', *Journalism and Mass Communication Quarterly*, 73 (1996), 445–66 https://doi.org/10.1177/107769909607300214

Rowbotham, Judith, Kim Stevenson, and Samantha Pegg, *Crime News in Modern Britain*: *Press Reporting and Responsibility, 1820–2010* (Basingstoke: Palgrave Macmillan, 2013) https://doi.org/10.1057/9781137317971

Royle, Edward, 'Introduction: Regions and Identities', in *Issues of Regional Identity*: *In Honour of John Marshall*, ed. by Edward Royle (Manchester: Manchester University Press, 1998), pp. 1–13.

Rubery, Matthew, *The Novelty of Newspapers*: *Victorian Fiction After the Invention of the News* (Oxford: Oxford University Press, 2009).

Russell, Dave, 'Culture and the Formation of Northern English Identities from c.1850', in *An Agenda for Regional History*, ed. by Bill Lancaster, Diana Newton, and Natasha Vall (Newcastle upon Tyne: Northumbria University Press, 2007), pp. 271–88.

—, *Football and the English*: *A Social History of Association Football in England, 1863–1995* (Preston: Carnegie, 1997).

—, '*The Heaton Review*, 1927–1934: Culture, Class and a Sense of Place in Inter-War Yorkshire', *Twentieth Century British History*, 17 (2006), 323–49 https://doi.org/10.1093/tcbh/hwl018

—, *Looking North*: *Northern England and the National Imagination* (Manchester: Manchester University Press, 2004).

Said, Edward W., *Orientalism* (London: Penguin, 2003).

Salmon, Edward G., 'What the Working Classes Read', *Nineteenth Century*, XX (1886), pp. 108–17.

Salveson, Paul, 'Region, Class, Culture: Lancashire Dialect Literature, 1746–1935' (unpublished PhD dissertation, University of Salford, 1993), http://usir.salford.ac.uk/14672/

Savage, Michael, *The Dynamics of Working-Class Politics: The Labour Movement in Preston 1880–1940* (Cambridge: Cambridge University Press, 1987) https://doi.org/10.1017/cbo9780511898280

Scannell, Paddy, *Radio, Television, and Modern Life: A Phenomenological Approach* (Oxford: Blackwell, 1996).

Schudson, Michael, 'The Objectivity Norm in American Journalism', *Journalism*, 2 (2001), 149–70, https://doi.org/10.1177/146488490100200201

Scott, John William Robertson, *The Day before Yesterday: Memories of an Uneducated Man* (Methuen, 1951).

Scott-James, Rolfe Arnold, *The Influence of the Press* (London: S. W. Partridge & Co., 1913), https://archive.org/details/influenceofpress00scotiala

Secord, James A., *Victorian Sensation : The Extraordinary Publication, Reception, and Secret Authorship of Vestiges of the Natural History of Creation* (Chicago: University of Chicago Press, 2003).

Sell's Dictionary of the World's Press, 1887, https://archive.org/details/bub_gb_DksCAAAAYAAJ

Seymour-Ure, Colin, *The British Press and Broadcasting since 1945* (Oxford: Blackwell, 1996).

Shamai, Shmuel, and Zinaida Ilatov, 'Measuring Sense of Place: Methodological Aspects', *Tijdschrift Voor Economische En Sociale Geografie*, 96 (2005), 467–76 https://doi.org/10.1111/j.1467-9663.2005.00479.x

Shannon, Mary L., *Dickens, Reynolds, and Mayhew on Wellington Street: The Print Culture of a Victorian Street* (London: Routledge, 2015) https://doi.org/10.4324/9781315577067

Shansky, Jean M., *Yesterday's World* (Penwortham: Smiths, 2000).

Shattock, Joanne, ed., *The Cambridge Bibliography of English Literature. Vol.4* (Cambridge: Cambridge University Press, 1999) https://doi.org/10.1017/cbo9780511518683

Shep, Sydney, 'Books in Global Perspectives', in *The Cambridge Companion to the History of the Book*, ed. by Leslie Howsam (Cambridge: Cambridge University Press, 2014), pp. 53–70, https://doi.org/10.1017/CCO9781139152242.005

Sherman, Stuart, *Telling Time: Clocks, Diaries, And English Diurnal Form, 1660–1785* (Chicago, IL: University of Chicago Press, 1997).

Shorrocks, Graham, 'Non-Standard Dialect Literature and Popular Culture', in *Speech Past and Present: Studies in English Dialectology in Memory of Ossi Ihalainen*, ed. by Juhani Klemola, Merja Kyto, and Matt. Rissanen (Frankfurt am Main: P. Lang, 1996), pp. 385–411.

—, 'A Phonemic and Phonetic Key to the Orthography of the Lancashire Dialect Writer, Teddy Ashton', *Journal of the Lancashire Dialect Society*, 27 (1978), pp. 45–59.

Silberstein-Loeb, Jonathan, *The International Distribution of News: The Associated Press, Press Association, and Reuters, 1848–1947* (New York: Cambridge University Press, 2014) https://doi.org/10.1017/cbo9781139522489

—, 'The Structure of the News Market in Britain, 1870–1914', *Business History Review*, 83 (2009), 759–88 https://doi.org/10.1017/s0007680500000908

Singleton, Frank, *Tillotsons, 1850–1950: Centenary of a Family Business* (Bolton: Tillotson, 1950).

Smith, David, 'Tonypandy 1910: Definitions of Community', *Past and Present*, 87 (1980), 158–84 https://doi.org/10.1093/past/87.1.158

Smith, Mary, *The Autobiography of Mary Smith, Schoolmistress and Nonconformist, a Fragment of a Life (Volume 1); With Letters from Jane Welsh Carlyle and Thomas Carlyle* (Carlisle: Wordsworth Press, 1892), http://archive.org/details/autobiographyma00smitgoog

Smith, Tom, '"Let Justice Be Done and We Will Be Silent": A Study of Preston's Catholic Voters and Their Parliamentary Elections Campaigns, 1832 to 1867', *North West Catholic History*, 28 (2001), pp. 5–54.

—, 'Religion or Party? Attitudes of Catholic Electors in Mid-Victorian Preston', *North West Catholic History*, 33 (2006), pp. 19–35.

Snape, Robert, *Leisure and the Rise of the Public Library* (London: Library Association, 1995)

Sommerville, Charles John, *The News Revolution in England: Cultural Dynamics of Daily Information* (Oxford: Oxford University Press, 1996).

St Clair, William, 'Following up *The Reading Nation*', in *The Cambridge History of the Book in Britain, Volume 6, 1830–1914*, ed. by David McKitterick (Cambridge: Cambridge University Press, 2009), pp. 704–35 https://doi.org/10.1017/CHOL9780521866248.022

Stafford, Fiona J., *Local Attachments: The Province of Poetry* (Oxford: Oxford University Press, 2010).

Stam, David H., and Deirdre C. Stam, 'Bending Time: The Function of Periodicals in Nineteenth-Century Polar Naval Expeditions', *Victorian Periodicals Review*, 41 (2008), 301–22, https://doi.org/10.1353/vpr.0.0054

Stamm, Keith R., Arthur G. Emig, and Michael B. Hesse, 'The Contribution of Local Media to Community Involvement', *Journalism & Mass Communication Quarterly*, 74 (1997), 97–107, https://doi.org/10.1177/107769909707400108

[Stephen, James Fitzjames], 'Journalism', *Cornhill Magazine*, 6 (1862), pp. 52–63.

Stephens, William B., *Education, Literacy and Society, 1830–1870*: *The Geography of Diversity in Provincial England* (Manchester: Manchester University Press, 1987)

Stephenson, Tom, *Forbidden Land*: *The Struggle for Access to Mountain and Moorland* (Manchester: Manchester University Press, 1989)

Stetz, Margaret D., 'Internationalizing Authorship: Beyond New Grub Street to the Bookman in 1891', *Victorian Periodicals Review*, 48 (2015), 1–14, https://doi.org/10.1353/vpr.2015.0011

Sutton, Charles W., and William Credland, eds. *Manchester Literary Club*: *Index to Publications, Catalogue of the Library and List of Members 1862–1903*. Manchester: Sherratt & Hughes, 1903. http://archive.org/details/indexpapers00mancuoft,

Swann, Joan, 'Style Shifting, Codeswitching', in *English*: *History, Diversity and Change*, ed. by David Graddol, Dick Leith, and Joan Swann (London: Routledge, 1996), pp. 301–37.

'Tackling the Threat to High-Quality Journalism in the UK', GOV.UK, https://www.gov.uk/government/news/tackling-the-threat-to-high-quality-journalism-in-the-uk

Tate, Steve, 'The Professionalisation of Sports Journalism, c.1850 to 1939, with Particular Reference to the Career of James Catton' (unpublished PhD dissertation, University of Central Lancashire, 2007), http://clok.uclan.ac.uk/7711/

Taylor, William Cooke, *Notes of a Tour in the Manufacturing Districts of Lancashire*: *In a Series of Letters to His Grace the Archbishop of Dublin* (London: Duncan and Malcolm, 1842), https://babel.hathitrust.org/cgi/pt?id=hvd.32044088916259;view=1up;seq=5

Taylor, H. A., 'Politics in Famine Stricken Preston: An Examination of Liberal Party Management, 1861–65', *Transactions of the Historic Society of Lancashire & Cheshire*, 107 (1956), 121–39, https://www.hslc.org.uk/wp-content/uploads/2017/06/107-7-Taylor.pdf

Tebbutt, Melanie, 'Centres and Peripheries: Reflections on Place Identity and Sense of Belonging in a North Derbyshire Cotton Town', *Manchester Region History Review*, 13 (1999), 3–20, http://web.archive.org/web/20061209065627/http://www.mcrh.mmu.ac.uk/pubs/pdf/mrhr_13_tebbutt.pdf

Tewksbury, David, and Dietram A. Scheufele, 'News Framing Theory and Research', in *Media Effects*: *Advances in Theory and Research*, ed. by Jennings Bryant and Mary Beth Oliver (New York: Routledge, 2009), pp. 17–33 https://doi.org/10.4324/9780203877111

Thompson, James, *British Political Culture and the Idea of 'Public Opinion', 1867–1914* (Cambridge: Cambridge University Press, 2013) https://doi.org/10.1017/cbo9781139208611

Thompson, John Brookshire, 'Editor's Introduction', in Pierre Bourdieu, *Language and Symbolic Power*, ed. by John Brookshire Thompson, trans. Gino Raymond and Matthew Adamson (Cambridge: Polity, 1991), pp. 1–31.

Thompson, Michael, *Rubbish Theory: The Creation and Destruction of Value* (Oxford, New York: Oxford University Press, 1979) https://doi.org/10.2307/j.ctt1rfsn94

Tomlinson, V. I., 'The Lancashire and Cheshire Antiquarian Society 1883–1983', *Transactions of the Lancashire & Cheshire Antiquarian Society*, 83 (1985), 1–39.

Toplis, Alison, 'Ready-Made Clothing Advertisements in Two Provincial Newspapers, 1800–1850', *International Journal of Regional and Local Studies*, 5 (2009), 85–103 https://doi.org/10.1179/jrl.2009.5.1.85

Tulloch, John, 'The Eternal Recurrence of New Journalism', in *Tabloid Tales: Global Debates over Media Standards*, ed. by Colin Sparks and John Tulloch (Oxford: Rowman & Littlefield, 2000), pp. 131–46

Turner, Mark W., 'Periodical Time in the Nineteenth Century', *Media History*, 8 (2002), 2 https://doi.org/10.1080/1368880022000030540

—, 'Time, Periodicals, and Literary Studies', *Victorian Periodicals Review*, 39 (2006), 309–16 https://doi.org/10.1353/vpr.2007.0014

Vernon, James, *Politics and the People: A Study in English Political Culture, c. 1815–1867* (Cambridge: Cambridge University Press, 1993).

Vicinus, Martha, *The Industrial Muse: A Study of Nineteenth Century British Working-Class Literature* (London: Croom Helm, 1974).

Vickery, Amanda, 'Town Histories and Victorian Plaudits: Some Examples from Preston', *Urban History Yearbook*, 15 (1988), 58–64 https://doi.org/10.1017/s0963926800013924

Vincent, David, *Literacy and Popular Culture: England 1750–1914* (Cambridge: Cambridge University Press, 1989) https://doi.org/10.1017/cbo9780511560880

Wadsworth, Alfred Powell, 'Newspaper Circulations, 1800–1954', *Transactions of the Manchester Statistical Society*, 9 March (1955), 1–40.

Wahl-Jorgensen, Karin, 'The Construction of the Public in Letters to the Editor: Deliberative Democracy and the Idiom of Insanity', *Journalism*, 3 (2002), 183–204 https://doi.org/10.1177/146488490200300203

—, 'Letters to the Editor in Local and Regional Newspapers', in *Local Journalism and Local Media*, ed. by Bob Franklin (London: Routledge, 2006), pp. 221–31.

Wales, Katie, *Personal Pronouns in Present-Day English* (Cambridge: Cambridge University Press, 1996).

—, *Northern English: A Cultural and Social History* (Cambridge: Cambridge University Press, 2006) https://doi.org/10.1017/cbo9780511487071

Waller, P. J., 'Democracy and Dialect, Speech and Class', in *Politics and Social Change in Britain: Essays Presented to A. F. Thompson,* ed. by P. J. Waller (Brighton: Harvester Press, 1987), pp. 1–33.

Walton, John K., *Lancashire: A Social History, 1558–1939* (Manchester: Manchester University Press, 1987).

—, *The English Seaside Resort: A Social History, 1750–1914* (Leicester: Leicester University Press, 1983).

—, 'Visitors' Lists', in *Dictionary of Nineteenth Century Journalism,* ed. by Laurel Brake and Marysa Demoor, C19: The Nineteenth Century Index, online (London: ProQuest).

Waters, Catherine, '"Much of Sala, and but Little of Russia": 'A Journey Due North,' Household Words, and the Birth of a Special Correspondent"', *Victorian Periodicals Review,* 42 (2009), 305–23 https://doi.org/10.1353/vpr.0.0090

Waterhouse, Robert, *The Other Fleet Street: How Manchester Made Newspapers National* (Altrincham: First Edition, 2004).

Whates, Harold Richard Grant, *The Birmingham Post, 1857–1957. A Centenary Retrospect* (Birmingham: Birmingham Post & Mail, 1957).

Waugh, Edwin, *The Diary of Edwin Waugh: Life in Victorian Manchester and Rochdale 1847–1851,* ed. by Brian Hollingworth (Lancaster: Carnegie, 2008).

Whorlow, H., *The Provincial Newspaper Society. 1836–1886. A Jubilee Retrospect* (London: Page, Pratt & Co., 1886).

Wiener, Joel H., 'How New Was the New Journalism?', in *Papers for the Millions: The New Journalism in Britain, 1850s to 1914,* ed. by Joel H. Wiener (London: Greenwood, 1988), pp. 47–72.

—, *The Americanization of the British Press, 1830s–1914: Speed in the Age of Transatlantic Journalism* (Basingstoke: Palgrave Macmillan, 2011) https://doi.org/10.1057/9780230347953

Williams, J. R., *The Whitehaven News Centenary 1852–1952: An Outline of 100 Years* (Whitehaven: Whitehaven News, 1952), http://cultrans.com/centenary/index.htm

Williams, Raymond, *The Long Revolution* (Harmondsworth: Penguin, 1965).

—, 'Region and Class in the Novel', in *Writing in Society* (London: Verso, 1983), pp. 229–38.

—, *Television: Technology and Cultural Form* (London: Routledge, 1990).

Wilson, A. N., *The Victorians* (London: Arrow, 2003).

[Wilson, J. F.], *A Few Personal Recollections, by an Old Printer* (London: Printed for private circulation, 1896), http://archive.org/details/fewpersonalrecol00oldpiala

Windscheffel, Alex, *Popular Conservatism in Imperial London 1868–1906* (London: Royal Historical Society, 2007).

Winstanley, Michael, *The Shopkeeper's World, 1830–1914* (Manchester: Manchester University Press, 1983).

—, 'News from Oldham: Edwin Butterworth and the Manchester Press, 1829–1848', *Manchester Region History Review*, 4 (1990), 3–10, http://web.archive.org/web/20061209065627/ http://www.mcrh.mmu.ac.uk/pubs/pdf/mrhr_04i_winstanley.pdf

Wolff, Michael, and Celina Fox, 'Pictures from the Magazines', in *The Victorian City: Images and Reality, Vol. 2*, ed. by H. J. Dyos and Michael Wolff (London: Routledge and Kegan Paul, 1973), pp. 559–82.

Woolf, D., 'News, History and the Contraction of the Present in Early Modern England', in *The Politics of Information in Early Modern Europe*, ed. by Brendan Maurice Dooley and Sabrina A Baron (London: Routledge, 2011), pp. 80–118.

Wright, Thomas [The 'Journeyman Engineer'], 'Readers and Reading', *Good Words*, 17 (1876), pp. 315–20.

Zboray, Ronald J., and Mary Saracino Zboray, 'Political News and Female Readership in Antebellum Boston and Its Region', *Journalism History*, 22 (1996), pp. 2–14.

—, '"Have You Read...?": Real Readers and Their Responses in Antebellum Boston and Its Region', *Nineteenth-Century Literature*, 52 (1997), 139–70, https://doi.org/10.2307/2933905

List of Illustrations

Front cover

Cross Street Manchester, showing offices of rival newspapers the *Manchester Courier* and *Manchester Guardian/Manchester Evening News,* 1902 (image M56243). Courtesy of Manchester Libraries, Information and Archives, Manchester City Council. All rights reserved.

Introduction

Chapter 1

Chapter 2

Chapter 3

Chapter 4

Chapter 5

Chapter 6

Chapter 7

Chapter 8

Chapter 9

Chapter 10

Index

This book need not end here...

Share

All our books—including the one you have just read—are free to access online so that students, researchers and members of the public who can't afford a printed edition will have access to the same ideas. This title will be accessed online by hundreds of readers each month across the globe: why not share the link so that someone you know is one of them?

This book and additional content is available at:
https://doi.org/10.11647/OBP.0152

Customise

Personalise your copy of this book or design new books using OBP and third-party material. Take chapters or whole books from our published list and make a special edition, a new anthology or an illuminating coursepack. Each customised edition will be produced as a paperback and a downloadable PDF. Find out more at:

https://www.openbookpublishers.com/section/59/1

You may also be interested in:

The Life and Letters of William Sharp and "Fiona Macleod"
Volume 1: 1855-1894

By William F. Halloran

https://doi.org/10.11647/OBP.0142

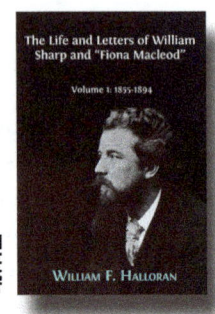

Verdi in Victorian London

By Massimo Zicari

https://doi.org/10.11647/OBP.0090

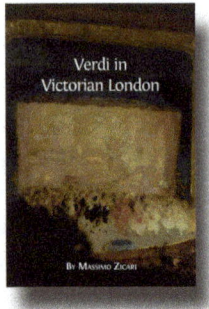

Dickens's Working Notes for *Dombey and Son*

By Tony Laing

https://doi.org/10.11647/OBP.0092